Helping Children
Learn Mathematics

Helping Children
Learn Mathematics

ROBERT E. REYS • MARILYN N. SUYDAM • MARY M. LINDQUIST
University of Missouri   *Ohio State University*   *National College of Education*

PRENTICE-HALL, INC., Englewood Cliffs, New Jersey 07632

Library of Congress Cataloging in Publication Data

Reys, Robert E.
    Helping children learn mathematics.

    Includes bibliographies and index.
    1. Mathematics—Study and teaching (Elementary).
I. Suydam, Marilyn N.   II. Lindquist, Mary Montgomery.
III. Title.
QA135.5.R49 1984   372.7   83-13775
ISBN   0-13-387027-8

Editorial/production supervision and interior design: Paul Spencer
Cover design: Wanda Lubelska Design
Page layout: Peggy Finnerty
Manufacturing buyer: Ron Chapman

ISBN 0-13-387027-8

Prentice-Hall International, Inc., *London*
Prentice-Hall of Australia Pty. Limited, *Sydney*
Editora Prentice-Hall do Brasil, Ltda., *Rio de Janeiro*
Prentice-Hall Canada Inc., *Toronto*
Prentice-Hall of India Private Limited, *New Delhi*
Prentice-Hall of Japan, Inc., *Tokyo*
Prentice-Hall of Southeast Asia Pte. Ltd., *Singapore*
Whitehall Books Limited, *Wellington, New Zealand*

Contents

Preface

Helping Children Learn Mathematics is for teachers of mathematics in elementary school. It is written to help you help children learn important mathematical concepts, skills, and problem-solving techniques. In the process we hope to challenge your thinking and further stimulate your interest in mathematics.

This book is divided into two main parts. The first part (Chapters 1-5) provides a base for understanding the changing mathematics curriculum and how children learn. It offers some guidelines for planning instruction and evaluating performance. Attention is directed to problem solving and technology, both of which have profound implications for mathematics teaching at all levels. Their importance is reflected throughout the book, as both problem solving and technology—especially calculators—are integrated within various chapters.

The second part (Chapters 6-16) discusses teaching strategies, techniques, and learning activities related to specific mathematical topics. Emphasis is on using models and materials to develop concepts and understanding so that mathematics learning is indeed meaningful. We believe meaning is most effectively achieved by helping students discuss mathematics as they move from concrete materials and examples to generalizations and abstractions.

Ten features provide a unique resource for you:

1. Problem solving, the single most important and challenging basic skill in mathematics, is addressed in a separate chapter, which not only discusses various problem-solving strategies but also presents a wide variety of problems with which the strategies are useful. You will also find a problem-solving spirit reflected in the Lesson and Activity Cards, as well as in many discussions throughout the book.

2. "Lesson Snapshots" provide a brief look into a variety of mathematical lessons at different grade levels. We opened most of the content-specific chapters (i.e., Chapters 6-16) with these "Snapshots" to remind you of the realities of teaching. The "Snapshots" not only demonstrate many effective classroom practices, but also illustrate the vital role that you as the teacher play in leading and promoting students to talk and learn about mathematics.

3. Lesson and Activity Cards are used to highlight a wide variety of instructional ideas. Lesson Cards summarize key questions and could serve as a skeleton outline for a specific lesson. Activity Cards also focus on specific mathematical topics but are more student-oriented; thus they could be used in group discussions or explored independently by children.

4. A research base has been threaded within many discussions. As a teacher you are often called upon to provide a rationale for curricular or instructional decisions, and we think you will find this integration of relevant research along with its implications useful.

5. Technology, such as the calculator, is widely available to everyone—including students. We recommend that calculators be used in schools. Furthermore, we have integrated calculator activities throughout this book. As you become more familiar with different uses of calculators, you will use them more freely and creatively.

6. Tedious computational algorithms, such as long division, are de-emphasized. The existence and use of technology demands changes in what we teach. We believe the operations must be taught, but our development focuses on meaningful understanding of the algorithm with less attention to the painfully laborious task of crunching large numbers.

7. Computational estimation skills are explicitly taught, with a chapter devoted to their systematic development. Technology has increased the importance of being able to estimate, and we have presented some new and effective strategies for developing basic estimation skills.

8. Throughout all discussions, provisions have been made for individual differences. This is reflected in many ways—from the wide range of student abilities in the Lesson Snapshots to the Lesson and Activity Cards. Our use of calculators and our integration and discussion of research findings provide further insight into individual differences. We think such discussions will help you implement the spirit of mainstreaming in your classroom.

9. "Things to Do" follow each chapter. These "Things" embody our active learning/teaching approach to mathematics. They are designed to engage you in investigating, inquiring, and thinking that will provide greater understanding and insight.

10. Many helpful references are provided to document research, ideas, and other points made within the chapter. Some discuss ideas that have been mentioned but that space did not allow us to develop to the extent we would like. Others elaborate and extend ideas that will promote greater insight and understanding.

This is not a "workbook," but it is an "ideabook." We feel you will learn much from reading and talking about what you have read. It is of course not possible—or even desirable—to establish exact steps to follow in teaching mathematics. Too much depends upon what is being taught to whom at what level. In your classroom, it is you who will ultimately decide what to teach, to whom to teach it, how to teach it, and the amount of time to spend. This book will not answer all of these questions for you, but we think you will find it very useful in helping you make these decisions wisely as you guide elementary school students in their learning of mathematics. We believe it will be a valuable teaching resource that can be used again and again in the classroom long after the "course" has been completed.

Upon completion of this book, we are reminded of the many—family, friends, colleagues, and students—who contributed in various ways. We thank our mathematics education colleagues at our schools, specifically Dale Clithero and Barbara Reys at the University of Missouri, and the following official reviewers who provided helpful direction: David Fitzgerald, Northeastern State University; Mary Anne Fowler, Northeastern Illinois University; Frank Lester, Indiana University; William D. Smith, James Madison University; Paul Trafton, National College of Education; and Margariete Montague Wheeler, Northern Illinois University. We especially thank our students for their willingness to read earlier drafts of this book and provide helpful comments and suggestions.

Robert E. Reys
Marilyn N. Suydam
Mary M. Lindquist

1

The Changing Elementary School Mathematics Program

INTRODUCTION

Soon you'll be walking into a classroom, responsible for teaching a group of children mathematics—as well as many other things. What mathematics will you be teaching? How will you teach it? This book will help you gain a clearer understanding of the answers to those two questions.

You'll also be asking other questions, as all teachers must:

- What mathematical knowledge will the children in my classroom have as they begin the year?
- What mathematical ideas do they need to learn?
- What am I expected to teach?
- How can each child, different in many ways from the others, be taught so that he or she will learn?

The answers to such questions provide the framework for the elementary school mathematics program in each classroom. From them, you can outline specific objectives to be accomplished, organize instructional materials, and plan daily lessons. No matter what age children you teach, you'll probably have several general goals:

- to teach children specific mathematical content—facts, skills, and concepts,
- to teach children how to apply mathematical ideas to solve problems, and
- to foster a positive attitude toward mathematics.

Developing lessons that teach a range of mathematical content to the children in your class will be considered in later chapters in this book. Here, our concern is with the curriculum—the scope and sequence of the mathematics program that has evolved through the years.

WHAT IS MATHEMATICS?

Frequently, people equate mathematics and arithmetic. Arithmetic is concerned with numbers. When considering the mathematics curriculum, there is a tendency to focus on the computational skills of arithmetic—addition, subtraction, multiplication, and division with whole numbers, fractions, and decimals—and consider that these constitute the full set of competencies that children must have in mathematics. But mathematics involves more than computation. Several statements delineate the broader scope of mathematics:

1. Mathematics is *a study of patterns and relationships*. Children need to become aware of recurring ideas and of relationships between and among mathematical ideas. This provides a unifying thread throughout the curriculum, for each topic is interwoven with others that have preceded it. Children must come to see how one idea is like or unlike other ideas already learned. For instance, we have children in second grade consider how knowledge of one basic fact (say $3 + 2 = 5$) is related to another basic fact (say $5 - 3 = 2$). Or, we have children in fifth grade consider how multiplication with decimals is like multiplication with whole numbers.

2. Mathematics is *a way of thinking*. It provides us with strategies for organizing, analyzing, and synthesizing data, largely but not exclusively numerical. People who are comfortable with mathematics use it as they meet everyday problems. For example, some people use it to write an equation to solve an everyday problem. Others use it to form tables to record information, or to develop an analogy with several related items.

3. Mathematics is *an art,* characterized by order and internal consistency. Many children come to think of mathematics as a confusing set of discrete facts and skills that must be memorized. Because of a tendency to focus on developing the skills required to "do" mathematics, we forget that children need to be guided to realize and to appreciate the underlying orderliness and consistency.

4. Mathematics is *a language,* using carefully defined terms and symbols. These enhance our ability to communicate about science and about other real-life situations.

5. Mathematics is *a tool*. It is what mathematicians use, and it is also used by everyone in the course of daily life. Thus, children can come to appreciate why they are learning the facts, skills, and concepts that the school program involves. They, too, can use mathematics to solve both abstract and practical problems, just as mathematicians do. It is useful in many vocations, serving as a "critical filter": mathematics is a prerequisite to many occupations.

WHAT MATHEMATICS SHOULD BE TAUGHT?

Mathematics has a prominent role in the elementary school program. It is second only to reading in the amount of time devoted to it and in the amount of money spent for curricular materials (13). Its importance is, in fact, reflected in the degree of concern recurrently voiced about it by parents and other members of the public.

What is the curriculum about which people are concerned? There is no such thing as a national curriculum guide for elementary school mathematics in the United States. Yet there is a great deal of similarity in the content of most elementary school mathematics textbook series. Both state and local curriculum guides (when they exist) tend to parallel this same content. There are some differences in sequence, but nevertheless for the most part there is a surprising degree of agreement on the order in which topics will be introduced.

How did this consensus come about? Three general factors influence the curriculum and play roles in its evolution:

1. The needs of the subject.
2. The needs of the child.
3. The needs of society.

Needs of the Subject

The nature of mathematics has helped to determine what is taught and when it is taught. Whole numbers are the basis for many mathematical ideas; moreover, experiences with them arise long before children come to school. Thus, whole-number work is stressed first. Work with rational numbers logically follows work with whole numbers. Such seemingly "natural" sequences are the result of long years of curricular evolution. This process has involved much analysis of what constitutes a progression from "easy" to "difficult," based in part on what is deemed to be needed at one level for the development of ideas at later levels.

Once a curriculum is in place for a long time, however, people tend to consider it the only "proper" sequence. Thus, to omit a topic or to change the sequence of topics often involves a struggle for acceptance.

Sometimes this process is aided by an event, as when the Russians sent the first Sputnik into orbit. The shock of this evidence of another country's technological superiority speeded up curriculum change. The "new math" of the 1950s and 1960s was the result, as millions of dollars were channeled into mathematics and science education to strengthen the programs of children in our schools. Mathematicians became integrally involved in developing curriculum, and, because of their interests and the perceived weaknesses of previous curricula, developed curriculum determined by the needs of the subject. Emphasis was shifted from social usefulness to such unifying themes as the structure of mathematics, operations and their inverses, systems of notation, properties of numbers, and set language. Not only was new content added at the elementary school level, but some old topics were introduced at lower grade levels.

Needs of the Child

Clearly influencing the curriculum have been beliefs about how children learn. Until the early years of this century, mathematics was taught to train "mental faculties" or provide *mental discipline.* Struggling with mathematical procedures was thought to exercise the mind, helping it work more effectively.

Around the turn of the century, mental discipline was replaced by *connectionism,* dominated by the thinking of Edward Thorndike. The stimulus-response theory, in which it was necessary to establish strong bonds or connections, resulted in an emphasis on speed and accuracy, attained by repeated drill. Much stress was placed, therefore, on identifying specific skills to be mastered and on the relative difficulty of the various topics. Precise placement of topics seemed vital, leading to such practices as introducing 7 X 3 a full year before introducing 3 X 7. Standardized tests were developed and normed, so that children could be precisely graded according to their attainment of mathematical skills. This in turn led teachers to resort to endless drill in order to ensure high scores.

During the late 1920s, a committee of school superintendents and principals from midwestern cities surveyed pupils to find out when topics were mastered (15). They then suggested the mental age at which each topic should be taught. Thus, subtraction facts under 10 were to be taught to children with a mental age of 6 years 7 months, and those over 10 at 7 years 8 months, while subtraction with borrowing or carrying was to be taught at 8 years 9 months. The Committee of Seven had a strong impact for years on the sequencing of the curriculum.

In reaction to the strictures of a drill-based program, and under the influence of writers such as John Dewey, the Progressive Movement in the 1920s advocated *incidental learning.* It was believed that children would learn as much arithmetic as they needed and would learn it better if arithmetic was not systematically taught. Rather, the teacher waited for situations to arise, or created situations in which arithmetic would arise.

Another change in thinking occurred in the mid-1930s, as the *field* or *Gestalt theory* was advanced. Greater emphasis was placed on a planned program to encourage the development of insight, relationships, structure, patterns, interpretations, and principles. This contributed to a shift to concern for *meaning and understanding,* with William Brownell as a prominent spokesperson. Learning was seen as a meaningful process. The value of drill was noted, but it was placed after understanding, instead of being the major means of sequencing the curriculum and providing instruction.

Changes in psychology have continued. We came to believe that the developmental level of the child is also a factor in determining the sequence of the curriculum—topics cannot be taught until a child is developmentally ready to learn them. Or, from another point of view, topics must be taught so that children at a given developmental level are ready to learn them. Such ideas and inferences have been taken into consideration as the curriculum has evolved. These factors will be considered in Chapter 4.

Needs of Society

The practicality and usefulness of mathematics in everyday situations and in vocations has also affected what is taught and when it is taught. This has been true ever since colonial times, when mathematics was considered necessary primarily for clerks and bookkeepers. The curriculum was limited to counting, the simpler procedures for addition, subtraction, and multiplication, and some knowledge of measures and of fractions. Much of the computation was with denominate numbers (such as "3 feet 5 inches") involving measures in commercial use.

By the late nineteenth century, business and commerce had increased to the point where mathematics was considered important for everyone. The arithmetic curriculum expanded to include such topics as percentage, ratio and proportion, powers, roots, and series.

The emphasis on teaching what was needed for use in occupations continued into the twentieth century. One of the most vocal advocates of *social utility* was Guy Wilson. He and his students conducted numerous surveys to determine what arithmetic was actually used by carpenters, shopkeepers, and other workers. He believed that the "dominating" aim of the school mathematics program should be to teach those skills, and only those skills.

We have already noted the outburst of public concern in the 1950s, when the anxiety to improve the curriculum lest we fall behind in the "space race" resulted in a wave of curriculum development and research in mathematics. Much of this effort was focused on the mathematically talented student. In the mid-1960s, however, concern was also expressed for the disadvantaged student, as our society renewed its search for equality of opportunity. With these changes—as, in fact, with *each* change—more and better mathematical achievement was promised.

In the 1970s, when it became apparent that once again the promise had not fully materialized, there was another swing in the curricular curve. Emphasis was renewed on skills needed for "survival" in the real world. The minimal-competency movement stressed "the basics." As these were embodied in sets of objectives and in tests, the "basics" were considered to be primarily addition, subtraction, multiplication, and division with whole numbers and fractions. Thus, the skills needed by children in colonial times were again considered by many to be the sole necessities for children living in a world with calculators and computers.

WHAT OTHER FORCES AFFECT THE MATHEMATICS CURRICULUM?

Besides the three general factors discussed above, seven other forces influence change in the curriculum.

Educational Organizations

Many educational organizations, such as the National Council of Teachers of Mathematics, the National Education Association, the Mathematical Association of America, and the Conference Board of the Mathematical Sciences, have at intervals established commissions, panels, or committees to provide a status report on the curriculum or some aspect of the curriculum, and to develop recommendations for proposed change. In the next section the efforts of several such committees will be summarized. A report that had a decided impact in the 1970s was prepared by the National Advisory Committee on Mathematical Education (NACOME) (9). It provided an extensive overview and analysis of school mathematics in kindergarten through grade 12. The curriculum reforms of 1955 to 1975 were analyzed and new curricular emphases considered. Both curriculum content and curriculum development were addressed. In introducing its recommendations on content, the report noted that:

> Curriculum content, subject to the flux of accelerating change in all areas of our society, cannot be viewed as a fixed set of goals or ideas; it must be allowed to emerge, ever changing, responsive to the human and technological lessons of the past, concerns of the present, and hopes for the future. With this in mind, no definitive curriculum can ever be recommended. (9, p. 138)

Five years later, the National Council of Teachers of Mathematics issued another set of recommendations in the form of *An Agenda for Action: Recommendations for School Mathematics of the 1980s* (1). The eight recommendations in the Agenda are found in Figure 1-1.

The emphasis on problem solving and the use of calculators and computers is clear in these recommenda-

RECOMMENDATIONS IN AN AGENDA FOR ACTION—1980

1. Problem solving must be the focus of school mathematics in the 1980s.
2. The concept of basic skills in mathematics must encompass more than computational facility.
3. Mathematics programs must take full advantage of the power of calculators and computers at all grade levels.
4. Stringent standards of both effectiveness and efficiency must be applied to the teaching of mathematics.
5. The success of mathematics programs and student learning must be evaluated by a wider range of measures than conventional testing.
6. More mathematics study must be required for all students and a flexible curriculum with a greater range of options should be designed to accommodate the diverse needs of the student population.
7. Mathematics teachers must demand of themselves and their colleagues a high level of professionalism.
8. Public support for mathematics instruction must be raised to a level commensurate with the importance of mathematical understanding to individuals and society.

Figure 1-1. From *An Agenda for Action* (1). Used by permission.

tions. As time passes, we will be able to judge the effectiveness with which the recommendations have been implemented.

Research

Research has influenced curriculum change, as we have noted. A noteworthy example currently is the testing program of the National Assessment of Educational Progress (2, 3), to which we will refer throughout this book. These assessments, occurring at intervals of several years, have provided evidence on how well students are learning certain content (for example, addition) and how poorly they are doing on other content (for example, problem solving). Concern about weakness in the latter has been voiced by many educators, and problem solving appears to be a leading candidate for curriculum change.

A survey of elementary and secondary teachers and principals, junior college and college teachers of mathematics, supervisors of mathematics, mathematics teacher educators, presidents of school boards, and presidents of parent-teacher organizations has provided information on current beliefs and reactions to possible mathematics curriculum changes during the 1980s (11). Not unexpectedly, there was strong support for topics now in the curriculum, with less support for most new topics. But the responses also indicated widespread support among all samples for a focus on problem solving. There was some evidence of support for a broad interpretation of basic skills as including more than computation. The sharpest differences between groups were found on calculator issues. It would appear that the curriculum could be changed much more smoothly to incorporate the use of computers than that of calculators. Thus, there is a need to inform parents (and teachers, too) about effective uses of calculators in concept development and comprehension. Research-based knowledge can be of help in implementing curriculum change.

Technology

Technology is changing patterns of production and behavior in people's everyday lives. It is not surprising that technology should affect what goes on in schools. Devices incorporating the use of microprocessors are of particular importance to teachers, for such devices led to the development of relatively low-cost calculators and microcomputers.

The long-term effect of technology on schools in general and mathematics programs in particular is unknown. There is feverish activity in this area, and it will be some time before the true effect on the curriculum is apparent. Many uncertainties exist, and the forecasting of future classroom implications is very speculative. Nevertheless, we know that many myths surround calculators and computers. Further, we recognize the importance of computer literacy among teachers, who will be called upon to utilize such technology and use it effectively. Therefore, we have devoted Chapter 2 to a discussion of the impact of technology.

Threats to Security

War is a threat to security that has affected the mathematics curriculum. During both the First and Second World Wars, concerns arose about the mathematical competency of draftees, leading to inquiries about change. In addition, wars have tended to generate new applications of mathematics and even new mathematics, thus spurring curriculum revision.

Another type of threat to security was raised by the flight of Sputnik: unexpectedly, it challenged the United States as the world's scientific leader. As a result, a massive curriculum development effort was instigated in the late 1950s. The "new math" projects resulted in cooperation among mathematics teachers and educators, mathematicians, and psychologists to develop new curricular materials. Most of these projects had some influence on activities you'll find in this and other books.

In the 1980s, another concern about security involves the amount of mathematics children in other countries—especially the Soviet Union and Japan—are given and how well they do on tests. It is feared that a better mathematics background may give them an advantage, especially in terms of technology and their ability to do better than we in applying mathematics.

Government

The major curriculum development projects noted above had federal funding for all or part of their activities. This was the first time federal agencies became involved in curriculum development on so massive a scale, and they attempted to fund a variety of types of projects in order to provide alternatives, rather than to control the direction of the development activities.

In addition to the creation of federal agencies such as the National Science Foundation and the National Institute of Education, responsible for funding multitudes of research, curriculum development, teacher training, and equipment proposals, other funds were supplied by acts of legislation. Thus, the National Defense Education Act funneled monies for equipment to schools, while the Elementary and Secondary Education Acts supplied funds for improving instructional programs. Money was earmarked for remedial teachers in such areas as mathematics.

Other laws directed new requirements at schools. For instance, metric education was furthered in most states by legislative action. Mainstreaming, involving the integration of children with handicaps into the regular classroom, was mandated—and, in many instances, so was minimal-competency testing.

Testing

It has long been apparent that tests can be a means toward controlling a curriculum or instigating curriculum change. If schools rely on tests for certain purposes, then they want their students to do well on those tests. To do this, they must teach the content that the tests cover. Thus, when the College Entrance Examination Board included "new math" content on its test, schools were forced to consider the new content seriously.

Tests can also act to retard curriculum change, however, by excluding new content. Thus, efforts to effect widespread use of calculators were slowed because tests (as well as textbooks) were slow to reflect the existence of new procedures.

Competency tests provide another example of tests acting to retard curricular change. Such tests have tended to focus on computation, therefore increasing the importance of computational skills rather than decreasing it, as so many recommendations suggest.

Economy

Restricted finances for a district can determine the extent to which a school can adopt curriculum changes. Not only is there likely to be less money for teachers to devote to curriculum development, but also there is likely to be less available for adopting new textbooks, even at five-year intervals. Without such new materials, curriculum change tends to be stifled.

WHAT CURRICULAR CONTENT HAS BEEN PROPOSED AS ESSENTIAL?

We will consider now four sets of suggestions about curricular content essential for all students. Each program is based on the assumption that the school mathematics program must meet societal needs by preparing individuals to live and work in the adult world.

The Drill Load of Arithmetic

This program was proposed by Guy Wilson in the 1940s on the basis of his surveys of the arithmetic actually used by workers (17). He concluded that:

> 90 percent of adult figuring is covered by the four fundamental processes, addition, subtraction, multiplication, and division [of whole numbers]. Simple fractions, percentage, and interest, if added to the four fundamental processes, will raise the percentage to over 95 percent (17, p. 7)

Thus, he arrived at "a very simple load for drill mastery." For example, for addition he proposed that all children master 100 primary facts, 300 related decade facts to 39 + 9, 80 other facts needed for carrying in multiplication to 9 × 9, simple columns and examples with sums to 39 + 9, and United States money.

Key Concepts for Postwar Programs

The Second World War not only demanded mathematical competencies at many levels, but also led to the development of new mathematical ideas and new applications of mathematics. The Commission on Post-War Plans of the National Council of Teachers of Mathematics developed a list of 29 key concepts that defined functional competence for junior high school mathematics students (7). In addition to such topics as computation, percents, ratio, square root, and geometric concepts, they included estimation, tables and graphs, statistics, algebra, and trigonometry. Practicality was also reflected in "first steps in business arithmetic" and "stretching the dollar."

Mathematical Competence and Skills Essential for Enlightened Citizens

Another NCTM committee was appointed in 1970 to draw up a list of basic mathematical competencies, skills, and attitudes necessary for citizens in contempo-

rary society (6). Their report noted continuing changes in mathematics and the added impact of technology. They presented a detailed list of skills and competencies needed by the majority of adults, characteristics of the nature of mathematics as a system, and understandings about the role of mathematics in society.

These ideas broadened the scope of what the mathematics curriculum should encompass—and suggested, in fact, teaching that mathematics is not merely a collection of facts and skills, but a necessary and enjoyable component of living.

Ten Basic Mathematical Skill Areas

In response to what mathematics educators perceived as a potentially dangerous narrowing of the mathematics curriculum by those advocating a "return to the basics" in the 1970s, the National Council of Supervisors of Mathematics prepared a "Position Paper on Basic Mathematical Skills" (10). Arguing that far more than computational skills are needed today, they identified ten basic skill areas (see Figure 1-2). They noted in their rationale for the expanded definition of basic skills that:

> The present technological society requires use of such skills as estimating, problem solving, interpreting data, organizing data, measuring, predicting, and applying mathematics to everyday situations. The changing needs of society, the explosion of the amount of quantitative data, and the availability of computers and calculators demand a redefining of the priorities for basic mathematics skills. (10, p. 1)

Changing needs are reflected in the four sets of suggestions. To Wilson, what was actually used in vocations provided the basis for determining curriculum. To the Post-War Commission, the use of mathematics as a tool in other subject areas was decisive in defining mathematical literacy for all who can possibly attain it. The suggestions of Edwards et al. went far beyond computation and were to some extent paralleled by the ten basic mathematics skills listed by the NCSM. Each program is based on the assumption that a mathematically literate population is not only desirable but vital to both society and the individual.

HOW HAS THE CURRICULUM ACTUALLY CHANGED?

We have noted some proposals for curriculum change and have listed some forces that interacted with curriculum planning. Curriculum change, as our brief history

TEN BASIC SKILL AREAS (NCSM)

Problem Solving

Learning to solve problems is the principal reason for studying mathematics. Problem solving is the process of applying previously acquired knowledge to new and unfamiliar situations. Solving word problems in texts is one form of problem solving, but students also should be faced with non-textbook problems. Problem-solving strategies involve posing questions, analyzing situations, translating results, illustrating results, drawing diagrams, and using trial and error. In solving problems, students need to be able to apply the rules of logic necessary to arrive at valid conclusions. They must be able to determine which facts are relevant. They should be unfearful of arriving at tentative conclusions and they must be willing to subject these conclusions to scrutiny.

Applying Mathematics to Everyday Situations

The use of mathematics is interrelated with all computation activities. Students should be encouraged to take everyday situations, translate them into mathematical expressions, solve the mathematics, and interpret the results in light of the initial situation.

Alertness to the Reasonableness of Results

Due to arithmetic errors or other mistakes, results of mathematical work are sometimes wrong. Students should learn to inspect all results and to check for reasonableness in terms of the original problem. With the increase in the use of calculating devices in society, this skill is essential.

Estimation and Approximation

Students should be able to carry out rapid approximate calculations by first rounding off numbers. They should acquire some simple techniques for estimating quantity, length, distance, weight, etc. It is also necessary to decide when a particular result is precise enough for the purpose at hand.

Appropriate Computational Skills

Students should gain facility with addition, subtraction, multiplication, and division with whole numbers and decimals. Today it must be recognized that long, complicated computations will usually be done with a calculator. Knowledge of single-digit number facts is essential and mental arithmetic is a valuable skill. Moreover, there are everyday situations which demand recognition of, and simple computation with, common fractions.

Because consumers continually deal with many situations that involve percentage, the ability to recognize and use percents should be developed and maintained.

Geometry

Students should learn the geometric concepts they will need to function effectively in the 3-dimensional world. They should have knowledge of concepts such as point, line, plane, parallel, and perpendicular. They should know basic properties of simple geometric figures, particularly those properties which relate to measurement and problem-solving skills. They also must be able to recognize similarities and differences among objects.

Measurement

As a minimum skill, students should be able to measure distance, weight, time, capacity, and temperature. Measurement of angles and calculations of simple areas and volumes are also essential. Students should be able to perform measurement in both metric and customary systems using the appropriate tools.

Reading, Interpreting, and Constructing Tables, Charts and Graphs

Students should know how to read and draw conclusions from simple tables, maps, charts, and graphs. They should be able to condense numerical information into more manageable or meaningful terms by setting up simple tables, charts, and graphs.

Using Mathematics to Predict

Students should learn how elementary notions of probability are used to determine the likelihood of future events. They should learn to identify situations where immediate past experience does not affect the likelihood of future events. They should become familiar with how mathematics is used to help make predictions such as election forecasts.

Computer Literacy

It is important for all citizens to understand what computers can and cannot do. Students should be aware of the many uses of computers in society, such as their use in teaching/learning, financial transactions, and information storage and retrieval. The "mystique" surrounding computers is disturbing and can put persons with no understanding of computers at a disadvantage. The increasing use of computers by government, industry, and business demands an awareness of computer uses and limitations.

Figure 1-2. From "Position Paper on Basic Mathematical Skills" (10). Used by permission.

suggests, is generally a slow, "push-pull" process. It is like the movement of a tide in which little change is apparent from moment to moment but, given time, the water does rise and fall. Moreover, there is a tendency for ideas about curriculum innovation to be cyclic—that is, suggestions made in one decade are likely to recur (frequently with a new label) two or more decades later.

The mid-1970s saw a turn away from the emphasis on structure and understanding, new content, and exploratory methods that had characterized curriculum development work for twenty years. Concern about public schools was widely publicized as a result of such factors as:

- Declines in scores on the Scholastic Achievement Test (SAT), a college-entrance examination.

- Low scores on portions of the National Assessment of Educational Progress (NAEP).

- Scores on state assessment tests that seemed to mirror the lower achievement reflected on the other tests.

The back-to-the-basics movement was a natural continuation of the movement to make schools and teachers accountable for children's learning. The minimal-competency movement grew apace, stressing a limited body of content that all students would be expected to master. Parallels can readily be drawn between it and the drill-for-mastery movement in the 1920s.

When we consider curriculum, it is imperative that we consider textbooks, for they are the primary determinant of the mathematics curriculum that is actually being taught throughout schools in this country. State curriculum guides present an outline that can be filled in by use of a textbook; local guides resemble textbooks in scope and sequence. More properly, we should refer to mathematics curricula, for textbooks do vary in what they cover at each grade level and the amount of attention they devote to each topic (8).

The evidence indicates that in most classrooms teachers use a single textbook with all students, rather than referring to multiple textbooks or varying text use to suit group or individual needs (13). Research also indicates that there appears to be a rather firm adherence to "covering the material" in the text, although sections that teachers do not consider important (and that may not be included on standardized tests) may be ignored. Nevertheless, the textbook does influence what is learned: different patterns of achievement have been associated with the use of different textbooks.

Research indicates also, however, that the effect of the teacher on children's achievement is great (5). One reviewer noted:

> It is the teacher, not the textbook, who can best control student motivation and self-concept, who can cultivate the development of logical reasoning through the interaction of students with peers, and who can capitalize on everyday situations and questions to nurture the growth of problem solving skills. (5, p. 5)

The textbook provides an outline or framework on which you can build a sound mathematics program. Along with experiences, activities, and manipulative materials, it contributes to mathematics learning. Teacher's guides for the textbook contain a wealth of background information, sequencing overviews (so you can fit a particular lesson into perspective), prelesson activities, and suggestions for using the book, including activities, questions, and ideas for helping children who need enrichment as well as those who need remediation. When you receive the teacher's guide you'll be using, look all the way through it to get a general idea of what it contains and where to look for specific help. Chapter 5 discusses how you can use the teacher's guide in lesson planning.

WHAT CURRICULUM CONCERNS ARE STILL UNRESOLVED?

At any point in time certain curricular concerns are unresolved. The curriculum is in a constant state of change, and therefore

> Curriculum work is a never-ending process. There needs to be on-going assessment of the content, ways of treating the content, and the effects of the curriculum on students (14, p. 13)

Today the curriculum is changing because the content and skills that students must have to meet societal needs have changed. In addition, new evidence about better ways of teaching is continuously being found.

Among the unresolved concerns noted in this chapter are the scope of curriculum content, the placement of topics, the role of computing technology, and the impact of competency testing. Trafton cites others, but concludes with a hopeful comment:

> The concern of the public for strong academic programs, the investigations on how students learn specific topics, the renewed interest in problem solving and applications, and the contributions that calculators can make are all factors providing possible beginning points for future curriculum considerations. (14, p. 26)

A GLANCE AT WHERE WE'VE BEEN

The mathematics curriculum is continuously changing to reflect the needs of the subject, the child, and society. This chapter has given examples of such changes. It has also considered seven other forces that affect the curriculum: educational organizations, research, technology, threats to security, government, testing, and the economy.

At intervals throughout American history, recommendations have been made on content considered essential for all students. This chapter has presented four sets of such suggestions to indicate their changing (and enlarging) scope. How the curriculum has actually changed is reflected by textbooks, and the chapter has noted their important role in the mathematics program. Finally, it has mentioned some unresolved curriculum concerns.

THINGS TO DO: ADDING TO YOUR PICTURE

1. What types of information can help you decide what mathematics to teach to a given group of children?

2. Give an illustration (in addition to those in this chapter) of how mathematics is: a study of patterns and relationships, a way of thinking, an art, a language.

3. Several educators have noted that the curriculum is in a continuous process of change in order to keep in balance as the needs of the subject, the child, and society pull it first one way and then another. Discuss this comment.

4. Discuss the role that testing can play in regard to the curriculum.

5. What elementary school curriculum content appears to have been constant for the past 100 years? Why? Is this likely to remain true? Why or why not?

6. Many countries have a national curriculum. Discuss this question: Does a national curriculum exist in the United States?

7. Identify some ways that a healthy economy stimulates curriculum changes in mathematics.

8. Read "The Teacher and the Textbook" by Driscoll (5) and summarize the points he makes. Present them to your class.

9. Which unresolved curriculum concerns do you consider of most importance? Why?

SELECTED REFERENCES

1. *An Agenda for Action: Recommendations for School Mathematics of the 1980s.* Reston, Va.: National Council of Teachers of Mathematics, 1980.

2. Carpenter, Thomas; Coburn, Terrence G.; Reys, Robert E.; and Wilson, James W. *Results from the First Mathematics Assessment of the National Assessment of Educational Progress.* Reston, Va.: National Council of Teachers of Mathematics, 1978.

3. Carpenter, Thomas P.; Corbitt, Mary Kay; Kepner, Henry S., Jr.; Lindquist, Mary Montgomery; and Reys, Robert E. *Results from the Second Mathematics Assessment of the National Assessment of Educational Progress.* Reston, Va.: National Council of Teachers of Mathematics, 1981.

4. DeVault, M. Vere, and Weaver, J. Fred. "Forces and Issues Related to Curriculum and Instruction, K-6." In *A History of Mathematics Education in the United States and Canada* (ed. Phillip S. Jones). Thirty-second Yearbook. Washington, D.C.: National Council of Teachers of Mathematics, 1970.

5. Driscoll, Mark J. "The Teacher and the Textbook." In *Research Within Reach: Elementary School Mathematics.* St. Louis: CEMREL, Inc., 1980.

6. Edwards, E. L., Jr.; Nichols, Eugene D.; and Sharpe, Glyn H. "Mathematical Competencies and Skills Essential for Enlightened Citizens." *Arithmetic Teacher,* 19 (November 1972), pp. 601-607.

7. "Guidance Report of the Commission on Post-War Plans." *Mathematics Teacher,* 40 (July 1947), pp. 315-339.

8. Kuhs, Therese M., and Freeman, Donald J. "The Potential Influence of Textbooks on Teachers' Selection of Content for Elementary School Mathematics." Research Series No. 48. East Lansing, Mich.: The Institute for Research on Teaching, 1979.

9. National Advisory Committee on Mathematical Education. *Overview and Analysis of School Mathematics Grades K-12.* Washington, D.C.: Conference Board of the Mathematical Sciences, 1975.

10. "Position Paper on Basic Mathematical Skills." National Council of Supervisors of Mathematics, 1977. *Arithmetic Teacher,* 25 (October 1977), pp. 18-22.

11. *Priorities in School Mathematics: Executive Summary of the PRISM Project.* Reston, Va.: National Council of Teachers of Mathematics, 1981.

12. Suydam, Marilyn N. "The Case for a Comprehensive Mathematics Curriculum." *Arithmetic Teacher,* 26 (February 1979), pp. 10-11.

13. Suydam, Marilyn N., and Osborne, Alan. *The Status of Pre-College Science, Mathematics, and Social Science Education, 1955-1975.* Volume II: *Mathematics Education.* Final Report, National Science Foundation. Columbus: The Ohio State University, 1977.

14. Trafton, Paul R. "Assessing the Mathematics Curriculum Today." In *Selected Issues in Mathematics Education* (ed. Mary Montgomery Lindquist). Chicago: National Society for the Study of Education; Reston, Va.: National Council of Teachers of Mathematics, 1980. Pp. 9-26.

15. Washburne, Carleton. "Mental Age and the Arithmetic Curriculum: A Summary of the Committee of Seven Grade Placement Investigations to Date." *Journal of Educational Research,* 23 (March 1931), pp. 210-231.

16. Wilson, Guy M.; Stone, Mildred B.; and Dalrymple, Charles O. *Teaching the New Arithmetic.* New York: McGraw-Hill, 1939.

17. Wilson, Guy M. "The Social Utility Theory as Applied to Arithmetic, Its Research Basis, and Some of Its Implications." *Journal of Educational Research,* 41 (January 1948), pp. 321-337.

2

Using Technology in Mathematics

INTRODUCTION

Technology greatly influences today's school programs, as well it should. Our instruction should be directed toward helping students cope with a changing world to ensure that they can function properly once their formal education is completed. It is no longer futuristic to describe a computerized society. It is here! We see it in homes, cars, and mass transit. We experience it in supermarkets, banks, hotels, and other businesses. We utilize it for recreational activities, such as those found in arcades and amusement parks as well as in homes. Historically schools have been slow to respond to societal changes. One might expect schools to be the last bastion of resistance, but this is not the case. An examination of current elementary school programs shows that dramatic changes have occurred. Here is some evidence of this technological impact:

1. Basal mathematics textbook series include calculator activities as a part of the regular student pages. In fact, every post-1980 major elementary mathematics series includes activities for use with calculators.
2. The second national mathematics assessment reported that more than 75 percent of nine-year-olds and 80 percent of 13-year-olds either have a cal-

culator of their own or access to a calculator at home (6).
3. Microcomputers are in schools as well as in many homes. A majority of all schools now have at least one microcomputer, and the number of microcomputers available, as well as the use made of them, is increasing greatly.

As you can see, the times are changing. We are in an exciting era that gives us the opportunity not only to experience many technological advances but also to help utilize them effectively in schools. This serves as a vivid reminder that education is an ongoing and continuous process. As teachers, we too must learn to cope effectively with a changing educational world.

WHAT IS COMPUTER LITERACY?

The term "computer literacy" was rarely mentioned as an instructional goal prior to 1970. Yet in the last ten years it has been included on every list of basic skills of school mathematics programs. It is generally recommended that the development of computer literacy should be started in elementary school. This does not mean that mathematics programs need to assume major responsibility for developing computer literacy, but it is generally agreed that mathematics programs will provide many natural opportunities for doing so.

Computer literacy should provide a general understanding of what computers can and cannot do. More specifically, as a computer-literate teacher, you should:

1. Be able to discuss different uses of computers in homes, business, and particularly in schools.
2. Know the basic operational plan of a computer.
3. Know and correctly use common computer terms.
4. Be able to run prepared programs on microcomputers.
5. Know the strengths and limitations of computers for classroom instruction.
6. Be able to help strip away the "black-box mystique" that surrounds computers. Computers must be recognized as tools—powerful, versatile, and subservient to human commands.

Unfortunately, the meaning of the term *computer literacy* is not universally agreed upon. It is in a developmental state, primarily because computer technology is changing so rapidly. We will need to refine and update regularly what is meant by computer literacy. Despite this ambiguity, computer literacy is an instructional goal endorsed by the National Council of Teachers of Mathematics and other professional organizations. It has been supported strongly by teachers—and even more strongly by lay persons. Parents recognize the impact of computers on society and want their children to be able to cope.

The goal of computer literacy in elementary school is to develop a general awareness and understanding of computers. Such experiences may encourage some students to acquire more sophisticated computer skills. However, the development of programming expertise is beyond what we are advocating today for elementary school.

CALCULATORS

Calculator Myths

Even though calculators are widely accessible, a tremendous inertia remains to be overcome before they will be used optimally in the classroom. Fears surrounding calculator use, founded on hearsay, half-truths, and innuendos, have created two myths that need to be dispelled.

Calculator Myth—Using Calculators Does Not Require Thinking. Calculators don't think, they only follow instructions. For example, the following problem can be solved with a calculator, but only if a correct problem-solving strategy is used.

In servicing a car the attendant used 5 quarts of oil at $1.45 a quart and 15 gallons of gas at $1.39 a gallon. What was the total cost for oil and gas?

If a calculator were used to find the answer, would it solve the problem? Does the calculator decide what keys to punch and in what order to punch them? Does the calculator interpret the result? A few problems such as this provide a vivid reminder that calculators don't solve problems—people do.

In fact, a very strong argument can be made that using calculators actually increases student thinking. More specifically, it frees students from tedious and laborious computation and allows them to dwell on the important problem-solving processes that generally precede the arithmetic computation.

Calculator Myth—Calculators Harm Student Mathematics Achievement. Many parents and some teachers have worried that students will become so dependent on calculators that they will forget how to compute. This concern is not supported by research. In the last ten years over 150 research studies have focused on the effects of calculator use, especially on whether use of calculators harms student mathematics achievement. Consistently the answer has been, "No, calculator use does not appear to affect achievement adversely" (21). In fact, not only are there no measurable ill effects, but "research is showing the calculator to be a powerful teaching and learning tool" (8). As teachers we must not only make effective use of calculators in our teaching but also help any skeptical parents put their fears to rest.

Calculator Recommendations

Calculators Should Be Used When Appropriate. We recognize that computation skills must be learned, but this does not preclude the use of calculators. Our recommendation is that calculators be used whenever computation is needed and the computational skills are not the main focus of instruction. Our recommendation provides for broad and creative use of calculators, as well it should. For example, it allows use of calculators in all problem-solving activities, yet also permits calculators to be used for developing basic facts. Clearly, the establishment of basic arithmetic facts should remain an important instructional goal in the primary grades. It is essential that rapid recall of basic facts (e.g., 4×7, $8 + 6$) be established. For one thing, these basic facts serve as natural stepping stones to mental computation (e.g., $40 \times 70, 800 + 600$) and estimation skills, both of which are important.

Can calculators be used to develop basic facts? Research evidence indicates that the development of basic facts is, in fact, enhanced in the primary grades through calculator use (7). Actual classroom practice shows that calculators can be used effectively in many different instructional activities as early as first grade.

Calculators provide a powerful computing tool; however, they can also be used in many developmental ways. For example, throughout this book we will show how calculators might be used in nontraditional ways to practice counting, basic facts, and mental computation. Problem solving and ways of searching for patterns with calculators will also be addressed.

Calculators Should Be Used on Some Tests. A calculator should be used to focus the students' attention on the concept being measured whenever paper-and-pencil computation is not being tested. The extent of calculator use on tests—both teacher-made and standardized—is changing for several reasons.

Research results (6) have indicated that calculator use alone has little effect on anything other than direct computation. Since most standardized tests have three distinct parts—concepts, computation, and problem solving—calculators could be used on two-thirds of the test without "contaminating" the results.

Many commercial tests have been or will be revised to accommodate calculator use. Revision often includes the provision of alternate forms that have been normed for calculator availability. Such forms help legitimize the use of calculators. They may also help us construct our regular teacher-made tests to accommodate calculator usage better.

Professional groups such as the National Council of Teachers of Mathematics have long advocated the use of calculators. More than ten years ago, one prestigious group recommended that "beginning no later than the end of eighth grade, a calculator should be available for each mathematics student during each mathematics class. Each student should be permitted to use the calculator during all of his or her mathematical work including tests" (18, p. 138). The spirit of this recommendation is reflected by businesses and employers when they ask prospective employees to bring a calculator to use on job application tests. Our schools must prepare students for such a future.

Getting Started with Calculators

As you might expect, students are excited when calculators are first used. This initial excitement will subside, but classroom experience confirms that both motivation and enthusiasm are long-term by-products of calculator use. Instruction should take advantage of and build on this excitement. To use calculators efficiently and effectively, students should understand the operation of the model they are using, along with its limitations. This knowledge will take them a long way in gaining computer literacy.

Here is a checklist of some things you might do *before* actually using calculators (5):

- Show the children several types of calculators.
- Ask how many children have used a calculator.
- Ask how many own their own calculator.
- Discuss with children what they think a calculator is for.
- If possible, show the students the inside of a calculator.

Now—some suggestions for introducing calculators to students in grades 1 through 8. The time you spend on various activities will depend on your students' level, interests, and background.

Free Play Time. Letting students experiment with their calculators (usually 3 to 5 minutes) will reduce the initial excitement to a manageable level. Most students will then be eager for guidance.

Explanation of Keys. After students have explored on their own, provide a brief description of the keys and how they are used. It is helpful to go over any special features (such as auto power-off, battery indicator, all clear versus clear entry key), adjusting your explanation to the students' level of understanding. Don't underestimate your students. Even young children are interested in this discussion, and their later understanding and use of a calculator may be enhanced. Also, do not overestimate your students. Some students will need to be reminded that the $\boxminus$ key is needed to find the sum or product.

Counting. Most calculators represent a powerful counting tool that provides the means for developing many important mathematical concepts. Counting with the calculator is a physical activity (a key is pressed each time a number is counted), through which students relate the size of a number to the amount of time needed to count it. Early calculator counting should emphasize the physical link between pressing the keys and watching the display, which helps students sense number size. For older students, counting by tenths (0.1) helps them understand the relative size of .1 and 1; similarly, counting by 100 and 1000 to a million helps develop a better understanding of large numbers. For example, Activity Card 2-1 shows that it takes over three minutes to count to 1000 by ones on a calculator, which is considerably longer than it takes to count to 100 but about the same amount of time as it takes to count by thousands to 1,000,000.*

Counting backward is a powerful but often difficult skill for young children. It is also one that can be aided by the calculator, as shown in Activity Card 2-2. Counting on from a particular number is another important skill, which leads to many patterns and is illustrated

*Activity Cards 2-1 through 2-6 are from *Keystrokes: Calculator Activities for Young Students: Counting and Place Value* (Palo Alto, California: Creative Publications, 1980). Used by permission.

Counting

Counting

Name _____

① How long did it take to count to 100? _____

② Guess how long it will take to count from 1 to 1000? _____

③ Count from 1 to 1000. How long did it take? _____

Counting Back
Patterns

Counting Backwards

Name _____

10, 9, 8, 7, 6, . . .

Fill in.

① 5 = ___ = ___ = ___ = ___ = ___
     4   3

② 15 = ___ = ___ = ___ = ___ = ___
      14

③ 20 = ___ = ___ = ___ = ___ = ___

④ 25 = ___ = ___ = ___ = ___ = ___

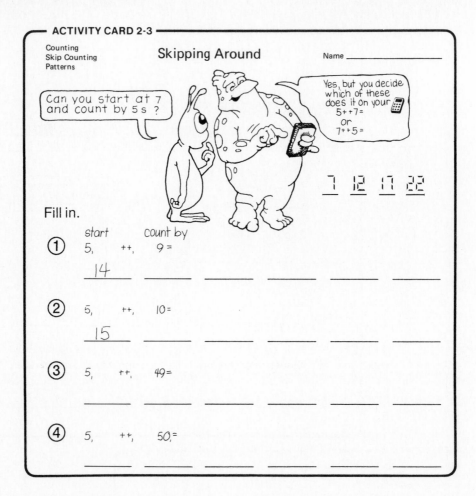

in Activity Card 2-3. These cards illustrate some of the potential of a calculator as a counter, which opens up many mathematical topics for exploration. The exact keystroking necessary to the counting varies among calculators. Helping and encouraging children to count with their calculator will promote many important problem-solving skills.

Overloading. A calculator can be overloaded in many ways. Any orientation should insure that the calculator sometimes overloads; otherwise the student may think it is broken when the display flashes or gives other overload indications. Many computational problems create an overload, and recognizing this limitation is an important aspect of computer literacy.

Activity Card 2-4 uses place-value patterns to lead to an overload situation. Ask students to answer question 6 by loading in the largest number their calculators will display. Have them add one to this number. Many calculators will flash when overloaded; others will display a single "E" or a series of "E's" across the display. Some calculators display an approximate answer when overloaded; in this case, proper positioning of the decimal point can provide a reasonable answer. Students

should recognize the overload signal, understand its importance, and learn how to cope with it.

Some Sample Calculator Activities

Children at all levels should do some counting activities, as these provide the basis for developing much mathematics. The calculator is an instructional tool to call upon in developing, practicing, and anchoring many topics in the elementary mathematics curriculum. Activity Card 2-5 provides a mental computation activity, while Activity Card 2-6 introduces some pattern exploration through problem solving. As you can see, these activities suggest a variety of different ways of using the calculator. Other activities will be integrated into topics throughout this book. We recommend, in fact, that whenever instruction is on a topic other than computational facts or algorithms, students have access to calculators.

What to Look for When Buying Calculators

The characteristics and prices of calculators vary tremendously. If your school or local parents' organiza-

Place Value
Regrouping
Patterns

How Much Will It Hold ?

Name _____

Enter in your 🖩   Write the number here.

① largest three-
digit number   _____ + 1 = _____

② largest four-
digit number   _____ + 1 = _____

③ largest five-
digit number   _____ + 1 = _____

④ largest six-
digit number   _____ + 1 = _____

⑤ largest seven-
digit number   _____ + 1 = _____

⑥ Enter the largest eight-digit number.

Add one. What do you see? _____

---

tion is considering buying a set for classroom use, there are a number of important characteristics to look for:

1. *Liquid crystal display.* Currently two types of display are available: LED (light-emitting diode) and LCD (liquid crystal display). The LCD provides for longer battery life and has a wider viewing angle.

2. *Automatic constant addend.* This feature allows users to count forward and backward as well as to hold a constant addend and/or multiplier; it is an absolute "must."

3. *Numerals on keys.* Numerals should appear *on* the keys, rather than above or below them. This is critical for younger students, less so for older ones.

4. *Slanted display.* Many calculators have a slightly angled display, allowing easy viewing even when the calculator is lying flat on a desk.

5. *A clear display.* The calculator's display should be easily readable and have an acceptable viewing angle.

6. *Distinct feel to buttons.* When buttons are pressed, the movement should be clearly felt by the user.

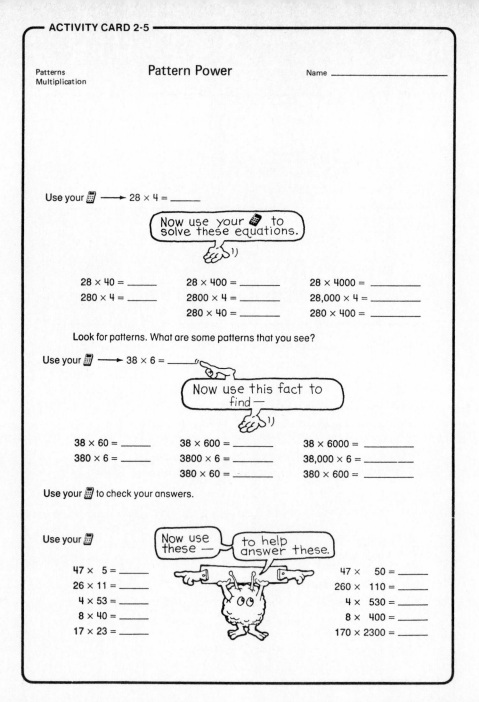

7. *Battery power source.* Automatic power-down displays and delayed power-off features maximize battery life. Batteries rather than adapters are recommended, simply because of the ease of use and access.

MICROCOMPUTERS

Computer Myths

Just as myths have been created about calculators, they have arisen also about microcomputers. These myths must be dispelled if microcomputers are to assume their role as a powerful instructional tool.

Computer Myth—Teachers Must Be Computer Experts to Use Microcomputers in Instruction. This untruth reflects the prevailing aura of computer anxiety. Some basic computer literacy skills are needed, of course, but not an extensive background in computer science and programming. In fact, most microcomputing equipment and accompanying software is directed toward people who have little or no such background. Most microcomputers are simple to operate, and the programming languages they use, such as BASIC and LOGO, are easy enough to learn by oneself.

Computer Myth—Computers Are Only for Exceptional Children. The computer is useful for all students, ranging from the academically talented to the below-average. Of course, the types of programs that students of differing ability experience and the ways they interact

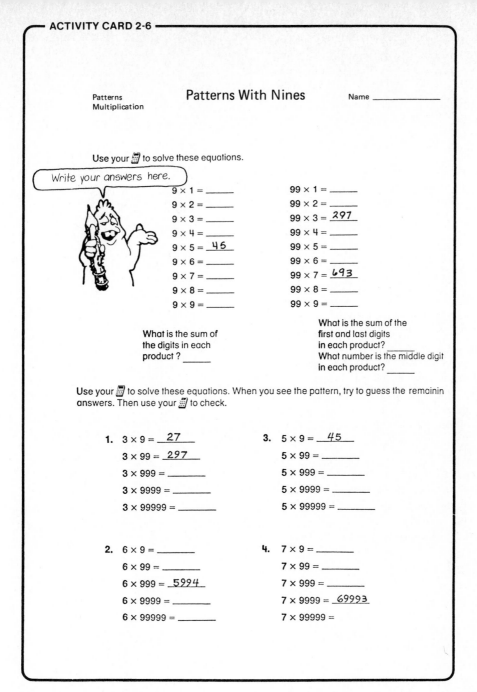

Patterns
Multiplication

Patterns With Nines

Name _____

Use your 🖩 to solve these equations.

Write your answers here.

9 × 1 = _____
9 × 2 = _____
9 × 3 = _____
9 × 4 = _____
9 × 5 = _45_
9 × 6 = _____
9 × 7 = _____
9 × 8 = _____
9 × 9 = _____

99 × 1 = _____
99 × 2 = _____
99 × 3 = _297_
99 × 4 = _____
99 × 5 = _____
99 × 6 = _____
99 × 7 = _693_
99 × 8 = _____
99 × 9 = _____

What is the sum of
the digits in each
product ? _____

What is the sum of the
first and last digits
in each product? _____
What number is the middle digit
in each product? _____

Use your 🖩 to solve these equations. When you see the pattern, try to guess the remainin
answers. Then use your 🖩 to check.

1. 3 × 9 = _27_
   3 × 99 = _297_
   3 × 999 = _____
   3 × 9999 = _____
   3 × 99999 = _____

3. 5 × 9 = _45_
   5 × 99 = _____
   5 × 999 = _____
   5 × 9999 = _____
   5 × 99999 = _____

2. 6 × 9 = _____
   6 × 99 = _____
   6 × 999 = _5994_
   6 × 9999 = _____
   6 × 99999 = _____

4. 7 × 9 = _____
   7 × 99 = _____
   7 × 999 = _____
   7 × 9999 = _69993_
   7 × 99999 =

with the system will vary, but all students can use the microcomputer. The immediate reinforcement available from the computer makes it an ideal teaching tool for slow learners, who often need more practice and immediate reinforcement.

Computer Myth—The Principal Reason to Use a Computer in School Is to Develop Programming Skills. It is a fact that programming skills are being learned by students of all ages as they interact with microcomputers. Such opportunities help students to do the following:

1. Develop computer literacy through firsthand experiences with the capabilities and limitations of computers.

2. Apply problem solving as they analyze the problem, plan steps toward a solution, check or debug their program, and then generalize or extend their program to handle entire classes of similar problems.

3. Seek a high level of understanding, as they must eventually "tell" the computer exactly what steps to follow in solving a problem.

4. Increase their motivation toward the study of mathematics as well as recognize the importance of persistence in their work and careful planning.

The opportunities to construct meaningful programs in elementary school mathematics are limited only by the ingenuity and creativeness of the teacher. Thus we see that programming skills can be developed. However, *there are other important instructional uses of the computer that should be experienced by all students.*

Instructional Uses of Microcomputers

Microcomputers are not a panacea or substitute for good teaching, but they do provide a valuable instructional tool to help teachers teach and children learn. Here are four of their very important instructional uses:

Tutorial. Many ready-to-use tutorial programs are commercially available. The student need only insert them in the microcomputer, which then provides direct instruction on specific topics, and the student responds. Good tutorial programs simulate a good teacher in their ability to introduce, explain, illustrate, question, diagnose, evaluate, and provide feedback. The programs available range in quality, so that a careful review should precede any decision to purchase one.

Drill and Practice. Programs are commercially available that allow the student to interact directly with the computer on specific skills. For example, basic facts can be presented on the monitor and timed to promote quick recall; or geometric shapes can be presented for students to name. Most of these programs keep track of the number of exercises attempted and the number correct. Such records help both students and teachers monitor progress.

The main purpose of drill and practice is to develop automatic recall, establish algorithmic responses, or recognize key aspects of ideas taught previously. These programs do not explain the mathematics but simply provide many opportunities to practice. This means that concepts and necessary understandings must be developed before such practice can become effective.

Simulations. Experiences that are important but too inconvenient or time-consuming to deal with directly can be illustrated via computers. Many mathematical concepts can be simulated, and probability models are particularly appropriate. For example, flipping coins and rolling dice can be simulated so that data from many observations can be generated quickly. This type of simulation is generally sandwiched within a lesson. Effective use of computer simulation, therefore, usually requires teachers to set up the lesson before data are collected and then initiate discussion afterward to ensure that important ideas from the simulation are understood.

Learning Games. Concepts and/or skills can often be established in gaming situations. Graphing (e.g., "Battleship"), basic facts (e.g., "Beat the Clock"), and consumer-related skills (e.g., "Lemonade") are only a few of the hundreds of computer-based games related to mathematics that are currently available. These gaming programs are typically simulations featuring competitive situations in which one or more persons can play, score, and win. By playing such games, children become less anxious about computers—one of the goals of computer literacy.

Although mathematics has been highlighted here, the uses of computers are interdisciplinary, cutting across other areas such as music, science, social studies, and reading. The computer must be recognized as a diverse and powerful instructional tool, taking the student far beyond any development of programming skills.

A GLANCE AT WHERE WE'VE BEEN

Technology is everywhere—including in our schools. Today's calculators and computers are powerful instructional tools. Although they must be used wisely, they must in fact be used, not ignored. Appropriate use of calculators has not hurt student learning of mathematics; often it has helped. Computers, too, in various ways can help increase the effectiveness of instruction for all students. First-hand experiences with computers will likely lead to higher levels of computer literacy. We are now witnessing many efforts to integrate the use of calculators and computers into the total K–12 mathematics curriculum. As teachers we must be aware of these developments and look for appropriate ways of using them as we plan instruction.

Direct applications to mathematics have been illustrated in this chapter, and many other examples are sprinkled throughout this book. Besides aiding directly the learning of some mathematical topics, the use of calculators and computers pays other, less obvious, yet very important dividends. For example, the value of following directions assumes a new level of significance, since these devices do exactly what they are instructed to do. Logical thinking skills are also sharpened as students apply statements such as IF-THEN.

Be alert for ways to use technology within the mathematics curriculum, not only as you read this book, but also as you visit, observe, and work in classrooms. To think ahead is to be ahead.

THINGS TO DO: ADDING TO YOUR PICTURE

1. Identify some characteristics of a teacher who is computer literate.
2. Check the NCTM *Agenda for Action* (1). How does it define computer literacy? Discuss some implications of this definition for elementary mathematics programs.
3. Examine the definition of computer literacy in three different resource materials listed in the references. Compare and contrast these definitions.
4. Describe how hands-on experience with calculators will help children become familiar with terms such as input and overload. Explain why familiarity with these terms contributes toward computer literacy.

5. Suppose your principal asked you to develop a school policy on calculator use. Prepare a statement that you feel would be appropriate and useful.

6. Read Wheatley's article, "Calculators in the Classroom: A Proposal for Curriculum Change" (25). Discuss the merit and consequences of implementing this proposal.

7. How would you respond to the following statement by a parent? "Calculators should not be used by children, because if they use them they will never have to think."

8. Examine a current elementary mathematics textbook series.
   (a) How early are calculator activities included?
   (b) Are calculator activities integrated into the regular lessons or relegated to ancillary materials?
   (c) Are any particular calculators endorsed or suggested by the series?

9. Examine a text at a given grade level to see how calculators are used. In particular, are they used to develop computational skills, to promote problem solving, and to build understanding of computational algorithms?

10. Choose some ancillary materials for calculator use —for example:

    Immerzeel, George; and Ockenga, Earl. *Calculator Activities—Books 1 and 2.* Palo Alto, Calif.: Creative Publications and Omron Corporation of America, 1977.

    Reys, Robert E.; Bestgen, Barbara J.; Coburn, Terrence G.; Schoen, Harold L.; Shumway, Richard J.; Wheatley, Charlotte L.; Wheatley, Grayson H.; and White, Arthur L. *Keystrokes: Calculator Activities for Young Students.* Palo Alto, Calif.: Creative Publications, 1979 and 1980.

    Select an activity related to a specific mathematical topic and describe how you might use it with a class.

11. Some valuable information is provided in the National Council of Teachers of Mathematics publication, *Guidelines for Evaluating Computerized Instructional Materials* (14). Highlight important issues that are discussed.

12. Get a calculator and apply it to the criteria on pages 15–16. Identify this calculator's strengths and weaknesses.

13. Try the calculator activities given in this chapter with students of the appropriate age. Keep a log of their reactions, the process they use, and whether the calculator assisted.

14. Identify and briefly describe several different instructional uses for a microcomputer.

15. Look at some of the suggested readings, such as the articles by Hatfield (13) and Wiebe (27) or the book by Malone and Johnson (16), for some samples of BASIC programs. Pick a program and describe how it might be used.

16. Describe how problem-solving skills could be enhanced in writing programs for a microcomputer.

17. Examine a recent commercial catalog listing microcomputer equipment. Decide what peripherals would be needed for a microcomputer, then determine about how much this "package" would cost.

18. If possible, visit an electronics store and try out one or more microcomputers.

SELECTED REFERENCES

1. *An Agenda for Action: Recommendations for School Mathematics of the 1980s.* Reston, Va.: National Council of Teachers of Mathematics, 1980.

2. *Arithmetic Teacher,* 23:7 (November 1976—Special Calculator Issue). 30:6 (February 1983—Special Microcomputer Issue).

3. Beardslee, Edward C. "Teaching Computational Skills with a Calculator." In *Developing Computational Skills* (ed. Marilyn N. Suydam and Robert E. Reys). 1978 NCTM Yearbook. Reston, Va.: National Council of Teachers of Mathematics, 1978.

4. Bell, Max S. "Calculators in Elementary Schools? Some Tentative Guidelines and Questions Based on Classroom Experience." *Arithmetic Teacher,* 23 (November 1976), pp. 502–509.

5. Bestgen, Barbara J. "Calculators—Taking the First Step." *Arithmetic Teacher,* 29 (September 1981), pp. 34–37.

6. Carpenter, Thomas P.; Corbitt, Mary K.; Kepner, Henry; Lindquist, Mary Montgomery; and Reys, Robert E. "Calculators and Computers." In *Results from the Second Mathematics Assessment of the National Assessment of Educational Progress.* Reston, Va.: National Council of Teachers of Mathematics, 1981.

7. Channell, Dwayne E. "The Use of Hand Calculators in the Learning of Basic Multiplication Facts." Columbus: The Ohio State University, May 1978.

8. Driscoll, Mark. "Calculators in the Classroom." In *Research Within Reach: Elementary School Mathematics.* St. Louis: CEMREL, Inc., 1980.

9. Dwyer, Thomas A., and Critchfield, Margot. *A Bit of Basic.* Reading, Mass.: Addison-Wesley, 1980.

10. Freeman, Donald J.; Kuhs, Therese M.; Porter, Andrew C.; Knappen, Lucy B.; Floden, Robert E.; Schmidt, William H.; and Schwille, John R. *The Fourth-Grade Mathematics Curriculum as Inferred from Textbooks and Tests.* Research Series No. 82. East Lansing, Mich.: The Institute for Research on Teaching, Michigan State University, July 1980. ERIC: ED 199 047.

11. Golden, Neal. *Computer Programming in the Basic Language,* 2d ed. New York: Harcourt Brace Jovanovich, 1980.

12. Hansen, Viggo P., ed. *The Impact of Technology on Mathematics Education.* 1984 NCTM Yearbook. Reston, Va.: National Council of Teachers of Mathematics, 1984.

13. Hatfield, Larry L. "A Case and Techniques for Computers: Using Computers in Middle School Mathematics." *Arithmetic Teacher,* 26 (February 1979), pp. 53–55.

14. Heck, William P.; Johnson, Jerry; and Kansky, Robert J. *Guidelines for Evaluating Computerized Instructional Materials.* Reston, Va.: National Council of Teachers of Mathematics, 1981.

15. Luehrmann, Arthur. "Computer Literacy—What Should it Be?" *Mathematics Teacher,* 74 (December 1981), pp. 682–686.

16. Malone, Linda, and Johnson, Jerry. *Basic Discoveries: A Problem Solving Approach to Beginning Programming.* Palo Alto, Calif.: Creative Publications, 1981.

17. Markuson, Carolyn and Tobias, Joyce. "LOGO Fever: The Computer Language Every Elementary School Is Catching." *Instructor,* 42 (January 1983), pp. 74–77.

18. National Advisory Committee on Mathematical Education. *Overview and Analysis of School Mathematics Grades K-12.* Washington, D.C.: Conference Board of the Mathematical Sciences, 1975.

19. *Position Statement on Computers in the Classroom. Position Statement on Calculators in the Classroom.* Reston, Va.: National Council of Teachers of Mathematics, 1976, 1978. ERIC: ED 153 782.

20. Shumway, Richard J. "Hand Calculators: Where Do You Stand?" *Arithmetic Teacher,* 23 (November 1976), pp. 569–572.

21. Suydam, Marilyn N. "The Use of Calculators in Pre-College Education: A State-of-the-Art Review." Columbus, Ohio: Calculator Information Center, August 1982.

22. Taylor, Ross. "Computers and Calculators in the Mathematics Classroom." In *Selected Issues in Mathematics Education* (ed. Mary M. Lindquist). National Society for the Study of Education. Berkeley, Calif.: McCutchan Publishing Company, 1980.

23. Usiskin, Zalman. "Are Calculators a Crutch?" *Mathematics Teacher,* 71 (May 1978), pp. 412–413.

24. Watts, Norman. "A Dozen Uses for the Computer in Education." *Educational Technology,* 22 (April 1981), pp. 18–22.

25. Wheatley, Grayson A. "Calculators in the Classroom: A Proposal for Curriculum Change." *Arithmetic Teacher,* 28 (December 1980), pp. 37–39.

26. Wheatley, Grayson A.; Shumway, Richard J.; Coburn, Terrence G.; Reys, Robert E.; Schoen, Harold L.; Wheatley, Charlotte L.; and White, Arthur L. "Calculators in the Classroom." *Arithmetic Teacher,* 27 (September 1979), pp. 18–21.

27. Wiebe, James H. "BASIC Programming for Gifted Elementary Students." *Arithmetic Teacher,* 28 (March 1981), pp. 42–44.

28. Zalewski, Don, ed. *Microcomputers for Teachers —With Application to Mathematics and Science.* Bowling Green, Ohio: School Science and Mathematics Association, 1982.

3

Focusing on Problem Solving

One day Mary Roberts read this story to her sixth-grade class:

Libby was walking up the stairs to her apartment.

"Hi, Libby," said Veronica. Veronica had just moved into the building and was in Libby's class at school. "Do you want to come over until dinner?"

"Sure," said Libby. "Just let me put these keys away."

"Why do you have so many keys?" asked Veronica.

"Because I walk dogs after school. Their owners work and I let myself into their apartments. I have five keys—one key fits each door."

"Oh," said Veronica. "By the way, did you finish the math homework?"

"Those word problems? Sure. I finished them in school. Get your math paper. I'll show you a trick. Then you can finish them in a flash," said Libby.

Veronica got her paper and started to read the first problem aloud.

Libby interrupted. "You're wasting your time reading the whole problem. All you have to do is look for the key word or words. They always tell you how to solve the problem. Just like the right key always opens the right apartment door."

"Are you sure?" asked Veronica.

"Positive. For example, look at number one. You see the word *more*. So you add. The answer is $55."

Veronica wasn't sure that Libby was correct. The problem read: "Joe has $15. He needs $40 to buy a new bike. How much more money does he need?"

"But $55 doesn't seem like the right answer. How can Joe need $55 more if the bike only costs $40?" asked Veronica.

"Hmmm . . . it always worked before," said Libby. "Let's try number two. The key words are *took away*. Whenever it says *less* or *take away*, you subtract. The answer is 10."

Veronica carefully read the problem to herself: "There were 12 baseball cards missing from Susan's set. Then her brother took away 2. How many are missing now?"

Veronica could see that the answer was 14.

"Maybe I'll finish these problems after dinner. Then I'll have more time to read each problem carefully," said Veronica.

"Suit yourself," said Libby. "But you're doing it the hard way."

When she had finished, Mrs. Roberts asked her class two questions: (1) Do you agree with Libby? (2) What do you think happened the next day in Libby's class?

INTRODUCTION

Every day, each of us must solve problems. We continually face situations in which there is an obstacle between us and something we want, and we must overcome or remove that obstacle. Not all the problems we face are mathematical, of course. Therefore, our goal as elementary teachers is to help children learn to solve a wide spectrum of problems: we help them to learn word attack and comprehension skills in reading, to use inquiry skills in science, to analyze the reasons why events occurred in social studies, and to cope with social interactions. And in mathematics, we present story or word problems and applications. We need to go one step further and develop children's ability to use various techniques and strategies for solving problems. Knowledge, skills, and understandings are important elements of mathematical learning, but it is in problem solving that the child synthesizes these components in order to answer a question, make a decision, or achieve a goal.

As the story about Libby and Veronica illustrates, we don't always produce problem solvers. Libby's problem-solving approach epitomizes the way many children attack problems: look for the numbers and the key words, and then go! They've decided there is no need to read, much less understand, the problem. They try to get an answer in the quickest way possible. Even after being wrong twice, Libby is still convinced her way is better than Veronica's. After all, it works at other times.

Teachers have difficulty teaching children how to solve problems, and children have difficulty learning how to solve problems. Some of this difficulty arises because "finding the answer" has been viewed as the sole objective. Children often misuse a technique intended to aid in problem solving because of this focus on the answer—as Libby misuses the key words. Increasingly, we have to recognize that the *process* of solving problems—that is, how we go about solving problems—is of primary importance. When answers are stressed, children may learn to solve particular problems. When process is stressed, children are more likely to learn how to attack other problems.

While problem solving has been of concern for many years, renewed attention was focused on it by two widely read reports. In 1977, the National Council of Supervisors of Mathematics prepared a position paper on basic mathematical skills (20) (see Figure 1-2). Listed first of ten skill areas was problem solving—"the principal reason for studying mathematics." In 1980, the National Council of Teachers of Mathematics issued *An Agenda for Action: Recommendations for School Mathematics of the 1980s*. The first recommendation was that "problem solving must be the focus of school mathematics in the 1980s" (1) (see Figure 1-1). They noted that:

True problem-solving power requires a wide repertoire of knowledge, not only of particular skills and concepts but also of the relationships among them and the fundamental principles that unify them. (1, p. 2)

Problem solving has long been the focus of numerous books, collections of materials, and research studies. But many questions continue to be raised about its nature and scope: What is a problem and what does problem solving mean? How can problem solving be taught effectively? What problem-solving strategies should be taught? How can problem solving be evaluated? This chapter will address these questions.

WHAT IS A PROBLEM AND WHAT IS PROBLEM SOLVING?

To gain skill in solving problems, one must have many experiences in solving problems. Research studies indicate that children who are given many problems to solve score higher on problem-solving tests than children who are given few (18). This finding has led many textbooks and teachers to offer a problem-solving program that simply presents problems—and nothing more. Children are expected to learn how to solve problems merely by solving problems, with virtually no guidance or discussion of how to do it. Thus, a typical page in a children's textbook would begin with exercises such as the following:

3194	5479	6754
5346	3477	8968
+ 8877	+ 6399	+ 7629

Next would appear "story problems" such as A, below:

(A) 7809 people watched television on Monday.
9060 people watched on Tuesday.
9924 people watched on Wednesday.
How many people watched in the three days?

That such story problems are really problems for most children is debatable. In effect, they are exercises with words around them. The biggest difficulty lies in doing the computation. The choice of what computation to perform is obvious: do what you've been doing most recently. If the past week's work has been on addition, solve the problems by adding; if the topic has been division, then find two numbers in the word problem and divide. The problems primarily provide practice on content just taught, with the mathematics placed in a more-or-less "real-world" setting. It is little wonder that children thus taught flounder on tests, where problems are not grouped so conveniently by operation.

Consider, as an alternative, problem B:

(B) Begin with the digits 1, 2, 3, 4, 5, 6, 7, 8, and 9. Use them to form three numbers with the sum of 1332.

To obtain a solution (or solutions), the children will have the desired practice in addition—but they will have to try many possibilities. They will be aided in reaching a solution if they apply some mathematical ideas. For instance, knowing that the sum of three odd numbers is odd will lead them to avoid placing 1, 3, and 5 all in the ones place. The children have the prerequisites for solving the problem—but the solution is not immediately apparent. They may have to guess and check a number of possibilities.

A problem involves a situation in which a person wants something and does not know immediately what to do to get it. If a "problem" is so easy that children know how to obtain the answer or know the answer automatically, there is really no problem at all. For children, the decision to add the three numbers in word problem A presents little if any challenge in terms of determining what to do: it becomes merely a computational exercise, providing practice with addition. They know what to do because the pattern has been set by the examples before it. With the second problem, however, they will probably have to try several alternatives. Interest in obtaining a solution or solutions and acceptance of the challenge of trying to do that which you have not done before (but believe you can do) are key aspects in problem solving.

Whether a problem is truly a problem or merely an exercise depends on the person faced with it—just as tying a shoelace is no longer a problem for you but is for a three-year-old. What is a problem for Ann now may not be a problem for her in three weeks, or it may not be a problem now for Dick. Problems that you select for children must be likely to be problems. Many teachers are prone to select only problems that can be solved immediately. This leads to presenting problems that are too easy for children. Children form the idea that problems should be solved readily—so that a problem where the route to solution is not immediately apparent is viewed as "impossible." Finding the right level of challenge for a student is not easy—but you can find it by trying out a range of problems, providing time, and then encouraging students to explore many ways around the obstacles initially posed.

A distinction is frequently made between routine and nonroutine problems. *Routine* problems involve an application of a mathematical procedure in much the same way as it was learned. *Nonroutine* problems often require more thought, for the choice of mathematical procedures to solve them is not as obvious. Results from the second national assessment showed that the majority of students had difficulty with any nonroutine problem that required some analysis or thinking (3). Students were generally successful in solving routine one-step problems like those found in most textbooks. They had great difficulty, however, in solving multistep or non-routine problems. The assessment results indicated that

> the primary area of concern should not be with simple one-step verbal problems, but with non-routine problems that require more than a simple application of a single arithmetic operation. (3, p. 147)

Unfortunately, problem solving in many mathematical programs has been limited to finding the answers to word problems in textbooks. Mathematical problem solving involves more. Whenever children are faced with providing a solution to a task they have not mastered, they are solving a problem.

HOW CAN PROBLEM SOLVING BE TAUGHT EFFECTIVELY?

Because problem solving is so difficult to teach and to learn, researchers have devoted much attention to it over the years. Their work has focused on characteristics of problems, on characteristics of those who are successful or unsuccessful at solving problems, and on teaching strategies that may help children to be more successful. On the basis of this research, several broad generalizations can be made (22):

- Problem-solving strategies can be specifically taught, and when they are, not only are they used more, but also students achieve correct solutions more frequently.

- No one strategy is optimal for solving all problems. Some strategies are used more frequently than others, with various strategies being used at different stages of the problem-solving process.

- Teaching a variety of strategies (in addition to an overall plan for how to go about problem solving) provides children with a repertoire from which they can draw as they meet a wide variety of problems. They should be encouraged to solve different problems with the same strategy and to discuss why some strategies are appropriate for certain problems.

- Students need to be faced with problems in which the way to solve them is not apparent, and they need to be encouraged to test many alternative approaches.

- Children's problem-solving achievement is related to their developmental level. Thus, they need problems at appropriate levels of difficulty.

A strong problem-solving program builds on the natural, informal methods that the child has upon entering school. Many of the best problem-solving situations come from everyday happenings. "How many more chairs will we need if we're having five visitors and two children are absent?" or "How many cookies will we need if everyone has two?" may be of concern to a group of first-graders; "Who has the higher batting average, Tom or Marianne?" or "What's the probability of our class winning the race?" may be urgent questions for a group of fifth-graders.

A problem-solving approach should pervade the mathematics curriculum. We need to use problem situations to introduce new topics, as a continuing thread throughout instruction, and as a culmination to ascertain whether children can apply what they have learned about how to solve problems. To teach problem solving effectively, we need to consider the time involved, planning aids, needed resources, the role of technology, and how to manage the class.

Time

Effective teaching of problem solving demands time. Attention must be focused on the relationships in the problem and on the thinking processes involved in reaching a solution. Thus, students must have time to "digest" or mull over a problem thoroughly: time to understand the task, time to explore avenues of solution, time to think about the solution. Moreover, teachers need to encourage students to extend the amount of time they are willing to work on a problem before giving up. It takes more time to tackle a problem that you do not know how to solve than to complete an exercise where you know how to proceed. (Consider problem B and exercise A on pages 22–23: how long did it take *you* to solve each?)

Some time for problem solving is already included as part of the mathematics program. Additional time can be gained by organizing instructional activities so that some of the time allotted for practicing computational skills is directed toward problem solving. This is logical, since students use computational skills and thus practice them as they solve many problems.

Planning

Instructional activities and time must be planned and coordinated so that students have the chance to tackle numerous problems, to learn a variety of problem-solving strategies, and to analyze and discuss their methods of attack. Since you will probably use a textbook when you teach mathematics, you need to consider how to use it most effectively to help you teach problem solving. For instance, you might (1) identify your objectives for using problem-solving materials in the textbook,

(2) examine the entire book for problems to use, (3) regroup textbook materials to suit your objectives, (4) use the textbook to develop questions to ask about problem solving, (5) extend textbook problems with materials you develop yourself, and (6) make use of "challenge problems" (found in some textbooks) with all children (13, 16).

As you plan, consider including problems that:

- Contain superfluous or insufficient information.

  (C) A bag contains 2 dozen cookies for 99¢. Andy bought 3 bags. How many cookies did she get?
  (D) Terry would like to be as tall as his uncle, who is 6 ft. 4 in. How much more must Terry grow?

- Involve estimation or are without well-defined answers.

  (E) Anita has 75¢. Does she have enough money to buy a candy bar costing 35¢ and a notebook costing 49¢?
  (F) How many times can you bounce a ball in one minute? in a day? in a month?

- Require students to make choices about the degree of accuracy required.

  (G) Which is the better buy, a 6-ounce jar of jelly for 79¢ or a 9-ounce jar for $1.14?

- Involve practical applications of mathematics to consumer or business situations.

- Require students to conceptualize very large or very small numbers.

  (H) Have you lived one million hours?

- Are based on students' interests or events in their environment, or can be personalized by adding the names of children in your class.

  (I) Some of you play soccer every Tuesday. If today were Wednesday, January 21st, what date would you next play?

- Involve logic, reasoning, testing of conjectures, and reasonableness of information.

  (J) Three children guessed how many jelly beans were in a jar. Their guesses were 80, 75, and 76. One child missed by 1. Another missed by 4. The other child guessed right. How many jelly beans were in the jar?

- Are multistep, or require the use of more than one strategy to attain a solution.

(K) Ellie had 95¢. She spent 34¢ for popcorn and 50¢ for the movies. How much did she have left?

- Require decision making as a result of the outcome (perhaps there are many answers—or no answers).

(L) Is a traffic light needed in front of the school?

Resources

Since many textbooks focus on routine word problems, you will need to acquire additional problems to stimulate and challenge your students. Fortunately, there are many sources of problems; the list of references at the end of this chapter includes several such sources. In addition, you can:

- Collect potential problems from newspapers, magazines, and so on.

(M)

America's 30 Most Densely Packed Cities...

Among cities with 1980 population of 100,000 or more—

	Area (sq. mi.)	People Per Square Mile
1. New York	302	23,453
2. Jersey City	13	16,934
3. Paterson, N.J.	8	16,623
4. San Francisco	46	14,633
5. Newark	24	13,662
6. Chicago	228	13,174
7. Philadelphia	136	12,413
8. Boston	47	11,928
9. Yonkers, N.Y.	18	10

- Write problems yourself (possibly using ideas from newspapers or from events in your community).
- Make use of situations that arise spontaneously— particularly questions children raise ("How tall is that building?").
- Attend problem-solving sessions at professional meetings.
- Share problems with other teachers.
- Have children write problems to share with each other.

(N) From a picture of items for sale (with prices), have children make up one problem using addition and one problem using subtraction.

It's not too soon to start a problem file, with problems grouped or categorized so you can locate them readily. File them by mathematical content, by strate-

gies—by how you're going to use the file. Laminating the cards permits them to be used over and over by students for individual or small-group problem solving.

Technology

Ever since hand-held calculators dropped in price and became feasible for use throughout the school program, their potential for increasing problem-solving proficiency has been recognized. In many problems we can now deal with more realistic numbers rather than merely with numbers that come out even. Calculators also help us to shift attention from computation to problem solving. However, research has indicated that use of calculators will not necessarily improve problem-solving achievement (22): the student must still be able to determine *how* to solve a problem *before* he or she can use a calculator to attain the solution.

Research also indicates that children tend to use more strategies when they use calculators (28). The main reason is that the time once spent on performing calculations can be spent on extending the use of problem-solving strategies. More problems can also be considered when calculations are no longer burdensome.

Consider using calculators whenever:

- They extend a child's ability to solve problems.
- They eliminate tedious computations and decrease anxiety about inability to do computations correctly.
- They allow time for considering more problems or for devoting extended attention to a problem.
- They allow consideration of more complex problems or of problems with realistic data.
- They provide motivation and confidence that a problem can be solved.

Microcomputers can be an important problem-solving tool. Like calculators, they allow for the processing of problems with realistic data. But microcomputers can also be used to present problems of different types —for instance, problems involving graphics and graphing. Programming itself involves problem solving, and problem-solving strategies can be learned and used as programs are being developed. Additional comments on the potential of technological tools may be found in Chapter 2.

Class Management

When you teach problem solving, you will find it useful at times to teach the whole class, at times to divide the class into small groups, and at times to have children work individually or with one other child. Large-group activities are effective for presenting and developing a new problem-solving strategy and for examining a variety of strategies for solving the same problem. You can focus children's attention on a problem's components, pose questions to help them use one strategy or find one solution, lead them to use other strategies or find other solutions, and encourage them to generalize from the problem to other problems. Individuals may suffer, however, because the faster students will tend to come up with answers before others have had a chance to consider the problem carefully. Moreover, what may be a problem to some students may appear trivial or impossibly difficult to others. Discussions *about* problem solving are feasible with large groups, but the process of solving problems should be practiced with small groups or individually.

Small-group instruction makes it possible to group students by problem-solving ability and interests. They have the opportunity to discuss problems, share ideas, debate alternatives, and verify solutions at an appropriate level of difficulty. In small groups, students can generally solve more problems than those who work alone, although the groups may take longer on each problem. Research indicates that when groups discuss problem meanings and solution paths, they achieve better than when they are told how to solve the problem (23).

When two children work together, they can be of comparable abilities, or they can differ slightly in abilities so that one child can teach the other. Usually, both children end up learning from the peer-teaching situation.

Some problem solving should be done individually. The child can progress at his or her own rate and use the strategies with which he or she is comfortable. You will also want to have in the classroom sources of problems to which individual children can turn in their free time: a bulletin board, a problem corner, or a file of problems (27).

WHAT PROBLEM-SOLVING STRATEGIES SHOULD BE TAUGHT?

One cannot consider problem solving without finding numerous references to the contribution of George Polya (19). He proposed a four-stage model of problem solving:

- First, *understand* the problem.
- Second, devise a *plan* for solving it.
- Third, *carry out* your plan.
- Fourth, *look back* to examine the solution obtained.

This model forms the basis for the problem-solving approach used in most elementary school mathematics textbooks. Thus, students are taught to SEE, PLAN, DO, and CHECK. Another variation on a plan can be seen in Figure 3-1, an example from a textbook teacher's guide.

Such an approach can help students see problem solving as a process consisting of several interrelated actions. They have a guide to help them attack a problem, for actions are suggested that will lead them to the goal.

However, the model can be misleading: except for simple problems, it is rarely possible to take the steps in sequence. Students who believe they can proceed one step at a time may find themselves as confused as if they had no model. Moreover, the steps are not discrete, nor is it always necessary to take each step. As students try to understand a problem, they may move unnoticed into the planning stage. Or, once they understand the problem, they may see the route to the solution without any planning stage. Moreover, the stages do not always aid in finding a solution: many children become trapped in an endless process of read, think, reread—and reread—and reread—until they give up.

Specific strategies are needed to help children move through the model (Polya himself delineates many of these). Such strategies are tools for solving problems, while the four-stage model is a blueprint of the points that must be covered. In this section we will consider a number of problem-solving strategies. This list is only one way of organizing and listing problem-solving strategies. It is not exhaustive, yet provides a set of strategies that seem particularly useful and can be applied in a wide variety of problem settings.

A plan is needed for introducing the strategies: it is not feasible for a teacher to introduce them all in a given year. Children need time to gain confidence in applying each. The plan will also assure that students are exposed to the range of strategies you want them to learn, and that they have the opportunity to practice them, at an appropriate level. Thus, you may decide to introduce "act it out" and "make a drawing" in grade 1, "look for a pattern" and "restate the problem" in grade 2, and so on. No one sequence is "best." In successive grade levels, children will practice and use the strategies they have already learned. For a plan from one school district, see (25).

Textbooks also outline the scope and sequence for any strategies they include. Use this to compare the scope of your textbook's program with what you may want to implement. Then you can devise a plan, if necessary, for extending children's learning beyond what the textbook covers.

The comments that follow include a number of illustrative problems, covering a range of mathematical topics and grade levels, that could be used to develop each problem-solving strategy. Usually the problem could also be solved with another strategy; it is rare that a problem can be solved by one and only one strategy.

Lesson 1-9
pp. 18-19

DAILY LESSON PLAN

Objective

Solve word problems using a four-step process.

Teaching the Lesson

- Distribute duplicated sheets of the first three columns of the problem-solving chart followed by five empty columns for students to write in. Explain that the four-step problem-solving method is a systematic way to solve problems. It may be used to solve any of the word problems in the book.

Work through the steps in the problem solving chart for the example in the text as follows.

1. *Understand the problem.* Explain that you must read the problem carefully to obtain all the given information and ascertain exactly what it asks. Ask: What do you know? Record: Fish for $2.79 and food for $.89; paid with a $5 bill. Ask: What do you want to know? Record: Amount of change.

2. *Make a plan.* Explain we must decide what arithmetic is necessary to solve the problem. Ask: What do you do to solve the problem? Record: Add $2.79 and $.89. Subtract sum from $5.00.

3. *Do the arithmetic.* Explain that you must do the arithmetic correctly. Tell students, show your work so that you may go back and check the arithmetic. Record:

$$\begin{array}{cc} \$2.79 & \$5.00 \\ + \ .89 & -3.68 \\ \hline \$3.68 & \$1.32 \end{array}$$

4. *Give the answer.* Ask: How much change? Record: $1.32.

Assignment

	Problem Solving
Basic	All
Average	All
Enriched	All

Problem Solving   Problem • Plan • Arithmetic • Answer

John bought 3 angel fish for $2.79 *The last lesson of each unit* and some fish food for $.89. He paid *focuses on problem-solving skills.* with a $5 bill. How much change did he receive?

These four steps may help you solve the problem.

1	Understand the problem.	What do you know? What do you want to know?	Spent $2.79, $.89. A $5 bill. How much change?
2	Make a plan.	What do you do to solve the problem?	Add $2.79 and $.89. Subtract sum from $5.00.
3	Do the arithmetic.	Show your work.	$2.79 $5.00 + .89 −3.68 $3.68 $1.32
4	Give the answer.	How much change?	$1.32

1. Sally spent $1.29 for a flea collar and $1.45 for cat food. She gave the clerk $3.00. How much change did she receive? **$.26**

2. Ron bought 2 rabbits for $5.99. He also spent $.89 for rabbit food. He gave the clerk $7.00. How much change did he receive? **$.12**

3. Carmela bought a parakeet for $4.25, a cage for $11.80, and some bird food for $.79. She gave the clerk $20.00. How much change did she receive? **$3.16**

4. Henry bought a steel pen for his puppy for $43.29. He also spent $2.79 for a brush. He gave the clerk $47.00. How much change did he receive? **$.92**

18   *See Resources chart at right.*

Figure 3-1. (From Ernest R. Duncan and others, *Mathematics—Book 6*, Teacher's Edition. Boston: Houghton Mifflin Company, 1978. Used by permission.)

This is what makes a repertoire of strategies useful. (On the other hand, not all strategies can be used effectively to solve a given problem.) Often more than one strategy *must* be used to solve a problem; thus, students may begin to "consider all possibilities" but find they need to record them in a table. By becoming familiar with possible strategies, a student acquires a repertoire that can be drawn on to start to attack a problem. And making a start is often the most difficult point. Moreover, when one strategy fails, the child has others to turn to—thus enhancing his or her confidence that a path to a solution can be found.

As you read, try to solve the problems!

1. Act It Out

This strategy helps children to visualize what is involved in the problem. They actually go through the actions, either themselves or by manipulating objects. This physical action makes the relationships among problem components clearer in their minds.

When teaching children how to use the act-it-out strategy, it is important to stress that other objects may be used in place of the real thing. Obviously, real money is not needed when a problem involves coins—only something labeled "25¢" or whatever. Since children are adept at pretending, they will probably suggest substitute objects themselves. Make sure they focus their attention on the actions, rather than on the objects per se.

Many simple real-life problems can be posed as you develop the act-it-out strategy in the early grades:

(1) Six children were standing at the teacher's desk. Five children joined them. How many children were at the teacher's desk then?

To make clear the value of "acting it out," however, problems need to be more challenging:

(2) Suppose you have 7 coins in your pocket that add up to $1.00. What are the coins?

(3) A man buys a horse for $60, sells it for $70, buys it back for $80, and sells it for $90. How much does the man make or lose in the horse-trading business?

(4) Gum balls cost 1¢ each. There are gum balls of 5 different colors in the machine. You can't see them, because it's dark. What would be the least number of pennies you'd have to spend to be sure of getting at least 3 gum balls of the same color?

(5) I counted 7 cycle riders and 19 cycle wheels go past my house this morning. How many bicycles and how many tricycles passed?

2. Make a Drawing or Diagram

Probably within the past week or so you've used this strategy to help you solve a real-life problem. Perhaps you had to find someone's house from a complicated set of directions: you drew a sketch of the route. Or maybe you were rearranging a room and drew a diagram of how the furniture was to be placed. This strategy provides a way of depicting the information in a problem to make the relationships apparent.

When teaching this strategy, stress to the children that there is no need to draw detailed pictures: draw only what is essential to tell about the problem. Thus, the appearance of the bus, the pattern of the upholstery, the presence of racks above the seats, and similar details are irrelevant in drawing a picture that will help to solve the bus problem:

(6) A bus had 10 rows of seats. There were 4 seats in each row. How many seats were there on the bus?

(7) You are riding on an elevator. You enter on the main floor. You go up 6 floors, down 3 floors, up 9 floors, down 7 floors, up 8 floors, down 2 floors, down 5 more floors. Then you get off the elevator. On what floor are you?

(8) How much carpet would we need to cover our classroom floor?

(9) When you buy stamps at the post office, they are usually attached to each other. How many different ways can you buy three attached stamps?

(10) It takes 3 minutes to saw through a log. How long will it take to saw the log into 4 pieces?

(11) Some acrobats are planning a new act. They want to build a human pyramid 15 acrobats wide and 15 acrobats high. How many acrobats will they need for the act?

At times you can reverse this strategy, presenting a picture for which the children have to make up a problem:

(12)

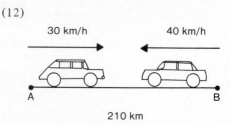

210 km

3. Look for a Pattern

In many early learning activities, children are asked to identify (passively observe) a pattern in pictures or numbers. As a strategy for solving problems, pattern recognition becomes a more active search. Often students will construct a table and then use it to look for a pattern.

(13) *Triangle dot numbers* are so named because that number of dots can be used to form a triangle with an equal number of dots on each side:

What triangle dot number has 10 dots on a side? What triangle dot number has 195 dots on a side?

(14) How long would it take to spread a rumor in a town of 90,000 people if each person who heard the rumor told it to 3 new people every 15 minutes?

(15) Little Island has a population of 1000 people. The population doubles every 30 years. What will the population be in 30 years? 60 years? 300 years? When will the population be over a million? over a billion?

(16) An explorer found some strange markings on a cave wall. Can you complete the table?

4. Construct a Table

Organizing data into a table helps us to discover a pattern and to identify information that is missing. It is an efficient way to classify and order large amounts of information or data, and it provides a record so that we need not retrace nonproductive paths or do computations repeatedly to answer new questions.

(17) Can you make change for a quarter using only 9 coins? only 17? only 6? How many ways can you make change for a quarter?

(18) How many ancestors have you had in the last 400 years?

(19) A carpenter makes only 3-legged stools and 4-legged tables. At the end of one day he had used 31 legs. How many stools and how many tables did he make?

(20) Ann, Jan, and Nan all like pizza. One likes her pizza plain. One likes pizza with mushrooms. One likes pizza with anchovies. Which kind of pizza does each girl like? Here are three clues:

    1. Ann doesn't know the girl who likes her pizza plain.

    2. Jan's favorite kind of pizza is cheaper than pizza with mushrooms.

    3. The one who likes mushrooms is Ann's cousin.

(21) Your teacher agrees to let you have 1 minute of recess on the first day of school, 2 minutes on the second day, 4 minutes on the third day, and so on. How long will your recess be at the end of 2 weeks?

Notice that the mathematical idea involved in this problem can be stated in terms of other situations. Such reformulation can alter the difficulty level of the problem. It can also give children practice in recognizing similarities in problem structure—an ability that appears to be closely allied to being a good problem solver. One alternative to the previous problem is:

(22) Suppose someone offers you a job for 15 days. They offer you your choice of how you will be paid. You can start for 1¢ a day and double the new amount every day. Or you can start for $1 and add $1 to the new amount every day. Which would you choose? Why?

Textbooks frequently teach part of this strategy: they have students *read* a table or *complete* a table already structured. It is important for students to learn to read a table, and thus such problems are presented as:

(23) Here is a bus schedule. What time does the bus from New York arrive? (Ask other questions about arrival, departure, and traveling times.)

But it is also vital that children learn how to construct a table. They need to determine for themselves what its form should be (for example, how many columns are needed), what the columns or rows should be labeled, and so on. For this purpose, we can present problems that require children to collect information and then organize it into a table in order to report it:

(24) Make a table that shows how many cars pass through the traffic lights at each intersection by the school.

5. Account Systematically for All Possibilities

This strategy is sometimes used with "look for a pattern" and "construct a table." We don't always have to *examine* all possibilities—rather, we have to account for all in some systematic way. We may be able to organize the possibilities into categories, then dismiss some classes of possibilities before beginning a systematic search of the remaining ones. Sometimes, however, we do need to actually check all possibilities.

(25) In how many different ways can a bus driver get from Albany to Bakersville? The driver always moves toward Bakersville.

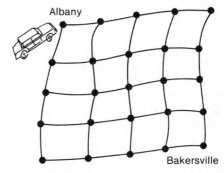

(26) In how many ways can you add 8 odd numbers to get a sum of 20? (You may use a number more than once.)

(27) Ask a friend to think of a number between 1 and 10. Find out what number it is by asking him or her no more than 5 questions that can be answered only by yes or no. How many questions would you need to ask to find a number between 1 and 20? between 1 and 100?

(28) If each letter is a code for digit, what is the following addition problem? Use 1, 2, 3, 6, 7, 9, and 0.

$$\begin{array}{r} SUN \\ + FUN \\ \hline SWIM \end{array}$$

(29) You need 17 lb. of fertilizer. What do you buy to obtain at least that amount at the lowest cost?

6. Guess and Check

For years, children have been discouraged from guessing. They've been told, "You're only guessing," in a derisive tone. But guessing is a viable strategy—when they are encouraged to incorporate what they know into their guesses, rather than doing "blind" or "wild" guessing.

An "educated" guess is based on careful attention to pertinent aspects of the problem, plus knowledge from previous related experiences. There is some reason to expect to be "in the right ballpark." Then one must check to be sure.

(30) Suppose it costs 13¢ to mail a postcard and 20¢ for a letter. Bill wrote to 12 friends and spent $2.05 for postage. How many letters and how many postcards did he send?

(31) Cut the circular region into two parts that have the same area but are not congruent.

(32) Place the numbers 1 through 9 in the cells so that the sum in each direction is 15.

(33) Margie hit the dart board with 4 darts. Each dart hit a different number. Her total score was 25. Which numbers might she have hit to make that score?

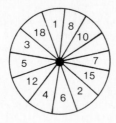

(34) This box has a volume of 2880 cubic centimeters. Find another box with the same volume.

(35) Use the numbers 1 through 6 to fill the 6 circles. You may use each number only once. Each row must add up to 9.

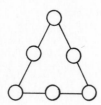

7. Work Backward

Some problems are posed in such a way that you are given the final conditions of an action and are asked about something that occurred earlier. In other problems you may be able to determine the endpoint and work backward (many mazes are like that).

(36) Complete the following table:

		3			
	12		11	15	
6		6			7
2			5	9	
					13
5					14

(37) If two whole numbers have a sum of 18 and a product of 45, what are the numbers?

(38) Sue baked some cookies. She put one-half of them away for the next day. Then she divided the remaining cookies evenly among her three sisters, so that each got 4. How many cookies did she bake?

8. Identify Wanted, Given, and Needed Information

This strategy has long been used in some textbook series, and research evidence indicates that it is valuable to many children (29). Instead of just "doing something with the numbers in a problem," they are encouraged to sort out relevant and irrelevant information. They select from what is available those facts that are needed. Most real-life problems are "messy," and a first task is to select the information that you have, determine the goal for which you're headed, and ascertain the information you'll need to reach that goal. You need to determine the question to be answered, select specific information necessary for solution, and choose the appropriate process.

An adjunct to this strategy is to provide experiences in which the child must formulate the question to be answered. This situation parallels many everyday problems, where you must ask questions before you begin working on a solution.

Children also need to meet problems for which they must collect information or data. The typical textbook problem gives all the necessary facts. For everyday situations you often must obtain necessary data. Problems from the USMES Project (Unified Science and Mathematics in the Elementary School) provide such situations (26):

(39) Challenge: Determine which brand of a product is the best buy for a certain purpose.

(40) Challenge: Recommend and try to have a change made which would improve the safety and convenience of a pedestrian crossing near your school.

9. Write an Open Sentence

This strategy is often taught in textbooks; in some, in fact, it is the *only* strategy taught. Research indicates that it is useful (23) but not that it is so useful that it should be taught exclusively. Once you can write an open sentence, you can probably solve the problem—true; but writing the sentence in the first place may be difficult. Thus some problems cannot be solved easily with this strategy, and sometimes other problem-solving strategies may need to be used first to clarify the problem. In particular, we must be able to perceive a relationship between given and sought information in order to write the sentence. Also, children need to learn that more than one sentence may be formed to solve some problems.

(41) An ant travels 33 cm in walking completely around the edge of a rectangle. If the rectangle is twice as long as it is wide, how long is each side?

(42) Two-thirds of a number is 24 and one-half of the number is 18. What is the number?

(43) David put $3 in his bank account today. Now he has $55 in the bank. How much money did he have in the bank yesterday?

10. Solve a Simpler or Similar Problem

Some problems are made difficult by large numbers or complicated patterns, so that the way to solve them is unclear. For such a problem, making an analogous but simpler one may aid in ascertaining how to solve it. Thus, for the following problem you might have second or third graders consider what they would do if Jen had 3¢ and Jeff had 5¢:

(44) Jen saved $3.56. Jeff saved $5.27. How much more money has Jeff saved?

You may need to break some problems down into manageable parts. When problems require a series of actions, children often fail to realize the need to answer one question before another can be answered. They need help in identifying the questions that must be answered.

Many kinds of problems are interrelated. Knowing how to solve one problem usually means that we can solve another problem that is somewhat similar. The insight and understanding that permit us to solve more complicated problems are built through solutions of easier problems, where relationships are easier to see and

possibilities for solving can be readily considered. Momentarily, we can set aside the original problem to work on a simpler case; if that problem can be solved, then the procedure used can be applied to the more complicated problem.

(45) Place the numbers 1 to 19 into the 19 circles so that any three numbers in a row will give the same sum.

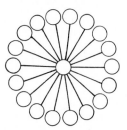

(46) How thick is a sheet of paper? Find the answer using only a ruler as your measuring instrument.

Often children need to restate a problem, expressing it in their own words. Sometimes this will indicate points at which they don't understand the problem, and you can then help them to clarify it. At other times the rephrasing will help them to ascertain what the problem means or requires, so that they see a possible path of solution. It can be a way of getting rid of unimportant words, or of changing to words that are more easily understood.

(47) Find 3 different integers such that the sum of their reciprocals is an integer.
(How can this be reworded so that children will understand the terms?)

(48) I bought some items at the store. All were the same price. I bought as many items as the number of cents in the cost of each item. My bill was $2.25. How many items did I buy?
(How can this be restated so that children will understand the process?)

11. Change Your Point of View

Often this strategy is used after several others have been tried without success. When we begin to work on most problems, we tend to adopt a particular point of view or make certain assumptions. Often we quickly form a plan of attack and implement it to determine whether it produces a plausible solution. If the plan is unsuccessful, we tend to return to the problem with the same point of view to ascertain a new plan of attack. But there may be some faulty logic that led us to adopt that point of view. We need to try to redefine the problem in a completely different way. Ask yourself such questions as, "What precisely does the problem say and not say? What am I assuming that may or may not be implied?"

The pizza problem (number 20) is one version of a set of logic problems that are useful in presenting this strategy. Following are some other problems that most students will rather quickly attack in a particular way. Only when it is apparent that an incorrect answer has been obtained (or no answer) will they see the value of looking at the problem from another point of view.

(49) How many squares are there on a checker-board?

(50) Without lifting your pencil from the paper, draw four straight line segments through the 9 dots.

· · ·

· · ·

· · ·

(51) A state with 750 schools is about to begin a "single elimination" basketball tournament— one loss and you're out. How many games must be played to determine a champion?

THE IMPORTANCE OF LOOKING BACK

Some of the best learning about problem solving may occur after the problem solution has been attained. It is important to think about *how* a problem is solved. In fact, research indicates that time spent discussing and reconsidering our thinking may be more important than any other strategy in helping children become better problem solvers (23). Thus, this step should be included regularly in our instructional planning.

Generalize. We use this strategy to extend the solution to more general and far-reaching situations. Analyzing the structural features of a problem rather than focusing only on details often results in insights more significant than the answer to the specific situation posed in the problem. Such insights can be applied to whole classes of similar problems. Being able to see similarities across problems is one of the characteristics of good problem solvers, according to research (12).

(52) First solve: A boy selling fruit has only three weights and a double pan balance. But with them he can weigh any whole number of pounds from 1 pound to 13 pounds. What weights does he have? Then consider: Should he buy a fourth weight? How many additional weighings could be made with the four weights?

(53) When 5 consecutive numbers are added together, their sum is 155. Find the numbers. How can this be symbolized so that other totals could be considered?

Getting children to focus on the relationships involved in a problem and then generalizing can sometimes be accomplished by giving children problems without numbers.

(54) A store sells pingpong balls by the box. For the amount of money Dot has, she can buy a certain number of boxes. What price does she pay per ball?

Check the Solution. Checking has long been advocated as a way to help children pinpoint their errors— provided they do not simply make the solution and the check agree. One way of checking is going through the procedures again. Another is verifying the reasonableness of the answer: is it plausible as the answer to the question posed in the problem? Estimating the answer before obtaining the solution will aid in this verification process.

Find Another Way to Solve It. Most problems can be solved with many different strategies. Use of each adds to understanding of the problem. You have probably felt uncomfortable with the classification of some of the problems in this chapter under one or another strategy. But even for those problems where you felt the classification was satisfactory, there's probably another way each could be solved. (Try it and see!)

Find Another Solution. Too often, children are given problems for which there is one and only one correct solution. Almost all textbook problems are like that. In real-life situations, however, there may be two or more answers that are acceptable (depending, sometimes, on the circumstances or the assumptions). You probably noticed that some of the problems already given have several solutions. For many others, each person tackling the problem will have a different answer.

(55) Find out how many days (or minutes) old you are.

Study the Solution Process. This strategy aims to help the child put the problem into perspective: the thinking used at each stage, the facts that were uncovered, the strategies that were employed, and the actions that were productive and nonproductive. Again, giving the same problem without numbers provides a useful way of helping children to focus on the process they followed, as well as the relationships in the problem, as they describe how they would go about finding the answer. Different students can also be asked to share with the group the varying ways in which they proceeded to reach the same solution.

USING PROBLEM-SOLVING OPPORTUNITIES

This chapter has presented a variety of problems, some of them typical of those found in textbooks, others not. We have noted also the possible use of nonverbal problems, embodied in pictures or materials. Real-world problems arise also in a variety of other modes, offering opportunities for teaching. Make use of problems posed spontaneously by children or by situations in which you find yourself. Bring in games that present good problem-solving situations, where children will have the opportunity to use problem-solving strategies. And be aware that personalizing problems—by, for instance, substituting the names of children in your class—can help many children to accept a problem that otherwise would seem remote or uninteresting.

Throughout your instruction, you need to encourage an enjoyment in solving problems. You achieve this in part when children believe that they *can* solve a problem—they need an atmosphere in which they feel both free and secure. Your positive attitude toward problem solving will stimulate a similar attitude on the part of the children.

HOW CAN PROBLEM SOLVING BE EVALUATED?

It is more difficult to evaluate problem solving than many other topics in the mathematics curriculum. As NCTM's *Agenda* (1) states:

> An emphasis on problem solving demands more flexibility and creativity in assessment than is possible within the restrictions of most current test formats. (p. 15)

We need to go beyond the open-ended or multiple-choice format of a paper-and-pencil test.

It takes a long time to develop problem-solving skills. Therefore, evaluation is a long-term process, not accomplished solely with short-term measures. It needs to be continuous over the entire school mathematics program.

Evaluation of problem solving should be based on your goals, using techniques consistent with those goals. If the mathematics program encompasses the ability to solve both routine and nonroutine problems, then evaluation measures must include both types of problems. If the program includes emphasis on the process of problem solving, then evaluation measures must incorporate ways of evaluating children's use of the process.

As you plan each lesson, consider how you will evaluate whether or not its objectives have been attained. Paper-and-pencil measures have a place in such evaluation. But consider also such procedures as:

- Facing students with a problem-solving situation and observing how they meet it.
- Interviewing students.

- Having students describe to a group how they solved a problem.
- Having one student teach another how to solve a problem.

You will need to evaluate as you go along, for you'll want to ascertain understanding and nonunderstanding, for guidance in developing the next lesson. But problem solving cannot be learned in any one lesson: the process must develop and thus be assessed over time.

Observations. As children work individually or in small groups, you can move about the room, observing them as they work, listening as they talk among themselves, making notes, questioning, offering suggestions. Focus on how each goes about the task of solving a problem. You might want to consider such points as:

- Is there evidence of careful reading of the problem?
- Do individual children seem to have some means of beginning to attack a problem?
- Do they apply a strategy, or do they try to use the last procedure you've taught?
- Do they have another strategy to try if the first one fails?
- How consistent and persistent are they in applying a strategy?
- Are careless errors being made, and if so, when and why?
- How long are they willing to keep trying to solve a problem?
- How well are they concentrating on the task?
- How quickly do they ask for help?
- What strategies does each child use most frequently?
- Do they use manipulative materials?
- What do their behaviors and such factors as the expression on their faces indicate about their interest and involvement?

Then make a brief note that describes the situation and the behaviors you've observed—an anecdotal record.

Interviews. An interview is an attempt to remove the limitations of writing—your own limitations in developing a written test item and the child's in developing a written answer. An interview lets you delve further into how a student goes about solving a problem. You can follow the thought patterns as the child describes what he or she does, and why.

Basically, you need to (1) present the student with a problem; (2) let the student find a solution, describing what he or she is doing; and (3) challenge the student, eliciting specific details on what he or she is doing and why. Make notes as the student works and talks: sometimes it's helpful to have an exact record of the replies.

You may want to have a student use a tape recorder when working alone. Or have a group of students discuss various ways of solving a problem. You can play the tape back later and analyze student thinking more carefully and from a different perspective than you can if you're involved in the interview.

Inventories and Checklists. An inventory can be used to check on what a student knows about problem-solving strategies. You might give students one or several problems and ask them to solve each with a specified strategy, or to solve each using two or three specified strategies. Your aim is to find out whether or not the student can apply each strategy—not what the answer to the problem is. You can also record your observations on a checklist, which then serves as an inventory.

Paper-and-Pencil Tests. You will also want to use written tests to assess children's ability to solve problems. Make sure that those you develop follow the guidelines of your problem-solving program—that is, select good problems that are interesting and challenging, allow sufficient time for the process, and so on. Of particular interest are paper-and-pencil tests that assess the stages of problem solving [see (21)].

Evaluation should be an ongoing component of the problem-solving program. You use it not just to assess where a student is, but also to help you plan what to do next. If children do not use a strategy you have taught, you need to consider why, and then try again. If they try to use a strategy, you have evidence on how well they use it and whether they need more practice. Don't let evaluation become just a recording process: it's a way of helping you solve the problem of how to teach problem solving more effectively!

A GLANCE AT WHERE WE'VE BEEN

Problem solving should pervade the mathematics curriculum. Children need many experiences with problems that they do not immediately know how to solve. Moreover, they should be taught to use a variety of problem-solving strategies, providing them with a repertoire from which they can draw. You will need to provide not only a large resource of good problems, but also enough time for problem solving. Your instruction must coordinate textbook materials with the use of calculators and other technology, as well as large-group, small-group, and individual work.

An overall strategy for approaching problems is desirable (understand, plan, carry out, look back), plus specific strategies that give children ways to begin to attack a problem. The chapter has described such strategies, provided sample problems, and discussed the evaluation of problem solving by means of observations, interviews, inventories, and tests.

THINGS TO DO: ADDING TO YOUR PICTURE

1. What other questions might Mary Roberts pursue with her class after reading the story that opens this chapter?
2. Describe why the four-step plan on page 26 is inadequate for helping students become good problem solvers. Why is it useful?
3. Discuss: "We don't teach textbook word problems any more because no one has to solve that kind of problem."
4. Identify levels (e.g., primary, intermediate) for problems posed in the chapter.
5. Identify problems posed in the chapter for which calculators would be of aid.
6. Answer true or false, then defend your answer: "Before solving a problem, pupils should be required to draw a picture for it."
7. Solve problems 5, 11, and 41 using two different strategies for each.
8. Why isn't finding the answer the final step in solving a problem?
9. Choose a problem from this chapter and pose it to two children. Identify the strategies each child uses, and write an evaluation of their efforts.
10. Start a file with problems from this chapter. Categorize them in a way you find most useful.
11. Make up problems using newspaper or magazine articles. Add them to your file.
12. Think of your activities for the past week. List the problem-solving strategies you used to solve each of five mathematical problems you faced.
13. Search textbooks for a particular grade level. Find at least one problem that could be solved by using the following strategies: make a drawing or diagram, act it out, solve a simpler or similar problem.
14. Choose a content topic for a particular grade level. Make up at least one interesting problem for that topic that can be solved by each of these strategies: look for a pattern, make a drawing or diagram, construct a table.
15. Plan a bulletin board focused on problem solving.

SELECTED REFERENCES

1. *An Agenda for Action: Recommendations for School Mathematics of the 1980s.* Reston, Va.: National Council of Teachers of Mathematics, 1980.
2. Bruni, James V. "Problem Solving for the Primary Grades." *Arithmetic Teacher,* 29 (February 1982), pp. 10–15.
3. Carpenter, Thomas P.; Corbitt, Mary Kay; Kepner, Henry S., Jr.; Lindquist, Mary Montgomery; and Reys, Robert E. *Results from the Second Mathematics Assessment of the National Assessment of Educational Progress.* Reston, Va.: National Council of Teachers of Mathematics, 1981.

4. *Didactics and Mathematics.* Palo Alto, Calif.: Creative Publications, 1978.

5. Duea, Joan, and Ockenga, Earl. "Classroom Problem Solving with Calculators." *Arithmetic Teacher,* 29 (February 1982), pp. 50–51.

6. Greenes, Carole, et al. *Successful Problem Solving Techniques.* Palo Alto, Calif.: Creative Publications, 1977.

7. Greenes, Carole E., et al. *Problem Solving in the Mathematics Laboratory: How To Do It.* Boston: Prindle, Weber & Schmidt, 1972.

8. *How to Solve Math Word Problems* (Levels A–F). Columbus, Ohio: Weekly Reader, 1981.

9. Immerzeel, George, et al. *Iowa Problem Solving Project Resource Decks.* Cedar Falls: University of Northern Iowa, 1978.

10. Krulik, Stephen. "Problem Solving: Some Considerations." *Arithmetic Teacher,* 25 (December 1977), pp. 51–52.

11. Krulik, Stephen, and Reys, Robert E., eds. *Problem Solving in School Mathematics.* 1980 Yearbook. Reston, Va.: National Council of Teachers of Mathematics, 1980.

12. Krutetskii, V. A. *The Psychology of Mathematical Abilities in Schoolchildren* (ed. Jeremy Kilpatrick and Izaak Wirszup, trans. Joan Teller). Chicago: University of Chicago Press, 1976.

13. LeBlanc, John F. "Teaching Textbook Story Problems." *Arithmetic Teacher,* 29 (February 1982), pp. 52–54.

14. Lindquist, Mary Montgomery. "Problem Solving with Five Easy Pieces." *Arithmetic Teacher,* 25 (November 1977), pp. 7–10.

15. *Mathematics Resource Project.* Palo Alto, Calif.: Creative Publications, 1977.

16. Meiring, Steven P. *Problem Solving . . . A Basic Mathematics Goal.* Columbus: Ohio Department of Education, 1979. (Available from Dale Seymour Publications.)

17. Morris, Janet. *How to Develop Problem Solving with a Calculator.* Reston, Va.: National Council of Teachers of Mathematics, 1981.

18. Pace, Angela. "Understanding and the Ability to Solve Problems." *Arithmetic Teacher,* 8 (May 1961), pp. 226–233.

19. Polya, George. *How to Solve It.* Princeton, N.J.: Princeton University Press, 1973 (1945, 1957). (Available from Creative Publications.)

20. "Position Paper on Basic Mathematical Skills." National Council of Supervisors of Mathematics, 1977. *Arithmetic Teacher,* 25 (October 1977), pp. 18–22.

21. Schoen, Harold L., and Oehmke, Theresa. "A New Approach to the Measurement of Problem-solving Skills." In *Problem Solving in School Mathematics* (ed. Stephen Krulik and Robert E. Reys). 1980 Yearbook. Reston, Va.: National Council of Teachers of Mathematics, 1980. Pp. 216–227.

22. Suydam, Marilyn N. "Update on Research on Problem Solving: Implications for Classroom Teaching." *Arithmetic Teacher,* 29 (February 1982), pp. 56–60.

23. Suydam, Marilyn N., with Weaver, J. Fred. *Using Research: A Key to Elementary School Mathematics.* Columbus, Ohio: ERIC Clearinghouse for Science, Mathematics and Environmental Education, 1981.

24. Thornton, Carol A., and Bley, Nancy S. "Problem Solving: Help in the Right Direction for LD Students." *Arithmetic Teacher,* 29 (February 1982), pp. 26–27, 38–41.

25. Tobin, Alexander. "Scope and Sequence for a Problem-Solving Curriculum." *Arithmetic Teacher,* 29 (February 1982), pp. 62–65.

26. *The USMES Guide.* Newton, Mass.: Education Development Center, 1974.

27. Van de Walle, John A., and Thompson, Charles S. "Fitting Problem Solving into Every Classroom." *School Science and Mathematics,* 81 (April 1981), pp. 289–297.

28. Wheatley, Charlotte L. "Calculator Use and Problem-Solving Performance." *Journal for Research in Mathematics Education,* 11 (November 1980), pp. 323–334.

29. Wilson, John W. "The Role of Structure in Verbal Problem Solving." *Arithmetic Teacher,* 14 (October 1967), pp. 486–497.

30. Worth, Joan. "Problem Solving in the Intermediate Grades: Helping Your Students Learn to Solve Problems." *Arithmetic Teacher,* 29 (February 1982), pp. 16–19.

4

Understanding How Children Learn Mathematics

INTRODUCTION

How is mathematics learned? This important question has no simple answer. Teachers provide their "answers" through classroom practices. In fact, every instructional activity within the classroom expresses the teacher's view of learning.

The way lessons are planned, topics presented, and questions answered tells how a teacher's view of learning is actually translated into classroom action. Teachers' beliefs about learning mathematics, whether true or false, have tremendous influence on what happens in their classrooms.

For example, consider this exchange about the amount of homework needed:

S: Do we have to do all thirty exercises for homework?

T: Yes, do every exercise on that page. Why do you think they are there if you're not supposed to do them?

A common pitfall in assignments is too much practice too soon. Research confirms that students rarely need all the practice exercises provided in a textbook (10); in fact, doing 30 to 50 percent of them produces

the same level of performance as doing all of them. Far more important than the quantity of exercises done is the developmental instruction that precedes them. One teaching-learning approach confirmed by research "sandwiches" practice between carefully planned instruction and discussions (7). (This approach is discussed in Chapter 5.)

Because teachers' beliefs about the learning process make such a difference in the classroom, a thoughtful study and understanding of how mathematics is learned should have high priority for every elementary teacher. It might surprise you that when a group of experienced teachers was asked, "How do your students learn?" 37 percent said they had not thought about it. The purpose of this chapter is to stimulate your thinking about how children learn.

HOW DO CHILDREN LEARN MATHEMATICS?

Early in the twentieth century, John Dewey asserted that learning comes from experience. Although much has been discovered since then about how children learn mathematics, the importance of meaningful experience remains unchallenged. Such experience can be acquired in many different ways, ranging from actual real-world situations to hands-on experience with models. It is ironic that much mathematics is introduced through definitions. Consider, for example, this experience with "daffy definitions":

> S: What is a pentagon?
> T: A five-sided figure.
> S: What is a figure?

Definitions are important in mathematics, but they must evolve naturally from previous knowledge, models, or real experiences that the child can relate to. Otherwise, confusion reigns. Mathematical definitions are generally very concise, contain technical terms, and require an immediate synthesis of the formation if understanding is to result. Yet, research confirms that most children cannot operate on an abstract or formal level until junior high school (4).

Classroom practice must recognize that most early learning moves from specific examples to generalizations. For instance, it would be foolish to develop the concept of "round" through definitions. A more appropriate approach is to make available various models that exhibit roundness, such as marbles, balls, and balloons. Thus, the notion of roundness gradually evolves, and as it does, children become aware of other objects, such as oranges, that also have this property. Classifying objects and citing examples of things that possess a particular property should precede any formal definitions.

Children may become so involved with the models that they never abstract the concept of round. This "I-can't-see-the-forest-for-the-trees" syndrome highlights the importance of guidance and direction. Teachers are essential at this developmental stage to insure that key issues are recognized, irrelevant variables ignored, important questions considered, abstractions formulated, and generalizations made.

Of course, mathematics can be learned in ways other than through hands-on experience. Children learn by watching, listening, reading, following directions, imitating, and practicing, to name a few. These activities can contribute to learning mathematics. However, each should be mixed with a proper balance of modeling and teacher guidance to insure that the mathematics being learned has meaning.

Learning is influenced also by factors peculiar to the individual, such as previous experience, innate ability, maturation, and motivation, so that no comprehensive learning theory can be unequivocally applied to any student at any level with any content. The situation is complex but not hopeless, as you will find. Many pragmatic questions about how children learn mathematics have been answered and are discussed throughout this book.

BUILDING LEARNING BRIDGES

Learning bridges have very valuable functions. Here are three important purposes of building and using learning bridges:

1. Bridges provide a way of linking real-world applications with "textbook mathematics." This bridging not only can clarify concepts, but often increases motivation for learning.
2. Bridges provide a connection between instructional models or physical embodiments and mathematical symbols. The abstract nature of mathematics demands that proper concept formation be based on a variety of different concrete models that embody or illustrate the concept.
3. Bridges provide a path that can be traveled many times—in either direction—to reach greater understanding. Frequent use of bridges seems to shorten the gap between concrete and abstract, thereby promoting meaningful learning and greater retention. Thus, bridges are effective from early introduction through review stages.

Mathematical applications surround our lives, but bridges are often needed to make the connection. For example, we have all seen manhole covers on streets. Have you ever considered why a manhole cover is a circle rather than a square? The reason rests on a mathematical property of a circle, namely that it is a curve of constant width. This property guarantees that the cover won't fall through the hole.

Much learning of mathematics depends on quick recognition and effective use of symbols. For example,

$$3\tfrac{1}{2} \times \tfrac{4}{5} < \square$$

requires knowledge of the mixed number $3\tfrac{1}{2}$, the fraction $\tfrac{4}{5}$, use of the operation of multiplication, and understanding of the relational symbol $<$ (less than), as well as the placeholder $\square$. Few children in elementary school are capable of operating only at the symbolic level when learning mathematical topics. If they are to handle symbols comfortably, the symbols must have meaning. Meaning arises only to the extent that the symbols are directly linked (physically and/or mentally) to the mathematical knowledges and skills being developed. Concrete materials provide the initial referent, and there are no vicarious substitutes. The connection of concrete materials to the symbols is often made through descriptive representation. This connection or "bridge" from the concrete to the abstract is essential. When provided with appropriate concrete materials, some children can move to the symbolic level with little or no further guidance.

TWO-WAY BRIDGES

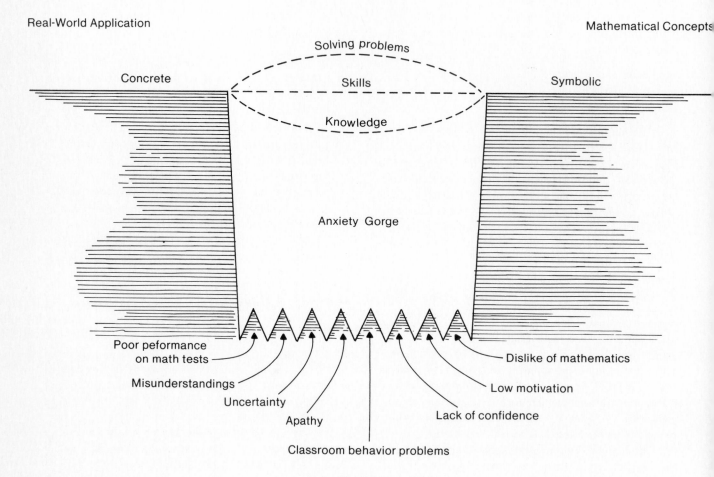

Figure 4-1

Children pushed into early symbolization or given symbols prematurely are likely to fall into the "Anxiety Gorge" (see Figure 4-1). Victims generally find it very difficult to recover, and the gorge can claim victims at any age. Young children are particularly vulnerable, although some of the classic symptoms don't surface until these children reach secondary school. Bridges, along with carefully constructed guard rails, are needed to connect the real-world models with the more abstract mathematical ideas. Such bridges must be established and crossed regularly in learning mathematics. Thus, the teacher's role is not to build a bridge from the concrete to the abstract, but rather to conduct a continual process of bridge building that applies to all grades as well as to different mathematics learning. Research has consistently documented the teacher's essential role, not only in establishing these bridges, but also in helping children make the transition (8).

Let us look at an instructional sequence that illustrates this process. It is designed to bridge the gap and help develop the concept of a missing addend.

The drawings at the top of the next page depict a sequence of activities. Each is a bit different and each plays an important role in moving from the concrete to the abstract. Carefully examine the sequence before reading the description of each stage.

(a) Enclose a number of beans (in this case, 7) in a ring of yarn.

(b) Use the same arrangement of beans and place over some of them a box whose top and bottom have been cut away. The box serves as a referent for the placeholder and partitions the beans into two groups. The sentence $2 + \boxed{5} = 7$ provides a descriptive representation of the arrangement of beans as viewed by the child.

(c) Same as step (b) but cover the box with a colored transparency. The child can still "see" the beans, so the transparent box is a visual reminder of the role the placeholder serves.

(d) Same as (c) but give the box a top, so it literally covers the beans. The box is hiding a number of

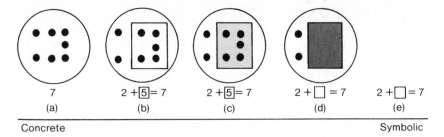

7	2 + ⬚5 = 7	2 + ⬚5 = 7	2 + ☐ = 7	2 + ☐ = 7
(a)	(b)	(c)	(d)	(e)

Concrete   Symbolic

beans and the child must determine the missing number.

(e) $2 + \square = 7$ is a mathematical sentence that typically is troublesome for children. Although abstract and completely symbolic, it can be solved by children who experience the genesis of the symbols.

We have now seen how a model can be used in different stages to help bridge over to symbolization. We would need to use the model for other examples, of course, to insure that the task is understood.

Point 3 listed earlier reminds us that the concrete is linked to the symbolic with two-way bridges. Children must be able to cross the bridges in both directions. Look again at the instructional sequence on missing addends. The reverse direction becomes particularly important when the solution path is unclear. Consequently, reversing directions is a powerful and useful problem-solving process. Consider this missing addend:

$$56 + \square = 104$$

Since it is not a basic fact, it may require careful thinking. Perhaps the student will need to reconstruct a mental or physical model of the problem. Such an approach would occur to students who understand the concept of missing addends. It testifies to the power of building two-way rather than one-way bridges.

SOME SUPPORT
FROM LEARNING THEORIES

Several theories of learning support the approach to teaching we have just sketched. The two major learning camps are behaviorists and developmentalists. Each view holds some key implications for learning and teaching. Consequently, you will find ideas from both in the next section ("Some Planks for the Bridges").

Behaviorism has its roots in stimulus-response and conditioned learning. This theory asserts that behavior can be shaped through rewards and punishments. Over the years it has marshalled a number of distinguished advocates, including E. L. Thorndike, B. F. Skinner, and R. Gagné.

Taking the behaviorist view of learning into the mathematics classroom has many interesting outcomes— some good, others highly questionable. The hierarchical nature of mathematics makes it a popular candidate for a behavioral approach. The first step is to state precisely the goal of instruction. This gives teachers direction in planning instruction and gives the student clear expectations—both valuable outcomes, consistently supported by research. Once an objective has been clearly stated, behaviorists recommend that the prerequisites for achieving that goal be identified and used as building blocks in planning instruction. Consider this example:

Objective: Correctly use the formula $A = \frac{1}{2}ba$ to find the area of a triangle.
Some prerequisite questions:
    What is area?
    What is base?
    What is the altitude?

Clear answers to these prerequisite questions are necessary if the objective is to be reached. However, this particular task analysis could be extended to include:

What is a triangle?
How do you multiply by a fraction?
How do you multiply by whole numbers?

It is hard to imagine ever constructing a complete task analysis for any objective, no matter how simple it may seem. Clearly, important prerequisites must be considered in preparing lessons, but we must be guided by common sense, not by zeal to construct "the" task analysis.

An examination of mathematics programs will show the heavy influence of behaviorism. It is found in daily, unit, grade, and total program objectives. The behaviorist approach has many attractive features: it is simplistic, provides instructional guidelines, allows for short-term progress, and lends itself well to accountability pressures. It is also reflected in technology, especially in instructional software materials for microcomputers.

Unfortunately, some of its strengths also limit the behaviorist approach. For example, emphasis on simple, short-term objectives that are easily measured may dominate instructional planning. If that happens, something must be deemphasized, and it is generally long-term goals and higher-level cognitive processes such as problem solving.

In our judgment, behavioristic psychology must be considered and used in teaching. However, it would be indefensible to rely exclusively on behaviorism, which is why we now extend this discussion to a very different interpretation of how children learn.

Let us examine some theory in developmental psychology and mathematics education. Both Jerome Bruner and Jean Piaget have characterized specific levels of cognitive development. Less well known, except in mathematics, are the levels of mental development proposed by Zoltan Dienes. Frameworks briefly highlighting these schemes of levels are shown in Figure 4-2.

The three schemes differ in the terms they use and in the number of levels they specify. However, rather than contrasting their differences, let's consider two striking similarities:

1. Each framework suggests that learning proceeds from the concrete to the abstract. Of course, concrete is a relative term. To one child, joining two blocks and four blocks is concrete but 2 + 4 is not, while another child may view 2 + 4 as concrete and $\triangle + \bigcirc$ as abstract.
2. Several characteristic and identifiable stages of thinking exist, through which children pass as they

grow and mature. The journey through most of these stages begins with concrete materials during the elementary school. Not until adolescence do children grow out of the stage where they are totally dependent on perceptions and concrete experiences.

Taken collectively, these theories in developmental psychology help us considerably in planning instruction and developing curriculum material. They provide a strong argument for using appropriate models and concrete materials to illustrate mathematical concepts and establish learning bridges.

Several other areas of current research activity may eventually hold significant implications for mathematics learning. For example, recent research has revealed that certain parts of the brain have very specialized functions—the left side is linguistically and algorithmically oriented, the right side spatially and problem-solving oriented (15). Other research has focused on brain growth; the findings suggest that there are predictable periods of rapid brain growth and other periods of little or no growth (13). It is interesting and perhaps not coincidental that one of these plateaus occurs at 12 to 14 years of age. Although the findings are not definitive, it is worth noting that none of this research conflicts with the description of learning presented here.

Figure 4-2. Frameworks of the learning process.

Formal Operational—Considers the possible rather than being restricted to concrete reality. Capable of logical thinking that allows children to reflect on their own thought processes.	*Symbolic*—Manipulation of symbols. Child manipulates and/or uses symbols irrespective of their enactive or iconic counterparts.	*Formalization*—Provides an ordering of the mathematics. Fundamental rules and properties are recognized as structure of the system evolves.
		Symbolization—Describes the representation in language and/or mathematical symbols.
Concrete Operational—Thinking may be logical but is perceptually oriented and limited to physical reality.	*Iconic*—Representational thinking based on pictures, images, or other representations. Child is involved with pictorial and/or verbal information based on the real world.	*Representation*—Provides a peg on which to hang what has been abstracted. Images and pictures are used to provide a representation.
		Generalization—Patterns, regularities, and commonalities are observed and abstracted across different models. These structural relationships are independent of the embodiments.
Pre-Operational—Represents action through thought and language but is prelogical in development.	*Enactive*—Firsthand manipulating, constructing, or arranging of real-world objects. Child is interacting directly with the physical world.	*Free Play*—Interacts directly with physical materials within environment. Different embodiments provide exposure to the same basic concepts, but at this stage few commonalities are observed.
LEVELS OF THINKING BY ELEMENTARY SCHOOL CHILDREN AS CHARACTERIZED BY PIAGET	*LEVELS OF DEVELOPMENTAL LEARNING AS CHARACTERIZED BY BRUNER*	*LEVELS OF MATHEMATICAL LEARNING AS CHARACTERIZED BY DIENES*

Early ——→ Advanced

Introductory ——→ Abstractions

SOME PLANKS FOR THE BRIDGES

Teaching occurs only to the extent that learning occurs. Therefore, effective teaching of mathematics rests heavily on considerations about how children learn. The process of building bridges from the concrete to the symbolic and helping children cross them is at the heart of good teaching. It is a continual challenge, and many factors must be considered as instructional decisions are made.

Here are some practical principles based on a blend of research, teaching experience, and our thoughts about how children learn mathematics. Since each addresses a specific issue, they are presented separately. No priority of importance is suggested by this ordering; in fact, it will soon be clear that these principles are intermingled with each other. A working knowledge requires that each principle be understood, and more importantly, that the total learning Gestalt be maintained.

Principle 1: Mathematics Learning Should Be Meaningful

The notion of meaningful learning, advanced by William Brownell in the first half of the 20th century, provides the cornerstone for a quality school mathematics program. Brownell conceived of arithmetic as a closely knit system of ideas, principles, and processes— a structure that teaching should not only take advantage of, but emphasize, so that "arithmetic is less a challenge to the pupil's memory and more a challenge to his intelligence" (1, p. 32).

Here is an example of meaningless learning:

S: What is 6 divided by 0?
T: You can't divide by zero.
S: Why?
T: You just can't.

Although the student has been told a rule, the rule lacks an explanation and is unaccompanied by understanding. Research confirms that such isolated "learnings" are not retained (9).

Meaningful learning is equally important for all content (from arithmetic to statistics) in the elementary school mathematics program. Mathematics can and should make sense. If it does, it has meaning, is understood as a discipline with order, structure, and numerous relationships, and is likely to be called upon in a variety of problem-solving situations. In fact, research has confirmed that teaching for meaning generally leads to greater retention, greater transfer, and increased ability to solve problems (4). Meaningful learning not only serves as the central plank for building learning bridges but is the principal goal of instruction.

Principle 2: Mathematics Learning Is a Developmental Process

Effective and efficient learning of mathematics doesn't just happen. It takes time and must be planned. An awareness of mathematical concepts occurs through exploration, both physical and mental. The teacher plays a critical role in establishing a rich environment to explore and providing the necessary direction in insure that mathematical ideas are recognized. One idea builds on another, and, as these interconnections are established, the need for symbols to represent ideas becomes clear and meaningful learning occurs.

It takes time to extract mathematics from real-life experiences and concrete materials, then to move from abstract to symbolic thinking. Yet this time is well spent, as it helps develop a lasting facility in mentally manipulating mathematical ideas and recording thought processes. This approach leads to meaningful learning, which interestingly enough is often evidenced by returns to concrete or intuitive levels for clarification. In fact, easy interplay among different levels of thinking (concrete to symbolic and vice versa) is one of the clearest signs that meaningful learning has occurred. (Remember the two-way bridges!)

Principle 3: Curriculum Organization Affects the Learning Process

Mathematics must be organized so that it is appropriate and comprehensible to students. In no other discipline is the ordering more important and previous learning more critical. For example, it is impossible to do long division if you cannot multiply. It is fruitless to estimate a distance in kilometers if you don't know what a kilometer is.

The mathematics program in K–8 basal textbook series is organized to provide continuous development and help students to understand the basic structure of mathematics. Scope and sequence charts provide a good overview of how a particular program is arranged. A careful examination of these charts will show how a sequence of activities is organized by a spiral approach.

The spiral approach to topics provides many opportunities over time to develop and broaden concepts. More specifically, it incorporates and builds on earlier learning to help guide the child through continued but increasingly more intricate study of related topics. Angle measurement, for example, is informally introduced in primary grades and returned to many times. As the concept of angle appears in later grades, greater levels of sophistication are required. The diagram in Figure 4-3 shows how previous experience influences the concept.

The spiral approach holds profound implications for learning and teaching. Instructional planning must

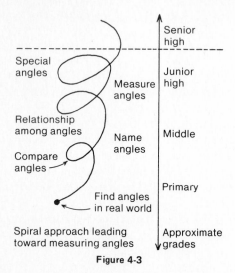

Figure 4-3

consider the prerequisites for success on the current lesson, and the instructor must check to see if students have them. It is not unusual to find students who have skipped, never learned, forgotten, or learned incorrectly topics that are prerequisites. Detecting these weaknesses early and quickly allows the inclusion of reviews, so that later lesson development is not hampered by students' lack of prerequisites.

Just as we must know what has happened in earlier grades, we must look ahead to learn what will be expected of our students tomorrow, next month, and next year. Third-grade teachers must know what has happened in kindergarten, first, and second grade, as well as what will be expected of their students in later years. This broad perspective helps each of us better understand and appreciate the importance of our role. It also demands that we guard against learning gaps in mathematics and, whenever they are detected, do our best to fill them.

Principle 4: Student Movitivation Affects the Learning Process and Vice Versa

Kindling sparks within students' minds and building fires of interest in mathematics are important responsibilities of teachers. There are no shortcuts to such motivation, but teaching that builds meaningful understanding is one major contributor. Success is another, so instructional planning should provide learning activities in which students are likely to be successful. Research shows that learning experiences that are interesting, challenging, and successful build student self-confidence and contribute significantly to positive motivation (4). Students who feel the excitement and satisfaction of learning new mathematical ideas demonstrate a motivation for learning that makes teaching a joy. Research has demonstrated the awesome role teachers play in affecting student motivation (4).

Principle 5: Students Need to Know What Is to Be Learned in Mathematics Classes

Students generally want to please teachers. They will work hard for realistic goals that have been clearly spelled out. For example, if a teacher says, "I expect everyone to be able to measure the length of their book when this lesson is done," probably every student will be able to do so. Why? Because it is a realistic goal, it is understood by the children, and the teacher has made specific expectations clear. Research has consistently confirmed that teacher expectations greatly affect student performance (6).

Student values are greatly influenced by their teachers. Thus, if mathematics classrooms place heavy emphasis on computational skills, students will view them as very important. If teachers reward creative solutions or approaches to problems, then students will develop respect for divergent thinking. Likewise, if teachers make it clear that problem solving is valued and respected, then problem solving will be viewed as important by students. Establishing what is important and valued within each mathematics classroom will greatly influence how students spend their time and, ultimately, what is learned.

Principle 6: Active Involvement Should Be Provided

This well-established learning principle is based on the conviction that active involvement will improve motivation toward mathematics as well as develop keener insight and greater understanding. Active involvement may provide for physical activity but always demands mental involvement. It takes many forms, including interaction with other children and teachers and use of materials, such special learning materials as textbooks, and such technology as calculators and microcomputers. One of the daily challenges of teaching is to select experiences that will encourage, promote, and reward active involvement.

Principle 7: Verbalization Is an Integral Part of Learning Mathematics

Models, manipulatives, and real-world examples provide many opportunities for thinking, talking, and listening. At all levels students must learn how to use mathematical words or phrases orally before they are expected to represent the mathematics symbolically. Just as speaking precedes writing for children, so should the oral language of mathematics precede its symbolization.

For example, the sentence $L < G$ may cause some confusion. Students often don't know what the symbol $<$ means, or they get mixed up on whether to read it as "less than" or "greater than." Prior experiences compar-

Lucy

Gary

ing and describing relationships are essential. To provide one such experience, students could look at the accompanying picture and describe a size relationship. Here are two ways:

English Word	Mathematical Symbols
Gary's weight is greater than Lucy's.	$G > L$
Lucy's weight is less than Gary's.	$L < G$

Both statements are correct, so either may be used to describe the situation. Such oral verbalization and discussion help clarify the mathematics and prepares the way for later symbolization. Remember, however, that precision in mathematical language is a product of learning; it is not necessarily a tool for the learning of mathematics. Be careful about pushing for too much precision in language too soon.

In talking about mathematics, students are likely to provide valuable insights into their thinking. You can use this feedback in many different ways. For example:

Student Comment	Possible Teacher Action
"I know that to divide two fractions, you invert the divisor and multiply, but I don't know why."	Knowing a rule is not sufficient, so you can quickly clarify this confusion by showing what the rule involves and why it works.
"So every even number is composite."	Asking "What about two?" torpedos this overgeneralization immediately.
"I think every even number that can be divided by three can also be divided by six."	Recognize this as an insightful observation, ask for more examples, and then build upon this generalization.

Children can and will tell us much about what they know and don't know. In the process they are developing some important communication skills. Talking about mathematics makes it become more alive, thus heightening student interest. Listening carefully to what is being said, and also noticing what is not being said, allows us to better tailor our teaching.

Principle 8: Multiembodiment Aids Learning

Manipulative materials and models assume a critical role in helping students learn mathematics throughout the elementary school. Mathematical thoughts by their very nature are abstract, so any model that embodies them is imperfect and has limitations. The model is not the mathematics but at best illustrates the mathematical concept under consideration.

Suppose we were developing the concept of a circle. A plate could be used to illustrate this concept, but it would also illustrate many very different mathematical concepts: area, boundary, circumference, and diameter, to name but a few. Since the concept is being formed, the learner has no way of knowing which attributes characterize it. Thus, irrelevant variables (design on plate, its attractive finish, a chip or crack) may be the only things "seen." It will not be clear exactly what characterizes a circle. Other models, such as coins or lids, could be introduced, but even here the focus might be on the interior rather than the boundary of these models. Additional models, such as a rim of a wheel, a bike tire, a ring, and the core from a roll of paper towels would reinforce the roundness associated with a circle but would also make it clear that a circle is associated with the outer edge or boundary of the models (see Figure 4-4). Research has shown that mildly attracting

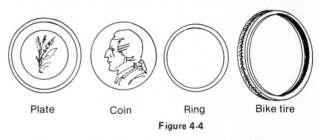

Plate   Coin   Ring   Bike tire

Figure 4-4

attention to the important attributes will enhance learning, so one might take a piece a chalk or a water-soluble pen and mark around the outer part of the coin or plate to highlight the circle (4).

The use of perceptually different models, such as those described for a circle, is called *multiple embodiment* or *multiembodiment*. The more divergent the models look, the more likely the students are to extract only the common characteristics and make abstractions. It is foolhardy to make abstractions from a single model in mathematics. The use of multiembodiments encourages students to abstract but to do so with discretion. It also decreases the likelihood of a mathematical concept's being uniquely associated with a particular model. Such associative learning can occur whenever a single model is used to illustrate a mathematical concept.

Although research has documented the value of providing multiembodiments, important questions remain:

1. *Which models are best for a particular concept?* There are many good models but rarely a best model. Research has been directed toward iden-

tifying models that have been successful in helping students learn mathematics. The embodiments described throughout this book are classroom tested. The selected references will provide additional ideas and suggestions of models for implementing a multiembodiment approach.

2. *How long should a model be used?* The length of time with a model depends upon both the student and the content. It is, however, safe to say that in general too little time is spent with a model. That is, students are rushed (dragged) too quickly through firsthand experiences with models and confronted with symbolizations. Students need to feel comfortable with the model and observe as well as talk about the key mathematical features it embodies. Even at this stage, leaving a model doesn't mean that it will never be used again. For example, periodic reviews are often more effective when linked to previous experience with specific models. Furthermore, the same model may be used at various levels throughout the elementary school to develop new and/or more sophisticated concepts.

Principle 9: Mathematical Variability Aids Learning

Mathematical learning depends heavily upon abstraction and generalization. The *multiembodiment* principle rests on the value of experiencing a mathematical concept in a variety of different physical settings. Within each embodiment, many attributes or characteristics appear. The use of *mathematical variability* insures that within a given embodiment, various mathematical features are allowed to change. Therefore, many different examples and nonexamples are needed before generalizations can be made.

For example, a parallelogram is a quadrilateral having its opposite sides parallel. We can vary its shape by changing the length of its sides and the size of its angles; the only crucial factor is that its opposite sides remain parallel. If exposed only to parallelograms having equal angular measure or only those having constant proportion relative to the length of the adjacent sides, a child would not develop a general concept of parallelogram. The mathematical variability principle suggests that in order to maximize the generalizability of a mathematical concept, as many irrelevant mathematical variables as possible (in this example the size of angle, length of side, and position on paper) should be varied while the relevant variables (opposite sides parallel) are kept intact. A student in the process of formulating a concept of parallelograms would, therefore, be exposed to at least the following different shapes:

Let's reconsider one of the embodiments—a plate —as shown in Figure 4-4 to develop a circle. In order to dispel the attention given to physical features, such as size or design of plate, chips, or other imperfections, several different kinds of plates could be used. Hopefully, these experiences would refocus attention on the plate's roundness. Thus, the model is unchanged but examples within it are varied. These changes within a given model enhance the prospects of the learner's concentrating on only the significant mathematical attributes.

Likewise, if rings were used, different designs, styles, and materials would provide a reminder that these rings model a circle. It would also be well to point out that some rings don't model a circle. Consider the "adjustable ring" shown in the accompanying sketch.

Although it is a ring, it does not model a circle. *Nonexamples* such as this play an important role in concept formulation. An oval serving platter could be used with the plates to provide a nonexample within that embodiment. Research confirms that students learn more when presented with a combination of examples and nonexamples of a mathematical concept than with examples only (11). Implementation of mathematical variability provides opportunities to vary examples and include nonexamples.

Principle 10: Forgetting Is a Natural Aspect of Learning, But Retention Can Be Aided

A very important aspect of learning is what is retained. For example, if students can read a clock in class but not when they get home, their retention of this clock-reading skill is so limited that it is virtually useless. *Retention* reflects the amount of knowledge retained, skill maintained, or problem-solving behaviors exhibited. With regard to the teaching of mathematics, retention refers to the mathematics learned that can be called upon and used when needed.

Forgetting is a problem in all disciplines, but the cumulative nature of mathematics increases its importance. Forgetting occurs over a summer, a spring vacation, a weekend, a day, or even shorter periods. The

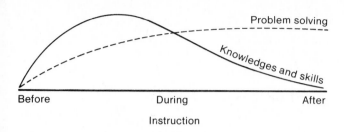

Figure 4-5. Typical learning retention curve.

graph in Figure 4-5 shows that skills and specific knowledge are subject to dramatic changes. Factual knowledge, such as:

What is a prime number?
State the transitive property.

is quickly forgotten when it isn't used regularly. Skills such as:

What is the quotient of $\frac{2}{3}$ and $\frac{1}{5}$?
Construct a square.

are also quickly lost without regular maintenance. Thus, classroom and achievement tests often report very volatile levels of performance on mathematical skill and knowledge.

The skill of problem solving, on the other hand, is less susceptible to big declines, and performance is more stable over time. One reason is that problem solving is a more complex behavior, requiring a number of higher-level thinking processes. Such processes take time to develop, but once established, not only are they retained longer, but performance may in fact improve as time goes by.

Retention is an important goal in mathematics education. Instructional efforts must recognize the importance of retention and try to maximize it. How can retention be improved? Research suggests several ways:

1. Meaningful learning is the best way to shore up retention. All phases of mathematics (knowledge, skill, and solving problems) that have been developed with meaning and learned with understanding are retained longer.

2. Daily lessons should include reviews of topics germane to the discussion. The value of systematically including brief reviews of topics prerequisite to the introduction of new knowledge, skills, or problem solving cannot be overestimated. Brief daily reviews improve immediate performance and contribute to higher levels of learning.

3. Periodic (weekly and monthly) reviews of selected key topics contribute substantially to the quantity of mathematics retained. These regular maintenance programs remove rustiness and provide refreshers that help improve retention (6).

A GLANCE AT WHERE WE'VE BEEN

Mathematics learning can and must have meaning. This is the cornerstone of all instructional planning and teaching in mathematics.

Although generalizations and abstractions are an integral part of mathematics learning, decades of research have revealed no single best path to teaching them. There are, however, several creditable learning theories to guide the teaching process. These theories recognize the importance of the concrete level and describe movements toward the abstract.

We know that what is "concrete" varies from learner to learner. We know that learning occurs from both physical and mental activity. We know that abstraction in mathematics is a slow process, requiring weeks, months, and generally years of development. We know that many individual differences exist; thus, the exact learning routes differ. Further, the rate of progress within a given route varies greatly among children. With due regard for these variables, the essential role of teachers is to help learners bridge from the concrete to the abstract. In performing this role, teachers must make effective use of appropriate models to involve pupils in experiencing, learning, and eventually abstracting the mathematics.

THINGS TO DO: ADDING TO YOUR PICTURE

1. State two reasons for developing learning bridges when teaching mathematics.
2. List some characteristics of mathematical anxiety.
3. Present an argument to support how the use of "two-way learning bridges" can save victims from "Anxiety Gorge."
4. Review Piaget's concrete operational level in Figure 4-2. What implications does this hold for using manipulative materials?
5. According to Bruner's scheme in Figure 4-2, what is the earliest level at which symbols are associated with mathematical concepts?
6. Explain how multiembodiment is an integral part of Dienes' generalizing level.
7. Give an example of meaningful learning in mathematics. Then give an example of nonmeaningful learning. State in your own words what distinguishes them.
8. The student comment, "What is a figure?", cited on page 37, illustrates nonmeaningful learning and the circular nature of many definitions in mathematics. Check definitions of some other mathematical terms and describe some potential difficulties students may have in understanding them.

9. How does the statement "If you don't know where you are going, how will you know when you get there?" relate to "Students need to know what is to be learned in mathematics classes"?

10. Why is it important to have children talk about the mathematics they are learning?

11. Distinguish between providing multiembodiment and mathematical variability for a concept.

12. Describe specific steps that teachers can take to improve retention of mathematics learning.

13. Select a topic from a scope-and-sequence chart for a current elementary mathematics textbook series. Describe how this topic is spiraled. For example, at what grade level is it introduced? How many years is it spiraled? During what year(s) does it receive the heaviest instructional attention?

14. Select a topic from a first-, second-, or third-grade textbook series. Read all the related suggested activities described in the teacher's manual. Consider these questions in your discussion. What concrete materials were used? Is multiembodiment reflected in these materials? How is mathematical variability provided?

SELECTED REFERENCES

1. Brownell, William A. "Psychological Considerations in the Learning and the Teaching of Arithmetic." In *The Teaching of Arithmetic.* Tenth Yearbook of the National Council of Teachers of Mathematics. Reston, Va.: National Council of Teachers of Mathematics, 1935.

2. Callahan, Leroy G., and Glennon, Vincent J. *Elementary School Mathematics: A Guide to Current Research.* Washington, D.C.: Association for Supervision and Curriculum Development, 1975.

3. Carpenter, Thomas P. "Research in Cognitive Development." In *Research in Mathematics Education* (ed. Richard J. Shumway). Reston, Va.: National Council of Teachers of Mathematics, 1980.

4. Driscoll, Mark J. *Research Within Reach: Elemen-tary School Mathematics.* St. Louis: CEMREL, Inc., 1980.

5. Ginsburg, Herbert. *Children's Arithmetic: The Learning Process.* New York: Van Nostrand Reinhold, 1977.

6. Good, Thomas L.; Biddle, Bruce; and Brophy, Jere E. *Teachers Make a Difference.* New York: Holt, Rinehart & Winston, 1975.

7. Good, Thomas L., and Grouws, Douglas A. "The Missouri Mathematics Effectiveness Project: An Experimental Study in Fourth-Grade Classrooms." *Journal of Educational Psychology,* 71 (June 1979), pp. 355–362.

8. Hiebert, James. "Children's Thinking." In *Research in Mathematics Education* (ed. Richard J. Shumway). Reston, Va.: National Council of Teachers of Mathematics, 1980.

9. Higgins, Jon L. *Mathematics Teaching and Learning.* Worthington, Ohio: Jones Publishing Company, 1973.

10. Maertens, Norbert, and Johnston, James. "Effects of Arithmetic Homework Upon Attitudes and Achievement of Fourth, Fifth, and Sixth Grade Pupils." *School Science and Mathematics,* 72 (1972), pp. 117–126.

11. Shumway, Richard J. "Students Should See 'Wrong' Examples: An Idea from Research on Learning." *Arithmetic Teacher,* 21 (April 1974), pp. 344–348.

12. Suydam, Marilyn N., and Higgins, Jon L. *Activity-Based Learning in Elementary School Mathematics: Recommendations from Research.* Columbus, Ohio: ERIC Clearinghouse for Science, Mathematics and Environmental Education, 1977.

13. Toepfer, Conrad F. "Brain Growth Periodization— A New Dogma for Education." *Middle School Journal,* 10 (August 1979), pp. 3–20.

14. Weber, C. A. "Do Teachers Understand Learning Theory?" *Phi Delta Kappan,* 46 (May 1965), pp. 433–435.

15. Wheatley, Grayson H., et al. "Hemispheric Specialization and Cognitive Development: Implications for Mathematics Education." *Journal for Research in Mathematics Education,* 9 (January 1978), pp. 19–32.

5

Planning for Mathematics Instruction

INTRODUCTION

At the heart of good teaching lies planning. Children learn best from lessons that are interesting and carefully sequenced, directed by thoughtful questions, and enriched by materials that develop ideas and provide practice. Research indicates that careful development of ideas, with clear explanations, careful questioning, and manipulative materials, is particularly important in teaching mathematical content (3, 15).

Teachers plan mathematics lessons in a variety of ways. Some write just the objectives they want children to attain, or take a step toward attaining. Some jot down key questions they want to ask. Some lay out the materials they want to use, or run off the worksheet they'll give the children. Others read the comments in the teacher's guide to the textbook. All these approaches require teachers to think through what they plan to do.

Few teachers have the time to write out a complete, detailed plan for every mathematics lesson they teach. Some do it occasionally, when they know the idea they want to teach must be developed particularly carefully. For someone just beginning to teach, however, writing detailed lesson plans is particularly worthwhile. Careful planning helps to make the initial experiences good ones, not only for the children but also for the beginning teacher. Plans give you the security of knowing what you'll do and say throughout the lesson, of

having interesting materials prepared and arranged for use, and of anticipating what the children will do. Your plan also gives you a way of judging how well the lesson went; even though you might not have been able to follow the plan precisely, it helps you evaluate your behaviors and the responses of the children. Moreover, through writing detailed plans you learn how to plan "in your head."

THE IMPORTANCE OF PLANNING

Planning for mathematics instruction is important for a number of reasons:

1. Planning establishes definite goals and helps to ensure that all essential content will be included, whether you are considering the year's work, a unit's work, or a day's work. The purposes of each lesson will be delineated clearly to help you to avoid omissions and mistakes.

2. Planning permits scheduling the work in feasible units of time and in a sensible sequence. The amount of time allotted to teaching a particular topic is determined on the basis of relative importance and relative difficulty. The sequence of topics is determined on the basis of the specific mathematics content and the developmental level of the children. Mathematics appears to be more highly sequenced than some other bodies of

knowledge. Thus, it is difficult to teach multiplication with fractions before children know how to multiply with whole numbers. On the other hand, sometimes a particular sequencing is not as mandatory as it seems. For instance, it was considered mandatory for many years to delay instruction on decimals until after instruction on whole numbers was well under way (that is, until the intermediate grades). As children use calculators, however, they encounter decimals much earlier, and we find that they learn decimal ideas before the intermediate grades. Developmental level must also be considered, however. The child who is at the concrete operations level, where ideas must be rooted in concrete illustrations and where it is difficult to manipulate abstract relationships, finds it difficult if not impossible to learn with understanding how to find the volume of a cube.

3. Planning helps to assure that a lesson begins interestingly, maintains a good pace throughout, and has a satisfying ending within the time allowed. Time is relatively flexible in most elementary schools, with no bells ringing to signify that students are to move on to the next class. Nevertheless, there are constraints, whether they be lunch time or another subject that must be taught. Often, however, you will be able to allow more time than you'd originally planned for a lesson in which the children are totally involved or in which they need more help in grasping an idea—or to end a lesson sooner than you'd thought when they have learned the content quickly or have met a difficulty so that you need to reconsider how to teach them. At the end, you'll probably want to emphasize a key point they should remember—or one they should think more about.

4. Planning aids in holding the children's interest and attention, whether they are working as a total class, in small groups, or individually. We know from research that "time-on-task" is associated with achievement gains (4). That is, the more time a student spends actively engaged in tasks related to the topic, the more he or she achieves on a test of that content. Thus, the teacher's goal is to have the children spend as much as possible of the time available for mathematics instruction actually working on that content. Moreover, children actively involved are less likely to create discipline problems.

5. Planning helps to avoid unnecessary repetition, while ensuring necessary repetition for review and practice. In most schools, with most textbooks, you will be using a spiral approach, in which mathematical ideas and skills are taught at several points in a year or over a several-year period. At each encounter a topic is approached in more depth, as children acquire the necessary background and developmental level to take another step toward mastery. As you plan, you'll need to consider the extent to which your pupils are ready for another look at a topic they've previously encoun-

tered. Sometimes you will want to delay instruction on a particular topic. But be wary of scheduling all the instruction on a given topic for a single period of time: children may need the "time between" to assimilate it. Some schools take a "mastery learning" approach, in which children are to master each topic or skill before they go on to the next. This has decided advantages, not the least of which may be achievement—but it also has some disadvantages, not the least of which is that children who do not learn a skill may be "stuck" at that point in the curriculum, unable to go on to new mathematical ideas with which they might be more successful. Frequently, a later topic will provide practice related to the earlier idea, and then the child learns it. The advantage of having all children master prerequisite topics before they go on to new material must be carefully weighed against the disadvantages—and the disadvantages must be compensated for.

6. Planning creates a feeling of confidence for you. You know what you want to do—and your class will recognize that you are prepared. If you think about the "good teachers" you've had, you will probably find that they were well prepared for teaching.

TYPES OF PLANNING

You must plan more than each day's mathematics lesson. At the beginning of the school year, you will need to consider what you want to have the children in your class accomplish during the year. These goals are not something you must develop on your own. Most schools have prepared a scope-and-sequence guide, or they rely on the one provided with the textbook series they use (see Figure 5-1). Familiarize yourself with this scope-and-sequence guide before you do any further planning. It is designed to ensure that a child will be taught the desired range of content across grade levels. It would be wise to check with your principal and other teachers to determine whether any changes have been made to meet the needs of children in your school, as well as the degree of flexibility you'll have in making changes for your class.

After ascertaining the goals of mathematics instruction and the order in which topics will be taught, you'll need to consider the approximate amounts of time you want to spend on each phase of the curriculum in terms of its relative importance. This allotment helps you to fit in all the mathematics content you want to include. Thus, if you want to include additional time for problem solving (as suggested in Chapter 3), indicate this in your planning.

The goals for the year need to be broken down by units (or "chapters"), with an outline of specific objec-

Scope and Sequence

4

Numbers and Numeration

Ones, tens, hundreds, 26-27
Thousands, 34-35
Millions, 38-39
Tenths, 342-343
Hundredths, 344-345
Reading and writing numerals, 26-27, 34-35, 38-41, 342-345
Comparing and ordering numbers, 28-29, 36-39, 346-347
Rounding to the nearest ten, hundred, 30-31, 56-57 thousand, ten-thousand, 56-57 dollar, 30-31
Roman numerals, 45
Expanded form, 85
Finite number system, 127
Prime numbers, 221
Base eight, 309
Other uses for numbers, 65
Odd and even, 103

Addition of Whole Numbers

Basic addition facts, 2-5
Addition properties, 4-5
Fact families, 18-19
Missing addends, 3, 18-19
Adding 2-digit numbers without regrouping, 48-49 with regrouping, 50-51
Adding larger numbers, 52-55, 60-61
More than two addends, 4-5, 62-63
Estimating sums, 58-59, 60-62, 78-79
Addition with money 52-55, 61, 63
Addition with subtraction, using grouping symbols, 23
Addition tables, 9

5

Numbers and Numeration

Ones, tens, hundreds, 32-33
Thousands, 34-35
Millions, 42-43
Billions, 44-45
Tenths, 256-257
Hundredths, 258-259
Thousandths, 270-271
Reading and writing numerals, 32-35, 42-47, 256-259, 270-271
Comparing and ordering numbers, 42-45, 260-261, 272-273
Rounding to the nearest ten, hundred. 38-39, 60-61 thousand, ten-thousand, hundred-thousand, million, 60-61, 72-73 dollar, 38-39, 60-61
Roman numerals, 51
Expanded form, 111-112
Prime numbers, 213
Composite numbers, 213
Base five, 279

Addition of Whole Numbers

Basic addition facts, 2-5
Addition properties, 4-5
Missing addends, 4-5, 81
Adding 2-digit or 3-digit numbers, 54-55
More than two addends, 56-59, 62-63
Adding larger numbers, 58-59, 72-73
Estimating sums, 62-63, 76-77
Addition with money, 58-59, 62-63, 72-75
Addition with subtraction, using grouping symbols, 29
Adding with a calculator, 353

6

Numbers and Numeration

Ones, tens, hundreds, thousands. 2-3
Millions, 6-7
Billions, 8-9
Tenths, hundredths, thousandths, 98-99
Ten-thousandths, hundred-thousandths, 100-101
Reading and writing numerals, 2-3, 6-7, 8-9, 98-101
Comparing and ordering numbers, 4-9, 102-103
Rounding through nearest billion, 24-27 decimals, 110-111, 134-135, 246-247 money, 24-25, 110-111
Roman numerals, 37
Expanded form, 67
Prime numbers, 229
Composite numbers, 229

Addition of Whole Numbers

Addition properties, 12-13
Adding larger numbers, 14-15, 26-27
More than two addends, 12-13
Estimating sums, 28-29
Addition with money, 14-17, 26-27, 30-33

Figure 5-1. (From *Series M: Macmillan Mathematics,* **Teacher's Edition, Level 6—Tina Thoburn and Jack E. Forbes, Senior Authors. Copyright © 1982 Macmillan Publishing Company. Used by permission.)**

CONCEPTS	PAGES	LESSONS	CLASS PERIODS ABOVE AVERAGE	AVERAGE	BELOW AVERAGE
Write addition sentence for number stories, facts to 10	26–27	2	1	1	2
Write addition sentences, facts to 10	28–29	2	1	2	2
Use commutative property of addition	30	1	1	1	1
Choose correct addition sentence	32	1	1	1	1
Addition, example form	33–34	2	2	2	3
Write addition sentences for number stories	36	1	1	1	1
Write subtraction sentences for number stories, facts to 10	37–38	2	1	1	2
Write subtraction sentences, facts to 10	39–40	2	2	2	2
Choose correct subtraction sentence	41	1	1	1	1
Subtraction, example form	42–43	2	2	2	3
Write subtraction sentences for number stories	45	1	1	1	1
Related addition and subtraction sentences	46	1	1	1	1
Related addition and subtraction examples	48	1	1	1	1
Supply correct operation sign	50	1	1	1	–
TOTALS		20	17	18	21

Figure 5-2. (From Bruce R. Vogeli and others, *Mathematics for Mastery 2,* **Teacher's Edition. © 1978 by Silver Burdett Company. Used by permission.)**

tives to be taught about each topic. The school's curriculum guide or the textbook will help you here. The time you assign to teaching each topic is again of importance. Most mathematics textbooks contain 130 to 150 lessons. Given the typical 180-day school year, you have some opportunity to spend extra time on some topics or to teach topics not included in the textbook. An example of a plan for a unit, with times noted, is given in Figure 5-2.

In planning for the unit, you have outlined what topics are to be taught, their sequence, and how much time you will spend on each. Now you can outline what you want to accomplish each week, and then you'll be ready to develop daily lesson plans. Some schools require teachers to maintain a lesson plan book in which they note the objectives (and sometimes other details as well) for each day's lessons for a week. Even if this is not required, it is a good idea. It keeps you aware of progress toward the goals for the year and gives you a guide to follow each day. As you plan each week, you can review the progress of the children in your class and vary or pace the content to be taught to meet their individual needs. Or you can plan to teach different content to small groups or to individuals.

COMPONENTS OF A LESSON PLAN

In preparing a lesson plan for a particular mathematical topic, you will need to:

- *State clearly the objective or objectives.* What mathematical skill or idea are you trying to teach? What do you want the children to learn? Is the purpose to introduce a new topic, develop understanding, or provide review? Do the children have the necessary prerequisites?
- *Determine the sequence.* What mathematical ideas logically come first, second, and so on?
- *Decide how the class is to be organized.* Should the lesson involve the total class, small groups, and/or individual work?
- *Determine the procedures to be followed.* What teaching strategy will be most effective? What type of motivation will capture the children's interest and attention? What must be reviewed to relate this lesson to previous work? What will you do and what will the children do? What questions will you ask? How will you and the children interact? What varied activities will be involved? What materials will you and the children use? How will the materials and activities be varied to meet individual needs? Should practice be assigned—and if so, will it be from the textbook, from worksheets, or from a follow-up activity? Will there also be homework? What and how much? (The assignment of homework depends on school policy: you'll need to check what role homework has in your school.)
- *Decide how much time to spend on each part of the lesson.* What is the lesson's relative importance in terms of the time available as well as the difficulty it might present to the children?
- *Decide how you will evaluate—both as the lesson proceeds and after it is completed.* What should you look for during the lesson? How will you and the children know what they have learned? Will each child meet with some success during the lesson?
- *Write the plan for the lesson.* Writing it down will help you clarify many of your ideas, and it also gives you a record that can be used in evaluating the lesson and in planning subsequent lessons. Moreover, if you diverge from the plan, you'll be able to pinpoint the point of divergency and return later to pick up where you left off.

In one school, teachers outlined their lesson plans in terms of four points: objectives, materials, procedures, and evaluation. One teacher's lesson plan using this model is found in Figure 5-3. Notice that it is designed to be used; the teacher who developed it is reminded quickly of the things to have ready and the steps to be taken. The plan does not indicate specifically what is to be said, however, so that you would probably find it difficult to carry out. Nor does it indicate prerequisites necessary for the lesson (e.g., children must be able to add three or more addends and divide by a one-digit divisor), since the teacher had already ascertained that the children had these skills.

Different forms of lessons are illustrated throughout this book. Many of them serve as chapter openers, highlighting key ideas and the materials necessary for the lesson. They are accompanied by a "snapshot" of actual behaviors and conversation of children and teachers.

Most teacher's guides follow a three-step lesson plan:

1. *Before using the textbook.* Prerequisites, motivation, and activities to develop the concept (often using manipulative materials) are described.
2. *Using the textbook.* The mathematical concept is developed systematically through pictures and words, with examples for practice.
3. *After using the textbook.* Suggestions are given for follow-up activities such as seatwork and games. Many guides also provide suggestions for remediation, enrichment, and variation for learning disabled and other handicapped children.

An example of a lesson from a textbook is given in Figure 5-4.

```
                    LESSON PLAN:   GRADE 4
ENTIRE CLASS

A.  Objectives:

    1.  To develop understanding of the term "average"

    2.  To teach one method of finding averages

B.  Materials:

    1.  Cutouts of trucks and cargo to tape on chalkboard

    2.  Objects from the room, such as books

    3.  Flannelboard and materials for use on it

    4.  Individual materials - small blocks, paper squares, chips

    5.  Textbook, page 167

C.  Procedure:

    1.  "Motivate" with truck story about average amount of cargo each will
        hold (told with cutouts on chalkboard), during which children
        will use and discover meaning of term "average"  (10 min.)

    2.  Use of objects and flannelboard materials to ascertain how to find
        an average  (15 min.)

    3.  Use of individual materials to provide practice and to ascertain
        individual understanding  (10 min.)

    4.  Practice with the procedure using textbook examples  (10 min.)

D.  Evaluation:

    1.  Observation of actions and responses in group and individually

    2.  Formulation of statement about averages
```

Figure 5-3

Figure 5-4. (From L. Carey Bolster and others, *Mathematics Around Us, Grade Four,* Teacher's Edition. Glenview, Illinois: Scott, Foresman and Company, 1978. Used by permission.)

Decimals: Place Value

page 292

objective
Give the place value for any digit in a decimal involving tenths or hundredths.

preliminary activities
Write a number such as 39.2 on the board but provide space between each digit. Insert a zero in different places in the numeral and let students discuss whether or how the value of the number changes. Some possibilities are 309.2, 39.02, 39.20, and 039.2. In the discussion bring out the value of each place in the numeral through the use of displays like the one at the top of the page. Also bring out such ideas as these:
1. 390.2 is the greatest of these numbers.
2. 39.02 is the least of these numbers.
3. 39.2, 39.20, and 039.2 all name the same number. (We seldom write 039.2.)

using page 292
After discussing Examples A-D, have students do the exercises on this page independently. Afterwards you might ask them to read aloud their answers to Exercises 13-18.

additional activities
Give sets of numbers, such as 8.1, 6.08, 8.01, 6.8, and 7.62. Ask students to arrange the numbers in order from least to greatest.

related resources
Practice, p. 111

hundreds tens ones tenths hundredths

208.43

A. In the decimal 208.43, the 4 is in the tenths place. This 4 means "4 tenths."

What does the 8 in 208.43 mean? 8 ones
What does the 3 in 208.43 mean? 3 hundredths
What does the 2 in 208.43 mean? 2 hundreds
What does the 0 in 208.43 mean? 0 tens

B. Both .6 and .60 name the same number.

What does the 6 mean in .6? 6 tenths
What does the 6 mean in .60? 6 tenths
What does the 0 mean in .60? 0 hundredths

C. Both 9 and 9.0 name the same number.

What does the 9 mean in 9? 9 ones
What does the 9 mean in 9.0? 9 ones
What does the 0 mean in 9.0? 0 tenths

D. .5 and .05 name different numbers.

What does the 5 mean in .5? 5 tenths
What does the 5 mean in .05? 5 hundredths
What does the 0 mean in .05? 0 tenths

Tell what each 6 means.

1. 176 ones   2. 17.6 tenths   3. 1.76 hundredths

Tell what each 9 means.

4. 12.9 tenths   5. .89 hundredths   6. 907 hundreds

Tell what each 1 means.

7. 152 hundreds   8. 2.13 tenths   9. 871.6 ones

Tell what each 4 means.

10. 4 ones   11. .04 hundredths   12. .4 tenths

Write the decimal.

Here's how

| 3 tenths |
| 8 ones | 8.34
| 4 hundredths |

13. | 7 tenths |
    | 9 ones |
    9.7

14. | 2 tens |
    | 6 tenths |
    20.6

15. | 7 hundredths |
    | 1 ten |
    10.07

16. | 8 tens |
    | 1 tenth |
    80.1

17. | 4 hundredths |
    | 3 ones |
    3.04

18. | 5 hundredths |
    | 5 hundreds |
    500.05

More practice
Set F, page 303

51

Research with fourth-grade classes has shown a pattern in lessons used by teachers whose classes had high achievement (9). It consisted of daily review, development of new content, seatwork, and homework assignment, with special reviews as needed (see Figure 5-5). One strength of this pattern lies in its emphasis on clarity.

GROUPING FOR INSTRUCTION

There are three basic patterns of grouping for mathematics instruction: (1) whole class with teacher guidance, (2) small group, either with teacher guidance or with pupil leaders, and (3) individuals working independently. The first is used most often.

In teaching reading, most teachers believe that children should be allowed to go as fast and as far as they can in developing skills and understanding. In contrast, the attitude toward mathematics instruction is that one should not go beyond the objectives for a given grade level. For reading, the teacher will work with three (or more) groups, but in mathematics the mode is one group—all children are given the same instruction despite individual differences in ability, achievement, needs, and interests.

It should be obvious that this is not logical. It occurs, in part, because of time pressures on the teacher: how can the school day include time for multiple groups in both reading and mathematics (and possibly other subject areas), and how does the teacher find time to plan for multiple groups? In response, we note that some

Figure 5-5. (From Good and Grouws (9). Copyright 1979 by the American Psychological Association. Reprinted by permission of the authors.)

Summary of Key Instructional Behaviors
_____

Daily Review (first 8 minutes except Mondays)

    a. review the concepts and skills associated with the homework
    b. collect and deal with homework assignments
    c. ask several mental computation exercises

Development (about 20 minutes)

    a. briefly focus on prerequisite skills and concepts
    b. focus on meaning and promoting student understanding by using lively explanations, demonstrations, process explanations, illustrations, etc.
    c. assess student comprehension
        1) using process/product questions (active interaction)
        2) using controlled practice
    d. repeat and elaborate on the meaning portion as necessary

Seatwork (about 15 minutes)

    a. provide uninterrupted successful practice
    b. momentum - keep the ball rolling - get everyone involved, then sustain involvement
    c. alerting - let students know their work will be checked at end of period
    d. accountability - check the students' work

Homework Assignment

    a. assign on a regular basis at the end of each math class except Fridays
    b. should involve about 15 minutes of work to be done at home
    c. should include one or two review problems

Special Reviews

    a. weekly review/maintenance
        1) conduct during the first 20 minutes each Monday
        2) focus on skills and concepts covered during the previous week
    b. monthly review/maintenance
        1) conduct every fourth Monday
        2) focus on skills and concepts covered since the 1st monthly review

teachers do find the time, both in the school day and for planning. You can probably learn to do it, too.

Other teachers compromise—keeping the whole group at approximately the same point in terms of introduction of new topics, so that many total-group lessons are possible, but using small-group instruction and individualized instruction at other times.

There are some guidelines to aid you in determining which grouping pattern to use:

1. Use large-group instruction:
    *   if the topic is one that can be presented to all pupils at approximately the same point in time (that is, if all pupils have the prerequisites for understanding the initial presentation)
    *   if pupils will need continuous guidance from the teacher in order to attain the knowledge, skill, or understanding
2. Use small-group instruction:
    *   if pupils can profit from pupil-to-pupil interaction with less teacher guidance
    *   if activities involve a few pupils at a time (which would leave the rest of the class merely watching and waiting their turn)
3. Use individual instruction:
    *   if pupils can follow a sequence or conduct an activity on their own
    *   if the focus is on individual practice for mastery

POINTS TO CONSIDER IN PLANNING (AND TEACHING)

In recent years much attention has been directed toward what actually goes on in classrooms and what factors are correlated with higher achievement. One research review described four categories of student responses that were correlated with achievement and suggested ways teachers can organize and present instruction to encourage such responses (1):

1. *Attention* ("on-task" behavior). When instruction is designed so that active participation in the learning activity is demanded, attention is usually higher. Thus, having all children hold up a card giving the sum of two numbers is better than having only one child give the answer.

Teachers' strategies for selecting students to participate during discussions influence attention and active participation. Thus, a teacher who calls only on volunteers to answer questions will find that other children will stop paying attention. For successful lessons, it seems desirable to keep the lesson moving at an even pace, try to prevent interruptions, and select activities that will not overstimulate children.

2. *Initiative.* Learning is most efficient when children can identify points where they need help and then obtain it. Thus, willingness to initiate contact with the teacher promotes learning. Some teachers discourage student-initiated contacts by lower-achieving students, who may interrupt at inconvenient times and with queries that are not directed toward the task. Therefore, these students are unable to get help when they need it. Teachers who were very specific about desired student behavior were more successful in promoting achievement. They let slower learners as well as other students know when they could and should demonstrate initiative, thus encouraging this behavior.

3. *Understanding* of how and why to do classroom work. Students who believe a task is worthwhile and understand clearly how to complete it are more likely to persist at it. Thus, teachers further students' understanding when they are explicit about how work should be done and what the reasons are for doing it.

4. *Success.* Not surprisingly, success in daily classroom tasks has been positively related to long-term achievement. Therefore:

*   Assignments should be matched to students' abilities.
*   Work in progress should be monitored and prompt feedback provided. (If a child makes an error and does not realize it, it may affect performance on the remainder of the task.)
*   Checking times should be incorporated into classroom activities (for example, by circulating through the room to look over children's shoulders as they work and being available to answer questions.)

In studies to identify patterns of behaviors that make a difference in student learning of mathematics at the fourth-grade level, one pair of researchers found that necessary skills for effective whole-class instruction include the ability to explain material clearly, to structure seatwork problems for the class, and to respond to individual students' need for help (8). Good teachers expected and even demanded work and achievement from students and moved through the curriculum quickly, thus increasing time on task. Students approached them readily to ask for help: they were more likely to get developmental, nonevaluative, and task-relevant feedback.

Do students learn best by direct, expository instruction by the teacher, such as that in Figure 5-5? Or by discovery, with the teacher posing the situation or problem and then letting children "solve" it more or less on their own? Or by guided discovery, with the teacher asking questions at key points as necessary? Research indicates that no one mode of instruction can be considered best (11). Teachers should learn as many instructional modes as possible and use them when appropriate.

The Importance of Questions

Questions can be aimed at checking children's knowledge of a fact or their ability to perform a skill. These are relatively low-level questions. At a higher level are questions requiring the analysis or synthesis of information—as when we ask a child to explain why a procedure works. In mathematics lessons, teachers often use questions of the first type and only infrequently those of the latter type (7, 10). While this is correlated with the ability of children to score high on achievement tests, it may give the child an erroneous picture of mathematics as involving only short answers, with one correct answer per question. We need to encourage children to do more talking about mathematics—about why a procedure works, about what would happen if something were changed in the problem, about how the mathematics could be applied in a real-life situation.

As you plan a lesson, give thought to the types of questions you ask. Try to include a range of them, with some requiring the child to think rather than merely to supply a fact from memory or to perform a learned procedure.

The Use of Manipulative Materials

All through this book, we stress the importance of having children use materials. While it has not yet shown why, research indicates that lessons using manipulative materials have a higher probability of producing greater mathematical achievement than do lessons without such materials (13). In short, children appear to gain a better understanding of mathematics when manipulative materials are used.

The Role of Drill and Practice

It should be obvious that students need drill and practice in order to be able to perform a desired behavior or procedure at will. Just as we practice learning to walk or drive a car, we practice basic addition facts or how to multiply fractions. The choice is not *if,* but *when.* Research has indicated that drill and practice should *follow,* not precede, the development of meaning (2). Research also indicates that drill and practice activities should not consume as much time as does developmental work that helps children to understand an idea or procedure (14).

Workbooks published to accompany textbook series provide practice on the content presented in the textbook, lesson by lesson. Whether to assign this practice material (perhaps in addition to the practice already presented in the textbook itself) is a decision you must make in terms of children's needs. Keep in mind that they must understand an idea or procedure before they are asked to practice it. Practicing a skill that has already been mastered doesn't appear to be harmful, except in one way: if the children become bored with the activity, then other outcomes than a completed workbook page may result.

Many teachers use worksheets in place of workbooks. When these are purchased, they are little different from the workbook. But when the teacher prepares them with the needs of particular children in mind, they can become a valuable tool. They can be used to aid slower learners by providing practice on subskills, to challenge faster learners with extension activities, and to provide personalized-for-this-class practice for everyone.

Many games can also be used to provide practice. They offer a motivating format and a competitive aspect that many children love. An example of such a game is Bingo—by changing the rules slightly, you can make it into a game that provides practice on place value ("The number has 3 tens and 2 ones") or for one of the operations ("The number is the sum of 50 and 24").

EVALUATION

Evaluation should be an integral aspect of mathematics instruction. We need to ascertain whether we have taught what we think we have taught and whether each child has learned what we think he or she has learned. We evaluate:

1. To assess the mathematics program in the classroom and in the school. Is the content appropriate for your students? How well are they progressing toward the goals and objectives you have set? Are they able to apply their knowledge and skills in new situations? Do they enjoy doing and using mathematics?

2. To assess the mathematics achievement of the children in each classroom.

3. To diagnose individual strengths and weaknesses.

Among the evaluation procedures you can use are: observations, interviews, inventories and checklists, criterion-referenced tests, norm-referenced tests, reports from parents, samples of a student's work, and attitude scales. Some of these procedures have already been discussed in Chapter 3 in relation to problem solving.

Observing is a way of ascertaining what children actually do. *Interviewing* provides information on what they say about what they do. The *inventory* or *checklist* serves as a means of collecting and recording information quickly. *Criterion-referenced* or *mastery tests* help you to evaluate a child in terms of individual achievement. If a child gets a predetermined percentage of the items correct, adequate mastery of the topic is assumed. [Specific suggestions for constructing paper-and-pencil tests can be found in (12).] *Norm-referenced tests* provide you with information on how well each child in your class achieves in relation to others at the same grade level. Instead of setting a mastery level, a scale is used: you expect a few students to do very well, a few to do poorly, but most to attain an "average" level. Most standardized achievement tests, given once or twice a year in many schools, are norm-referenced. *Standardizing* a test refers to developing prescribed, uniform requirements for administration and scoring and to the norms or average performance levels developed after the test is given to a large group of students.

Comments from parents, whether in written form or given in parent-teacher conferences, can provide the teacher with helpful clues as to what a child is learning. *Samples of a child's work* can be collected for use in such conferences, and they also provide the teacher with a means of analyzing progress over a period of time.

Attitudes involve many facets, ranging from awareness of the structural beauty of mathematics and of the important roles of mathematics, to feelings about the difficulty and challenge of learning mathematics, to interest in particular topics in mathematics or particular methods of being taught mathematics. We attempt to assess the child's attitudes toward mathematics by observing his or her expressions, comments, and behaviors; by asking the child to comment on the way he or she feels about mathematics; and by using an attitude scale. On such a scale, the child is asked to respond (using five responses from strongly agree to strongly disagree) to such items as:

- I usually feel happy when doing mathematics problems.
- My mind goes blank and I am unable to think clearly when working mathematics examples.

In the final analysis, all the information we collect is useful as we plan lessons. We know more about not only the achievement and progress of each child, but what his or her individual needs are.

Many teachers have found it helpful to keep another type of evaluative record. They jot down notes in their planbook or the teacher's guide about things that went well and things that didn't for each lesson. These notes help them to plan the following year. You may think you will remember, but you'll probably forget, without such a note.

Diagnosis

To meet the needs of children learning mathematics, you must first determine what their strengths and weaknesses are, using one or more of the procedures cited above or using a specific diagnostic test. The results of such evaluation are used to place students in instructional materials, to group students for instruction, and to decide just what needs to be taught or retaught to individuals and to the class.

Among the guidelines for diagnosis in mathematics are (5):

1. Make sure that a child's apparent mathematical deficiency is really a deficiency.
2. Remember that each child progresses through several stages of development before reaching an adult conceptual level.
3. Strengthen your diagnosis with the liberal use of manipulative materials.
4. Don't lose sight of the emotional side of students in your diagnosis.
5. Be both flexible and patient in piecing together an accurate picture of a child's thinking.
6. Maintain a climate of acceptance.
7. Distinguish between errors that are random and those that occur more systematically.

Both observations and interviews are highly effective in revealing behaviors not noticeable from paper-and-pencil tests. But tests are useful tools in diagnosis, especially when you analyze how the child reached an answer, not merely what the final score was.

Remediation

Effective remediation begins with effective diagnosis. Once you have a clear picture of a child's needs, you can plan activities to provide the missing prerequisites that are at the source of a difficulty, develop the understanding that has been missed, provide the practice that is needed, and give the encouragement that is so vital in effective remediation.

At times you'll be able to group pupils who all need help on a particular point; at other times you must work with individuals. Research has indicated some effective methods for remediation (6):

1. Involve the child in planning his or her remedial program.
2. Design remedial instruction to be different from previous instruction.

3. Provide multisensory experiences.
4. Guide the children from a concrete, intuitive understanding of mathematical ideas toward being able to represent their understanding verbally and symbolically.
5. Encourage the child to estimate answers.
6. Have children use calculators.

USING THE STRATEGIC MOMENT

Despite careful planning, teachers must make many minute-to-minute decisions. It would be very sad if you did not take advantage of a situation because had not planned for it (see Figure 5-6). Making use of "teachable" or "strategic" moments and events is imperative.

To some extent, you can encourage "strategic moments" by the way you arrange the environment—by bringing in something new and therefore exciting, for instance. The teacher must know exactly what concepts he or she wants to teach and how these develop for the child—and then recognize the strategic moment when it arises.

Experience will also help you as you make the many on-the-spot decisions that are a part of teaching. You will learn what works and what doesn't. Try to define for yourself the goals you want to attain and how to attain them, and try to work within that framework. Consider how children develop and learn. Observe the children in your class as individuals, and watch for their errors and their successes. These will help you diagnose their needs and plan their instruction. And when you

know your children well, you'll be more ready to see and grasp strategic moments and make valid decisions.

A GLANCE AT WHERE WE'VE BEEN

Planning lies at the heart of good teaching. Planning helps to insure that all essential content will be included, permits scheduling the work in feasible periods of time and in a sensible sequence, helps to control the pace of a lesson, aids in holding children's attention, helps to avoid unnecessary repetition while assuring necessary review and practice, and creates a feeling of confidence for you. Planning must be done for the year, the unit, and the day. Lesson plans should include clearly stated objectives, procedures, and evaluation; a pattern consisting of daily review, development of new content, seatwork, and homework assignment has been suggested as effective. Some guidelines to aid in determining which grouping pattern to use—large-group, small-group, or individual instruction—have been presented.

Observations in classrooms have indicated the importance of attention, initiative, understanding, and success in relation to achievement. We have also considered the ability to explain material clearly, skills in questioning, the use of manipulative materials, and the role of drill and practice. Evaluation procedures have been discussed briefly, with reference to diagnosis and remediation. The importance of using the strategic moment has been stressed.

THINGS TO DO: ADDING TO YOUR PICTURE

1. Compare two different scope-and-sequence charts for a particular grade level. How does the scope of

Figure 5-6

Several first-grade children come into the room all excited by the parade they saw yesterday, with "hundreds" and "thousands" of marchers. You've planned a lesson on measurement for that day. What do you do?

All the traffic lights in town are off. Why? The computer has failed. You've planned a lesson on multiplication with two-digit numbers. Do you discuss the computer's role in society instead?

You are teaching a lesson on estimation. You have the class use calculators to find "3760.5 x 795.8" quickly. A child asks, "Why is there no decimal point in the answer?" Do you continue the lesson on estimation?

the content included differ? What proportion is the same? How does the sequence differ?

2. Select a content topic. Compare the way it is taught in two different textbooks.

3. Select a content topic. Follow its development through three grade levels in a set of textbooks. Trace what is review and what is new development of mathematical content.

4. Select a topic and plan a week's work for it.

5. Write a lesson plan for the "snapshot" of the lesson at the beginning of Chapter 9.

6. Design a lesson using the five-step plan proposed by Good and Grouws (see Figure 5-5).

7. Observe in a classroom, recording the way teacher and pupils interact. What proportion of time does the teacher talk? What type of questions are asked? Is there evidence that children learned?

8. Plan a written test to evaluate learning resulting from the lesson at the beginning of Chapter 8.

SELECTED REFERENCES

1. Anderson, Linda M. "Short-Term Student Responses to Classroom Instruction," *Elementary School Journal,* 82 (November 1981), pp. 97–108.

2. Brownell, William A., and Chazal, Charlotte B. "The Effects of Premature Drill in Third-Grade Arithmetic." *Journal of Educational Research,* 29 (September 1935), pp. 17–28.

3. Bush, A. J.; Kennedy, J. J.; and Cruickshank, D. R. "An Empirical Investigation of Teacher Clarity." *Journal of Teacher Education,* 28 (March–April 1977), pp. 53–58.

4. Denham, Carolyn, and Lieberman, Ann, eds. *Time to Learn: A Review of the Beginning Teacher Evaluation Study.* Sacramento: Commission for Teacher Preparation and Licensing, 1980.

5. Driscoll, Mark J. "Diagnosis: Taking the Mathematical Pulse." In *Research Within Research: Elementary School Mathematics.* St. Louis: CEMREL, Inc., 1980.

6. Driscoll, Mark J. "Unlocking the Mind of a Child: Teaching for Remediation in Mathematics." In *Research Within Reach: Elementary School Mathematics.* St. Louis: CEMREL, Inc., 1980.

7. Evertson, Carolyn M.; Emmer, Edward T.; and Brophy, Jere E. "Prediction of Effective Teaching in Junior High Mathematics Classrooms." *Journal for Research in Mathematics Education,* 11 (May 1980), pp. 167–178.

8. Good, Thomas L.; Grouws, Douglas A.; and Ebmeier, Howard. *Active Mathematics Teaching.* New York: Longman, 1983.

9. Good, Thomas L., and Grouws, Douglas A. "The Missouri Mathematics Effectiveness Project: An Experimental Study in Fourth-Grade Classrooms." *Journal of Educational Psychology,* 71 (June 1979), pp. 355–362.

10. Meckes, Richard C. "A Study to Ascertain the Instructional Index and Questioning Strategy of Mathematics Teachers in Grade 6, and to Determine Their Relationship to Professional Characteristics and Situational Factors." Unpublished doctoral dissertation, Southern Illinois University, 1971. *Dissertation Abstracts International,* 32A (February 1972), pp. 4245–4246.

11. Robertson, Howard C. "The Effects of the Discovery and Expository Approach of Presenting and Teaching Mathematical Principles and Relationships to Fourth Grade Pupils." Unpublished doctoral dissertation, University of Pittsburgh, 1970. *Dissertation Abstracts International,* 31A (April 1971), pp. 5278–5279.

12. Suydam, Marilyn N. *Evaluation in the Mathematics Classroom.* Columbus, Ohio: ERIC Clearinghouse for Science, Mathematics and Environmental Education, 1974. ERIC: ED 086 517.

13. Suydam, Marilyn N., and Higgins, Jon L. *Activity-Based Learning in Elementary School Mathematics: Recommendations from Research.* Columbus, Ohio: ERIC Clearinghouse for Science, Mathematics and Environmental Education, 1977. ERIC: ED 144 840.

14. Suydam, Marilyn N., and Weaver, J. Fred. *Using Research: A Key to Elementary School Mathematics.* Columbus, Ohio: ERIC Clearinghouse for Science, Mathematics and Environmental Education, 1981.

15. Thornton, Carol D. "An Evaluation of the Mathematics-Methods Program Involving the Study of Teaching Characteristics and Pupil Achievement in Mathematics." *Journal for Research in Mathematics Education,* 8 (January 1977), pp. 17–25.

6

Developing Early Numbers

Key Ideas for an Early Lesson on Numbers:

1. Maintain and/or improve skill in small-group recognition.
2. Increase awareness of number patterns.
3. Develop counting skills.

Necessary Materials:

Each child should have about 20 counters.

Orientation:

A few minutes are spent each day helping the children recognize by sight small groups of objects. The teacher, Miss Blue, has just placed four beans on the face of the overhead. She turns on the overhead for two seconds, then turns it off.

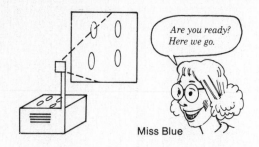

Are you ready? Here we go.

Miss Blue

Miss Blue: "How many beans did you see?"

Less than half the children raise their hands, so Miss Blue decides to do it again. This time nearly all the children raise their hands.

Miss Blue: "How many beans? Barry?"
Barry: "Four."

One child, Susan, is in obvious disagreement, so Miss Blue calls on her.

Susan: "Five."
Miss Blue: "O.K, let's check. I will turn on the overhead and Susan can count the beans for us."

Susan goes to the chalkboard and counts the images.

Susan: "There are only four. When I saw the pattern, I thought there was one in the middle."
Miss Blue: "I am glad Susan is looking for patterns. That is the key to recognizing groups of things. Let's try another one and be sure to look for patterns."

Miss Blue places five beans on the overhead, turns it on for two seconds, then turns it off.

Miss Blue: "How many beans?"

All the children have a hand up; Miss Blue points

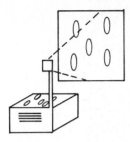

to one of them, who says five, and the others agree.

Miss Blue: "We will try one more."

Five beans are again placed on the overhead. Miss Blue then turns it on for two seconds.

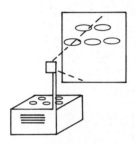

Miss Blue: "How many beans did you see? Bonny?"
Bonny: "Five, but it looks different than the other five."
Susan: "It is different because there are six. It fits the pattern for six."
Miss Blue: "Let's check it."

Miss Blue turns the projector on and Bonny confirms there are five. Susan and many other children are looking for patterns, but their recognition skills need sharpening. They see part of a pattern but are not sensitive to small differences. That's why this activity is used for a couple of minutes each day.

Miss Blue: "Thanks, Bonny, there are only five. We really have to watch those patterns carefully. That's enough for today."

Many children groan and plead for more. They really enjoy this activity, but Miss Blue realizes the value of not overdoing a good thing. Therefore, she is careful not to "burn them out" with too much at one time. Even though the children don't realize it, this activity reviews counting and provides readiness for addition and subtraction that follow.

INTRODUCTION

Children are aware of number names long before they begin to count.

> How old are you? "Two?"
> What channel should we watch? "Thirteen."
> On what floor is your father's office? "Four."
> How many sisters do you have? "One."

Such early experiences introduce number names as well as symbols—for example, "13" on the channel indicator or "4" on the elevator. They are memorized through sound and sight recognition and provide an important beginning, but these names alone tell us very little about the child's grasp of number.

For one thing, these experiences underscore a very important characteristic of number. It is an abstraction. It can't be illustrated uniquely in just one situation. For example, there is no way to describe the meaning of "two" other than providing many different examples of the property of two, namely "two-ness." The number "two" is used as an adjective to describe many different situations, such as two hands, two eyes, two feet, and two years old. Research into how children develop number makes it clear that the more varied and different the situations, the more likely it is that number concepts will be abstracted from the experiences (3). Helping children develop number concepts and counting skills has a high instructional priority. That's what this chapter is about.

PRENUMBER CONCEPTS

Numbers are everywhere, and thus children get a vast amount of early number experiences. In order to help children take advantage of these experiences, we often need to help them organize their prenumber development. Many different steps are involved in developing these prenumber concepts that will lead eventually to meaningful counting skills. Although the paths that children take may be very different, they all begin with classifying whatever is to be counted.

Classification

Children, in learning to count, become aware of number as a characteristic of different things. They must first know *what* to count. The ability to separate and distinguish one thing from another (whether it be books, toys, people, or money) is essential to number development. This is *classification* in action. It is a powerful process that begins early but is practiced and refined throughout our lives. Experience in classifying toys or any materials that interest children will be valuable in stimulating children's observational skills.

As children classify or sort materials, such as in Activity Card 6-1, they must decide whether or not each object has the given characteristic. Should children disagree on how an object is sorted, it forces them to defend their answer and perhaps further clarify how the classification process was done. At this point there may be no counting as materials are classified—yet words such as *more, few, many, most, none* will likely be used in describing the resulting collection.

Classification allows us to reach general agreement on what is to be counted. Look at Activity Card 6-1 and consider the question: How many pieces of fruit are shown? The answer is a number that tells *how many.* When a number is used in this way, it is called a *cardinal number.* However, before finding the specific cardinal number, we must first decide which are fruits. This means we must classify the fruit and distinguish it from other things on the table. Sometimes it is clear what should be counted. For example, it is clear that some things such as the silverware, doll, and cup are not to be counted as a fruit. What about the tomato? Is it a fruit? a vegetable? Once this is determined, then the members to be counted are well defined, the task is commonly understood, and the result should be the same.

Classification provides opportunities for children to sort objects according to "what belongs to what." Thus, in Activity Card 6-1, when the child sorts the glass into the roll box, the object has been classified. The child is saying this object belongs (is included or contained) in the set of things that roll.

Attribute blocks, sometimes called *logic blocks,* provide an excellent model for classification activities. These blocks may differ in color, shape, and size. For example, attributes for a set of 24 blocks may be as follows:

Color: red, black, green, yellow
Shape: triangle, square, pentagon
Size: small, large

Blocks are alike in some attributes, but no two are alike in all attributes. For example, there is only one large black triangle and there is only one small black triangle.

These blocks can be made from cardboard but are also commercially available in wood or plastic. They provide many opportunities to classify by size, shape, and color. Children at all grades can benefit from some structured activities with these materials. Attribute blocks almost guarantee student involvement, but they also require teachers to assume an active role. Directed questions and probes can provide clues about the children's thinking processes. Observing children's actions will tell you much about their maturity. For example, when asked to choose a piece that is red and a triangle, one child might choose a red piece but not a triangle. Another might select a triangle but not necessarily red. Still another child may without a moment's hesitation choose a red triangle. These responses may reflect only poor listening skills. However, additional questioning may show the first two children don't understand what the word "and" means or are unable to keep two different attributes in mind simultaneously. Carefully observing and questioning children as they are using materials such as attribute blocks will help us better understand what they are thinking, which in turn helps us design more appropriate learning activities.

Many different experiences are needed to sharpen observation skills and provide children the basis on which the notion of numbers is built. Consider another example. Count the money shown in the accompanying

ACTIVITY CARD 6-1

Primary   Classification

Sort these.

ROLL   WON'T ROLL

1¢   1¢   5¢

sketch. What answers might be given? Three, if coins were counted; seven, if cents were counted. This provides a reminder that rarely is a number name alone reported, such as three or seven. In this case "three coins" tells us both cardinality (i.e., how many) and what was actually counted. It also provides another reminder that what is to be counted must be well defined or clearly understood. If there is any confusion about what is being counted, then counting discrepancies are certain to happen.

Such discrepancies occur in many different forms but are particularly troublesome when working on a number line. For example, Figure 6-1 shows two children standing on a number line that has been made from a roll of adding machine tape and fastened to the floor. How far is it from Barb to Scott? Is it 4 or 3? The solution depends on what is to be counted. Should the intervals between the heavy dots be counted? All of the heavy dots? Confusion over what should be counted is a classification problem that must be resolved before any counting can begin. This is a very important step in developing effective counting skills.

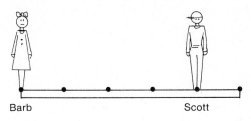

Barb   Scott

Figure 6-1

Comparisons

Comparison of quantities is the next important step toward counting and also is essential in developing number awareness. Comparisons are plentiful in classrooms as children use materials. Teacher-led activities occur frequently and provide opportunities for questions such as: Does everyone have a piece of paper? Are there more pencils or desks? These questions either directly or indirectly involve comparisons, which may lead to the very important and powerful mathematical notion of one-to-one correspondence.

Look at Figure 6-2a and consider this question: Are there more hearts or gingerbread cookies? Counting would provide a solution, particularly with the cookies scattered on a plate. However, if the cookies are arranged in an orderly fashion (Figure 6-2b), we can make direct comparisons and answer the question without

counting. Sometimes placing connectors (laying string or yarn; drawing lines or arrows) provides a visual reminder of the one-to-one correspondence that underlies many comparisons (Figure 6-2c).

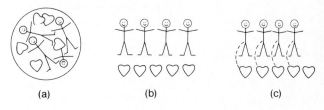

(a)   (b)   (c)

Figure 6-2

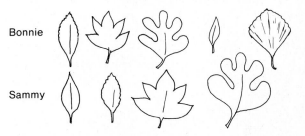

Bonnie

Sammy

When making comparisons, students must be able to discriminate between important and irrelevant attributes. In the accompanying sketch, for example, who has more leaves—Bonnie or Sammy? The leaves are very different; the size, shape, and color of them vary. Still the procedure for setting up a correspondence is the same, and establishing a connection would help answer the question. Sometimes to insure that members of two sets are arranged in an order, it is helpful to use squared paper or index cards. In this case placing each leaf on a card and then stacking the cards on a common base provides a helpful framework. This provides graphical representation of the information, and visual comparisons can be quickly and accurately made.

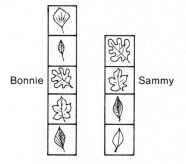

Bonnie   Sammy

Several different but equally valid verbal descriptions may be given for this situation. For example:

Bonnie has more leaves than Sammy.
Sammy has less leaves than Bonnie.

Children need to become familiar with descriptions of relationships such as "more than," "less (fewer) than," and "as many as." A grasp of these terms is followed by more explicit characterization.

> Bonnie has one more leaf than Sammy.
> Sammy has one less leaf than Bonnie.

In these cases the notion of order and succession are being developed. Children must come to realize that four is the number between five and three as well as one more than three and one less than five. Such relationships can evolve naturally as comparisons are made and discussed.

When comparisons are made among several different things, ordering is involved. For example, children can print their first names on some grid paper:

Children can physically compare their names with others to answer questions such as:

> Who has the longest name?
> Who has the shortest name?
> Can you find someone with a name the same length as yours?
> Can you find someone with one more (less) letter than your name?

Ordering often requires several comparisons, and a graph might help organize the information. The graph in Figure 6-3 was constructed by classifying children according to the length of their names. It summarizes much information and presents it in an organized form. The graph could also be used to answer the previous question. In addition, we could generate questions such as:

> Which length name is most popular?
> Greg wasn't here today. Where should his name go on our graph?
> Can you think of anyone you know who has a shorter name than Tim?

As more things are ordered, the ordering process becomes more complicated and most children need guidance to order things efficiently. That's why organiza-

tional techniques, such as graphing (see Chapter 14), are particularly helpful and will contribute toward the early development of numbers.

Group Recognition

Prior to counting, children are aware of small numbers of things: one nose, two hands, three wheels on a tricycle. Research shows that most children entering school can identify quantities of three things or less by inspection alone without the use of counting techniques (10). In fact, one instructional goal for first grade is to develop immediate recognition of groups up to five or six.

Sight recognition of quantities up to five or six is important for several reasons:

1. It saves time. Recognition of the number in a small group is much faster than counting each individual member of that group.

2. It is more accurate. Children often mess up counting small groups, even when their counting skills are well developed.

3. It is the forerunner of some powerful number ideas. Children naming small groups give evidence of knowing early order relations; e.g., three is more than two and one is less than four. Some may also realize that three actually contains a group of two and a group of one.

4. It helps develop more sophisticated counting skills. Children who recognize the number in a small group will more quickly begin counting from that point.

5. It accelerates the development of addition and subtraction. Early work with these operations involves manipulation with objects. Being able to recognize the quantity in small groups will free children of the burden of counting small quantities to be joined or removed and allow them to concentrate on the action of the operation.

The teacher in the opening "Snapshot" used beans and the overhead projector to address this goal. The emphasis was on sight recognition. The overhead projector allowed careful control of time so that the children

Figure 6-3

BRENT

PAT   STEVE   GERALD

TIM BILL KELLY ROBERT BARBARA

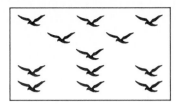  

Figure 6-4

could not count individual beans. The teacher placed the beans in different arrangements to encourage children to identify different arrangements and different patterns, and to do so quickly. Children do indeed develop early sight recognition of number patterns. Several different approaches were demonstrated as the children counted. Sight recognition is also evidenced by their skills in reading the number of dots on the face of a die or a domino. In fact, both of these materials provide natural as well as interesting models for developing and practicing this skill.

As children grow older, this ability to recognize quantities continues to improve but it is still very limited. For example, look at the birds in Figure 6-4. How many birds do you see? Few adults can recognize by inspection groups of more than six or eight, and even these groups need to utilize common patterns such as those found on cards or dominoes. Each picture shows 12 birds, but you probably used different processes to count them. The left picture provides no clear groups, so you could either count every bird or perhaps immediately identify the numbers in some subset of the birds and then count the rest. In the other two pictures, some natural groupings are suggested—for example, three groups of four and two groups of six. For larger numbers, it is even more difficult to recognize them without counting or forming some subsets of numbers. Nevertheless, small-group recognition is a powerful ally in counting larger groups.

COUNTING

Children may count apples, blocks, cards, rocks, stones, twigs, even petals on a flower. You should try counting the petals on the flowers shown in Figure 6-5. The photographs are from a fascinating book (13). They provide a very interesting setting for practicing counting, and they remind us that numbers are everywhere in nature.

The items we have been describing are *discrete objects*—that is, materials that lend themselves well to handling and counting. *Continuous quantities,* such as the amount of water in a glass or the weight of a person, are measured rather than counted; this is discussed in Chapter 10.

Figure 6-5. Reprinted with permission of the National Council of Teachers of Mathematics.

What is counting? It is a surprisingly intricate process by which children call number values by name. A close look at the counting process shows that finding how many objects are present involves two distinct actions. A child must *say* the number-name series, beginning with one, and *point* to a different object as each number name is spoken. Children exhibit several different but distinct stages of counting, as we shall soon see.

Counting Principles

How do children count? Let's look at an actual counting situation. Suppose seven blocks are to be counted. A child who is what we will call a "rational counter" might say each number name as the blocks are counted. The last number named, "seven," would report the total.

As adults we probably cannot recall our own struggle with counting. Yet observing young children can remind us how counting strategies vary and are developed sequentially over a period of years. Here are four important principles upon which the counting process rests:

1. Each object to be counted must be assigned one and only one number name. As shown in the sketch, a one-to-one correspondence between each block and the number name was established.

2. The number-name list must be used in a fixed order every time a group of objects is counted. The child started with one and counted two, three, . . . , seven in a specific order.

3. The order in which the objects are counted doesn't matter. The child can start with any block and count them in any order.

4. The last number name used gives the number of objects. There are seven blocks, but the fact that seven was associated with a particular block is not important. Regardless of which block was counted first or the order in which they were counted, the last block named would still be seven.

These principles help us recognize the levels of children's counting skills. Careful observation of children coupled with a good understanding of these principles will pinpoint counting errors. Once the trouble is diagnosed, instruction can focus on the specific problem.

Counting Strategies

Thus far we have mentioned only rational counters. Actually there are several identifiable stages of counting, and application of the previous counting principles will help identify some levels of sophistication. Here are several different stages of counting that children typically demonstrate during the primary grades.

Rote Counting. The number names and proper sequence are known up to a limit of ten or so, which is an important prerequisite for all counting. However, at this level the child is not always able to maintain a correct correspondence between the objects being counted and the number names. Thus a rote counter may say, "One, two, three, four, . . . ," but the rate of saying the number names is not coordinated with the objects being counted. Rote counters will continue to say number names until they perceive all the objects to be counted.

Point Counting. A correct number name is given as each object is pointed to in succession. A point counter will say the number-name string beginning with one and point to a different object as each number name is spoken. Although the one-to-one correspondence principle is well established, it is possible for a child to be able to point-count and still not know how many objects have been counted. For example, in response to the question, "How many toys are in the box?" Bev correctly counted "One, two, three, four." Although Bev could count, it was not clear to her that the last number named tells how many.

Rational Counting. Here, too, a correct number name is given as objects are counted in succession. However, rational counting includes being able to answer the question about the number of objects being counted. Thus, rational counters exhibit all four principles of counting.

Rational counting is an important skill for every primary child. It has the advantage that children notice their own progress and become proud of their accomplishments. Early in first grade, some children will count to 10, others to 20, some to 50, and a few to over 100 (8). No upper limit should be imposed, although a goal of 100 is clearly reasonable for most children by the end of first grade. Instruction should provide regular practice and encourage each child to count as far as he or she can.

Once mastery of rational counting to 10 or 20 has been reached, more efficient and sophisticated counting strategies should be encouraged, such as those which follow.

Counting On. Here correct number names are given as counting proceeds, but the starting point is flexible. Children can start at any number and begin counting. For example, they can begin with eight pennies and count nine, ten, eleven; or begin at seventy-eight and count seventy-nine, eighty, eighty-one; or begin at ninety-eight and count ninety-nine, one hundred, one hundred one. Such counting-on practice leads to the discovery of many valuable patterns. Counting on is also an essential strategy in developing addition.

Counting Back. Correct number names are given as children count backward from a particular point. For example, to count to solve the problem, "Bobbie had 22 rabbits and three were lost," a child might count twenty-one, twenty, nineteen, and conclude there are 19 left. At an early stage counting back can be related to rockets blasting off (i.e., counting down—five, four, three, two, one, blast off); later it becomes helpful in developing subtraction.

Skip Counting. Correct names are given, but instead of counting by ones, the child counts by twos, fives, tens, or other values. The starting point and direc-

tion are optional. In addition to providing many patterns, skip counting provides valuable readiness for multiplication and division.

Skip counting coupled with counting on and counting back provide excellent preparation for counting change. Thus, given the coins shown in the sketch, children would be encouraged to choose the largest-valued coin and then begin counting on—e.g., "twenty-

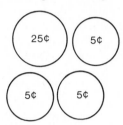

five, thirty, thirty-five, forty." Counting change is a very important skill whose usefulness children recognize. It holds great appeal for them and they find it interesting. It should be introduced and extended as far as possible in the primary grades. Interestingly enough, most of the difficulties associated with counting change can be traced to weaknesses in counting. This suggests that our teaching should take advantage of every opportunity to encourage accurate and rapid counting.

The hundred chart is an ideal model for developing skip counting both with or without a calculator. Activity Card 6-2 provides a record of what has been counted and makes patterns visible.

ON DEVELOPING NUMBERS

Most children develop many counting skills by the time they enter kindergarten. Today's children have experienced many direct attempts, primarily while watching television (e.g., "Sesame Street"), to develop counting skills, and our classroom instruction should be designed to build onto these experiences.

The development of the numbers one through five will be principally done through sight recognition of patterns coupled with immediate association with the oral name and then the written symbolization. For example, consider the question, "How many wheels?"

It is important that the number of wheels be linked to both oral name and written symbol. It is also important that different configurations ($\bullet\!\bullet\!\bullet$) as well as ($\bullet \bullet \bullet$) be used. Using 3 as well as ($\mathit{3}$) also helps broaden symbol recognition.

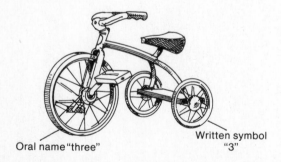

Oral name "three"   Written symbol "3"

Many valuable relationships are established as the numbers one through five are developed, but none are more useful than the notions of *one more* and *one less*. These relationships are fundamental in early counting and also in learning place value with larger numbers. The notions of one more and one less evolve from many different experiences, such as:

"He is one year younger."
"She has one more sister."
"They have one more cookie."

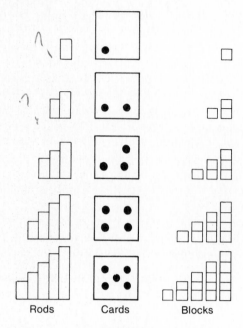

Rods   Cards   Blocks

Figure 6-6

These notions can be modeled nicely as shown in Figure 6-6. These arrangements provide the basis for discussing one more or one less and then how these relationships link numbers such as four and five together.

The dots on the cards and the trains of blocks provide a clear reminder of the numbers represented and the notion of one more or one less. Both the staircase of rods and the trains of blocks vividly illustrate not only the concept of more or less, but also an important yet subtle difference between the models. The staircase of rods illustrates the concept of more, but it is not absolutely clear how much more until the length of the rods has been made clear. If we used a single rod without identifying a unit rod, it would not be possible to associate the rod with a unique number. This illustrates how the rods provide a very different model to develop numbers than the dot cards or trains of blocks.

Instruction in counting should provide practice counting backward as well as forward. Counting backward, "Five, four, three, two, one," helps establish sequences and relates each number to another in a different way. Activity Card 6-3 illustrates how a problem setting can provide practice in counting either forward or backward. Solving this problem requires counting, but it also encourages higher-level thinking and logical reasoning. For example, questions such as "Should I count forward?" and "Is there more than one correct answer?" should be raised and discussed. The problem also illustrates that unique answers don't always exist. Such experiences may even encourage children to formulate similar problems.

Counting backward is also a good way to intro-

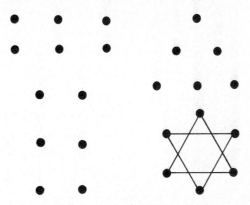

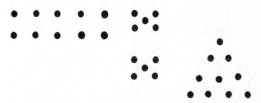

Figure 6-7. Some configurations of six.

duce zero. In Figure 6-6, it would be appropriate to include a blank card, and then the number of dots would be zero. Many telephone numbers include zero, so most children are introduced to zero early. Although this introduction helps visual recognition of zero, it provides a very narrow and limited experience.

Models should be used to develop the concept of zero, and some models illustrate zero more clearly than others. For example, a rod of length zero is more difficult to grasp than a card with zero dots. Care should be taken to introduce zero as soon as it becomes natural to do so, but select models appropriate for the purpose. Help children distinguish between zero and nothing by encouraging the use of zero to report the absence of something. For example, when reporting the scores of a game, it is better to say "Cardinals three, Bears zero" than to say "Three to nothing."

As the numbers six through ten are developed, it is important that various patterns within them be discovered, recognized, and used. For example, consider some of the patterns for six shown in Figure 6-7. At this stage the focus is on the number six and some of its configurations. Exploring some of these arrangements shows that six can be represented in different ways, such as two groups of three, three groups of two, or a group of three, two, and one. No mention will be made here of

addition or multiplication, but such observations are sure to be made by children and will be very helpful later when these operations are developed.

Similar illustrations and applications of the numbers seven through ten should be presented. For example, seven days in a week may also suggest a natural grouping; eight vertices (corners) of a cube suggest two groups of four; and the number of boxes in a tac-tac-toe grid suggest three groups of three.

Ten is a very special number, and children should realize this early. At this stage of development, the most unusual thing about ten is that it is the first number represented by two digits, 1 and 0. In addition to our having ten fingers, the number is evident in many different places, such as money exchanges. Figure 6-8 shows some different configurations of ten that suggest some number patterns. As you examine these, can you find two groups of five? Five groups of two? A group of four, three, two, and one? Ten provides the cornerstone for our number system, and its significance is developed further in the next chapter.

Figure 6-8. Common configurations of ten.

Children need much practice in counting discrete materials so that they establish efficient and accurate counting skills. Calculators are a valuable instructional tool in helping children learn to count and in further developing their concept of number. For example, Activity Card 6-4 shows how counting and number patterns are linked together in problem solving. In addition to the instructional suggestions on counting given in Chapter 2, other activities are available (12).

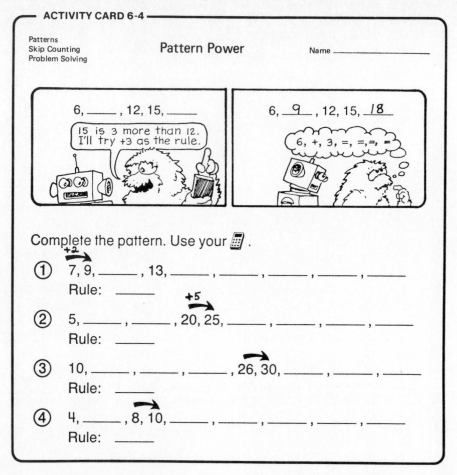

Patterns
Skip Counting
Problem Solving

Pattern Power

Name _____

6, _____ , 12, 15, _____

15 is 3 more than 12.
I'll try +3 as the rule.

6, _9_ , 12, 15, _18_

6, +, 3, =, =, =,

Complete the pattern. Use your ⌨ .

① 7, 9, _____ , 13, _____ , _____ , _____ , _____
   Rule: _____

② 5, _____ , _____ , 20, 25, _____ , _____ , _____
   Rule: _____

③ 10, _____ , _____ , _____ , 26, 30, _____ , _____
   Rule: _____

④ 4, _____ , 8, 10, _____ , _____ , _____ , _____
   Rule: _____

Children are often surprised to learn that it is as easy for a calculator to count backward as forward. Many children find it very difficult to count backward, just as many adults find it difficult to recite the alphabet backward. For such children the calculator provides a valuable instructional tool to help them improve their ability to count backward.

Similarly, children are surprised to learn that it is as easy to count by any given number on the calculator as to count by one. Thus a calculator can start at zero and count by two or three. Or start at one and count by two to get odd numbers. Or instead of counting by one, count by .1, 10, or 100.

Clearly the calculator represents a powerful instructional ally in helping children develop counting skills. However, the early developmental stages of counting—with or without a calculator—will remain intact. Children will be rote counters before rational counters and will need teacher guidance to develop more efficient counting strategies.

CONSERVATION OF NUMBER

The phenomenon of conservation of number reflects how children think. We need to be aware of the symptoms of the lack of conservation and its implications for early number development and counting. It occurs in different forms, but here is an example involving counting and numbers.

Two rows of blocks are arranged side by side, and a teacher and a five- or six-year-old child look at them together. The teacher asks:

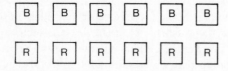

"How many blue blocks?"

After counting them, the child responds, "Six."

"How many red blocks?"

The child again counts and says, "Six."

"Are there more blue blocks or red blocks?"
"They are the same."

Now the red blocks are spread out.

"How many blue blocks?"
"Six."
"How many red blocks?"

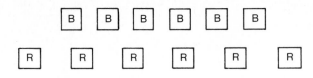

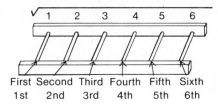

Figure 6-9

"Six."

"Are there more blue blocks or red blocks?"

"More red blocks."

"I thought you said there were six blue and six red."

"I did, but this (points to row of red blocks) six is bigger."

This is a typical case where a young child thinks the number varies and depends on the arrangement or configuration. Here the child believes that stretching out the row makes it longer; the fact that the number remains the same creates no conflict. Look now at the sketch of three groups of dots. Some children count six in each of these groups but report one group has more. For adults it seems inconceivable that "this six" could be more than "that six," but as this and other examples in this book show, children's logic and adults' logic are very different.

The phenomenon of conservation was described by Jean Piaget and has been the subject of much research (5). Rarely do children before five or six years of age conserve number; that is, they don't realize that moving the objects in a set has no effect on the number of the objects. This means that many children in kindergarten, first, and second grades and sometimes in much later grades are nonconservers. A child can be very adept at counting (i.e., be able to count by rote and rationally) and remain naive about conservation. Whenever this happens, instructional activities (such as the different configurations of five objects on the overhead in the opening "Snapshot") should be designed to increase the child's awareness of the invariance of number.

CARDINAL AND ORDINAL NUMBERS

So far we have discussed important considerations in number development and described how children think about the numbers 0, 1, 2, ... The emphasis has been on finding a correct number name for a given group. This aspect of number, *cardinal number,* answers the question, "How many?" Another important aspect of number emphasizes arranging things in an order and is known as *ordinal number*; it answers the question, "Which one?"

An emphasis on ordering, seriating, or arranging things in a given sequence leads to ordinal numbers. The order may be based on any criteria, such as size, time of day, age, or position in a race. Once an order is established, however, the counting process not only produces a set of number names but also names each object according to its position. Thus in counting the rungs on the ladder in Figure 6-9, number one is first, two is second, three is third, and so on. Research shows that many children know some ordinal numbers such as first, second, and third before they begin school (8). Encounters with statements such as

"The first letter of the alphabet is A."

"Bob is second in line."

"Cary was third in the race."

provide early and valuable experience with ordinal numbers.

It is important that the development of early number concepts provide opportunities to learn both ordinal and cardinal numbers. Don't worry about which to teach first; just be sure both are given attention.

It is possible for a child to recognize a pattern of four dots but not be able to count to four correctly.

Such a child could give cardinal number four to answer the question, "How many dots do you see?" For this child, the notion of cardinal number is very limited but has preceded the use of ordinal number in counting. Such instances are rare, and when they do occur, they are limited to small numbers.

The second counting principle suggests that counting cannot occur until a child knows which number name comes first, which second, and so on, even though

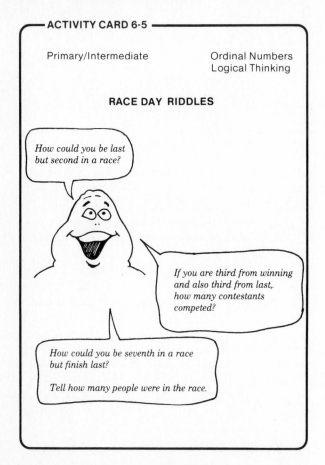

ACTIVITY CARD 6-5

Primary/Intermediate   Ordinal Numbers
                                        Logical Thinking

RACE DAY RIDDLES

How could you be last but second in a race?

If you are third from winning and also third from last, how many contestants competed?

How could you be seventh in a race but finish last?

Tell how many people were in the race.

(as mentioned in the third principle) the order in which things are counted is not important. The only way for the ordinal aspect of number to be present is for the things counted to be seen in order.

A knowledge of ordinal relationships along with logical thinking leads to more challenging experiences such as Activity Card 6-5. These questions are guaranteed to generate much discussion as they help children further clarify notions of ordinal numbers.

In using cardinal and ordinal numbers, children need not distinguish between the terms. It is important, however, that correct usage be established. Do this informally by asking questions within problem situations, such as, "How many checkers are on the board?" and "Which checker is third?" Such questions force children to recognize when ordering is important and when it isn't. They also help children think about where to begin. Often they are confused about whether to move right to left or left to right. Questions along the way will increase children's consciousness of order.

WRITING AND RECORDING NUMERALS

Young children typically have difficulty recording or writing numerals. If they are pressured into premature symbolization, it can create unnecessary frustrations and anxieties. Care should be taken to recognize these difficulties and not push children too rapidly. For children who initiate early writing of numerals on their own, fine. In fact many children get a feeling of great accomplishment from it.

First graders can usually recognize a number symbol and say it correctly long before they write it. It is recommended that formal writing of numbers be preceded by many developmental number experiences, including much practice counting. There are physical as well as psychological reasons for this delay. The lack of development of small muscles needed to write numerals presents a problem, and another results from the limited eye-hand coordination of many young children. Both of these make it difficult or impossible for young children to write numerals. For such children calculators can be helpful. The calculator display provides a visual reminder of the number being counted and removes the burden of writing complicated numerals at this stage. When numerals are written, the display serves as a visual model to be copied. Even though calculator numerals look different from those traditionally written, their widespread use requires that children learn to recognize and use them effectively.

The writing of numerals should be supervised to insure that proper skills are being formed and poor habits avoided. It is recommended that when children are learning to write numerals, this skill be developed aside from "mathematics." Children should master these skills and use them freely before applying them in computational situations—otherwise the writing task consumes all their concentration and they forget about the mathematics being done.

Many children develop the necessary writing skills on their own. These youngsters need monitoring and maybe some occasional guidance. Others, however, need systematic step-by-step procedures to help them. For these children it should be realized that there is no one best way to form a numeral, but there are some patterns that may help. Guiding a child's hand until the child takes the initiative in writing helps him or her get started. Later, dittos with numerals on them can be provided for children to trace. Here are some additional suggestions; these will not be necessary for everyone, but some children will profit from them.

1. Use the overhead projector and cut out numerals. Project a numeral on the chalkboard and have

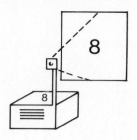

children come to the board and trace the numeral's silhouette.

2. As one child is tracing the numeral at the chalkboard, have class members trace it in the air. As the tracing is being done, describe it verbally such as "down one way and back another." Dots can also be used to show patterns for the children to follow.

3. Have a child who can make numerals stand behind someone who cannot. Ask the child to use a finger and gently "write" a numeral on the other child's back. The child in front should identify the numeral and either trace it on the chalkboard or write it in the air. This calls upon the tactile sense and helps some children better develop their writing skills.

4. Use numerals that have been cut from sandpaper and pasted to cards. Or take heavy fishing cord and glue it in the shape of numerals. Place a mark on each numeral to show the child where to begin tracing it. This is particularly helpful with children who persist in reversing numerals.

5. Cover numerals to be traced with a transparency. Then give the children a water-soluble pen and have them practice tracing the numerals.

The fact that numerals take different forms should also be mentioned but not belabored. This will help avoid confusion when a four appears as 4 and 4 or on a calculator as 4. The wide use of calculator numerals in everyday living demands planned instruction to make children familiar with them.

A GLANCE AT WHERE WE'VE BEEN

Good number sense is prerequisite to all later computational development. Young children need to recognize small groups of objects (up to five or six) by sight and name them properly. Activities involving sight recognition of the numbers of objects in small groups provide many opportunities to introduce and use key terms such as *more, less, after, before, one more, one less.* A good start with the numbers through five will focus on patterns and develop recognition skills that will accelerate the learning of longer numbers.

Counting skills are started before children begin school but must be developed by careful and systematic instruction before written work is appropriate. Counting processes reflect various levels of sophistication, beginning with rote counting, which should eventually lead to rapid skip counting forward and backward. Although the four counting principles are established in the primary grades, counting skills are extended in the intermediate grades and often are further refined throughout our lives.

Competence with and understanding of the numbers zero through ten is essential for meaningful later development of larger numbers. The relation of the sets of objects, the number names, the written symbols, and the order between numbers must be well understood. This knowledge is the basis for the successful study of elementary mathematics, and it prepares children for the necessary understanding of large numbers and place value.

THINGS TO DO: ADDING TO YOUR PICTURE

1. Describe why classification is an important prenumber skill.

2. Suppose you send a note home to parents encouraging them to help their child improve sight-recognition skills. One parent responds, "Why should my child learn to recognize a group of five? After all, you can just count them." How would you respond?

3. Suppose you observe a child counting rocks, "One, two, three, . . . six," and touching the rocks one at a time. What type of counting is being used?

4. Describe how the following activity could help children sharpen their understanding of ordinal and cardinal numbers.

   How many ordinal numbers are in this sentence? "The 500 residents of Centerville celebrated the 100th anniversary of the town's founding by setting off a $200 fireworks display at the corner of Fifth and Broadway on January 1."

5. There are four fundamental principles of counting. Describe in your own words what each means and why it is necessary.

6. Several different levels of counting exist. Distinguish between rote, point, and rational counting.

7. It is an educational maxim that active involvement with materials of interest to students will result in meaningful learning. Describe how the comparison activity illustrated in Figure 6-4 puts that maxim into practice.

8. What is meant by conservation of number? Why is its development important for counting?

9. Describe how counting could be used to answer these questions:
   (a) How many floors are between the seventh and fifteenth floors?
   (b) If Willy has read to the bottom of page 16, how many pages must he read to reach the top of page 21?
   Describe another procedure besides counting that could be used.

10. Read the article by Yvon and Spooner (14). Describe how the "Pincushion" activity could help develop counting and early number concepts.

11. We recommend that the skill of writing numerals "be developed aside from mathematics." Isn't writing numerals part of mathematics? What do you think is the spirit of this recommendation?

12. Suppose you have children who reverse their numerals, writing Ɛ instead of 3. Describe some instructional activities that could be used to help these children.

13. Find the films related to counting listed in *Films in the Mathematics Classroom* (2). Use the film description and reviews to identify a film on counting appropriate for kindergarten. For intermediate grades.

14. Observe some young children counting. Describe how the four counting principles are reflected in their actions.

15. Read the article by Lettieri (9) and react to several of the Activity Cards. Describe some ways these cards could be used to sharpen classification skills.

16. Examine the article by Huntsberger (7) or a resource such as the following to learn some specific ways of using attribute pieces or blocks to help children learn mathematics.

> Connolly, Austin, *Keymath Attribute Blocks Manual*. Circle Pines, Minn.: American Guidance Service, 1980.
>
> Dienes, Z. P., and Golding, E. W. *Learning Logic, Logical Games*. New York: Herder and Herder, 1966.
>
> Marolda, Maria. *Attribute Games and Activities*. Palo Alto, Calif.: Creative Publications, 1976.

17. Examine two different textbook series and find how far they expect children to be able to count when they begin first grade and when they complete first grade.

18. Examine a post-1980 textbook series. Describe how calculators are used to develop counting skills in the first three grades.

19. Suppose you decide to use the calculator to do some counting activities with children. In addition to some recent articles in the *Arithmetic Teacher*, you should examine Reys et al., *Keystrokes: Calculator Activities for Young Students: Counting and Place Value* (12). Pick out several counting activities to present and discuss in class.

20. If you examine a textbook series for first and second grade, you will find lessons devoted to the development of ordinal and cardinal numbers, but these terms are not likely to be found on pupil pages. Find lessons designed to develop ordinal and cardinal numbers. Which lesson appeared first? Explain how one served as a prerequisite for the other.

SELECTED REFERENCES

1. Baratta-Lorton, Mary. *Mathematics Their Way.* Palo Alto, Calif.: Addison-Wesley, 1976.

2. Bestgen, Barbara J., and Reys, Robert E. *Films in the Mathematics Classroom.* Reston, Va.: National Council of Teachers of Mathematics, 1982.

3. Driscoll, Mark J. "Counting Strategies." In *Research Within Reach: Elementary School Mathematics.* St. Louis: CEMREL, Inc., 1980.

4. Ginsburg, Herbert P. *Children's Arithmetic: The Learning Process.* New York: Van Nostrand Reinhold, 1977.

5. Ginsburg, Herbert P. "Children's Surprising Knowledge of Arithmetic." *Arithmetic Teacher,* 28 (September 1980), pp. 42-44.

6. Hiebert, James. "Children's Thinking." In *Research in Mathematics Education* (ed. Richard J. Shumway). Reston, Va.: National Council of Teachers of Mathematics, 1980.

7. Huntsberger, John P. "Using Attribute Blocks with Children." *Science and Children,* 15 (January 1978), pp. 23-25.

8. Liedtke, W. W. "Rational Counting." *Arithmetic Teacher,* 26 (October 1978), pp. 20-26.

9. Lettieri, Frances Massara. "Meet the Zorkies: New Attribute Material." *Arithmetic Teacher,* 26 (September 1978), pp. 36-39.

10. Payne, Joseph N., and Rathmell, Edward C. "Number and Numeration." In *Mathematics Learning in Early Childhood* (ed. Joseph N. Payne). Reston, Va.: National Council of Teachers of Mathematics, 1975.

11. Rea, Robert E., and Reys, Robert E. "Competencies of Entering Kindergarteners in Geometry, Number, Money, and Measurement." *School Science and Mathematics,* 71 (May 1971), pp. 389-402.

12. Reys, Robert E.; Bestgen, Barbara J.; Coburn, Terrence G.; Marcucci, Robert; Schoen, Harold L.; Shumway, Richard J.; Wheatley, Charlotte L.; Wheatley, Grayson H.; and White, Arthur L. *Keystrokes: Calculator Activities for Young Students: Counting and Place Value.* Palo Alto, Calif.: Creative Publications, 1980.

13. Wahl, John, and Wahl, Stacey. *I Can Count the Petals of a Flower.* Reston, Va.: National Council of Teachers of Mathematics, 1976.

14. Yvon, Bernard R., and Spooner, Eunice B. "Variations in Kindergarten Mathematics Programs and What a Teacher Can Do About It." *Arithmetic Teacher,* 29 (January 1982), pp. 46-52.

7

Emphasizing Place Value

Key Ideas for a Second-Grade Lesson on Place Value:

1. Illustrate the place-value concept with two different physical models.
2. Provide concrete representation of two-digit numbers and their corresponding symbolization.

Necessary Materials:

- *Bean Sticks.* Each child should have a set of bean sticks, where ten lima or butter beans are glued on tongue depressors (or other similar model).

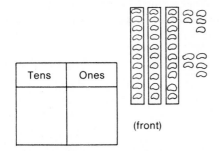

(front)

- *Place-Value Mat.* This is a piece of heavy construction paper with tens and ones positions that has been laminated so children can write on it with water-soluble pens. Also have a transparency of the mat for use on an overhead projector.

Orientation:

In previous lessons, children have been practicing counting by ones and tens as well as counting on. They have glued beans on their own sticks, thereby convincing themselves that there are indeed ten beans on a stick. It has also increased pride in ownership of these sticks among the children. Mrs. Williams places some (less than ten) beans and bean sticks on a table for all children to see. They begin counting aloud as sticks and beans are individually moved (sticks first, then beans) from the table and placed in the proper position on the overhead.

Mrs. Williams: "How many beans do you see? Jack?"

Jack has been waving his hand frantically but when called upon didn't have an answer.

73

Mrs. Williams: "Jack, how many beans are on each stick?"

Jack: "Ten."

Mrs. Williams: "Good—and how many sticks have been used?"

Jack: "Three. There are three sticks so there are three tens."

Mrs. Williams: "Okay—there are three tens and now, Jack, can you tell us how many ones there are?"

Jack: "Four."

Mrs. Williams: "Fine. There are three tens and four ones or thirty-four. Please show this number on your mat and then write it."

Tens	Ones
⦚⦚⦚ 3	⬭ ⬭ ⬭ ⬭ 4

[Check for any difficulties in modeling the number or writing the correct numerals. Writing the numerals under the manipulatives helps children not only naturally associate the symbol with the model, but also understand the significance of place value in a concrete way.]

Mrs. Williams: "Here are some practice exercises:

25
52
forty-one
89

I want you to show each of them on your mat. Be sure to model the number with your beans and sticks and then write the number. When you finish, hold up your hand so I can check each number before you clear the mat and do the next problem."

OUR NUMERATION SYSTEM

There are many different numeration systems and various procedures to use in building new number systems. "Our" system is ours only to the extent that it is a part of our cultural heritage. History tells us that "our numeration system" is really the result of continuous development and refinement over many centuries.

Called the Hindu-Arabic system, it was probably invented in India by the Hindus and transmitted to Europe by the Arabs, but many different countries and cultures contributed to its development.

Our numeration system has four very important characteristics:

1. *Place value.* The position of a digit represents its value.
2. *Base of ten.* Base simply means a collection. Thus, in our system, ten is the value that determines a new collection and it has ten digits, 0 through 9.
3. *Use of zero.* A symbol for zero exists.
4. *Additive property.* 123 names the number 100 + 20 + 3.

These properties make our number system efficient. That is, once these characteristics are understood, the formation and interpretation of numbers—either large or small—is an easy task. Each of these characteristics will be developed, discussed, and used throughout this chapter, but place value will be given the most attention. The reason is simple. If the notion of place value is well developed and understood, these other characteristics

will fall into place. Furthermore, all the place-value models provide opportunities for illustrating and clarifying the other characteristics.

THE NATURE OF PLACE VALUE

Place value is an essential feature of our number system. In fact, together with base ten it forms the cornerstone of our Hindu-Arabic numeration system. It allows us to read, symbolize, and manipulate both large and small numbers. A thorough understanding of place value is necessary if computational algorithms for addition, subtraction, multiplication, and division are to be developed and learned in a meaningful way. It sharpens a sense of reasonableness about computational results, becoming particularly useful for learning computational estimation strategies (see Chapter 13).

Place value rests upon two key ideas:

1. Explicit grouping or trading rules are defined and consistently followed. These ideas are implicit in the bulletin board sketch shown in Figure 7-1. Such a display provides a constant reminder of the importance to place value of grouping by ten. Our base-ten system is characterized by trading ten ones for one ten (or one ten for ten ones), ten tens for one hundred, ten hundreds for one thousand, and so on. The two-way direction of these trades (i.e., ten tens for a hundred or one hundred for ten tens) should be stressed, since there are times when each type of trade must be used. It should also be noted that similar trading agreements are followed with numbers less than one, namely

Figure 7-1. Sketch of bulletin board for place value.

decimals. Thus, one can be traded for ten tenths (or ten tenths for one); ten hundredths for one tenth (or one tenth for ten hundredths), and so on.

2. Position of a digit determines the number being represented. Thus, the 2 in 3042 and in 2403 represents completely different quantities. It represents two ones in 3042 and two thousands in 2403. Furthermore, the 0 in each of these numbers plays a similar yet different role. It has positional value in each case, but it reports the lack of a quantity for that place. Although the notion of zero will continue to be expanded and developed throughout the study of elementary school mathematics, the role of zero in place value should be experienced early and often.

In our number system, place value means that any number can be represented using only ten digits (0-9). Think about the problems of representing numbers without place value! Each number would require a separate and unique symbol. Our memory storage would be quickly exceeded, and we would probably have to use only the few numbers whose symbols we could remember. Nevertheless, place value is difficult for some children to grasp. Oral counting and rote recitation of numbers by young children is often interpreted as understanding of place value. Yet many such children have absolutely no idea of the concept of number, let alone place value. In most cases the confusion or misunderstanding can be traced to a lack of counting and trading experiences with appropriate materials and the subsequent recording of these results. Early and frequent hands-on counting activities, similar to those described in the previous chapter, are essential in establishing this concept.

Place-value concepts are started very early in work with numbers. For example, before starting school, many children distinguish between the one- and two-digit numbers on a channel indicator of a television dial, or a timer for a microwave. Some pushbutton entries require that four be entered as 04. These early experiences with place value provide the foundation upon which all later development will rest.

USING PHYSICAL MODELS

Let's look at some physical models for establishing and developing the concept of place value. Although each of these models may be proportional or nonproportional, they all rest upon groups of ten (see Figure 7-2). More will be said in the next section about the importance of grouping or trading rules. In proportional models for base ten such as popsicle sticks, the material for 10 is ten times the size of 1; 100 is ten times the size of 10, and so on. Nonproportional models, such as money, do not maintain any size relationships. Although both types of embodiments are important and should be represented, proportional models are more concrete, and we recommend that children use and clearly understand them before moving to the nonproportional models.

Of the nonproportional models shown in Figure 7-2, the abacus and the chips are very similar. In each model, a set of different colored beads (chips) provides the basis for trading. For example, ten white beads

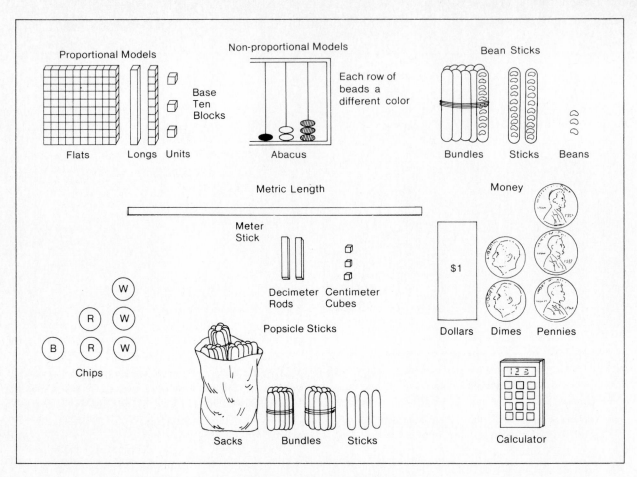

Figure 7-2. Place-value models.

(chips) might be traded for one red, ten red for one blue, and so on. Use of a trading mat can help keep the chips in order. In a similar manner the beads on an abacus are arranged in a fixed order. This color distinction is important for the early establishment of proper trades, but it should be dropped as soon as possible so that attention will shift from color of the beads (chips) to their position. It is only the position of the bead (chip) that has long-range significance.

In developing place value and establishing number names it is far better to skip beyond the tens and start with the larger numbers. The names for the numbers eleven through nineteen are not consistent with the names for other numbers, even though the symbolization or visual pattern is wholly consistent. This is be-

cause the numbers eleven, twelve, . . . , nineteen do not exhibit the place-value characteristic in their names that other numbers do. To do so they should be renamed, such as onety-one (i.e., one ten and one one), onety-two, . . . , onety-nine, which would make them consistent with larger numbers such as forty-one, forty-two, . . . , forty-nine.

What does 25 mean? It is important that children think of numbers in various ways. In this case, 25 might be thought of as two tens and five ones or twenty-five ones and later as one ten and fifteen ones, five times five, or four times six plus one. Let's use metric length to illustrate several of these interpretations, employing only decimeter rods and centimeter cubes.

If we require that the least number of pieces (rods

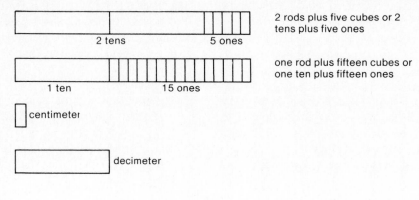

and cubes) be used to represent 25, seven pieces are needed, namely two rods and five cubes. This notion of representing a quantity with the least number of pieces for a particular model is critical in place value. Establishing it here will eliminate some later algorithmic errors, such as:

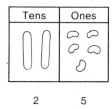

	Tens	Ones
	1	15

$$\begin{array}{r} 1\ 6 \\ +\ \ 9 \\ \hline 115 \end{array}$$

Since ten or more of something (namely ones) exist in one column on the mat, a trade must be made. Making the ten-for-one trade results in the least number of pieces, and thus 25 becomes the only representation that is meaningful. This notion will surface again during our development of computational algorithms.

	Tens	Ones
	2	5

$$\begin{array}{r} 1\ 6 \\ +\ \ 9 \\ \hline 2\ 5 \end{array}$$

The next diagram highlights the advancement from a concrete model to the symbolic representation. The bridges from the physical models to the symbolic representation must be crossed back and forth many times if meaningful learning is to occur.

the resulting numbers—25 and 52—are very different. Children should compare the modeled numbers to appreciate better the magnitude of the differences. Such comparisons lead to ordering and provide a natural introduction to *greater than* or *less than*. Thus, 25 < 52 is read, "Twenty-five is less than fifty-two," and 52 > 25 is read, "Fifty-two is greater than twenty-five."

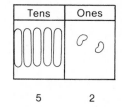

Lesson Card 7-1 highlights an activity that extends the modeling to larger numbers and provides some opportunities to order numbers according to place value. Modeling these numbers establishes more clearly the importance of position for each digit. It also helps establish a "front-end" procedure for ordering and comparing numbers. Activity Card 7-1 provides a slightly different approach to establishing the "front end" of a number. The importance of working from the front end will be further developed when we discuss computational estimation strategies in Chapter 13.

The front-end approach can be extended and applied to ordering larger numbers. Try it on this problem:

Norway has an area of 125,181 square miles. New

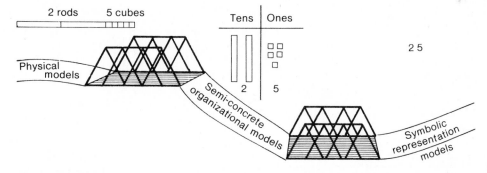

Careful attention must be given to the process of meaning, in this case calling each rod a ten. The further transition from 2 tens and 5 ones to 25 requires equal care in development. For it is this code or representation that allows the position of the digits to tell us precisely how to read each number and then interpret what it means.

Many children reverse the digits of a number. Although this is generally an error of carelessness, it may be symptomatic of a disability known as dyslexia. In either case it is very important that children understand the consequences of such reversals. That's the reason the first two practice exercises were included at the end of the opening lesson. Although the same digits are used,

Mexico has an area of 121,400 square miles and Greece an area of 50,944 square miles.

Why is it easy to tell which has the least area? Can you tell which has the greater area by comparing the first front-end digits?
the second?
the third?
Which has the greater area?

This problem reminds us of the importance of place value when comparing numbers. For example, the front-end approach is used only when the numbers have the same number of digits. It is not needed to compare 125,181 square miles with the area of Greece of 50,944 square miles, because the numbers of digits are different.

LESSON CARD 7-1

MAKE THAT NUMBER

Materials: A deck of 40 index cards with the numerals 0-9 or discard face cards
from a regular deck and let an ace be one and 10 be zero

Activity: Shuffle the cards and select two, three,or four cards at random. Pose
questions for children to model the resulting numbers possible. For
example, suppose these
three cards were selected:

| 3 | | 1 | | 4 |

• Show the smallest number with the cards. Model it.

| 1 | | 3 | | 4 |

• Now show the largest number and model it.

| 4 | | 3 | | 1 |

• Show a number between the largest and smallest number.

• Show the number closest to 400.

• How many different numbers can you make with these three cards?

ACTIVITY CARD 7-1

Intermediate   Place Value

Make a three-digit number creature with a "5" on the front end.

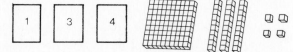

*Here is a three-
digit number
creature.*

| 4 | 3 | 1 |

*A four is
on the front end.*

Make a three-digit number creature with a "5" on the
front end.

Make a different three-digit number creature with a
"5" on the front end.

Make a six-digit number creature. What digit is on the
front end?

Make a different six-digit number creature. What digit
is on the front end?

Make two five-digit number creatures where the first
three front-end digits are the same.

Seven different models are shown in Figure 7-2 to represent the same number, namely 123. The value of using different embodiments is that a child will be less likely to associate place value with a particular model. In fact, our instructional goal is to develop concepts to a level that does not depend on any physical model yet provides for abstraction of the commonality among all the models.

We can combine each of the proportional models with a place-value chart and use the additive property to illustrate expanded notation. For example:

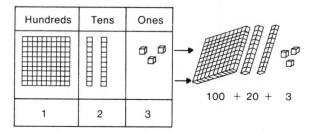

Hundreds	Tens	Ones
1	2	3

100 + 20 + 3

Here is one way to illustrate an expanded form of a number while reenforcing the concept of place value. And for an effective review of key ideas, we can use a variety of strips similar to those in the accompanying sketch.

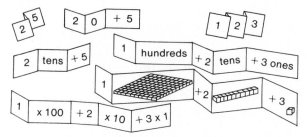

A different embodiment of the same concept can also be made from a set of cards similar to those illustrated. The use of a different color for each group of cards is recommended because it serves as a vivid reminder of the place value of each digit. Then 142 can be built by choosing the appropriate cards and stacking them together. Keeping the right edge of the cards

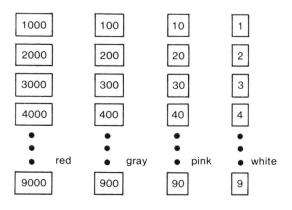

1000	100	10	1
2000	200	20	2
3000	300	30	3
4000	400	40	4
•	•	•	•
•	•	•	•
• red	• gray	• pink	• white
9000	900	90	9

100		
40	or	100	+	40	+	2
2		

aligned is easily done and is a very important reminder to watch the position of each digit carefully. Once the numbers are illustrated, the cards can be rearranged to show this relationship a different way.

Activity Card 7-2 reinforces place value and also provides practice in important mental computational skills. In the targets on the card, the X represents a dart and must be used to find or show a particular score. This provides practice counting by ones, tens, and hundreds.

A calculator provides many opportunities to practice and develop important place-value concepts. Activity Card 7-3* shows how counting by hundreds provides challenging practice in pattern development and place value. Similar experiences should be provided with other powers of ten.

"Wipe Out" is a place-value game that involves either addition or subtraction using a calculator. The goal is to change (wipe out!) a predetermined digit by subtracting or adding a number.

Kelly entered

Sally wiped out the 3

Sally wiped out the   by subtracting 30, which also left the other digits unchanged.

SALLY'S RECORD

Enter	Wipe Out	Keys Pressed	Display
431	3	−30	401
24	4		
849	8		
206	6		

This can be made into a competitive game for two people. Have players take turns entering a number; the other player must change a specific digit to 0. Score a point if you change the digit to 0 on the first try.

*Activity Card 7-3 is from Reys (10), by permission of Creative Publications.

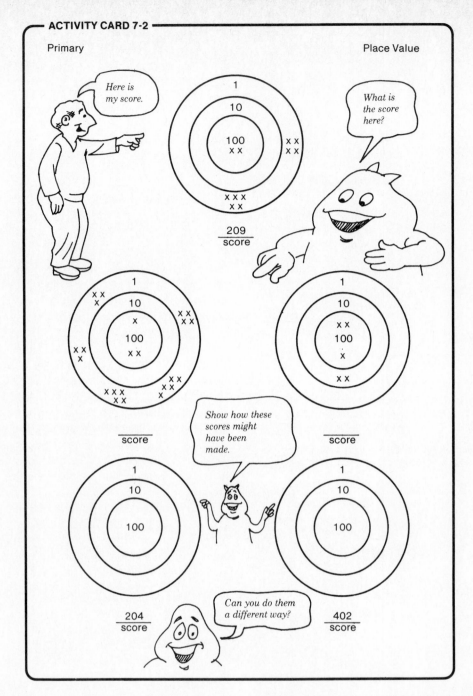

Wipe Out can be played without a calculator, but it is much more exciting with one. Children don't get bogged down with computation: the focus remains on place value. Furthermore, they are often surprised—and thus reminded—by what happens when they do make a place-value error.

ESTABLISHING GROUPING OR TRADING RULES

Children in the first three grades need much experience in counting piles of objects, trading for as many groups of ten as possible, and then describing the results. Using the mats and bean sticks or other materials to model

numbers as they are counted will help children understand and use proper trading procedures. As in the opening lesson, let students model each number on their mats as a long sequence of numbers is counted aloud.

Look, for example, at Figure 7-3. This activity demonstrates the changes resulting each time another number in this sequence is counted. Other patterns are suggested here, but the most important is observing what happens when the number after nine (nineteen, twentynine, etc.) is modeled on the mat. Trading occurs in every case and must be practiced. The pattern involved in bridging from one decade to another should be recognized and clearly understood by children.

Piles of materials, say between 20 and 100, should be counted for practice, and children should be encour-

Patterns
Problem Solving

Hunting Hundreds

Name _____

Which target will you hit?

	Start	Rule	Which target?		Guess	🖩 Check
①	20	+100	(200)	(220)	_____	_____
②	35	+100	(335)	(500)	_____	_____
③	41	+100	(410)	(441)	_____	_____
④	86	+100	(586)	(580)	_____	_____
⑤	97	+100	(897)	(970)	_____	_____
⑥	169	+100	(469)	(696)	_____	_____
⑦	123	+100	(321)	(323)	_____	_____

Write what your 🖩 shows.

Figure 7-3

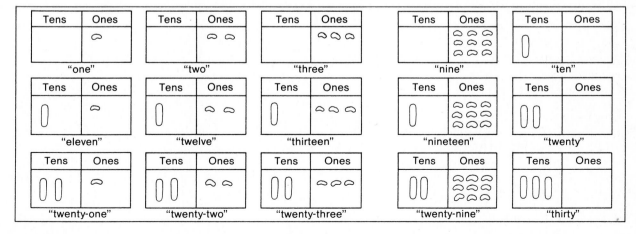

aged to form groups of ten as they go along. Asking children to group by tens as they count the larger piles serves several valuable purposes. First, if a child loses count, correction is easier if these smaller groups have been formed. It is also easier to check for errors by inspecting groups of ten than to recount the entire pile. However, the most important value of this practice is the organization it suggests for children (2), changing an unknown quantity into a form that can be interpreted by inspection. This process of sorting by ten is the framework for place value.

As we mentioned earlier, it is important that children recognize the reversibility of this trading process and its relationship to renaming. That is, a pile of ten beans can be traded for one bean stick, but also a bean stick can be traded for ten beans. Thus, trading and then trading back not only provides valuable practice, but anchors fundamental place-value concepts.

Calculators can also be useful in grouping and pattern recognition. Seeing each value displayed on the calculator helps develop important insight into what digits are changing and when. For example, when counting on the calculator by ones, children observe that the digit on the right (ones place) changes every time they "count," while the next digit (tens place) changes less frequently, and it takes much counting to change the third digit (hundreds place).

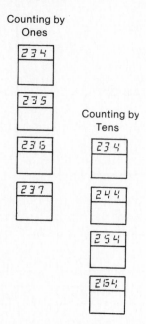

Counting by
Ones

Counting by
Tens

On the other hand, counting on by tens never changes the ones place. However, the tens place changes on each count and the next digit (hundreds) changes every ten counts. Observing these changing patterns in counting larger and larger numbers helps children better

understand the trading rules that represent the fundamental concepts of place value. Counting with powers of ten also develops and practices important mental computational skills. (See Activity Card 7-3.)

One fifth-grade calculator counting activity asked pupils to record how long it took to count from 0 to 1000 by ones (Activity Card 2-1). In a later activity they were asked to find how long it took to count from 0 to 1,000,000 by thousands. Many pupils were surprised to learn that it took about the same time. One child said, "That means there are as many thousands in one million as ones in one thousand." A profound observation—of the type that leads to a better understanding of both place value and large numbers.

REGROUPING AND RENAMING

Regrouping and place value are intertwined in all later development of computational algorithms. This happens whenever bridging occurs, as from one ten to another (such as 29 to 30) or from one hundred to another (such as 799 to 800). Regrouping also happens when 6 tens 7 ones are considered as 5 tens 17 ones, or 245 is thought of as 24 tens 5 ones, or 40 pennies are traded for 4 dimes. The importance of clearly understanding this regrouping process cannot be overstressed. Understanding is most likely to develop when children experience this bridging with physical models.

This regrouping-through-trading process should be mastered *before* introduction of most of the paper-and-pencil computation approaches presented in Chapter 9. So it would be done in the first three grades and again later as needed. For example, examine the stages in Figure 7-4 to see how regrouping affects digits and then place value.

Whenever trading occurs, there are accompanying changes in how the number is recorded. An understanding of this symbolization requires much structured practice with problems involving the trading and related recording process.

Figure 7-5 further illustrates this process with two different models. It should be extended to larger numbers as soon as children have grasped the trading principles involving ones, tens, and hundreds. In fact, it is this extension process that demonstrates the power of mathematical abstraction. Extending to thousands should be done with proportional models to illustrate the dramatic size increase that continues to occur as new places are used. This helps children appreciate that it soon becomes very cumbersome to model large numbers with proportional models.

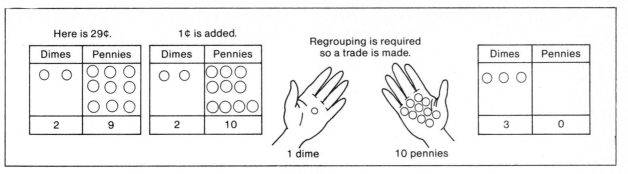

Figure 7-4

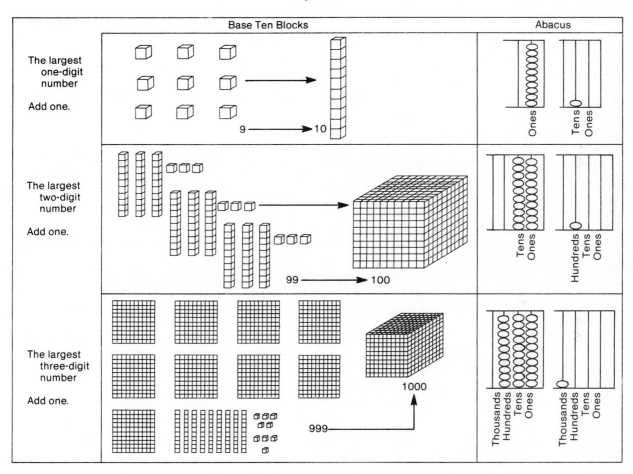

Figure 7-5. Models illustrating some relationships between regrouping and place value.

The calculator can be used with very large numbers, as was shown in Activity Card 2-4. It is only through nonproportional models and later abstractions that large numbers can be conceptualized. Even then it is very difficult for most of us to comprehend large numbers. For example, it is hard for most adults to distinguish conceptually among millions, billions, and trillions. That's why references to large numbers are usually accompanied by other explanatory comments to help us better understand their magnitude. Consider the plight of the United States federal debt, which in 1982 went over one trillion dollars! In an effort to help readers better comprehend the size of a thousand billion or a million million, *Time* magazine reported that a trillion one-dollar bills laid end to end would reach 94,696,960 miles—1.8 million miles past the sun. If they were distributed among the population of the United States, every man, woman, and child would receive $4,415. Happily, we don't have to conceptualize such large numbers very often, but the point is that it is not an easy task. The strongest foundation for conceptualizing numbers of any size is a clear understanding of how numbers up to thousands can be modeled; then we can rely on established patterns to generalize and handle larger numbers.

Such experiences serve as a reminder that although we may have difficulty conceptualizing large numbers, our minds can handle numbers too big for many calculators. For example, most inexpensive four-function calculators display a maximum of eight digits. Any greater number exceeds the calculator's capability to handle it. Therefore, it is impossible for this calculator to do 99,999,999 + 1, yet a clear understanding of regrouping and place-value patterns allows us to solve this problem—without a calculator!

READING NUMBERS

Let's consider things we know about place value and examine some implications for reading numbers. Take, for example, the number 463. We can identify the places (hundreds, tens, ones) as well as what value is in each (4, 6, and 3). We know that the 4 means 4 hundreds. We also know that 63 is both 6 tens, 3 ones and 63 ones or that 463 is 4 hundreds, 6 tens, 3 ones; 46 tens, 3 ones; and 463 ones. Look at this grid and see how we can read these interpretations directly from it.

This skill of reading numbers in different ways (and the understanding of the grouping that allows us to do that) can be useful in many operations with whole

numbers. This is especially true if, from the reading, the child can write the number. For example:

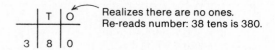

Realizes there are no ones.
Re-reads number: 38 tens is 380.

As you can see, this leads to multiplying a number by 10.

Although it seems logical to write number words as they sound, this procedure can lead to difficulty. If this were done, sixty-one would be incorrectly written as 601, and one hundred twenty-three as 100203. The exercise in the opening lesson where children were asked to show "forty-one" was aimed at detecting this error. If anyone made this mistake, the models could again be called upon as a reminder that forty-one is this:

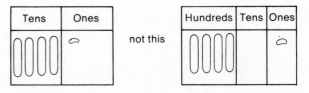

Modeling the number on the mat will help clarify this notion.

The second national assessment provided an unexpected outcome related to place value and the naming of numbers. Suppose nine-year-olds were given a number such as 3076 and asked to choose:

The digit in the tens place	56% were correct
What the 7 represents	80% were correct

It might be expected that performance on these two questions would be very similar, yet the results show a difference of 24 percent. These two tasks are almost logically opposite: "Given the place, state the digit," and "Given the digit, state its value" (5). Such a wide disparity in performance is indeed surprising. These results remind us that as teachers we cannot assume that if a student can do a task in one direction, he or she can do it in the logically opposite manner.

The naming of numbers is an important skill that is aided by place-value charts. They can be naturally expanded to represent larger numbers such as:

	H	T	O	
	4	6	3	

4 hundred 6 tens 3 ones

	H	T	O	
	4	6	3	

46 tens 3 ones

	H	T	O	
	4	6	3	

463 ones

BILLIONS			MILLIONS			THOUSANDS			ONES		
Hundreds	Tens	Ones	Hundreds	Tens	Ones	Hundreds	Tens	Ones	Hundreds	Tens	Ones

In order to develop facility in reading large numbers, children need careful instruction and practice in actually naming them aloud. For example, would you read 12,345,678 as "one ten million two million three hundred thousand four ten thousand" and so on? Certainly not! You would use the period names and read it as "twelve million, three hundred forty-five thousand, six hundred seventy-eight." This is a clear application of an organizing strategy; namely, the digits within each period are read as hundreds, tens, ones as was done with "three hundred forty-five thousand." This is why children need to think of larger numbers (those more than three digits) in blocks of three digits always beginning at the decimal point.

Recognition and understanding of the hundreds, tens, ones pattern provides a powerful organizational strategy that can be called upon in naming numbers. Only the key terms—ones, tens, and hundreds—along with the recognition of the periods for thousands, millions, and billions are needed to name very large numbers.

Did you know that in many countries a comma is not used to separate blocks of three digits? Thus 2,346,457 is written as 2 346 457. The blocks of digits remain visible but are separated by spaces rather than commas. Some newspapers, journals, and textbooks in the United States are now printing numbers this way. This change has instructional implications for both reading and writing numbers. In particular, children must become even more sensitive to the importance of writing numbers clearly and distinctly.

Naming numbers is clearly an important skill. Yet with the widespread existence and use of calculators, a needed and far more efficient way to read a multidigit number is being used. For example,   would be read as "three two seven six four" and   would be read as "four point three four two five." Each of these readings is correct. Furthermore, it is much easier to say them this way than to name the respective periods. There is the danger that digits will simply be mimicked without any realization of the value of the numbers involved, but such interpretations are not necessary at every stage of the problem-solving process. If it is only desired to copy the number displayed on a calculator, then a direct translation of digits is without a doubt the best way to read the number. Rather than require children to read numbers in a specific way, it is far better to recognize the value of each technique and encourage children to choose wisely—namely, to select the technique that is most appropriate for a given situation.

ROUNDING

Rounding is an important skill that combines place value and naming numbers. It is introduced around fourth grade and should follow the process of truncation presented in Chapter 13. In fact, both truncation and rounding take on great importance as estimation skills are developed.

As rounding skills are developed, children should come to realize that rounding "rules" may vary and are not universal. For example, here are two different rules from current textbooks for rounding a number ending in 5:

(a) Increase the previous digit by one.
(b) If the digit preceding the five is even, leave it alone; whereas if it is odd, increase it to the next even digit.

In either case, 75 would round to 80. However, 85 would round to 90 using rule (a) and 80 using rule (b). Neither rule is "right" or "the best," but such variability across textbooks can confuse children. Checking to make sure everyone understands the specific rules of rounding that are to be applied avoids later confusion.

Now let's examine several different models that could be used to develop rounding skills. The roller coaster shown in Activity Card 7-4 represents a model familiar to all children. Labeling it as shown provides an effective tool, but one that requires an understanding of the number line. Children know what happens when the coaster stops at certain points. The model also suggests that something special happens at the top; i.e., the coaster could roll either way. This provides an opportunity to discuss a rule of rounding, such as if it ends in 5 you go over the hump to the next valley. In rounding, attention is given to the "back-end" digit or digits, and Activity Card 7-4 is designed to introduce rounding.

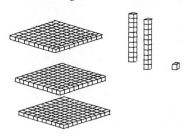

The blocks are also an excellent model for rounding. For example, showing 321 provides clear evidence that it is closer to 300 than 400. Adding more ones and tens would help children become more aware that 350 is halfway between 300 and 400. As a specific rounding rule is stated, its similarity with the roller coaster model should be mentioned. These rounding ideas could be sequenced in steps as shown in Activity Card 7-5 for grade six.

Perhaps the biggest difficulty related to rounding is knowing whether to round to the nearest ten, hundred, thousand, or whatever. Normally this decision

ACTIVITY CARD 7-4

Intermediate　　　　　　　　　　　　　Rounding

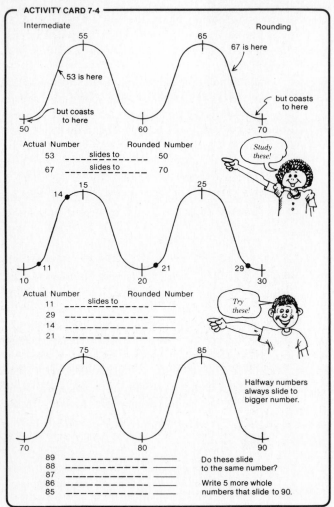

Actual Number　　　　Rounded Number
53 ___slides to___ 50
67 ___slides to___ 70

Study these!

Actual Number　　　Rounded Number
11 ___slides to___ ___
29 ___ ___
14 ___ ___
21 ___ ___

Try these!

Halfway numbers always slide to bigger number.

89 ___
88 ___
87 ___
86 ___
85 ___

Do these slide to the same number?

Write 5 more whole numbers that slide to 90.

ACTIVITY CARD 7-5

Intermediate　　　　　　　　　　　Rounding

The Netherlands is 321 feet above sea level. How would you express this height to the nearest hundred feet?

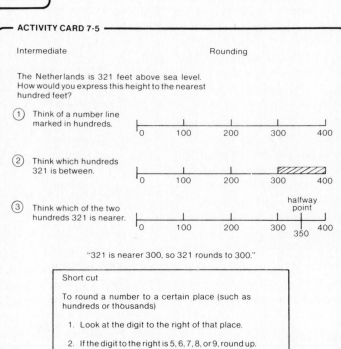

1. Think of a number line marked in hundreds.

2. Think which hundreds 321 is between.

3. Think which of the two hundreds 321 is nearer.

"321 is nearer 300, so 321 rounds to 300."

Short cut

To round a number to a certain place (such as hundreds or thousands)

1. Look at the digit to the right of that place.

2. If the digit to the right is 5, 6, 7, 8, or 9, round up.

3. If the digit to the right is 0, 1, 2, 3, or 4, round down.

depends on the purpose of rounding and the context of the problem. For example, suppose the attendance at a game was 59,784 and someone asked, "How many were at the game?" An answer of 60,000 would not only be reasonable but more realistic than either 59,780 (rounding to tens) or 59,800 (rounding to hundreds). Knowing how much precision is necessary and what to round to will improve through practice in many different problem contexts.

A GLANCE AT WHERE WE'VE BEEN

Children must have a clear understanding of our number system if they are going to be mathematically literate. Many counting and trading (particularly, grouping by tens) experiences are necessary. As these skills become established with the aid of various models (such as bean sticks, base-ten blocks, and abacus), it becomes necessary to organize the results in some systematic fashion and record them. Trading mats and pocket charts serve as a visual reminder of the quantities involved and provide a bridge toward the symbolic representation of larger numbers. Establishing these bridges from the concrete to the abstract is the heart of good teaching. It is particularly critical in place value, whose importance is second to none in all later development of number concepts.

Place-value concepts are developed over a long period of time. The trading rules help plant the seeds early, but recognition of the power as well as importance of place value is developed, refined, extended, and expanded throughout our study of mathematics. Thus, systematic study over a long period is essential. For example, review of important place-value concepts must be provided as computational algorithms are being established. Such study also provides an opportunity not only to maintain but also to extend many earlier place-value concepts. The point here is that place value is not just taught for a couple of days in one or two grades; rather, systematic instruction on place value must be planned and integrated throughout the elementary school mathematics program.

THINGS TO DO: ADDING TO YOUR PICTURE

1. Identify four characteristics of our number system. Select one characteristic and make a visual representation of it.
2. Many lessons in the primary grades involve trading. Tell why trading activities are so important with respect to place value. Describe several materials that could be used for trading.
3. Show how 201 would be represented with three different place-value models.
4. Read "Some Aids for Teaching Place Value" by Jensen and O'Neil (8). Compare and contrast the place-value models discussed with those illustrated in Figure 7-2.
5. Distinguish between proportional and nonproportional models. Name an example of each.
6. Read "A Two Dimensional Abacus—The Papy Minicomputer" by Van Arsdel and Lasky (13). Is this a proportional or nonproportional model? Describe how it would be used to represent several three-digit numbers.
7. Examine the model shown on page 76. Make some strips to illustrate the expanded form of a three-digit number. Then illustrate a four-digit number.
8. Examine a primary-level mathematics textbook. How many different models are illustrated in developing place value? Which model appears to be used the most? Do you think the textbook writers made a good choice of models? Defend your position.
9. Find a scope-and-sequence chart for an elementary mathematics textbook series. Is place value identified as a strand? If so, are place-value concepts included in all grade levels (K–8)? Identify the grades where place value receives the most attention.
10. Examine the films listed under "Place Value" in *Films in the Mathematics Classroom* (4). Read the reviews and recommend a place-value film you would use with a third-grade class.
11. It has been suggested that centuries and decades can be used to demonstrate some notions of place value. Describe how this could be done.
12. Examine the sequence 10, 21, 32, 43, 54 for patterns. Mark these numbers on this hundred chart and describe a pattern. What are the next two values in this sequence? What are you counting by? Describe the pattern in the tens place, then in the ones place.

1	2	3	4	5	6	7	8	9	10
11	12	13	14	15	16	17	18	19	20
21	22	23	24	25	26	27	28	29	30
31	32	33	34	35	36	37	38	39	40
41	42	43	44	45	46	47	48	49	50
51	52	53	54	55	56	57	58	59	60
61	62	63	64	65	66	67	68	69	70
71	72	73	74	75	76	77	78	79	80
81	82	83	84	85	86	87	88	89	90
91	92	93	94	95	96	97	98	99	

13. Examine Lesson Card 7-1. Show the six different numbers that could be made with the three cards. Which is closest to 400? Which number less than 400 is also the closest to 400?
14. Examine an elementary textbook series and find the grade level at which rounding is first introduced. Trace the development of rounding to tens, hundreds, thousands, and so on and summarize the specific rules for rounding that are stated. Are rounding rules also stated for decimals? for fractions?

15. Read the chapter on "Base and Place Value" in *Experiences in Mathematical Ideas* (7). Select one of the activities and set up the stations described.

16. Use your calculator. Enter the largest number possible in the display and name this number. How many digits does it have? Add one to this number and describe how your calculator behaves.

17. Make a board using base five and also make bean sticks using base five. Describe how to demonstrate any number up to twenty-four with your sticks.

18. Read "Ancient Systems of Numeration—Stimulating, Illuminating" by Cowle (6) or "Numeration Systems and Their Classroom Roles" by Rudnick (12). Describe a project that could be used to provide enrichment for several able students.

SELECTED REFERENCES

1. Baker, Beverly Elizabeth. "The Effect of Sequencing Levels of Representation on the Learning and Retention of Place Value Skills." Doctoral Dissertation, University of South Florida, 1977.

2. Barr, David Campbell. "A Comparison of Three Methods of Introducing Two-Digit Numeration and the Effects of These Methods on Certain Groups of Children." Doctoral Dissertation, University of Illinois at Urbana-Champaign, 1975.

3. Bell, Max S. "Early Teaching for Effective Numeracy." *Arithmetic Teacher,* 28 (December 1980), p. 2.

4. Bestgen, Barbara J., and Reys, Robert E. *Films in the Mathematics Classroom.* Reston, Va.: National Council of Teachers of Mathematics, 1982.

5. Carpenter, Thomas P.; Corbitt, Mary Kay; Kepner, Henry S., Jr.; Lindquist, Mary Montgomery; and Reys, Robert E. *Results from the Second Mathematics Assessment of the National Assessment of Educational Progress.* Reston, Va.: National Council of Teachers of Mathematics, 1981.

6. Cowle, Irving M. "Ancient Systems of Numeration—Stimulating, Illuminating." *Arithmetic Teacher,* 17 (May 1970), pp. 413–416.

7. *Experiences in Mathematical Ideas,* Vol. 1. "Base and Place Value." Reston, Va.: National Council of Teachers of Mathematics, 1970.

8. Jensen, Rosalie, and O'Neil, David R. "Some Aids for Teaching Place Value." *Arithmetic Teacher,* 29 (November 1981), pp. 6–9.

9. Makurat, Phillip A. "A Look at a Million." *Arithmetic Teacher,* 25 (December 1977), p. 23.

10. Reys, Robert E.; Bestgen, Barbara J.; Coburn, Terrence G.; Marcucci, Robert; Schoen, Harold L.; Shumway, Richard J.; Wheatley, Charlotte L.; Wheatley, Grayson H.; and White, Arthur L. *Keystrokes: Calculator Activities for Young Students: Counting and Place Value.* Palo Alto, Calif.: Creative Publications, 1980.

11. Ronshausen, Nina L. "Introducing Place Value." *Arithmetic Teacher,* 25 (January 1978), pp. 38–40.

12. Rudnick, Jesse A. "Numeration Systems and Their Classroom Roles." *Arithmetic Teacher,* 15 (February 1968), pp. 138–147.

13. Van Arsdel, Jean, and Lasky, Joanne. "A Two Dimensional Abacus—The Papy Minicomputer." *Arithmetic Teacher,* 19 (October 1972), pp. 445–451.

14. Wilcutt, Robert; Greenes, Carole; and Spikell, Mark. *Base Ten Activities.* Palo Alto, Calif.: Creative Publications, 1975.

8

Beginning Whole-Number Operations: Meaning and Basic Facts

———————————————— A LESSON PLAN ————————————————

Purpose:

To provide initial experiences with multiplication (as repeated addition) and division (as repeated subtraction).

Needed Materials:

Flannelboard; flannel "candies"—20 small yellow, 15 medium orange, and 12 large red; discs for each child —25 yellow, 20 orange, and 15 red.

Procedures:

Read story to children, stopping to ask questions and model each situation on flannelboard.

Once upon a time there was a little old lady who lived in a little old house in the middle of a little old town. She was such a nice little old lady that all the children who lived in the town liked to come to visit her. For a special treat, she would often given them candy. She had three kinds, each wrapped in a different color:

- small yellow ones   [Put sample of each
- medium orange ones   on flannelboard.]
- large red ones

She let the children choose the kind they wanted, but she realized there could be a problem—everyone might want the largest. So she made a rule: each child could have

- 4 yellow, or   [Put each on chalkboard.]
- 3 orange, or
- 2 red.

1. One day 3 children came to visit. They all took *red* candies. Who can show how many pieces one child took? the other? How many altogether? [Expected response: 2 + 2 + 2 = 6; possibly 3 groups of 2, 3 twos are 6, or 3 × 2 = 6. Have child show and count.]

2. 2 children took red.
   (a) How many pieces?
   (b) How do you know?
   (c) Is there any other way to know?

89

3. 3 children—orange.
4. 2 children—yellow.
5. 4 children—orange.
6. 3 children—yellow.
7. *If needed:*
   2 children—orange. 4 children—yellow.
8. 6 children—3 took yellow, 3 red.
9. 4 children—2 took red, 2 orange.
10. 5 children—2 took orange, 3 yellow.
11. *If needed:* 5 children, all took yellow. 6, all took red.

[Ask (a), (b), (c) questions. After several examples with whole group watching flannelboard, have each child use discs.]

Suppose she had 8 pieces of yellow candy. How many children could choose yellow? How do you know?

1. 15 orange
2. 10 red
3. 12 red
4. 12 yellow
5. 12 orange
6. 9 orange
7. 8 red

[After several examples with flannelboard, have each child solve with discs.]

Practice:

Worksheet paralleling lesson:
[Use to evaluate.]

> 3 children.
> All took red.
> Make a drawing.

Extension:

1. If she gave away 2 candies, how many children came? What color candies did she give? What if she gave 9 candies? 15?
2. Pretend you see boots all lined up outside a classroom. How many children were in the room if there were 18 boots and each child left boots? [Use 2–9.]
3. Have children make up similar problems.

INTRODUCTION

Computation with whole numbers continues to be the focus of most elementary school mathematics programs. Thus, when you observe in a classroom, there is a high probability you will find a lesson related to computation being taught. The preceding lesson incorporates several essential components of a well-planned classroom activity. First and foremost, it involves the student in an active way in manipulating objects to answer questions. It provides problem-solving experiences that promote reasoning and discussion. Also, it poses mathematical ideas in a potentially real situation.

These components are important in other elementary school mathematics lessons but are of particular importance as understanding of the relevance and meaning of computational ideas is developed. In particular, an understanding of the operations of addition, subtraction, multiplication, and division and knowledge of the basic facts for each operation provide a foundation for all later work with computation. To be effective in this later work, children must develop broad concepts for the operations. This is more likely to happen if each operation is presented through a multiembodiment approach using various physical models. Such experiences help children recognize that an operation can be used in several different types of situations. Children must also understand the properties that apply to each operation and the relationships between operations.

Learning the basic facts is one of the first steps children take as they refine their ideas about each operation. By using the facts, plus an understanding of place value and mathematical properties, one can perform any addition, subtraction, multiplication, or division with whole numbers. Understanding the operations and attaining immediate recall of number facts are essential in doing both mental computation and pencil-and-paper algorithms; they continue to be essential as calculators and similar computing devices are used. Without such devices, the basic facts form the building blocks for performing more difficult, multidigit calculations; with calculational devices, the basic facts provide a means of quickly checking the reasonableness of answers. Moreover, knowing the basic facts lets us perform calculations or estimate answers in many everyday situations where it would be slower to use a calculator. So, no matter what type of computation a child is using—mental computation, estimation, paper-and-pencil computation, or a calculator—quick recall of the basic facts for each operation is essential.

PREREQUISITES

Ultimately, our goal is that children know not only how to add, subtract, multiply, and divide, but more importantly *when* to apply each in a problem-solving situation. We also expect children to recall quickly the basic facts when needed.

How do we help them to attain these skills and understandings? We begin by finding out what each child knows. Then we capitalize on this knowledge as we help them to continue to build upon the number concepts they already have. Most children entering school will be ready in some ways and not ready in other ways for formal work on the operations. Of the prerequisites for such work, three seem particularly important.

1. Counting

Children use counting to solve problems involving addition, subtraction, multiplication, and division long before they come to school, as research has indicated (18). Any problem with whole numbers can be solved by counting, provided there is sufficient time. We do not always have the time to solve problems by counting, however. So we use the more efficient operations, and the procedures that help us cope with more difficult computation, especially with multidigit numbers (see Figure 8-1).

Counting nevertheless remains an integral aspect of children's beginning work with the operations. They need to know how to count forward, backward, and by twos, threes, and other groups (see Chapter 6). They need to count as they compare and analyze sets and arrays and as they affirm their initial computational results. But they need more than counting to become proficient in computing.

2. Concrete Experiences

Children need to have many experiences in real-life situations and in working with physical objects in order to develop understandings about the operations. Research has indicated that work with actual physical objects promotes achievement for most children (17). Understanding improves if they can relate the symbols to some experience each has had or can visualize. Thus,

a basic fact cannot be learned with meaning unless it has been experienced in a situation that gives it meaning.

Manipulative materials serve as a referent for later work with the operations, as well as establishing the basic facts. They also provide a link to connect the operation to real-world problem-solving situations. And whenever a child wants to be sure that an answer is correct, materials can be used for confirmation.

3. Language

Children need to talk about mathematics: experiences to develop meanings need to be put into words. Manipulative materials can be a vehicle for talking about mathematics. Such talking about and discussion of mathematics is a critical part of meaningful learning. All early phases of instruction on the operations and basic facts should reflect the important role language plays in their acquisition.

Frequently, the move to symbols is made too quickly and the use of materials dropped too soon. Instead, the use of materials should both precede and then parallel the use of symbols. Recording the symbols should be done as materials are manipulated. As illustrated in the lesson that opened this chapter, language should be used to describe what is happening in a given situation. Then and only then will children see the relation of the symbols to the manipulation of materials.

The language that is learned as children communicate about what they are doing and what they see happening as they use materials helps them to understand the symbolism related to the operation. Thus, the referent for each symbol is being strengthened. Children should begin their work with operations after having had a variety of experiences about which they have talked. They need to be encouraged to continue talking about the mathematical ideas they meet as they work with the operations.

Figure 8-1

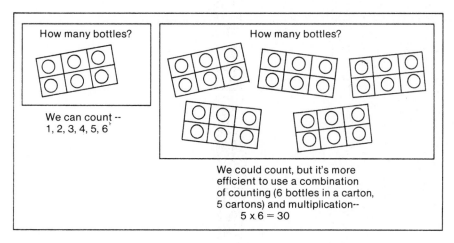

MODELS FOR THE OPERATIONS

Development of the basic facts and later work with multidigit examples are based on clear understanding of the operations. Models help children to understand addition, subtraction, multiplication, and division by representing the situation and portraying the action involved in an operation.

While the four operations are clearly different, there are relationships among them that children must come to understand:

- Addition and subtraction are inverse operations; i.e., one undoes the other.

$$5 + 8 = 13 \quad\text{———}\quad 13 - 5 = 8$$

- Multiplication and division are inverse operations.

$$4 \times 6 = 24 \quad\text{———}\quad 24 \div 4 = 6$$

- Multiplication can be viewed as repeated addition.

$$4 \times 6 \quad\text{———}\quad 6 + 6 + 6 + 6$$

- Division can be viewed as repeated subtraction.

$$24 \div 6 \quad\text{———}\quad 24 - 6 - 6 - 6 - 6$$

These relationships can be developed through careful instruction with a variety of different experiences.

Addition and Subtraction

A variety of models can be used to represent addition (see Figure 8-2). In all, the idea that addition means putting together quantities is depicted.

The models for addition can also be used in subtraction. Each can be applied in the three situations that lead to subtraction:

1. Separation or "take away" involves having one quantity, removing a specified quantity from it, and noting what is left. Research indicates that this is the easiest subtraction situation for children to learn (8).

Peggy had 7 balloons. She gave 4 to other children. How many did she have left?

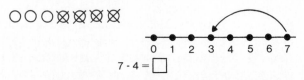

$$7 - 4 = \square$$

2. Comparison or "finding the difference" involves having two quantities, matching them one-to-one, and noting the quantity that is the difference between the first two.

Peggy had 7 balloons. Richard had 4 balloons. How many more balloons did Peggy have than Richard did?

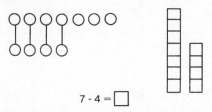

$$7 - 4 = \square$$

3. "How many more are needed" involves having the total quantity, knowing one of the parts, and ascertaining the remaining part.

Peggy had 7 balloons. Four of them were red and the rest were blue. How many were blue?

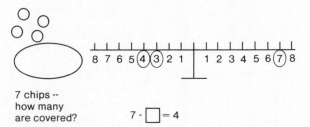

7 chips -- how many are covered?

$$7 - \square = 4$$

The importance of providing many varied experiences where children use physical objects to model or act out examples of each operation cannot be overemphasized. The lesson at the beginning of this chapter provided one such experience. It illustrates a way to in-

Figure 8-2

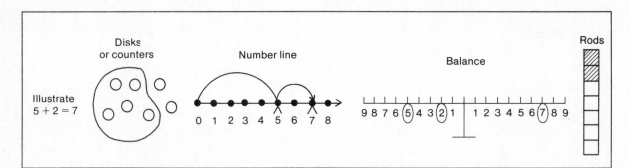

volve each individual child in forming equal-sized groups. Writing symbols for each action is not necessary at this early stage: moving, counting, and questioning are the important components.

Lesson Card 8-1 illustrates a slightly more symbolic activity. The children solve problems in a variety of ways using the dot sticks, followed by individual practice (see Activity Card 8-1). Similar activities can be done using the abacus, rods, and other objects.

Initially, symbols are given as a complement to the physical manipulation of objects. They are a way of showing the action with materials and should be introduced along with the materials. As the work progresses, the amount of symbolization you offer and encourage will increase. The symbols should always be introduced in relation to a concrete material or model.

The number line is used in many textbooks as a model for addition and subtraction, but it must be used with caution. The second national assessment indicated that there is misunderstanding of how to use and interpret this model (4). For example, consider:

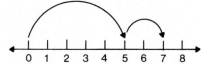

About twice as many nine-year-olds responded that "5 + 7" was pictured as responded with the correct answer, "5 + 2 = 7." Thirty-nine percent of the 13-year-olds made the same error. It was suggested:

> Since the model does not seem to clearly suggest the operation, the meaning must be developed or misunderstandings may occur. The mathematics curriculum should be constructed to ensure that students have a meaningful development of the basic operations. Certainly, many types of models can help this development, but they must be carefully selected and meaningfully taught. (4, p. 19)

Whatever the model used to illustrate the ideas of addition and subtraction, the desired sequence is clear:

1. Use a variety of problem settings and manipulative materials to act out and model the operation.
2. Provide representations of objects in pictures, diagrams, and drawings to move a step away from the concrete toward symbolization.
3. Finally, use symbols to illustrate the operation.

Thus, children move through experiences from the concrete to the semiconcrete to the abstract.

Multiplication and Division

The same three steps are followed for multiplication and division. Many different models can be used to represent multiplication. The three most commonly used

---

LESSON CARD 8-1

DOT STICKS

Materials: Each child needs a set of dot sticks (6 popsicle sticks labeled 1-6, each with the appropriate number of dots).

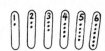

Activity: Pose questions for children to model, solve, and discuss.

- Pick up 4 dots. (Most children will pick up the 4 stick.)

  Is there another way to pick up 4 dots?

- This time, pick up 6 dots.

  How many ways can you do it?
  Can you pick up 6 dots using 3 sticks?

- Pick up 11 dots.

  Can you do it with 2 sticks? 3 sticks? 4 sticks?

- Pick up 8 dots using only 3 sticks.

- How many different ways can you find to pick up 10 dots?
  (List them on the chalkboard.)

ACTIVITY CARD 8-1

PICKING UP STICKS

are (1) equivalent groups of objects, (2) the number line, and (3) the array, in which equivalent groups are joined together.

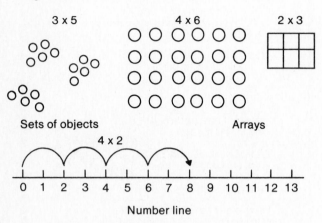

Occasionally, multiplication is considered in terms of Cartesian products. For example, consider the number of different sundaes possible with four different ice cream flavors and two toppings.

	Vanilla	Cherry	Mint	Chocolate
Pineapple	✕			
Butterscotch				

The array model for multiplication can be especially effective. It may serve as a natural extension to children's prior work in making and naming rectangles using cubes, geoboards, or graph paper.

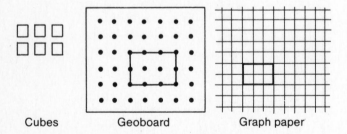

Cubes   Geoboard   Graph paper

The accompanying illustrations show a 2-by-3 or 3-by-2 rectangle. Thus, each contains 6 small squares. Asking children to build and name numerous rectangles with various numbers provides a good readiness experience for the concept of multiplication. Activity Cards 8-2 through 8-5 illustrate several experiences designed for this purpose.

ACTIVITY CARD 8-2

Take 12 cubes.

Make a rectangle using all 12 cubes.

Draw it here.

Do it another way.

Have you tried a 6 by 2 rectangle? How about a 12 by 1?

How many different ways did you do it?

ACTIVITY CARD 8-3

How many ways can you make a rectangle with these blocks?

List the ways.

1 block

2 blocks

3 blocks

4 blocks

5 blocks

8 blocks

ACTIVITY CARD 8-4

You try these. Draw each rectangle, color it in, then tell how many squares.

5 x 3 = _____   4 x 4 = _____

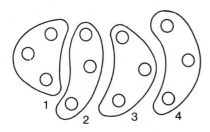

4 x 1 = _____   2 x 3 = _____

ACTIVITY CARD 8-5

For this activity, you'll need 2 dice or 2 cubes labeled 1-6. (Use this pattern to make a cube.)

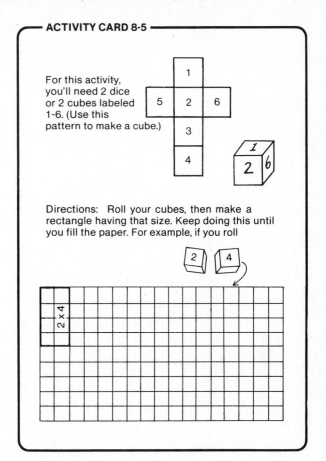

Directions: Roll your cubes, then make a rectangle having that size. Keep doing this until you fill the paper. For example, if you roll

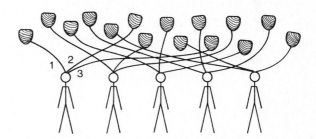

Just as sets of objects, the number line, and arrays were useful in representing multiplication, they can be useful in representing division. However, in division two different types of situations must be considered: measurement and partition.

1. In *measurement* situations, one knows the number in each group and must determine the number of groups.

    Jenny had 12 candies. She gave 3 to each person. How many persons got candies?

2. *Partition* situations are those in which a group is separated into a given number of equivalent groups, and one seeks the number in each group.

Gil had 15 shells. If he wanted to share them equally among 5 friends, how many should he give to each?

Partitioning is very difficult to show in a diagram, but relatively easy to have children act out. Dealing cards for a game is another instance of a partition situation.

It is not necessary for children to learn the terms and to name problems as measurement or partition division situations. To identify when a problem requires division is vital, however, and that means being able to identify both types of situations as division situations.

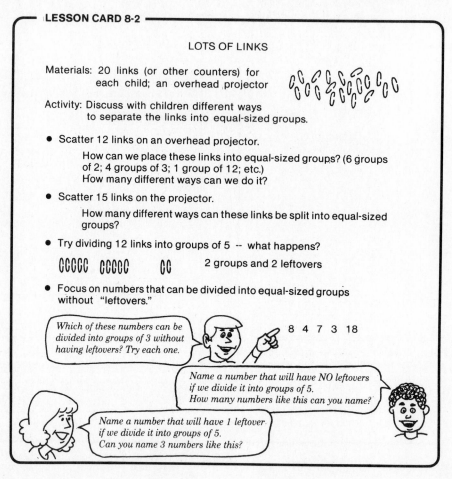

Lesson Card 8-2 illustrates an early activity that can be used to introduce the idea of division to children in a meaningful way.

MATHEMATICAL PROPERTIES

Understanding of the mathematical properties that pertain for each operation is vital to the child's understanding of the operation and how to use it. This understanding is not a prerequisite to work with operations, but it must be developed as a part of the understanding of the operations.

In elementary school we are not concerned that children state these properties precisely or that they identify them by name. Rather, our goal is to help them understand the commutative, associative, distributive, and identity properties and to use them when it is efficient. Figure 8-3 gives the meaning of each property, states what we hope children will understand, and provides examples of each to illustrate how it can make learning and using the basic facts easier.

Understanding these properties also implies knowing when they apply. For example, while both addition and multiplication are commutative, neither subtraction nor division is. That is,

$$7 - 3 \text{ is } not \text{ equal to } 3 - 7$$
$$28 \div 7 \text{ is } not \text{ equal to } 7 \div 28$$

Many children have difficulty with this idea. They tend to "subtract the smaller number from the larger" or to "divide the larger number by the smaller" regardless of their order. Care needs to be taken to develop correct notions.

THE BASIC FACTS

As children develop concepts of the meaning of the operations, instruction begins to focus on certain number combinations. These are generally referred to as the *basic facts*.

- *Basic addition facts* each involve two one-digit addends and their sum. There are 100 basic addition facts.

- *Basic subtraction facts* rely on the inverse relationship of addition and subtraction for their

Property:	In mathematical language:	In the child's language:	How it helps:
Commutative	For all numbers *a* and *b*: $a + b = b + a$ and $a \times b = b \times a$	If $4 + 7 = 11$, then $7 + 4$ must equal 11, too. If I know 4×7, I also know 7×4.	The number of addition and multiplication facts to be memorized is reduced from 100 to 55.
Associative	For all numbers *a, b,* and *c*: $(a + b) + c = a + (b + c)$ and $(ab)c = a(bc)$	When I'm adding or multiplying three or more numbers, it doesn't matter where I start.	When more than two numbers are being added or multiplied, combinations that make the task easier can be chosen; for example: $37 \times 5 \times 2$ can be done: $37 \times (5 \times 2)$ or 37×10 rather than $(37 \times 5) \times 2$
Distributive	For all numbers *a, b,* and *c*: $a(b + c) = ab + ac$	$8 \times (5 + 2)$ is the same as $(8 \times 5) + (8 \times 2)$. $24 \div 3$ is the same as $(12 \div 3) + (12 \div 3)$.	Some of the more difficult basic facts can be split into smaller, easier-to-remember parts. For example: 8×7 is the same as $(8 \times 5) + (8 \times 2)$ or $40 + 16$
Identity	For any whole number *a*: $a + 0 = a$ and $a \times 1 = a$	0 added to any number is easy; it's just that number. 1 times any number is just that number.	The 19 addition facts involving 0 and the 19 multiplication facts involving 1 can be easily remembered once this property is understood and established.

Figure 8-3

definition. The 100 subtraction facts result from the difference between one addend and the sum for all one-digit addends.

- *Basic multiplication facts* each involve two one-digit factors and their product. There are 100 basic multiplication facts.

- *Basic division facts* rely on the inverse relationship of multiplication and division. There are only 90 division facts. Since division by zero is not possible, there are no facts with zero as the divisor.

Development and mastery of the addition and subtraction facts begins in grades 1 and 2 and continues as multiplication and division facts are developed and practiced in grades 3 and 4. Some children, however, have not mastered the facts several years later. Children's difficulty in attaining this competency may have two causes. First, the underlying numerical understandings may not have been developed; thus, the process of memorizing the facts becomes merely manipulation of symbols. Second, the skill of memorizing itself may not be taught by teachers or understood by children, result-

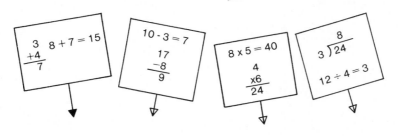

ing in inefficient strategies. Teachers can do something about both of these lacks. Thus, we will consider:

- Start from where the children are: Get Ready
- Build understandings: Get Set
- Focus on how to memorize: Go

GET READY: The Starting Place

Many children come to school knowing some basic facts. For instance, the chances are great that they can say "one and one are two," "two and two are four," and maybe even "five and five are ten." They may know that 2 and 1 more is 3, and that 6 and "nothing more" is still 6. But they probably don't know that $6 + 7 = 13$. Nor do they have a clear concept of the meaning of "+" and "=".

Similarly, they may know that if you have 3 and take away 2, you have only 1 left. But they probably won't know $3 - 2 = 1$ (or "three minus two equals one"). They may know that buying 3 pieces of gum at 2¢ each will cost 6¢, but they won't know that $3 \times 2 = 6$. They may know that 8 cookies divided among 4 children means that each child will get 2 cookies, but they won't know that $8 \div 4 = 2$.

In other words, they can solve simple problems involving facts, but they are not likely either to recognize or write the facts. Nor do many children understand *why* $5 + 5 = 10$, or realize that $4 + 2 = \square$ asks the same question as

$$\begin{array}{r} 4 \\ + 2 \\ \hline \end{array}$$

It is our task to help them organize what they know, fill in the gaps, and, in the process, develop meaning.

We need to begin by determining what each child knows, using responses from group discussions, observations of how each child works with materials and with paper-and-pencil activities, and individual interviews. Many teachers use an inventory at the beginning of the year, administered individually to younger children and in a test format in later grades. We want to know whether the children have the concept of an operation ("What does it mean to add?" "Why did you subtract?" "When can you multiply?"), what basic facts they understand (e.g., by drawing a picture to illustrate or by writing the fact for an illustration), what strategies they use to find the solution to combinations ("How did you know $7 + 9$ is 16?"), and what basic facts they have memorized [by giving a speed test; see (11)].

We use this information to plan instruction. Do some children need more work with manipulative materials in order to come to understand what multiplication means? Do some children need help in seeing the relationship of $17 - 8$ and $8 + 9$? Do some children need to be taught that counting on from a number is quicker than counting each number? Which children need regular practice in order to master the facts? We can group them to meet individual needs (as suggested in Chapter 5) and provide activities and direct instruction to fill in the missing links and strengthen understanding and competency.

GET SET: Presenting the Facts

The emphasis in helping the children to learn the facts is on aiding them in organizing their thinking and seeing relationships among the facts. We want them to use strategies for remembering the facts, prior to drill for memorizing them.

The basic facts have been classified as "easy" or "difficult" in a variety of studies (18). But relative difficulty is not a simple matter to determine with accuracy: while we know that *generally* the facts with both addends or factors greater than 5 are more difficult for most children, what is difficult for an individual child is really the important point. While most textbooks and workbooks emphasize practice on the generally difficult facts, many also encourage the child to keep a record of those facts that are difficult for him or her, and suggest extra practice on those. If the textbook does not do this, the teacher should.

Some research has focused on the use of mathematical properties and analysis of relationships among the facts to determine the order in which to present them to children and ways of helping children understand them (18). It should be kept in mind, however, that no one order for teaching the basic facts has been shown to be superior to any other order. Thus, the teacher can use professional judgment about what each group of children needs, choosing to use or not use the sequence in a given textbook.

How can the basic facts for an operation be organized meaningfully? Many textbooks present facts in small groups (e.g., facts with sums to 6: $0 + 6 = 6$, $1 + 5 = 6$, $2 + 4 = 6$, etc.). Other textbooks organize the facts in "families" (e.g., facts in the "2-3-5 family" are $3 + 2 = 5$, $2 + 3 = 5$, $5 - 3 = 2$, and $5 - 2 = 3$). Still other textbooks organize the facts by "thinking strategies" (e.g., all facts where 1 is added, doubles such as $7 + 7$, etc.).

A variety of thinking strategies can be used to recall the answer to any given fact. *Thinking strategies* are efficient methods for determining answers to the basic facts. The more efficient the strategy, the more quickly the student will be able to construct the correct answer for the sum, difference, product, or quotient of two numbers and, eventually, memorize these facts so he or she can quickly recall them.

Research has shown that certain thinking strategies help children learn the basic facts (14, 20). Understanding of the facts develops in a series of stages characterized by the thinking children use. Some of these thinking strategies involve using concrete materials or counting. Others are more mature strategies in the sense that a known fact is used to figure out an unknown fact. We want to help children develop these mature, efficient strategies to help them recall facts.

Many children rely heavily on counting—in particular, on finger counting—and fail to develop more efficient ways of recalling basic facts. For example, a child may count 4 fingers and then 5 more to solve "4 + 5." This is a perfectly acceptable strategy for a while. However, this counting process should not be repeated every time "4 + 5" is given. We want the child to move to counting on from 4, to thinking "4 + 4 = 8, so

4 + 5 is 9," or other thinking strategies. Eventually, we want the child to memorize "4 + 5 = 9" for quick recall.

Some children discover new thinking strategies on their own, but most children need explicit instruction. In the following sections, thinking strategies and ways to teach them are illustrated.

Thinking Strategies for Addition Facts. The 100 basic facts for addition are shown in Figure 8-4. They are not presented to children in this completed form; rather, the children gradually and systematically learn the facts and may fill in or check off the facts on the table.

Lesson Card 8-3 presents questions that a teacher might use to help children see the orderliness of the

Figure 8-4

+	0	1	2	3	4	5	6	7	8	9
0	0	1	2	3	4	5	6	7	8	9
1	1	2	3	4	5	6	7	8	9	10
2	2	3	4	5	6	7	8	9	10	11
3	3	4	5	6	7	8	9	10	11	12
4	4	5	6	7	8	9	10	11	12	13
5	5	6	7	8	9	10	11	12	13	14
6	6	7	8	9	10	11	12	13	14	15
7	7	8	9	10	11	12	13	14	15	16
8	8	9	10	11	12	13	14	15	16	17
9	9	10	11	12	13	14	15	16	17	18

LESSON CARD 8-3

THE BIG PICTURE

Materials:　Activity Sheet for each child; a transparency of it for use on the overhead projector.

Activity:　To discover the orderliness of the basic addition facts to be memorized.

● Ask each child to study carefully examples on the activity sheet.

　What is alike about the examples?
　What patterns are apparent?

● Discuss the top row of examples -- those involving 0. Have the children fill in each of the sums.

● Discuss the second row of examples.
　Why isn't $\frac{0}{+1}$ included? (It is in the top row.)
　How can each sum be found quickly? (By counting on one)

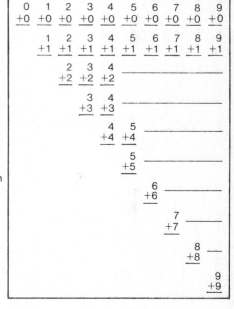

● Look at the diagonal. Find these sums.

● On the overhead projector quickly fill in the remaining sums. Then focus attention on the entire table.

　What patterns are apparent?
　What is the largest sum? What are its addends?
　What is the smallest sum? What are its addends?
　Circle all examples whose sum is 8.
　Where are they?
　What patterns do you see in the addends?
　Why isn't $\frac{5}{+7}$ in the chart?

● Continue discussing patterns as long as you feel your children are benefitting from the experience. Encourage the children to understand that all the basic facts to be memorized are included on this sheet.

basic addition facts. This overview will help children see their goal as they begin to memorize.

The thinking strategies that can be used when teaching basic addition facts include commutativity; adding 0, 1, and doubles; counting on; and adding to 10. For many facts, more than one strategy is appropriate.

1. Commutativity. The task of learning the facts is simplified because of the commutative property: changing the order of the addends does not affect the sum. Children encounter this idea when they note that the 2 black objects and 3 white objects form the same quantity as 3 black objects and 2 white objects.

In work with the basic facts, children see or write:

$$\begin{array}{cc} 2 & 5 \\ +5 & +2 \end{array} \quad \text{or} \quad 2 + 5 = \square \text{ and } 5 + 2 = \square.$$

We want them to realize that "the same two numbers will have the same sum, no matter which comes first." We want them to be able to put this idea into their own words: they do not need to know the term "commutative property." We want them to *use* the idea as they work with basic facts, not merely parrot a term.

We encourage the use of commutativity by using materials such as a chain of loops:

Have the children note that "5 is followed by 2" and "2 is followed by 5" all around the chain. Later, the chain can be turned as they read and add: $5 + 2 = 7$, $2 + 5 = 7$, $5 + 2 = 7$, and so on. Activity Card 8-6 presents another way of helping them develop and use the idea of commutativity.

The blank boxes in Figure 8-5 indicate that 45 addition facts can be learned readily if the children apply commutativity.

2. Strategies for 0, 1, and Doubles. The strategy for *adding zero* applies to facts that have zero as one addend. These facts are learned as a generalization: 0 added with any number does not change the number. This follows from many concrete examples in which children see that any time they add "no more" (zero) they have the same amount. Activities then focus on the pattern:

+	0	1	2	3	4	5	6	7	8	9
0	0	1	2	3	4	5	6	7	8	9
1		2	3	4	5	6	7	8	9	1
2			4	5	6	7	8	9	10	1
3				6	7	8	9	10	11	1
4					8	9	10	11	12	1
5						10	11	12	13	1
6							12	13	14	15
7								14	15	1
8									16	1
9										18

Figure 8-5

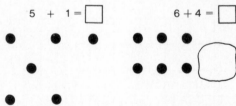

1 + 0 = ☐   0 + 1 = ☐
2 + 0 = ☐   etc.
3 + 0 = ☐
4 + 0 = ☐

Adding one to a number is easy for most children: in fact, most learn this idea before they come to school, and they have to practice only the recognition and writing of it rather than develop initial understanding. To reinforce their initial concept, experiences with objects come first, followed by such paper-and-pencil activities as:

5 + 1 = ☐   6 + 4 = ☐

Recognition of the pattern is then encouraged:

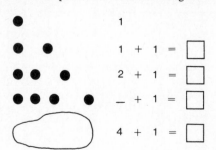

1
1 + 1 = ☐
2 + 1 = ☐
_ + 1 = ☐
4 + 1 = ☐

100

ARRANGING AND REARRANGING

Materials: Counters, string for rings (or rings drawn on a sheet of paper), graph paper.

Activity:
A   B

How many counters are in Ring A? _____

How many counters are in Ring B? _____

Make your counters and rings show the same numbers.

Now move 1 counter from Ring A to Ring B.

How many counters are now in Ring A? _____

How many counters are in Ring B? _____

How many different ways can you put 10 counters in the two rings? (Use your counters and rings.)

List the ways here: <u> 4 + 6 </u> _____ _____
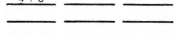

Plot the ways on graph paper. 4 + 6 and 3 + 7 are marked.

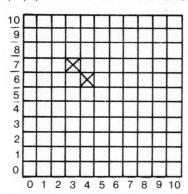

(The number of counters can be varied to develop other combinations. Then have children compare the graphs.)

Doubles refers to facts where both addends are the same number; e.g., 4 + 4 or 9 + 9. Most children learn these facts quickly, often parroting them before they come to school. They can profit from work with objects followed by drawings:

4 + 4 = ▢   8 + 8 = ▢

Another strategy, *one more or one less,* can be used for the facts that are 1 more or 1 less than the doubles.

Think:	
7 + 8 = ▢	7 + 6 = ▢
7 + 7 = 14	7 + 7 = 14
So 7 + 8 is one more.	So 7 + 6 is one less.
7 + 8 = 15	7 + 6 = 13

Lesson Card 8-4 shows one way of presenting this strategy.

The four thinking strategies in this section can be used with the addition facts shown in Figure 8-6.

LESSON CARD 8-4

- Have children put a group of 6 objects on the flannelboard.
- Have them add a second group of 6.

  How many?

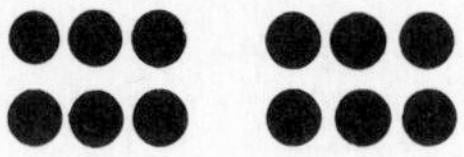

- Add one more object to the second group. Now how many are in this group? How many in all?
- Then, 6 + 7 = 13.

3. Counting On. The *counting-on* strategy is most easily used when one of the addends is 1, 2, or 3.

> *Think:*
>
> 2 + 6 = □
> 6 . . . 7, 8
> 2 + 6 = 8

Initially, children count all objects in a group:

1, 2, 3, 4, 5, ... 6, 7, 8

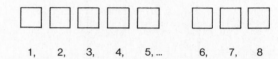

They need to learn to start with the larger addend, 5, and count on, 6, 7, 8. (Notice that understanding of the commutative property is assumed.) Research indicates that young children will count on, but not necessarily from the larger addend (9). Thus, the strategy must be taught to many children, using activities such as:

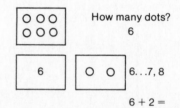

The counting-on strategy can be used with the addition facts noted in Figure 8-7.

Figure 8-6

+	0	1	2	3	4	5	6	7	8	9
0	0	1	2	3	4	5	6	7	8	9
1	1	2	3	4	5	6	7	8	9	10
2	2	3	4	5						
3	3	4	5	6	7					
4	4	5		7	8	9				
5	5	6			9	10	11			
6	6	7				11	12	13		
7	7	8					13	14	15	
8	8	9						15	16	17
9	9	10							17	18

Figure 8-7

+	0	1	2	3	4	5	6	7	8	9
0										
1		2	3	4	5	6	7	8	9	10
2		3	4	5	6	7	8	9	10	11
3		4	5	6	7	8	9	10	11	12
4		5	6	7						
5		6	7	8						
6		7	8	9						
7		8	9	10						
8		9	10	11						
9		10	11	12						

4. Adding to 10. With the *adding-to-10* strategy, one addend is increased and the other decreased, to make one of the addends 10. It is used most easily when one of the addends is 8 or 9, although some children also find it useful when adding 6 or 7.

> *Think:*
>
> $8 + 4 = \square$
> $8 + 2 = 10$, and $4 - 2 = 2$
> So $10 + 2 = 12$, and
> $\qquad 8 + 4 = 12$

Children must know the sums to 10 well in order to use this strategy. Practice with regrouping to 10 is needed to help them become proficient. They also need to realize that it is easier to add a number to 10 than to work with some other number.

Which is easier?

$$10 + 5 \quad \text{or} \quad 9 + 6$$
$$7 + 8 \quad \text{or} \quad 5 + 10$$

Change this to an easier problem:

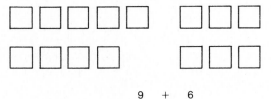

$$9 \quad + \quad 6$$

Talk the strategy through with drawings as well as objects:

$$8 + 4 \qquad\qquad 10 + 2$$

Similarly, put up objects showing $5 + 5$, then remove 1.

$$9 \quad + \quad 5 \quad = \quad \square$$

OOOOOOOOO OOOOO

Ask: 9 is close to what number that's easy to work with? Have a child move one of the 5 objects to the group of 9.

OOOOOOOOO OOOOO

Now:

$$10 + 4 = 14$$
$$\text{so} \quad 9 + 5 = ?$$

The adding-to-10 strategy can be used with the facts shown in Figure 8-8.

In many cases, more than one strategy can be used to aid in recalling a fact. This point should be made with the children; it encourages them to try different ways of recalling a fact, and it may strengthen their understanding of the relationships involved.

Notice from Figure 8-9 that, when the strategies for 0, 1, and doubles, counting on, and adding to 10 have been taught, only six basic facts remain. These can

+	0	1	2	3	4	5	6	7	8	9
0										
1										
2										11
3									11	12
4									12	13
5									13	14
6									14	15
7									15	16
8			11	12	13	14	15	16	17	
9		11	12	13	14	15	16	17	18	

Figure 8-8

Figure 8-9

+	0	1	2	3	4	5	6	7	8	9
0	0	1	2	3	4	5	6	7	8	9
1	1	2	3	4	5	6	7	8	9	10
2	2	3	4	5	6	7	8	9	10	11
3	3	4	5	6	7	8	9	10	11	12
4	4	5	6	7	8	9			12	13
5	5	6	7	8	9	10	11		13	14
6	6	7	8	9		11	12	13	14	15
7	7	8	9	10			13	14	15	16
8	8	9	10	11	12	13	14	15	16	17
9	9	10	11	12	13	14	15	16	17	18

be derived using one of the strategies (and commutativity), or simply taught separately. Children form relationships: this can be done with almost all the 100 basic addition facts.

It should also be noted that children may invent strategies of their own, such as:

	Think:				*Think:*
6 + 7 = □	6 is 5 + 1	or	6 + 8 = □		8 + 3 + 3
	7 is 5 + 2				11 + 3
	So 10 + 3				14
	13				

Encourage this!

Thinking Strategies for Subtraction Facts. For each basic addition fact, there is a related subtraction fact. In some mathematics programs the two operations are taught simultaneously; the relationship between them is then readily emphasized, and learning of the basic facts for both operations proceeds as if they were in the same "family." Even when they are not taught simultaneously, however, the idea of a "fact family" is frequently used:

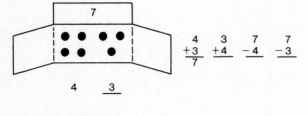

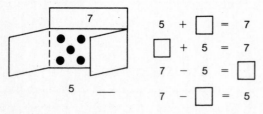

The addition facts form the major thinking strategy for learning and recalling the subtraction facts. Encourage children to recognize, think about, and use the relationships between addition and subtraction facts.

Think:
15 − 7 = □
7 + 8 = 15
So 15 − 7 = 8

Other strategies for finding subtraction facts can also be taught: using 0 and 1, doubles, counting back, and counting on.

1. Using 0 and 1. As for addition, most children find it rather easy to learn the subtraction facts involving 0 and 1. They can profit from work with materials and from observing patterns similar to those used for addition facts.

2. Doubles. The strategy for *doubles* may need to be taught more explicitly for subtraction facts than for addition facts. It rests on the assumption that children know the doubles for addition.

Think:
16 − 8 = □
8 + 8 = 16
16 − 8 = 8

3. Counting Back. The *counting-back* strategy is most effectively used when the number to be subtracted is 1, 2, or 3.

Think:
9 − 3 = □
9 . . . 8, 7, 6
9 − 3 = 6

As for other strategies, use problems and a variety of manipulative materials to help children gain facility in counting back from given numbers. Focus especially on the numbers involved in subtraction facts.

Write the numbers in order backward:

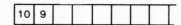

Write the numbers you say when you count back. Write the answer.

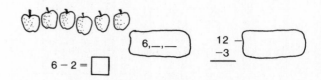

4. Counting On. The *counting-on* strategy is used most easily when the difference is 1, 2, or 3.

Think:
8 − 6 = □
6 . . . 7, 8
8 − 6 = 2

Activities for developing the strategy include:

Begin with 9. Count on until you reach 12. How many?

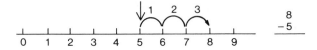

$$\begin{array}{r} 8 \\ -5 \\ \hline \end{array}$$

Begin with 5. Count on until you reach 8. How much?

The emphasis in using this strategy can also encompass "adding on": how much more would I need? Thus the child is encouraged to use the addition facts to reach the solution. This is particularly valuable with missing-addend situations, such as $6 + \square = 9$.

Thinking Strategies for Multiplication Facts. Multiplication is frequently viewed as a special case of addition in which all the addends are of equal size. The solution to multiplication problems can be attained by adding or by counting, but we use multiplication because it is so much quicker.

Instruction on multiplication ideas begins in kindergarten as ideas about groups, numbers, and addition are developed. In grades 1 and 2, counting by twos, threes, fours, fives, tens, and possibly other numbers is taught. Such expressions provide a basis for understanding the patterns that will occur with the basic multiplication facts. Use of the calculator as described in Chapter 6 can aid teachers in developing ideas about these patterns of multiplication.

The basic multiplication facts pair two one-digit factors with a product, as in Figure 8-10.

The basic multiplication facts should not be *given* in toto to the children in the form of a table or chart of facts until they have been meaningfully introduced. Rather, the facts should be developed through problem situations, experiences with manipulative and other materials, and the use of various thinking strategies. The table thus becomes the end result of this process of developing understanding of the operations and of the facts.

The thinking strategies for multiplication facts provide an efficient way for a child to solve each fact. These strategies include: commutativity, using 1 and 0, skip counting, repeated addition, splitting into known parts, and patterns.

1. Commutativity. Commutativity applies to multiplication just as it does to addition; it is therefore a primary strategy for helping students learn the multiplication facts. Activity Cards 8-3 through 8-6 (presented earlier) emphasize this property. The calculator also is useful in reinforcing the idea; children can multiply 4×6, then 6×4, and realize that the answer to both is 24.

$$3 \times 6 = 18 \longrightarrow 6 \times \square = 18$$
$$7 \times 5 = 35 \longrightarrow \square \times 7 = 35$$

After they have tried many combinations, they should be able to verbalize that the order of the factors is irrelevant.

Figure 8-11 indicates that, as for addition, 45 of the facts remain to be learned after commutativity is applied.

Figure 8-10

	0	1	2	3	4	5	6	7	8	9
0	0	0	0	0	0	0	0	0	0	0
	0	1	2	3	4	5	6	7	8	9
	0	2	4	6	8	10	12	14	16	18
	0	3	6	9	12	15	18	21	24	27
	0	4	8	12	16	20	24	28	32	36
	0	5	10	15	20	25	30	35	40	45
	0	6	12	18	24	30	36	42	48	54
	0	7	14	21	28	35	42	49	56	63
	0	8	16	24	32	40	48	56	64	72
	0	9	18	27	36	45	54	63	72	81

Figure 8-11

×	0	1	2	3	4	5	6	7	8	9
0	0	0	0	0	0	0	0	0	0	0
1		1	2	3	4	5	6	7	8	9
2			4	6	8	10	12	14	16	18
3				9	12	15	18	21	24	27
4					16	20	24	28	32	36
5						25	30	35	40	45
6							36	42	48	54
7								49	56	63
8									64	72
9										81

2. *Using 0 and 1.* The facts with zero and one are generally learned from initial work with multiplication. We want children to be able to generalize that "multiplying with 1 does not change the other number" and that "multiplying by 0 results in a product of 0."

Figure 8-12 indicates the facts that can be learned with these strategies.

X	0	1	2	3	4	5	6	7	8	9
0	0	0	0	0	0	0	0	0	0	0
1	0	1	2	3	4	5	6	7	8	9
2	0	2								
3	0	3								
4	0	4								
5	0	5								
6	0	6								
7	0	7								
8	0	8								
9	0	9								

Figure 8-12

3. *Skip Counting.* This strategy works best for the multiples children know best, twos and fives, but it may also be applied to threes and fours (or other numbers) if children have learned skip counting by them.

> *Think:*
>
> $4 \times 5 = \square$
> 5, 10, 15, 20
> $4 \times 5 = 20$

The facts that can be solved with the skip-counting strategy are noted in Figure 8-13.

4. *Repeated Addition. Repeated addition* can be used most efficiently when one of the factors is less than 5. The child changes the multiplication example to an addition example.

> *Think:*
>
> $3 \times 6 = \square$
> $6 + 6 + 6 = 18$
> $3 \times 6 = 18$

X	0	1	2	3	4	5	6	7	8
0									
1									
2			4	6	8	10	12	14	16
3			6			15			
4			8			20			
5			10	15	20	25	30	35	40
6			12			30			
7			14			35			
8			16			40			
9			18			45			

Figure 8-13

ACTIVITY CARD 8-7

①

What multiplication problem is shown?
How many dots in all? Count them: 5, 10, 15, 20.
4 x 5 = 20.

②

Ring sets of 7. Count them? 7,___,___,___.
How many sevens? How many in all? 4 x 7 = □

③

Do these using a calculator: 7+7+7+7+7 = □

5+5+5+5 = □

Can you find a simpler way?

Since this strategy is based on one interpretation of multiplication, children should have had many experiences with objects and materials. Drawings and the calculator can be used to provide additional experiences to help to develop the strategy as well as the concept for the operation. Activity Card 8-7 illustrates several ideas that can be used.

×	0	1	2	3	4	5	6	7	8	9
			4	6	8	10	12	14	16	18
			6	9	12	15	18	21	24	27
			8	12	16	20	24	28	32	36
			10	15	20					
			12	18	24					
			14	21	28					
			16	24	32					
			18	27	36					

Figure 8-14

On Figure 8-14, note the facts that can be learned with this strategy.

5. Splitting the Product into Known Parts. As children gain assurance with some basic facts, they can use those facts to derive others. *Splitting the product* is based on the distributive property of multiplication. It can be approached in terms of one more set, twice as much as a known fact, or known facts of 5.

(a) The *one-more-set* idea can be used for almost all facts. If one multiple of a number is known, the next multiple can be determined by adding a single-digit number. Each fact in turn can be used to help learn the next multiple of either factor. The greatest difficulty arises when renaming is needed.

> *Think:*
>
> $8 \times 7 = \square$
> $7 \times 7 = 49$
> $8 \times 7 = 49 + 7$
> $8 \times 7 = 56$

Illustrating this strategy using an array model will be helpful:

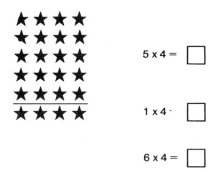

$5 \times 4 = \square$

$1 \times 4 = \square$

$6 \times 4 = \square$

Have children name each part of the array and write the multiplication fact for the whole array.

(b) *Twice as much as a known fact* is a variation of the above strategy. It can be applied to multiples of 4, 6, and 8, because an array with one of these numbers can be split in half. The product is twice as much as each half. Note, however, that a difficulty may arise when renaming is needed.

> *Think:*
>
> $6 \times 8 = \square$
> $3 \times 8 = 24$
> 6×8 is twice as much—$24 + 24$.
> $6 \times 8 = 48$

Again, using models will clarify this strategy:

2 sevens is _____

2 sevens is _____

$4 \times 7 = \square$

Have children work with already divided arrays.

Have children divide an array, write about each part, and write the multiplication fact for the whole array.

(c) Working from *known facts of 5* will also aid children. It can be helpful for any problem with large factors but is most useful for multiples of 6 and 8. Five 6's or five 8's is a multiple of 10, so it is rather easy to add on the remaining part.

> *Think:*
>
> $7 \times 6 = \square$
> $5 \times 6 = 30$
> $2 \times 6 = 12$
> So 7×6 is $30 + 12$, or 42.

To illustrate this strategy, the array is divided so that five 6's or 8's (or other number) are separated from the remaining portion:

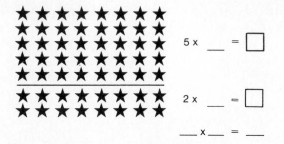

5 x ___ = □

2 x ___ = □

___ x ___ = ___

Call attention to how the array is divided. Have them work with other arrays, determining when it seems reasonable to work with particular numbers.

The facts that can be solved by splitting the product into known parts are shown in Figure 8-15.

X	0	1	2	3	4	5	6	7	8	9
0										
1										
2										
3										
4						24	28	32	36	
5						30	35	40	45	
6					24	30	36	42	48	54
7					28	35	42	49	56	63
8					32	40	48	56	64	72
9					36	45	54	63	72	81

Figure 8-15

The preceding strategies account for all the multiplication facts. One more is mentioned, however, because it can provide help with some difficult facts.

6. Patterns. Finding patterns is helpful with a number of facts. One of the most useful aids concerns 9's:

$$1 \times 9 = 9 \qquad 0 + 9 = 9$$
$$2 \times 9 = 18 \qquad 1 + 8 = 9$$
$$3 \times 9 = 27 \qquad 2 + 7 = 9$$
$$4 \times 9 = 36 \qquad 3 + 6 = 9$$

The tens digit is 1 less than 4.

The *sum* of the digits of 36 is 9.

So, for 5 × 9—
the tens digit is one less than 5 → <u>4</u>
the sum of the digits is 9—so 4 + □ = 9 → <u>5</u>
5 × 9 = 45

Try 7 × 9 = □.

Challenge children to find patterns on a table such as the one in Figure 8-10. They should note, for instance, that the columns (and rows) for 2, 4, 6, and 8 contain all even numbers, while the columns for 1, 3, 5, 7, and 9 alternate even and odd numbers.

You will probably find that children also enjoy "finger multiplication" (see Figure 8-16).

Thinking Strategies for Division Facts. The teaching of division has consumed a large portion of time in the elementary school—so much that, with the increased use of calculators, some thought is being given to reducing the attention accorded to it. Nevertheless, children will continue to need an understanding of the division process and the division facts. The facts help them to respond quickly to simple division situations and to understand better the nature of division and its relationship to multiplication.

The multiplication facts form the primary thinking strategy to aid children in understanding and recalling the division facts. Division is the inverse of multiplica-

Figure 8-16

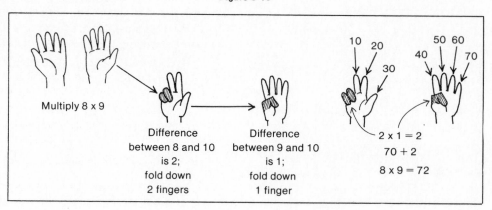

tion; that is, it seeks the unknown factor when the product and one factor are known. The multiplication table can be used for division facts. And just as "fact families" could be developed for addition and subtraction, so can they be useful for multiplication and division:

$$8 \times 4 = 32$$
$$4 \times 8 = 32$$
$$32 \div 8 = 4$$
$$32 \div 4 = 8$$

Because of its relationship to multiplication, division can be stated in terms of multiplication:

$$42 \div 6 = \square \longrightarrow 6 \times \square = 42$$

Thus, children must search for the missing factor. Since multiplication facts are usually encountered and learned first, children can use what is known to solve the more difficult division fact.

Moreover, division is related to subtraction, and division problems can be solved by repeated subtraction:

$$12 \div 3 = 12 - 3 - 3 - 3 - 3$$

$$12 \div 3 = 4$$

0 1 2 3 4 5 6 7 8 9 10 11 12

four threes

However, repeated subtraction and the related strategies of counting backward or skip counting are confusing for many children. You may present them as ideas children might like to try, but don't be surprised if only a few children actually use them.

Think:

$15 \div 3 = \square$
$15 \ldots 12, 9, 6, 3, 0.$
That's 5 numbers.
$15 \div 3 = 5$

Think:

$28 \div 7 = \square$
$28 - 7,$
$21 - 7,$
$14 - 7,$ } 4 subtractions
$7 - 7,$ $28 \div 7 = 4$
0

Splitting the product into known parts relies heavily on knowledge of multiplication facts, as well as on the ability to keep in mind the component parts:

Think:

$35 \div 7 = \square$
$2 \times 7 = 14$
$3 \times 7 = 21$
$14 + 21 = 35$, and $2 + 3 = 5$.
So $35 \div 7 = 5$

As with multiplication, work with arrays helps children to relate the symbols to the action.

In general, children have little difficulty in dividing by 1. They need to exercise caution when 0 is involved, however. Division by zero and division of zero present two different situations. We can divide 0 by 6 ($0 \div 6$): the result is 0. We can check this by multiplying: $6 \times 0 = 0$. But division *by* zero cannot be checked. For example, to solve $6 \div 0 = \square$ requires the solution of the sentence $6 = \square \times 0$. However, there is no value for $\square$ that would make this sentence true. Therefore, $6 \div 0$ has no solution, and division by zero is undefined in mathematics. Just as you may have difficulty remembering which one is possible, division *of* 0 or division *by* 0, so children have difficulty and need to be given practice in remembering.

Thus, thinking strategies for division are far more difficult for children to learn than are the strategies for the other operations. The child must remember more, and regrouping is necessary so frequently. In skip counting, for instance, the child must keep track of the number of times a number is named even as the struggle to count backward proceeds.

Therefore, the primary burden falls on the child's facility with the multiplication facts. Being able to recall those facts quickly will facilitate recall of the division facts.

GO: Mastering the Basic Facts

Pairs of children are keying numbers on a calculator and passing it back and forth. Other pairs are seated at a table, some playing a card game and others playing board games. Still others are working individually with flashcards. What are they all doing? Probably they are practicing basic facts.

If children are to become skillful with the algorithms for addition, subtraction, multiplication, and division, they must learn the basic facts to the level of immediate or automatic recall. When should this mastery level be attempted? As soon as children have a good understanding of the meanings of the operations and the symbols, the process of memorizing can begin. Thus, they should be able to (1):

- State or write related facts, given one basic fact.

- Explain how they got an answer, or prove that it is correct.
- Solve a fact in two or more ways.

Research has shown that drill increases speed and accuracy on tests of basic facts (22). However, drill will not change a child's thinking strategies so that they become efficient. Drill will, therefore, be most effective when the child's thinking is already efficient.

Some principles for drill have been proposed, based on research with primary-grade children (5). They include:

- Children should attempt to memorize facts only after, but soon after, understanding is attained.
- They should participate in drill with the *intent* to memorize. Remembering should be emphasized: this is not the time for explanations.
- Drill lessons should be short—5 to 10 minutes—and should be given almost every day. Children should try to memorize only a few facts in a given lesson and should constantly review previously memorized facts.
- They should feel confidence in their ability to memorize and should be praised for good efforts. Records of their progress should be kept.
- Drill activities should be varied, interesting, challenging, and given with enthusiasm.

Increasingly, new technology is being used to present drill work. Calculators, preprogrammed devices, and microcomputers or computers provide a natural complement to more traditional materials and activities for establishing the quick recall of basic facts, such as flashcards, games, and audiotaped practice tests. The progress made in learning basic facts is easy to document with short tests that are carefully timed. Children must respond quickly to basic fact questions (within 4 seconds). A short response time is very important, because it rewards efficient strategies and encourages children to memorize for quick recall. Posting the results of regular tests of basic facts provides a cumulative record of children's individual progress. This allows children to diagnose for themselves the basic facts they do and don't know. It also provides a source of motivation, as each student can compete against himself or herself, with the goal of complete mastery always clearly in mind. Similarly, when using flashcards, have the child go through the entire set and separate them into a pack of those known and those unknown. Each time the child works with the cards, he or she should review those in each pack, moving newly learned facts to the "known" pack. Thus, progress is evident.

The Activity Cards that follow illustrate several types of drill and practice procedures. Activity Card 8-8 provides examples of individual activities. Games are noted on Activity Cards 8-9 through 8-13.* These activities supplement the many others that you will find widely available in textbooks, journals, computer software, and other sources.

A GLANCE AT WHERE WE'VE BEEN

Skill in computation with whole numbers, the continuing focus of elementary school mathematics programs, is developed through concrete-based experiences. In this chapter the prerequisites of counting, concrete experiences, and language have been considered, and models for each operation described. Mathematical properties to be developed as part of the understanding of the operations have been presented. The remainder of the chapter has focused on the basic facts for each operation. Starting from what children know, the facts have been developed using experiences that range from concrete to pictorial to symbolic. Thinking strategies for the basic facts for each operation have been described, to help children move from counting to more mature, efficient ways of solving the facts. Finally, how to help children master the basic facts for quick recall has been discussed, with specific suggestions for drill and activities to provide practice and promote mastery.

THINGS TO DO: ADDING TO YOUR PICTURE

1. What are the four or five most important guidelines you should follow in helping children learn the basic facts?
2. Discuss:
   (a) When you teach multiplication, you begin preparation for learning division.
   (b) Children should not be allowed to count on their fingers when they start addition.
   (c) With the wide use of calculators, there is little need for children to attain prompt recall of the basic facts.
3. What prerequisites must children have before being taught the opening lesson?
4. What properties of addition and multiplication are especially helpful in teaching the basic facts?
5. Describe the thinking strategies a child might use with the following:

$$8 + 0 = \square$$
$$18 \div 3 = \square$$
$$8 \times 5 = \square$$
$$16 - 7 = \square$$
$$7 + 8 = \square$$

*Activity Card 8-11 is from Romberg et al. (16). Activity Card 8-13 is from Reys et al. (15), by permission of Creative Publications.

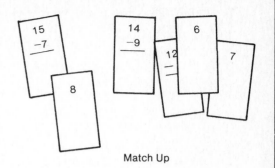

Match Up

- The leader deals 5 cards to each player, and puts the rest of the cards in the center of the table.

- The object of the game is to match examples with answers, making pairs. When a player has a pair, he or she puts them down during a turn.

- Each player may draw 1 card from the center during a turn. When the center cards are gone, the player may draw 1 card from the player to the right.

- The player with most pairs is the winner.

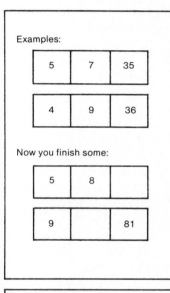

Examples:

| 5 | 7 | 35 |

| 4 | 9 | 36 |

Now you finish some:

| 5 | 8 | |

| 9 | | 81 |

Scramble and rematch:

Put a number in each empty box to make the next number correct.

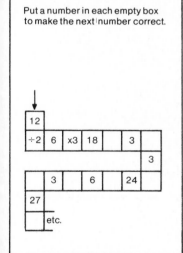

Multiply each number in the middle ring by the number in the center.

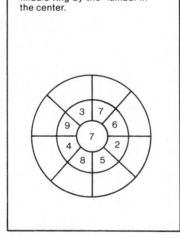

9	6	17	11	5
5	8	10	3	7
15	11	Free	13	14
7	9	2	1	12
2	13	11	18	17

Addition Bingo!

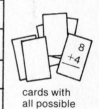

cards with all possible combinations

- The leader should give each player a card and some macaroni (markers).

- The leader then draws one card and reads the addends on it.

- Each player covers the sum on his or her card.

- Not all sums are given on each card.

- Some sums are given more than once on a card. The player may cover only one answer for each pair of addends.

- The winner is the first with 5 in a row.

ACTIVITY CARD 8-11

MULTIG

Materials: spinner, chips

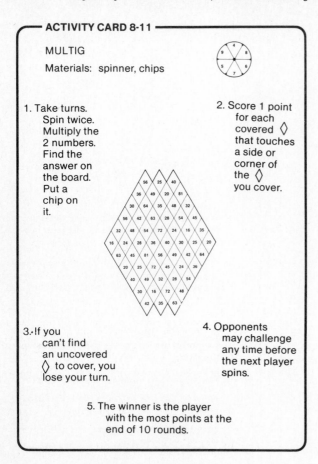

1. Take turns.
   Spin twice.
   Multiply the
   2 numbers.
   Find the
   answer on
   the board.
   Put a
   chip on
   it.

2. Score 1 point
   for each
   covered ◊
   that touches
   a side or
   corner of
   the ◊
   you cover.

3. If you
   can't find
   an uncovered
   ◊ to cover, you
   lose your turn.

4. Opponents
   may challenge
   any time before
   the next player
   spins.

5. The winner is the player
   with the most points at the
   end of 10 rounds.

ACTIVITY CARD 8-12

Materials: two identical sets of 20 cards, with
             numbers (depending on operation
             being practiced)

Sample:

| 7 | 8 | 17 | 10 |

1. Deal 4 cards to each player. Put remaining
   cards face down in center.

2. The goal is to add or subtract the numbers on
   the 4 cards to equal 0.

3. The first player draws a card and discards a
   card, face up. Other players can draw from
   either the face-down or the discard pile.

4. The first player to get 0 wins.

(Multiplication and division can be used along
with addition and subtraction. Players can agree
to reach some number other than 0.)

ACTIVITY CARD 8-13

21 or Bust

Enter 1, 2, 3, 4, or 5 in your

Give the   to your opponent, who adds 1,

2, 3, 4, or 5 to the displayed number.

Take turns adding 1, 2, 3, 4, or 5 to the total.

The first player to reach 21 wins.

If you go over 21, you "bust," or lose.

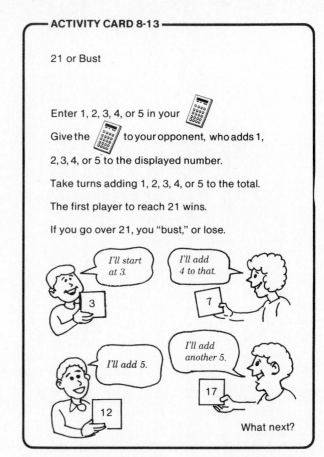

I'll start at 3.

I'll add 4 to that.

3

7

I'll add 5.

I'll add another 5.

12

17

What next?

---

6. When is "counting back" an effective strategy in
   subtraction?

7. List the specific thinking steps a child goes through
   in using a "doubles" strategy to find the sum of
   $9 + 4$.

8. Design a game that provides practice on basic
   division facts.

9. Plan a bulletin board to help children learn about
   one or more thinking strategies for subtraction.

SELECTED REFERENCES

1. Ashlock, Robert B., and Washbon, Carolynn A.
   "Games: Practice Activities for the Basic Facts."
   In *Developing Computational Skills* (ed. Marilyn
   N. Suydam and Robert E. Reys). 1978 Yearbook.
   Reston, Va.: National Council of Teachers of
   Mathematics, 1978. Pp. 39–50.

2. Baratta-Lorton, Mary. *Mathematics Their Way.*
   Reading, Mass.: Addison-Wesley, 1976.

3. Bruni, James V., and Silverman, Helene. "Let's Do
   It!: Making and Using Board Games." *Arithmetic
   Teacher,* 22 (March 1975), pp. 172–179.

4. Carpenter, Thomas P.; Corbitt, Mary Kay; Kepner,
   Henry S., Jr.; Lindquist, Mary Montgomery; and
   Reys, Robert E. *Results from the Second Mathe-
   matics Assessment of the National Assessment of*

Educational Progress. Reston, Va.: National Council of Teachers of Mathematics, 1981.

5. Davis, Edward J. "Suggestions for Teaching the Basic Facts of Arithmetic." In *Developing Computational Skills* (ed. Marilyn N. Suydam and Robert E. Reys). 1978 Yearbook. Reston, Va.: National Council of Teachers of Mathematics, 1978. Pp. 51–60.

6. Driscoll, Mark. J. "Counting Strategies." In *Research Within Reach: Elementary School Mathematics.* St. Louis: CEMREL, Inc., 1980.

7. Folsom, Mary. "Operations on Whole Numbers." In *Mathematics Learning in Early Childhood* (ed. Joseph N. Payne). Thirty-seventh Yearbook. Reston, Va.: National Council of Teachers of Mathematics, 1975. Pp. 162–190.

8. Gibb, E. Glenadine. "Children's Thinking in the Process of Subtraction." *Journal of Experimental Education,* 25 (September 1956), pp. 71–80.

9. Ginsberg, Herbert. *Children's Arithmetic: The Learning Process.* New York: Van Nostrand Reinhold, 1977.

10. Golden, Sarah R. "Fostering Enthusiasm Through Child-Created Games." *Arithmetic Teacher,* 17 (February 1970), pp. 111–115.

11. Inskeep, James E., Jr. "Diagnosing Computational Difficulty in the Classroom." In *Developing Computational Skills* (ed. Marilyn N. Suydam and Robert E. Reys). 1978 Yearbook. Reston, Va.: National Council of Teachers of Mathematics, 1978. Pp. 163–176.

12. Leutiziinger, Larry P., and Nelson, Glenn. "Using Addition Facts to Learn Subtraction Facts." *Arithmetic Teacher,* 27 (December 1979), pp. 8–13.

13. Litwiller, Bonnie H., and Duncan, David R. *Activities for the Maintenance of Computational Skills and the Discovery of Patterns.* Reston, Va.: National Council of Teachers of Mathematics, 1980.

14. Rathmell, Edward C. "Using Thinking Strategies to Teach the Basic Facts." In *Developing Computational Skills* (ed. Marilyn N. Suydam and Robert E. Reys). 1978 Yearbook. Reston, Va.: National Council of Teachers of Mathematics, 1978. Pp. 13–38.

15. Reys, Robert E.; Bestgen, Barbara J.; Coburn, Terrence G.; Schoen, Harold L.; Shumway, Richard J.; Wheatley, Charlotte L.; Wheatley, Grayson H.; and White, Arthur L. *Keystrokes: Calculator Activities for Young Students: Addition and Subtraction, Multiplication and Division.* Palo Alto, Calif.: Creative Publications, 1980.

16. Romberg, Thomas A.; Harvey, John G.; Moser, James M.; and Montgomery, Mary E. *Developing Mathematical Processes.* Chicago: Rand McNally, 1974–1976.

17. Suydam, Marilyn N., and Higgins, Jon L. *Activity-Based Learning in Elementary School Mathematics: Recommendations from Research.* Columbus, Ohio: ERIC Clearinghouse for Science, Mathematics, and Environmental Education, 1977. ERIC: ED 144 840.

18. Suydam, Marilyn N., and Weaver, J. Fred. *Using Research: A Key to Elementary School Mathematics.* Columbus, Ohio: ERIC Clearinghouse for Science, Mathematics and Environmental Education, 1981.

19. Thompson, Charles S., and Dunlop, William P. "Basic Facts: Do Your Children Understand or Do They Memorize?" *Arithmetic Teacher,* 25 (December 1977), pp. 14–16.

20. Thornton, Carol A. "Emphasizing Thinking Strategies in Basic Fact Instruction." *Journal for Research in Mathematics Education,* 9 (May 1978), pp. 214–227.

21. Wills, Herbert. "Diffy." *Arithmetic Teacher,* 18 (October 1971), pp. 402–405.

22. Wilson, Guy M. "New Standards in Arithmetic: A Controlled Experiment in Supervision." *Journal of Educational Research,* 22 (December 1930), pp. 351–360.

9

Extending Whole-Number Operations: Algorithms

On the chalkboard, the teacher has drawn a problem:

136 boxes
in all

How many boxcars
are needed?

Teacher: "As you can see, I've put a problem on the board. Can your group solve it using the materials in front of you? [Each group has a different type of material.] After you've had a chance to try, we'll share the ways we attacked it."

After 7 or 8 minutes, all the groups are ready to tell how they solved the problem:

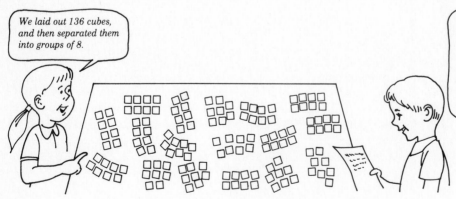

We laid out 136 cubes, and then separated them into groups of 8.

We keyed 8 on the calculator, then the division sign, then 136--but the answer was less than 1! So we knew we'd used the wrong order. We had to key 136, then the division sign, then 8--136 divided by 8.

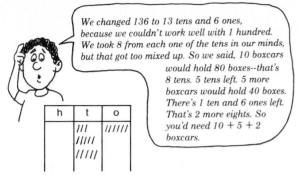

We changed 136 to 13 tens and 6 ones, because we couldn't work well with 1 hundred. We took 8 from each one of the tens in our minds, but that got too mixed up. So we said, 10 boxcars would hold 80 boxes--that's 8 tens. 5 tens left. 5 more boxcars would hold 40 boxes. There's 1 ten and 6 ones left. That's 2 more eights. So you'd need 10 + 5 + 2 boxcars.

Teacher: "Good work! Now, how would you write this problem?"

Several children write:

$$136 \div 8 \qquad \frac{136}{8} \qquad 8\overline{)136}$$

Teacher: "Yes, all show 136 divided by 8. We will use the third way when we work with paper and pencil. We know now that the answer is 17—will you put the answer in place, Karen?"

Karen writes:

$$\begin{array}{r} 17 \\ 8\overline{)136} \end{array}$$

Several other children say "No!" They are asked why.

Children: "The answer has 1 ten and 7 ones, so it must be written in those places."

Teacher: "Good. I hope you'll always remember that. Now, suppose you didn't know what the answer was. Can you find it using just the numbers?"

$$\begin{array}{r} 7 \\ 10 \\ \hline 8\overline{)136} \\ 80 \\ \hline 56 \\ 56 \\ \hline 0 \end{array} \;\rightarrow 17$$

We know there are at least 10 eights in 136, because 10 x 8 = 80. When I subtract, there are 56 left. 56 ÷ 8 is 7.

Teacher: "Great! Now try: 259 ÷ 6."

INTRODUCTION

For hundreds of years, computational skill with paper-and-pencil procedures called *algorithms* has been viewed as an essential component of children's mathematical achievement. Calculators are now readily available to relieve the burden of computation, but the ability to use algorithms is still considered essential. Gradually, however, the curriculum changes to reflect events and needs outside the school. In *An Agenda for Action* (1), the National Council of Teachers of Mathematics suggested that

> Common sense should dictate a reasonable balance among mental facility with simple basic computations, paper-and-pencil algorithms for simple problems done easily and rapidly, and the use of a calculator for more complex problems or those where problem analysis is the goal and cumbersome calculating is a limiting distraction. (1, p. 6)

More specifically, the Agenda supports decreased emphasis on performing paper-and-pencil calculations with numbers of more than two digits. We support this position, so the development in this chapter reflects that framework.

Over the years, we have learned much about teaching computation. Some of these ideas are summarized in the ten tenets in Figure 9-1. These represent key ideas that continue to guide the role of computational skills in the curriculum and will guide our discussion of teaching computation as well. Patient and consistent application of these tenets will promote computational proficiency. Research shows, however, that high levels of proficiency in computational skills are not acquired at the time of initial instruction (3). Instead, instruction over several years is needed to reach "stability," the point at which 80 to 90 percent of the students attain mastery.

Role of Materials in Learning Algorithms

As with other mathematical ideas, the use of manipulative materials in developing understanding of the algorithms is essential. In the "snapshot" of the lesson that opens this chapter, the use of materials of one kind or another was the basis on which work with symbols was formed. The materials form a bridge between the real-life situation and the abstract application of the algorithm, helping to forge the recognition that what is written down represents real objects and actions.

Importance of Place-Value Ideas

Each of the algorithms for whole-number computation is based on place-value ideas, many of which were discussed in Chapter 7. Children need to have a firm understanding of these ideas before they can work effectively with the algorithms. Linking place-value ideas directly with renaming ideas, such as those in Figure 9-2, is a necessary step as the algorithms for each operation are introduced.

TENETS ON THE TEACHING OF COMPUTATION

1. Computational skill is one of the important, primary goals of a school mathematical program.

2. All children need proficiency in recalling basic number facts, in using standard algorithms with reasonable speed and accuracy, and in estimating results and performing mental calculations, as well as an understanding of computational procedures.

3. Computation should be recognized as just one element of a comprehensive mathematics program.

4. The study of computation should promote broad, long-range goals of learning.

5. Computation needs to be continually related to the concepts of the operations and both concepts and skills should be developed in the context of real world applications.

6. Instruction on computational skills needs to be meaningful to the learner.

7. Drill-and-practice plays an important role in the mastery of computational skills, but strong reliance on drill-and-practice alone is not an effective approach to learning.

8. The nature of learning computational processes and skills requires purposeful, systematic, and sensitive instruction.

9. Computational skills need to be analysed carefully in terms of effective sequencing of the work and difficulties posed by different types of examples.

10. Certain practices in teaching computation need thoughtful reexamination.

Figure 9-1. From *An Agenda for Action* **(1), by permission of the National Council of Teachers of Mathematics.**

ADDITION

Addition without Regrouping

Children can readily learn to add two two-place numbers without regrouping. This process involves no new ideas, since they need only apply basic addition facts and write the sum in the appropriate column. It is vital that they understand what they are doing. They need to understand that for

$$\begin{array}{r} 24 \\ + 35 \\ \hline \end{array}$$

they are adding 4 *ones* and 5 *ones*; they write this sum in the *ones* place. Then they add 2 *tens* and 3 *tens* and write the sum in the *tens* place. We allow bad habits to develop when children just add the numbers in each column and do not think of tens and ones.

We recommend that children be given relatively little practice with addition without regrouping before they move to addition with regrouping, or that addition with regrouping be taught first. If the latter is done, then addition without regrouping is merely a simpler case of addition with regrouping. Attention is focused on the meaning of what they are doing, rather than on the mechanical procedure.

After review practice has been given with renaming (as suggested in the introduction to this chapter), a problem can be posed to the children:

> Jill and Jeff both collected baseball cards. Jill had 24 cards and Jeff had 35. How many did they have together?

The children need to have a variety of experiences with materials. Lesson Card 9-1 presents an effective sequence.

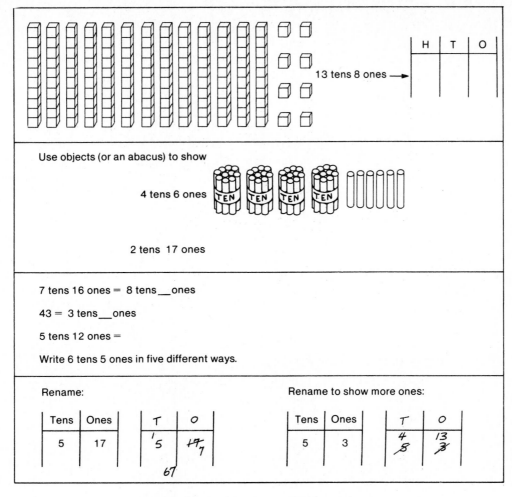

Figure 9-2. Linking place value and renaming.

We want to build a bridge between the materials and the written form. So the materials should be matched with written forms, using extended algorithms and then the final algorithm. Thus, after extensive work with materials, questions such as those on Lesson Card 9-2 need to be asked.

The addition of

$$\begin{array}{r} 437 \\ + 521 \end{array} \quad \text{or} \quad \begin{array}{r} 437 \\ + 21 \end{array}$$

is simply an extension of the procedure to the hundreds place. Adding multiples of 10, 100, and so on is another simpler case.

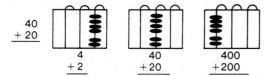

As children work with addition (as well as the other operations), they should be encouraged to estimate to ascertain whether the answer they reach is approximately correct. Activity Card 9-1 illustrates how an estimation activity provides practice with adding multiples of 10. Use of compatible numbers is a powerful estimation strategy, as will be discussed more fully in Chapter 13.

Addition with Regrouping

Teaching addition with regrouping (sometimes called *carrying*) parallels the teaching of addition without regrouping, although children not unexpectedly find it more difficult. A sequence for instruction is found on Lesson Card 9-3. After the work with materials, children need to be able to relate the written form of the algorithm with the materials.

LESSON CARD 9-1

1. <u>Pose a problem:</u> Jill and Jeff both collected baseball cards. Jill had 24 cards and Jeff had 35. How many did they have together?

2a. <u>Use manipulative materials, ungrouped:</u>

Lay out 24 cards (or slips of paper, popsicle sticks, or other objects), then lay out 35 more. Count to find the sum.

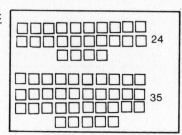

2b. <u>Use manipulative materials, grouped:</u>

Lay out 2 bunches of ten and 4 ones, then 3 tens and 5 ones. Regroup these to 5 tens and 9 ones. Name the sum. (Rods, multibase blocks, or similar place value materials could be used.)

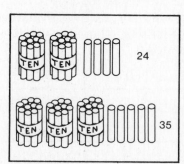

3. <u>Use the pocket chart:</u>

Show 24 and then add 35 in a pocket chart. Name the sum. (Alternatively, use an abacus.)

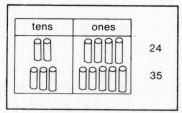

4. <u>Use the place value chart:</u>

Write 24 and then 35 in a place value chart. Write the sum.

tens	ones
2	4
3	5

Sample of questions to ask children:

How could you rename 24?

How could you rename 35?

What is the sum of 4 ones and 5 ones?

Where do you suppose the 9 should be written?

What is the sum of 2 tens and 3 tens?

Where do we write the 5?

What is the answer?

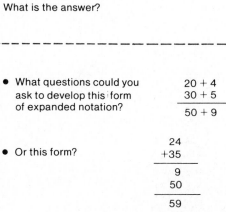

2 tens 4 ones
3 tens 5 ones
———————
        9 ones

↑

5 tens

- -

- What questions could you ask to develop this form of expanded notation?

$$20 + 4$$
$$30 + 5$$
———————
$$50 + 9$$

- Or this form?

$$\begin{array}{r} 24 \\ +35 \\ \hline 9 \\ 50 \\ \hline 59 \end{array}$$

$3.09 $5.15

$17.95

$4.99

$7.05

$13.11

You can use compatible numbers to help add.

I see many pairs of compatible numbers -- which should I take?

compatible numbers basket

Name 2 numbers that add to about $10.

Name 2 numbers that add to about $20.

Name 2 numbers that add to about $30.

How many different pairs of compatible numbers can you find?

1. Pose a problem: Mr. Gregory sold 37 popsicles on Monday and 46 on Tuesday. How many did he sell during the two days?

2a. Use manipulative materials, ungrouped:

Lay out 37 popsicle sticks, then 46 more. Count the sum.

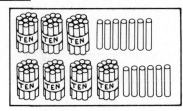

37

46

2b. Use manipulative materials, grouped:

Lay out 3 tens and 7 ones, then 4 tens and 6 ones. Regorup 6 ones and 7 ones to form 13 ones--or 1 ten and 3 ones. (Alternatively, use multibase blocks.)

3. Use the pocket chart:

Show 37 and then 46 in a pocket chart. Name the sum.

tens	ones

4. Use the place value chart:

Write 37 and then 46 in a place value chart. Write the sum.

tens	ones
3	7
4	6
~~7~~	~~13~~
8	3

119

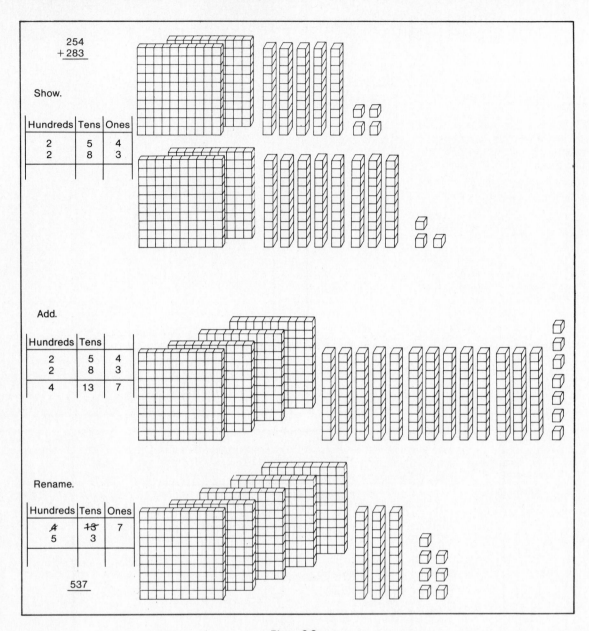

Figure 9-3

Children also need to have experiences with regrouping from tens to hundreds, or regrouping in both places, as indicated in Figure 9-3.

Some textbooks have children keep track of the regrouping by writing a small number in the appropriate column, as in Figure 9-3. Ideally, this "crutch" should not be suggested automatically to all children, but used only when a child has difficulty recalling the number. A crutch once introduced is very difficult to remove, yet many children can work more quickly (as well as accurately) without it. Encourage children to view it as a way the book shows the regrouping, not necessarily as something they should use.

Some problem-solving activities to practice mental computation and sharpen estimation skills, as well as deepen understanding of addition algorithms, are found on Activity Card 9-2.

Column Addition

Column addition with three or more one-digit addends is often introduced after some of the basic addition facts are learned, so that it may be used to provide varied practice.

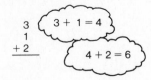

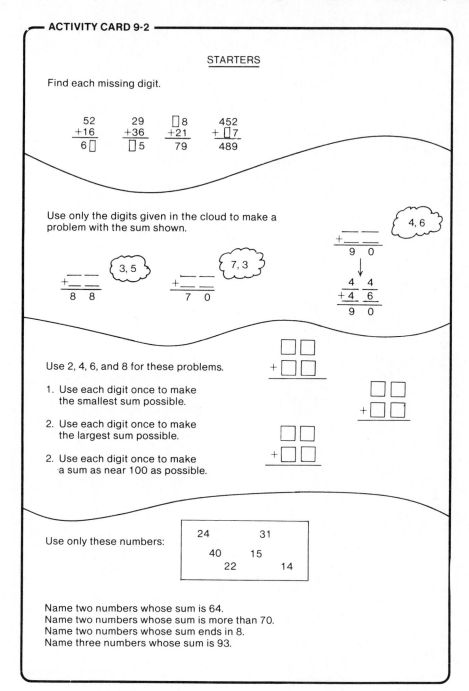

ACTIVITY CARD 9-2

STARTERS

Find each missing digit.

```
  52        29        □8       452
+16       +36       +21      +□7
 6□        □5        79       489
```

Use only the digits given in the cloud to make a problem with the sum shown.

```
3, 5          7, 3          4, 6
  __ __        __ __          __ __
+ __ __      + __ __        + __ __
  8  8        7  0            9  0
                               ↓
                              4  4
                            + 4  6
                              9  0
```

Use 2, 4, 6, and 8 for these problems.

1. Use each digit once to make the smallest sum possible.

2. Use each digit once to make the largest sum possible.

2. Use each digit once to make ·a sum as near 100 as possible.

Use only these numbers:

24		31
40	15	
	22	14

Name two numbers whose sum is 64.
Name two numbers whose sum is more than 70.
Name two numbers whose sum ends in 8.
Name three numbers whose sum is 93.

One new skill is required: adding an unseen addend. In this example, the 4 resulting from the addition of 3 + 1 must be added mentally to 2.

As with other topics, column addition is introduced through a problem situation, such as:

Joey bought a pencil for 3¢, an eraser for 1¢, and gum for 2¢. How much did he spend?

Using manipulative materials, flannelboard objects, or drawings will help children to visualize the situation:

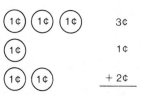

The materials or pictures help the child to bridge from the situation to the solution with symbols.

The number line provides another model (although caution in using the number line is suggested, as noted in Chapters 6 and 8).

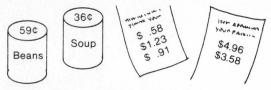

Many other activities can provide needed practice with unseen addends. Activity Card 9-3 contains four such activities.

Many textbooks present longer columns of addends as children learn the basic facts. Multidigit addends are usually introduced in connection with money, one of the real-life situations in which they must be added.

Is it better to teach children to add down, to add up, or to group numbers that add to 10 (using the associative property)? Research has indicated that adding either up or down, and using the opposite to check, is better than grouping (20). Fewer errors of omitting numbers or using a number more than once are likely to occur. "Be consistent" is the best rule.

ACTIVITY CARD 9-3

● Find the sum for this magic square. Add rows, columns, and diagonals. Put in the missing number.

8	1	6
3	5	7
4	9	

● Find the sum of each line.

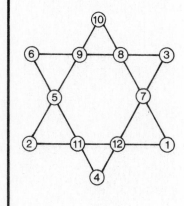

● Add each ▷ . Then change the number in the middle. How does that change the sums?

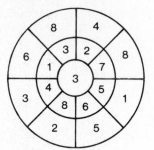

● You need 3 beanbags and a garment marked on the floor.

mat

	5	
3		4
1		2

Each player tosses the beanbag. Another player records the numbers. Score 0 if the bag misses the mat. Add to find the winner.

With children who find it difficult to keep the unseen sums in mind, other algorithms can be used (10):

$$
\begin{array}{l}
8 \\
5 \\
^{1}9^{3} \\
^{1}7^{2} \\
\hline
29
\end{array}
$$

8 + 5 = 13; write 3 on ones side, 1 on tens side

3 + 9 = 12; write 2 on ones side, 1 on tens side

2 + 7 = 9; write 9 as the sum of the ones, then add the two 1's from the tens side

Long columns of multidigit numbers can be added if the children enjoy this type of activity. However, these additions are almost always done more efficiently by using a calculator.

Higher-Decade Addition

Combinations like 17 + 4 or 47 + 8 or 3 + 28 are called *higher-decade* combinations, or referred to as "adding by endings." Note that the two-digit number may come either before or after the one-digit number.

The need for higher-decade addition arises in real-life problems; for instance, adding 6¢ tax to a purchase of 89¢. The skill is also necessary in column addition and in multiplication. To help children learn how to do such addition readily, experiences with manipulative materials, place-value charts, and the abacus are useful. Then, attention is focused on the relationship of 9 + 5 and 19 + 5, 29 + 5, and so on, as shown on Activity Card 9-4. We want children to realize that:

- In each example, the sum has a 4 in the ones place because 9 + 5 = 14, and the tens place has 1 more ten.
- The sum of 9 + 5 is more than 10, so the sum of 19 + 5 is more than 20, and 29 + 5 is more than 30.
- For 59 + 5, there is a 4 in the ones place and (5 + 1) in the tens place.

Children need to learn to perform these additions automatically, without adding ones and then tens as they do with examples such as 27 + 32. Such experiences not only encourage mental computation but greatly increase this skill.

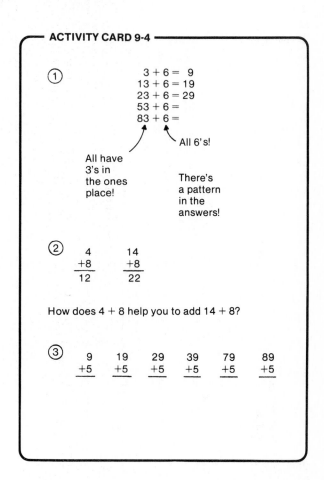

SUBTRACTION

Subtraction of multidigit numbers requires only knowledge of the basic subtraction facts and of place value. Just as addition without regrouping is comparatively easy for most children, so is subtraction without regrouping. For addition, we have suggested that you might begin with regrouping and then consider addition without regrouping as a simpler case. You might do the same for subtraction.

Subtraction with Regrouping

Subtraction with regrouping (sometimes called *borrowing*) is difficult for many children. It is wise to make sure that they are proficient with place value and basic facts (especially those with sums greater than 10)

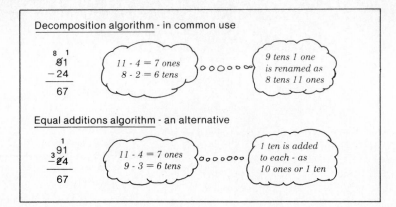

Decomposition algorithm - in common use

$$\begin{array}{r} {}^{8}\;{}^{1}\\ \cancel{9}1 \\ -24 \\ \hline 67 \end{array}$$

11 - 4 = 7 ones
8 - 2 = 6 tens

9 tens 1 one is renamed as 8 tens 11 ones

Equal additions algorithm - an alternative

$$\begin{array}{r} {}^{1}\\ 91 \\ -\,{}_{3}\cancel{2}4 \\ \hline 67 \end{array}$$

11 - 4 = 7 ones
9 - 3 = 6 tens

1 ten is added to each - as 10 ones or 1 ten

Figure 9-4

LESSON CARD 9-4

1. <u>Pose a problem:</u>   Frankie collected 91 coupons for dogfood. He gave his mother 24 coupons when she went to the store. How many did he have left?

2. Use manipulative materials:

Show:

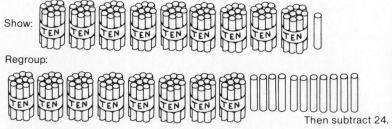

Regroup:

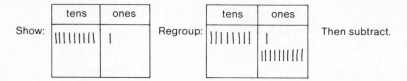

Then subtract 24.

3. <u>Use the pocket chart:</u>

Show:

tens	ones
│││││││││	│

Regroup:

tens	ones
││││││││	│
	││││││││││

Then subtract.

4. <u>Use the place value chart:</u>

tens	ones
$\cancel{9}\,^{8}$	$\cancel{1}\,^{11}$
2	4

Subtract.

5. <u>Use symbols alone:</u>

9 tens 1 one = 8 tens 11 ones
2 tens 4 one = 2 tens 4 ones
        6 tens 7 ones

$$\begin{array}{r} 91 \\ -24 \\ \hline 67 \end{array}$$

124

and to plan on systematically developing the algorithm with materials and then matching the materials with the symbolic representation.

Two algorithms for subtraction with regrouping have been used in this country during the past five or so decades. The one in common use is the *decomposition algorithm*; the other, the *equal additions algorithm,* provides an alternative that can be used for enrichment work. Figure 9-4 shows the two algorithms. Research has confirmed that both are effective in terms of speed and accuracy—when taught meaningfully (4).

Again, lessons follow the progression from materials to symbols, after introduction with a problem, as shown on Lesson Card 9-4. Emphasis should be placed on the child's asking, "Do I have enough ones (tens,

etc.)? If not, I must regroup or rename." In other words, using the algorithm is a decision-making process.

Experiences with regrouping from tens to hundreds, or regrouping in both places, are also necessary, as shown in Figure 9-5. Activity Card 9-5 presents several activities to provide practice with multidigit subtraction.

Another algorithm to aid children who find it difficult to follow the regular algorithm adds an extra step (10):

$$\begin{array}{r} 652 \\ -487 \end{array}$$ 652 is renamed, place by place, then the subtraction is performed.

$$\begin{array}{r} 6\ 5\ 2 \\ \hline \\ \hline -\ 4\ 8\ 7 \end{array} \qquad \begin{array}{r} 6\ 5\ 2 \\ \hline 2 \\ \hline -\ 4\ 8\ 7 \end{array} \qquad \begin{array}{r} 6\ 5\ 2 \\ \hline 4^{1}2 \\ \hline -\ 4\ 8\ 7 \end{array} \qquad \begin{array}{r} 6\ 5\ 2 \\ \hline 5^{1}4^{1}2 \\ \hline -\ 4\ 8\ 7 \\ \hline 1\ 6\ 5 \end{array}$$

Figure 9-5

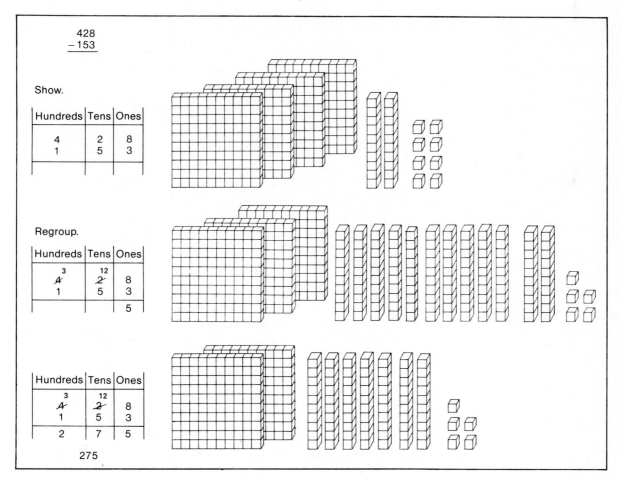

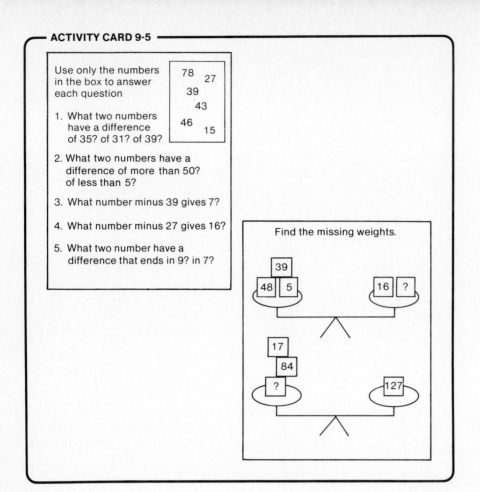

Use only the numbers in the box to answer each question

78	27
39	
	43
46	
	15

1. What two numbers have a difference of 35? of 31? of 39?

2. What two numbers have a difference of more than 50? of less than 5?

3. What number minus 39 gives 7?

4. What number minus 27 gives 16?

5. What two number have a difference that ends in 9? in 7?

Find the missing weights.

Figure 9-6

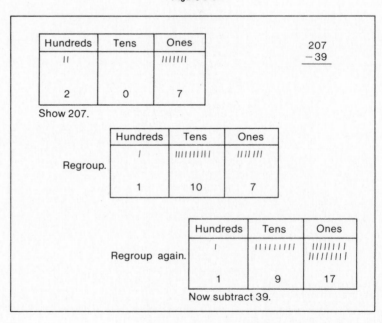

Hundreds	Tens	Ones
II		///////
2	0	7

Show 207.

$$\begin{array}{r} 207 \\ -39 \end{array}$$

Regroup.

Hundreds	Tens	Ones
/	/////////	///////
1	10	7

Regroup again.

Hundreds	Tens	Ones
/	//////////	////////// //////////
1	9	17

Now subtract 39.

Zeros in the Sum

The presence of zeros in the sum demands special attention. If the zero is in the ones place, it causes little difficulty. Thus, 50 in this example

$$\begin{array}{r} 850 \\ -287 \end{array}$$

is renamed as 4 tens and 10 ones. Zero in the tens place is slightly more difficult, especially when regrouping in the ones place is also necessary. The steps are shown in Figure 9-6.

The biggest difficulty lies with numbers having more than one zero. One alternative is multiple renaming, from hundreds to tens, then tens to ones:

Place-value experiences are important in preparing children to cope with these problems. They must clearly understand that 500 can be renamed as 4 hundreds and 10 tens, or as 4 hundreds, 9 tens, and 10 ones. If this understanding is clear, they will find it easier to recognize the need for multiple regrouping when they see multiple zeros, and they can do all the renaming at once:

$$\begin{array}{r} 500 \\ -283 \end{array} \qquad \begin{array}{r} \overset{4\ \ 9}{\cancel{5}}\ \overset{}{\cancel{0}}{}^{1}0 \\ 283 \end{array} \qquad 500 = 49 \text{ tens } 10 \text{ ones}$$

(In the example, 207 − 39, they could similarly have renamed 207 as 19 tens and 17 ones in one step. However, the need to do this was not readily recognizable to all children; those who need to do the double renaming should be allowed to do so.)

Higher-Decade Subtraction

As with addition, combinations like 17 − 4 and 59 − 6 are called higher-decade combinations. Subtracting a one-digit number from another number is facilitated by focusing attention on the pattern, as on Activity Card 9-6.*

*Activity Card 9-6 is from Reys (14), by permission of Creative Publications.

127

MULTIPLICATION

Before children tackle the multiplication algorithms, they must have a firm grasp on place value, expanded notation, and the distributive property, as well as the basic facts of multiplication. As with other operations, it is wise to provide review practice on each of these before beginning work on each aspect of the multiplication algorithm.

Multiplication without Regrouping

Multiplication without regrouping causes relatively little difficulty for children—but there are comparatively few times when no regrouping is required. It provides practice on basic multiplication facts and also an opportunity to have children gain initial understanding of the algorithm. The meaning of multiplication is reinforced with materials:

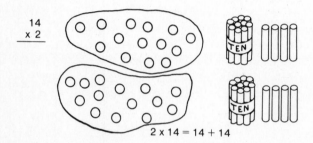

$$2 \times 14 = 14 + 14$$

Use of the distributive property is pointed out:

$$2 \times 14 = 2 \times (10 + 4) = (2 \times 10) + (2 \times 4)$$
$$= 20 + 8 = 28$$

Thus, arrays can be used to develop meaning:

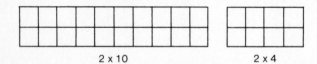

Place-value ideas are noted along with materials:

Tens	Ones			Tens	Ones
/ 1	4	////		1	4
/ 1	4	////		x	2
2	8			2	8

Expanded algorithms can be developed easily:

				14	
	1 ten	4 ones		× 2	
×		2		8	
	2 tens	8 ones		20	
				28	

Multiplication with Regrouping: One-Digit Multiplier

A number of activities help children to gain understanding of the algorithm. The relationship with addition, the use of arrays, the use of expanded notation, and the writing of all partial products each help to teach the meaning of the final algorithm (see Figure 9-7).

The distributive property helps children understand the algorithm. Activity Card 9-7 illustrates one way of using the property in providing mental computation and serves to sharpen estimation skills. The calculator also promotes a focus on estimation, while decreasing the amount of time spent on computation. Some activities with that focus are found on Activity Card 9-8.*

Multiplication with Regrouping: Two-Digit Multiplier

As children work with two-digit multipliers, the use of manipulative materials begins to become cumbersome. Some materials are used to tie the work to previously learned procedures, but increasingly the emphasis shifts to work with symbols (see Figure 9-8). This is possible because of the earlier base built on the use of materials.

Two activities for using calculators with multidigit multipliers can be found on Activity Cards 9-9 and 9-10. One aids in strengthening the meaning of the algorithms, while the other presents a problem-solving situation.

Multiplying by 10 and Multiples of 10

Multiplying by 10 comes easily to most children, and it is readily extended to multiplying by 100 and 1000 as children gain understanding of larger numbers. The basic teaching consists of showing the children a series of examples, then having them generalize, noting that when there is a zero in the ones place, each digit moves one place to the left in the product. Activity Card 9-11[†] shows how a calculator can help children develop ideas about the effect of zero.

Multiplying by 20, 30, 100, 200, and so on is an extension of multiplying by 10 and 100. The emphasis is placed on comparing what happens across examples and generalizing from the pattern. Thus, we have children consider 3×50:

$$3 \times 5 = 15$$
$$3 \times 5 \text{ tens} = 15 \text{ tens} = 150$$
$$3 \times 50 = 150$$

*Activity Cards 9-8, 9-9, and 9-10 are from Miller (12), by permission of Cuisenaire Company of America, Inc.

[†]Activity Card 9-11 is from Reys (14), by permission of Creative Publications.

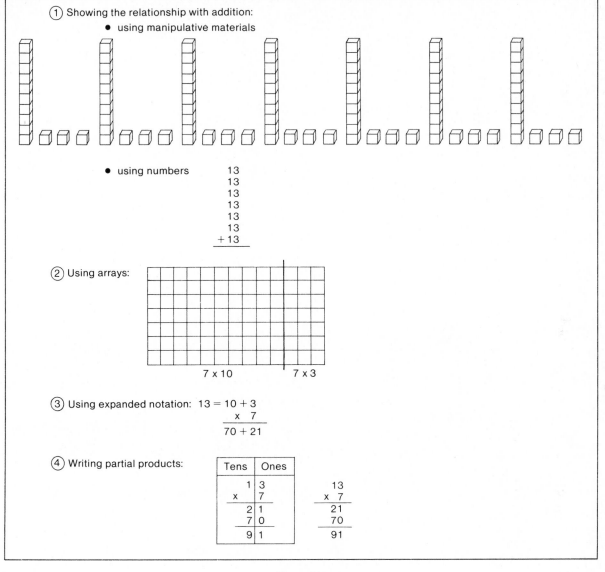

① Showing the relationship with addition:
  • using manipulative materials

  • using numbers   13
                         13
                         13
                         13
                         13
                         13
                       + 13

② Using arrays:

                    7 x 10   7 x 3

③ Using expanded notation: 13 = 10 + 3
                              x   7
                             70 + 21

④ Writing partial products:

Tens	Ones
1	3
x	7
2	1
7	0
9	1

         13
       x 7
         21
         70
         91

Figure 9-7

Then consider 4 × 50:

$$4 \times 5 = 20$$
$$4 \times 5 \text{ tens} = \_\_\_ \text{ tens} = \_\_\_$$
$$4 \times 50 = \_\_\_$$

After several more examples, they are given other examples for which they are to find the pattern:

20	70	90	...	36	52
× 7	× 6	× 8		× 20	× 30

A similar sequence is followed for examples with hundreds, such as 2 × 300:

$$2 \times 3 = 6$$
$$2 \times 3 \text{ hundreds} = \_\_\_ \text{ hundreds} = \_\_\_$$
$$2 \times 300 = \_\_\_$$

Finally, examples such as these are given:

273	418
× 50	× 80

It is tremendously useful for children to be able to use multiplication by rounded numbers in making estimates. Suppose they are to estimate 19 × 427.

The child thinks:

That's about 20 × 400.
2 × 4 = 8.
2 × 400 = 800.
So 20 × 400 would be 8000.

In conjunction with this, they need to answer such questions as: How do I know how many zeros will be in the

USE WHAT YOU KNOW!

Rename the larger factor.

Then multiply.

1. 3×99 ⟶ Think "3 hundreds − 3" =
   $300 - 3 = 297$

2. 7×104 ⟶ Think "7 hundreds + 7 fours" =

3. 6×49 ⟶

4. 5×95 ⟶

5. 4×24 ⟶

FIND WHAT'S MISSING

1. Find the missing digits. use only 2, 3, and 4.

$$\begin{array}{r} \square\square \\ \times\ \square \\ \hline 4\ 6 \end{array} \qquad \begin{array}{r} \square\square \\ \times\ \square \\ \hline 6\ 6 \end{array} \qquad \begin{array}{r} \square\square \\ \times\ \square \\ \hline 8\ 4 \end{array} \qquad \begin{array}{r} \square\square \\ \times\ \square \\ \hline 1\ 2\ 6 \end{array}$$

2. Use only 4, 6, 8, and 9.

Make the largest product.

$$\begin{array}{r} \square\square\square \\ \times\quad\ \square \\ \hline \end{array}$$

Make the smallest product.

$$\begin{array}{r} \square\square\square \\ \times\quad\ \square \\ \hline \end{array}$$

3. Guess the numbers that will go into the circles and boxes. Write your estimate and then check it on a calculator. Score 2 points if correct on the first try and 1 point if correct on the second try.

(4) (6) (7) (8)   [32] [48] [68] [82]

1) ○ × □ = 408

2) ○ × □ = 476

3) ○ × □ = 384

4) ○ × □ = 272

5) ○ × □ = 336

6) ○ × □ = 492

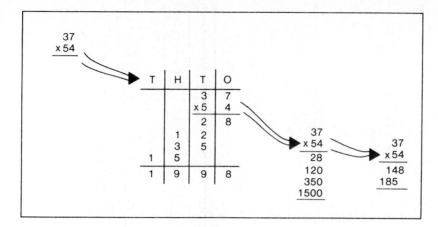

Figure 9-8

ACTIVITY CARD 9-9

Analyzing Multiplication

Study the completed problems and then use your arithmetic skills to help find the missing numbers MENTALLY.
Check your mental answers with a calculator.
Score one point for each correct answer.

1)

```
    387
  × 264
  1548
 23220
 77400
102168
```

```
    264
  × 387
  1848
 21120
 79200
102168
```

a) $387 \times 60 =$ _____

b) $2640 \times 70 =$ _____

c) $200 \times 387 =$ _____

d) $2640 \times$ ___ $= 79200$

e) $260 \times 387 =$ _____

f) $24 \times 387 =$ _____

ACTIVITY CARD 9-10

MAKING CONJECTURES

1. Multiply some 2-digit numbers by 99. Record your results and make a conjecture.

2. Multiply some 3-digit numbers by 999. Record your results and make a conjecture.

3. Multiply some 2-digit numbers by 999. Record your results and make a conjecture.

Now try these. Find the pattern.
   11 x 11
  111 x 111
 1111 x 1111

Predict 11111 x 11111 and check!

Zeros Count

1. Use your [calculator] ⟶ 8 × 10 = _____
   How many 0's in 10? _____   How many 0's in the product? _____

2. Use your [calculator] ⟶ 6 × 100 = _____
   How many 0's in 100? _____   How many 0's in the product? _____

3. Use your [calculator] ⟶ 9 × 1000 = _____
   How many 0's in 1000? _____   How many 0's in the product? _____

Complete this multiplication table. Use your [calculator] to check your answers.

X	10	100	1000
7			
14		1400	
28			28,000
247			
989			

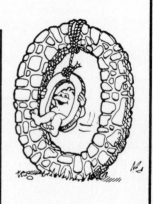

---

product? How is the number of zeros in the estimate related to the factors? How many digits will be in the estimated product?

Multiplying with Zeros

When zeros appear in the factor being multiplied, particular attention needs to be given to the effect on the product or partial product. Many children are prone to ignore the zero. Thus, for 9 × 306, their answer may be:

$$\begin{array}{r} 5 \\ 306 \\ \times\ \ 9 \\ \hline 324 \end{array}$$

When an estimate is made first, they have a way of determining whether their answer is "in the ballpark." Use of the place-value chart will help them to understand what the correct procedure must be, as will expanded notation:

$$\begin{array}{r} 306 \\ \times\ \ 9 \end{array}$$

Estimate:

$9 \times 3 = 27$
$9 \times 300 = 2700$

t	h	t	o
	3	0	6
			9
2	7	5	4

$9 \times 306 = 9 \times (300 + 6)$
$= (9 \times 300) + (9 \times 6)$
$= 2700 + 54$
$= 2754$

Multiplication with Large Numbers

How can the calculator be used to solve computations involving numbers that appear too big for the calculator? As children experiment with calculators and multiplication, there will come a time when they overload the calculator. Sometimes the number to be entered will contain more digits than the display will show. At other times the product will be too big for the display. Thus, if this example

$$\begin{array}{r} 2345678 \\ \times \quad 4003 \\ \hline \end{array}$$

is entered in a four-function calculator, an error message will result. When this happens, children should be encouraged to estimate an answer and then use the distributive property plus mental computation, along with the calculator:

Estimate:

$4000 \times 2,000,000 =$
$8,000,000,000$

$\begin{aligned} 4003 &= 4000 + 3 \\ &= (4 \times 1000) + 3 \end{aligned}$
$4 \times 2345678 = 9382712$ (with the calculator)
$9382712 \times 1000 = 9382712000$ (mentally)
Then add 3×2345678

Such examples show how an understanding of multiplication, plus problem-solving skills, can be used with calculators to reach a solution. They also remind us that calculator algorithms differ from the currently used paper-and-pencil algorithms.

DIVISION

Division is without doubt the most difficult of the algorithms for children to master—for a number of reasons:

- Computation begins at the left, rather than at the right as for the other operations.
- It involves not only the basic division facts, but also subtraction and multiplication.
- There are a number of interactions in the algorithm, but the pattern of them moves from one spot to another.
- Trial quotients, involving estimation, must be used, and may not always be successful at the first attempt—or even the second.

Teachers struggle to teach division, and children struggle to learn division; it is little wonder that the use of calculators is posed as a means of resolving the dilemma of the division algorithm. As *An Agenda for Action* indicates:

> For most students, much of a full year of instruction in mathematics is spent on the division of whole numbers—a massive investment with increasingly limited productive return . . . . For most complex problems, using the calculator for rapid and accurate computation makes a far greater contribution to functional competence in daily life. (1, p. 6)

On the second national assessment in mathematics, some exercises were given with and without the use of calculators (5). One exercise, $28\overline{)3052}$, was given only to 13- and 17-year-olds when calculators were not used, for nine-year-olds had not yet been taught division with a two-digit divisor. Thirteen-year-olds scored 46 percent and 17-year-olds scored 50 percent without calculators. With calculators, the scores rose dramatically, to 82 percent and 91 percent, respectively. And 50 percent of the nine-year-olds attained the correct answer when they used calculators! When you consider that half of the 17-year-olds could not perform the division even after years of practice, is it not reasonable to let them use the tool with which they are successful—and which they will use anyway for the rest of their lives?

We strongly recommend that development of the division algorithm with one-digit divisors should be the focus of instruction, followed by some work with two-digit divisors so that students understand how the algorithm works. Performing complex division—perhaps any that takes over 30 seconds to do—with paper and pencil is a thing of the past for adults; thus, we should not demand that children spend countless hours mastering an antiquated skill. We can't afford the instructional time for this. Instead, estimation skills, including the compatible-numbers strategy, should be taught to place bounds on the quotient, so that the approximate accuracy of calculator answers can be verified.

Division with Remainders

As long as problems remain on a concrete level, the concept of remainder is rather easy.

- Separate a class of 31 into 2 teams. The 1 left over is scorekeeper.
- Pass out 17 pieces of paper to 5 children. Each receives 3 sheets with 2 left over.
- How much change would you get when you buy some 4-cent pencils and give the clerk 15¢?
- Four children can ride in each car. If 30 children are going on the class trip, how many cars are needed?

The "part left over" is given a different task, discarded, saved, or rounded up. In other cases it is expressed as a fraction or a decimal. With calculators, the results of inexact division are expressed in decimal form, and children need to learn how to interpret the remainder when it is not an integer (see Chapter 11).

Initially, children are taught to write the remainder in one of the following ways:

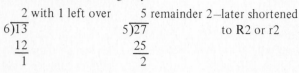

ACTIVITY CARD 9-12

A REMAINDER GAME

Number of Players: 2 to 4

Needed: 4 cards of each numeral 0 to 9, placed face down in a pile.

A counter for each player.

12	23	34	17
18	19	HOME	40
	10		20
START	31	27	14

Rules: The first player draws a card.

Divide the first number on the board by the number drawn.

Move the counter forward by the number of spaces indicated by the remainder. If the remainder is 0, no move is made.

Then the others go in turn.

To get "home" a player must be able to move the exact number of spaces left. First one home wins.

Figure 9-9

Distributive algorithm

```
      94  r 3
  4 ) 379      First think "How many 4's in 37?"
      36
      ---
      19
      16
      ---
       3
```

Subtractive algorithm

```
  4 ) 379
      200     50 x 4
      ---
      179
      160     40 x 4
      ---
       19
       16      4 x 4
      ---
       3      94 r 3
```

This algorithm is easier because correction of the quotient is seldom needed. The child can take out 1, 10, or any number of the divisor; it will just take longer:

```
  4 ) 379
       40     10 x 4
      ---
      339
       40     10 x 4
```

Sometimes the quotient is written above the dividend:

```
      40
      50
  4 ) 379
      200
      ---
      179    etc.
```

It is important to emphasize the real-life situations from which the examples arise.

Activities such as the game in Activity Card 9-12 provide practice in identifying the remainder.

Division with One-Digit Divisor

Children clearly need a good understanding of place value as they work with the division algorithm; understanding of the distributive property is essential. Two algorithms have been used for division in recent years (see Figure 9-9). The distributive algorithm is most common; the subtractive algorithm is easier to teach and to learn but is not so often taught as it was a decade or so ago.

Research indicates that both forms of the algorithm are effective (19). You might use the subtractive

algorithm as you develop the meaning of the algorithm, then move to the distributive algorithm. Or you might decide to "save" the subtractive algorithm for those children who are having undue difficulty with the distributive algorithm.

As with the other operations, it is important that children work with concrete objects, then move to less concrete materials, and finally work with the algorithm alone. At each of the earlier stages, the written form should be related to the objects or display. It is wise to work carefully with examples without remainders until children are at ease with the division idea (based on their earlier work with the basic facts) as well as with the algorithm form. Lesson Card 9-5 identifies the sequence of experiences that should be used to develop the division algorithm, in conjunction with problem situations.

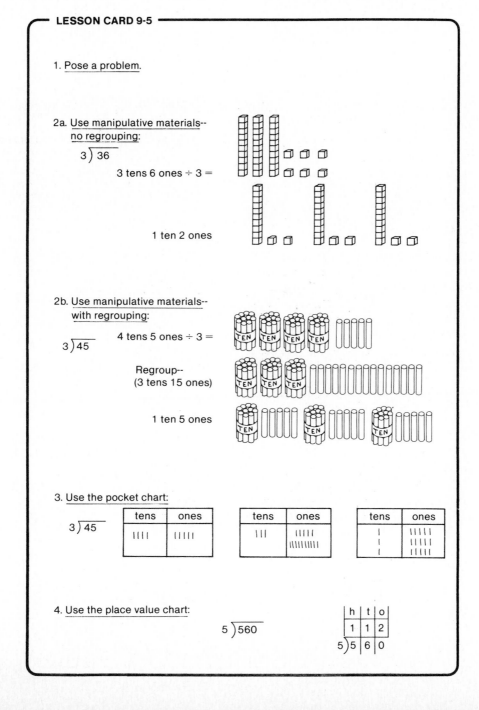

LESSON CARD 9-5

1. Pose a problem.

2a. Use manipulative materials--
   no regrouping:

   3)36

   3 tens 6 ones ÷ 3 =

   1 ten 2 ones

2b. Use manipulative materials--
   with regrouping:

   4 tens 5 ones ÷ 3 =

   3)45

   Regroup--
   (3 tens 15 ones)

   1 ten 5 ones

3. Use the pocket chart:

   3)45

tens	ones
||||	|||||

tens	ones
|||	||||| ||||||||||

tens	ones
|	|||||
|	|||||
|	|||||

4. Use the place value chart:

   5)560

h	t	o
1	1	2

   5)5 6 0

A variety of experiences and activities (see Activity Cards 9-13 and 9-14) may help children to gain facility with the division algorithm.

Division with Two-Digit Divisor

A necessary first step in determining the quotient is to estimate the number of places in the quotient:

$$6\overline{)839}$$

- Are there as many as ten 6's in 839? [Yes, ten 6's are only 60.]
- Are there as many as 100 6's? [Yes, 100 6's are 600.]
- Are there as many 200 6's? [No, 200 6's are 1200.]
- So the quotient is between 100 and 200—and probably closer to 100.

An alternative to this is the following teaching sequence:

- Are there enough hundreds to divide? $3\overline{)187}$ [No.]
- Are there enough tens? $3\overline{)187}$ [Yes.]
- So, the quotient has 2 digits—$3\overline{)187}$.

We now know the range of the answer:

- There are 6 tens—$3\overline{)187}$.
- The answer is between 60 and 70.

Such procedures help to develop an early recognition of the range for a quotient. They help to provide meaning to the algorithm while developing valuable estimation skill.

Both procedures are readily extended to multidigit examples. In work with multidigit divisors, there are also two procedures used in many textbooks that involve using an estimate as a trial divisor. Neither method works with all examples, but both the *apparent method* and the *rounding-off method* are widely taught.

Apparent Method. Only the first digit of the divisor is used as the trial figure:

$34\overline{)876}$ How many 3's in 8?

$57\overline{)472}$ How many 5's in 47?

Rounding-Off Method. When the second digit from the left in the two-digit divisor represents a 4 or less, the rounding-off method is the same as the apparent method. When that digit is 5, 6, 7, 8, or 9, the tens digit is increased by 1 and used as the trial divisor.

$34\overline{)876}$ How many 3's in 8?

$57\overline{)472}$ How many 6's in 47?

ACTIVITY CARD 9-13

WHAT'S MISSING?

- Find the missing digits:

- A game--
--Without the other players looking, work out a division example.
--Put the pattern of the example on the board.

--Divide the players into 2 teams.
--A player on Team A asks a question like, "Are there any 2s?" If there are, put them in and give the team a point for each.

--Then Team B asks a question, and so on.
--If there are no boxes for a number, the team scores 0--and loses its turn.
--The winner is the team with the highest score. (At some point, a team could guess the example, and win with a bonus.)

ACTIVITY CARD 9-14

MAKE AN EXAMPLE

Make a division example with:

1. A quotient of 6 r2

2. A quotient of 10 r4

3. A quotient of 23 r5

4. A dividend of 47 and a divsior of 3

5. A dividend of 81 and a divisor of 5

6. A divisor of 6 and a quotient of 15 r3

7. A divisor of 3 and a quotient of 25 r2

8. A dividend of 83 and a quotient of 11 r6

Since 57 is closer to 60 than to 50, using 60 will lead to a more accurate estimate.

Either method needs corrections. When the tens digit is 5 or greater, the trial quotient (if incorrect) will be too small by rounding off and too large by the apparent method. When the tens digit is less than 4, the trial quotient (if incorrect) will be too large by both methods.

Activity Card 9-15* suggests one idea for making estimates for division to determine whether the calculator answer is "in the right ballpark." The calculator is used to judge the successfulness of estimates necessary for performing the algorithm.

The development of division with two-digit divisors proceeds through the stages from concrete to abstract, paralleling the work with one-digit divisors. Much practice is needed with the symbolic form, but if children have had the procedure developed with materials, they are likely to attain proficiency sooner. Use of the calculator is interwoven in the activities, as indicated on Activity Card 9-16.[†]

CHECKING

Just as it is important to estimate before computing, it is important to check after computing. Ordinarily, addition and subtraction are used to check each other, as are multiplication and division. Unfortunately, checking does not always achieve its purpose of ascertaining correctness: research has indicated that children frequently "force the check"—that is, make the results agree without actually performing the computation (8). Obviously, children must come to understand the purpose of checking, as well as what they must do if the solution in the check does not agree with the original solution.

While checks by other procedures are possible (e.g., casting out nines), the existence of calculators has made teaching them less important except for enrichment. While the calculator can serve many other functions, its use in checking has not been overlooked by teachers.

Nevertheless, we do not recommend that the calculator be used primarily to have children check paper-and-pencil computation. It insults students to ask them to spend large amounts of time on a computation, and then use a machine that does the computation instantly. We do recommend that estimation be used extensively, both as a means of identifying the "ballpark" for the answer *and* as a means of ascertaining the correctness

*Activity Card 9-15 is from Reys (14), by permission of Creative Publications.
[†]Activity Card 9-16 is from Miller (12), by permission of Cuisenaire Company of America, Inc.

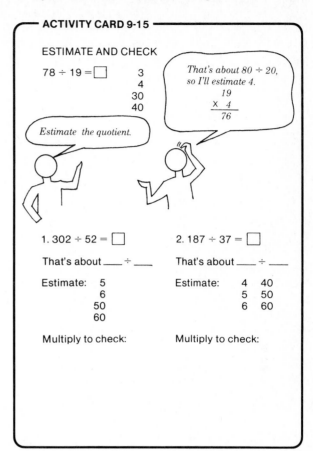

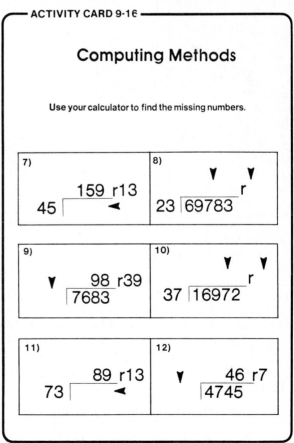

of the calculator answer. While the words "use your calculator to check" appear in some Activity Cards, it is
almost always when the calculator is to perform the
computation following an estimate.

OTHER SOURCES

Textbooks give extensive attention to the development
of computational algorithms, and you should analyze
this development carefully as you teach. Countless articles and books also provide suggestions and activities
for developing and practicing computation, as well as
offering alternative suggestions for those having difficulty. Three sources are called to your attention because
of the specific help they provide. One describes the development of addition and subtraction algorithms using
trading-chip activities and games (11). A second presents
a detailed plan for developing multiplication and division
algorithms (9). For children with learning disabilities,
the third article provides many helpful suggestions (13).
Each of these, as well as other references, gives you the
results of others' experience to help you become proficient in teaching computation.

A GLANCE AT WHERE WE'VE BEEN

While computational skill is viewed as an essential
component of children's mathematical achievement, its
role in the curriculum is changing. Tenets that continue
to guide our teaching of computation have been presented. The development of each algorithm has emphasized the use of manipulative materials and place-value
ideas. Suggested sequences of topics and ideas for developing these algorithms have been provided, with discussion of points with which to take particular care. The
use of calculators has been interwoven into lessons,
with many activities being suggested that use calculators
as well as other materials.

THINGS TO DO: ADDING TO YOUR PICTURE

1. What prerequisites must the child have in order to
   succeed in the opening lesson?
2. Consider the distributive and equal-additions algorithms for subtraction. What are the advantages
   and disadvantages of each?
3. Choose a textbook for grade 3 or 4. Trace the development of the multiplication algorithm. How is
   it introduced? What steps do children go through?
4. Choose a textbook series. Trace the development
   of the division algorithm. What phases of the
   development have been or should be modified
   because of the use of calculators?
5. Choose a textbook for grade 2 and analyze a lesson plan in the teacher's guide. What stages from
   concrete to abstract are involved in the lesson?
6. List at least five ways to help children who are
   having difficulty subtracting two two-digit numbers with regrouping.

7. Design an Activity Card to provide experience
   with materials for multiplication with zero.
8. Plan a lesson to teach children how to multiply
   9876543 × 99.
9. Design a homework assignment to follow Lesson
   Card 9-3.
10. Read the article by Merseth (11). How are trading
    games helpful in teaching addition and subtrac-
    tion? How do trading games help to bridge the gap
    between materials and the symbolic representation
    for 37 + 95?
11. Develop three test items that would assess stu-
    dents' understanding of adding two two-digit
    numbers with regrouping.
12. Discuss: "All students should be able to divide a
    seven-digit number by a three-digit number using
    a paper-and-pencil algorithm."
13. Select an algorithm for one operation. List ways
    in which you could help children to master it.
14. Consider each example. Describe what a child
    would think as he or she worked. What questions
    might you ask to develop or explain the proce-
    dure? How could manipulative materials be used?

    (a)
    $$\begin{array}{r} 1 \\ 536 \\ 279 \\ +\ \ 83 \\ \hline 8 \end{array}$$

    (b)
    $$\begin{array}{r} 2\ 14 \\ \not{3}\ \not{4}\ 9 \\ -1\ 8\ 4 \\ \hline 5 \end{array}$$

    (c)
    $$\begin{array}{r} 14 \\ 73\not{4} \\ 7 \\ -2\not{6}9 \\ \hline 5 \end{array}$$

    (d)
    $$\begin{array}{r} 45 \\ \times\ 3 \\ \hline 15 \\ 120 \\ \hline \end{array}$$

    (e)
    $$\begin{array}{r} 5 \\ 79 \\ \times\ 6 \\ \hline 4 \end{array}$$

    (f) $38\overline{)291}^{\ 9}$

15. An old procedure that children having difficulty
    may find useful is the lattice method. Can you
    figure it out? What do children need to know?

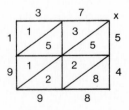

SELECTED REFERENCES

1. *An Agenda for Action: Recommendations for School Mathematics in the 1980s.* Reston, Va.: National Council of Teachers of Mathematics, 1980.

2. Brandau, Linda, and Easley, Jack. *Understanding the Realities of Problem Solving in Elementary School, with Practical Pointers for Teachers.* Columbus, Ohio: ERIC Clearinghouse for Science, Mathematics and Environmental Education, 1979.

3. Bright, George W. "Assessing the Development of Computation Skills." In *Developing Computational Skills* (ed. Marilyn N. Suydam and Robert E. Reys). 1978 Yearbook. Reston, Va.: National Council of Teachers of Mathematics, 1978. Pp. 148–162.

4. Brownell, William A. "An Experiment on 'Borrowing' in Third-Grade Arithmetic." *Journal of Educational Research,* 41 (November 1947), pp. 161–171.

5. Carpenter, Thomas P.; Corbitt, Mary Kay; Kepner, Henry S., Jr.; Lindquist, Mary Montgomery; and Reys, Robert E. *Results from the Second Mathematics Assessment of the National Assessment of Educational Progress.* Reston, Va.: National Council of Teachers of Mathematics, 1981.

6. Driscoll, Mark J. "Algorithms in Elementary School Mathematics." In *Research Within Reach: Elementary School Mathematics.* St. Louis: CEMREL, Inc., 1980.

7. Folsom, Mary. "Operations on Whole Numbers." In *Mathematics Learning in Early Childhood* (ed. Joseph N. Payne). Thirty-seventh Yearbook. Washington, D.C.: National Council of Teachers of Mathematics, 1975. Pp. 162–190.

8. Grossnickle, Foster E. "The Effectiveness of Checking Subtraction by Addition." *Elementary School Journal,* 38 (February 1938), pp. 436–441.

9. Hazekamp, Donald W. "Teaching Multiplication and Division Algorithms." In *Developing Computational Skills* (ed. Marilyn N. Suydam and Robert E. Reys). 1978 Yearbook. Reston, Va.: National Council of Teachers of Mathematics, 1978. Pp. 96–128.

10. Hutchings, Barton. "Low-Stress Algorithms." In *Measurement in School Mathematics* (ed. Doyal Nelson and Robert E. Reys). 1976 Yearbook. Reston, Va.: National Council of Teachers of Mathematics, 1976. Pp. 218–239.

11. Merseth, Katherine Klippert. "Using Materials and Activities in Teaching Addition and Subtraction Algorithms." In *Developing Computational Skills* (ed. Marilyn N. Suydam and Robert E. Reys). 1978 Yearbook. Reston, Va.: National Council of Teachers of Mathematics, 1978. Pp. 61–77.

12. Miller, Don. *Calculator Explorations and Problems.* New Rochelle, N.Y.: Cuisenaire Company of America, 1979.

13. Moyer, John C., and Moyer, Margaret Bannochie. "Computation: Implications for Learning Disabled Children." In *Developing Computational Skills* (ed. Marilyn N. Suydam and Robert E. Reys). 1978 Yearbook. Reston, Va.: National Council of Teachers of Mathematics, 1978. Pp. 78–95.

14. Reys, Robert E.; Bestgen, Barbara J.; Coburn, Terrence G.; Schoen, Harold L.; Shumway, Richard J.; Wheatley, Charlotte L.; Wheatley, Grayson H.; and White, Arthur L. *Keystrokes: Calculator Activities for Young Students: Addition and Subtraction, Multiplication and Division.* Palo Alto, Calif.: Creative Publications, 1980.

15. Suydam, Marilyn N., and Dessart, Donald J. *Classroom Ideas from Research on Computational Skills.* Reston, Va.: National Council of Teachers of Mathematics, 1976.

16. Swart, William L. "Teaching the Division-by-Subtraction Process." *Arithmetic Teacher,* 19 (January 1972), pp. 71–75.

17. Trafton, Paul R., and Suydam, Marilyn N. "Computational Skills: A Point of View." *Arithmetic Teacher,* 22 (November 1975), pp. 528–537.

18. Tucker, Benny F. "The Division Algorithm." *Arithmetic Teacher,* 20 (December 1973), pp. 639–646.

19. Van Engen, Henry, and Gibb, E. Glenadine. *General Mental Functions Associated with Division.* Educational Service Studies, No. 2. Cedar Falls: Iowa State Teachers College, 1956.

20. Wheatley, Grayson H., and Wheatley, Charlotte L. "How Shall We Teach Column Addition? Some Evidence." *Arithmetic Teacher,* 25 (January 1978), pp. 18–19.

10

Measuring

A sixth-grade class of 29 students is studying area of rectangles. Today, they are in groups of two or three and working on task cards.

Mrs. Katz: "What did we do in math yesterday?"
Loren: "We found the area of rectangles using the base and the altitude."

After reviewing the procedure, Mrs. Katz explains that today they will be applying it to objects in the room. As the groups work on the task cards, Mrs. Katz circulates and helps the groups or asks questions of those who need challenging. Later we can hear conversations such as the following:

Pat: "Which is larger, the desk top or the top of the bookcase? That's easy, the bookcase is much longer."
Kim: "But it says area, Pat. We need to find the area and I think the desk is larger."
Wes: "I think it's the bookcase. Let's see."
Mrs. Katz: "Well, what did you find?"
Pat: "The desk was larger in area even though the bookcase was longer. When we covered them with squares the other day, the desk took more squares."

:

Kim: "Unless I remember that I'm trying to find how many squares, I forget why I'm measuring the lengths and whether to add or multiply."

Wes: "It really helps me to think of the number of rows and the number of squares in each row. All you have to do is to count the number of squares, and multiplying is an easy way to count."
Mrs. Katz: "Why don't you try a challenge card instead of the last one on your list?"
Pat: "I'll get it. It's a blue card, isn't it?"
Kim: "Oh, let's try this one. I've always wanted to cover the science table with a rug!"

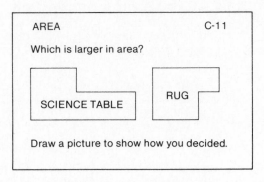

Wes: "These aren't rectangles. I don't want to get out that many squares."
Pat: "Look, we can make them into two rectangles. Remember when we cut those shapes apart? Let's cut the rug!"

140

Wes: "Funny, but you're right. Let's mark where we would cut them. Then we can find the area of each rectangle and add them."

.
.
.

Mrs. Katz: "What's the problem?"

Steve: "We don't know where to begin."

Mrs. Katz: "What are you trying to do?"

Steve: "We have to find something in the room that is about 120 square centimeters. That's awfully large. Are you sure there is something?"

Sue: "No, it isn't. A square centimeter is awfully small."

Jane: "Well, I just can't imagine 120 square centimeters. What can we do?"

Mrs. Katz: "Do you know how large your name card is?"

Sue: "Let me measure. It's about 7 cm by 11 cm. That would mean it's about 77 square centimeters. We need something larger."

Steve: "How about this sheet of paper?"

Jane: "That's way too much. It's about four times larger. We need something in between."

.
.
.

Maureen: "Mrs. Katz, can you help us?"

Mrs. Katz: "We'll see, what are you doing?"

Jose: "Well, we were talking and Maureen said the reading table was larger than this table. How can we tell?"

The reading table is a trapezoidal table.

Mrs. Katz: "Is the reading table a rectangle?"

Jose: "No, but can't we just measure the length and width?"

Mrs. Katz: "What would be the length?"

Maureen: "Wouldn't it be the longest side?"

.
.
.

Mrs. Katz: "Let's get back together and see what all of you have found."

Sue: "We found three things that were about 120 square centimeters. One was the task card, that was pretty sneaky."

Kim: "The science table is larger than the rug. Even if we could cut the rug, it wouldn't cover the table. Guess we won't have an easy-on-your-elbow table after all."

Jose: "We finally figured out the reading table. How about other shapes? How do you find the areas without covering them with squares?"

Mrs. Katz: "Jose, what do you mean you figured out the reading table?"

Jose: "Well, it isn't a rectangle, so we had to do some cutting. We cut off this triangle and put it there to make a rectangle."

Mrs. Katz: "Right. When things aren't rectangles, we need other ways to find the area. Tomorrow, we'll look at another shape. Some of you might wish to explore other shapes on your own. The area packet will help you."

BACKGROUND

We have just looked in on a lesson that could have happened in a sixth grade. What experiences should the children have before this lesson? What concepts and skills are important for children to learn? How do you help children to have these experiences? Before examining these questions and other things that you should consider as a teacher, we will discuss why measuring should be taught.

Stop and think about how you have used numbers in the past few days. Did you tell someone how long it took you to drive to school, how many calories are in a piece of chocolate cake, how far it is to the nearest store, or how many cups of coffee you drank? Any of these would be a measurement. In fact, we use measuring daily; it is probably the one topic in elementary mathematics that we use the most. Thus, one of the main reasons to include measuring is that it has many *practical applications in everyday life.*

Second, measurement can be used in *learning other topics* in mathematics. It is apparent that we need many of the other topics of mathematics to help us with measuring. For example, we may count the number of grams it takes to balance a scale, we may multiply to find the volume, we may divide to change minutes to hours, we may subtract to see how close our estimate was, or we may add to find the perimeter of a triangle. To report the number of units, we may use whole numbers, common fractions, decimals, and even negative numbers.

It is not quite as apparent that measurement can help teach some of these operations or types of numbers. However, many of the models that we use have a measurement base. For example, the number line is based on length. One model for multiplication is very close to an area model. Also, there are concepts and procedures that underlie both measurement and number ideas. As seen in Figure 10-1, measuring to the nearest unit is similar to rounding to a given unit. Thus, measurement ideas may be used to complement numerical ideas.

Not only is measurement useful in everyday life, it is *useful in other areas of the curriculum*. If you are trying to think of ways to bridge mathematics with other subjects, think of measurement. How do you use measurement in art, music, science, social science, and language arts?

Another reason that measurement is an important part of the mathematics curriculum is not as much

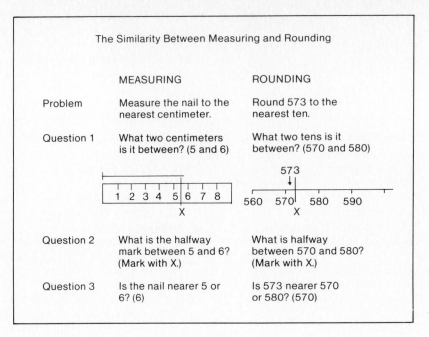

Figure 10-1

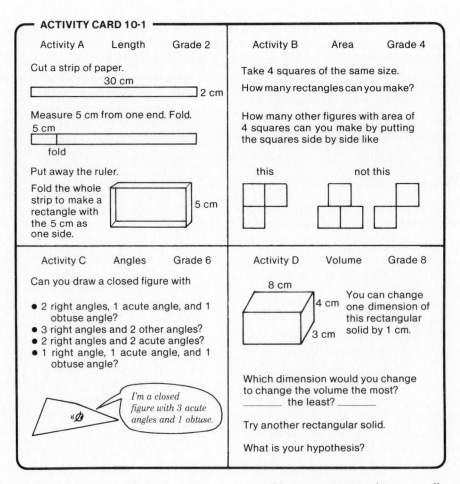

mathematical as pedagogical. It is a splendid way to *involve students* in activities that are often a *change of pace* from other mathematics topics. Look again at the opening lesson. Is this what you remember happening in a mathematics class?

Measurement provides an excellent way to present *problem-solving* experiences at every level. Activity Card 10-1 gives samples of some problems at various levels. They could be used at the grade level suggested or with older students.

HOW TO TEACH

Some measurable attributes considered in most elementary mathematics programs are length, capacity, weight, area, volume, time, and temperature. While each of these is different, there are some overall similarities in how to teach children to measure them. Based upon the measuring process, here is an outline of steps needed for each attribute.

I. Identifying the attribute by comparing objects
   A. Perceptually
   B. Directly
   C. Indirectly through a reference
II. Choosing a unit
   A. Arbitrary
   B. Standard
III. Comparing the subject to the unit
IV. Finding the number of units
   A. Counting
   B. Using instruments
   C. Using formulas
V. Reporting the number of units

If a new attribute is being introduced, it is recommended that you cycle through I–V several times—the first time using only arbitrary units and counting, the next time using standard units and counting before introducing instruments or formulas. When children are first learning about measurement, this cycling may take place over several years, but after several attributes have been introduced, the length of the cycling may be shortened.

Identifying Attributes

One of the first steps in measuring is knowing what you are measuring. This may sound trivial, but it is often a source of difficulty. Take, for example, a measure of attitude. What are you actually measuring? Do you see why scores on attitude tests may be difficult to interpret? We do not really understand the attribute, attitude, being measured. For young children, measuring the area of an object may be difficult if they really do not understand what area is. Thus, one of our first tasks is to build an understanding of the attribute. We will do this through comparing: first by comparing objects that are perceptually different, next by comparing them directly, and then by comparing them indirectly. These three types of comparisons are described more fully as we discuss length.

As children are doing these types of comparisons, not only are they gaining an understanding of the attribute and the associated vocabulary but also they are

learning procedures that will help them in assigning a number. This stage is often called *premeasurement,* since no numbers are involved. Since this is a crucial stage, we will examine each attribute separately.

Length. Length is one of the most perceptual attributes of objects. Children come to school with some concept of length and some vocabulary associated with it. However, they often have what adults may consider misconceptions about length. For example, they may say that a belt is shorter when it is curled up than when it is straight. These misconceptions disappear as children develop cognitively and are given constructive experiences.

Contrast the activities on Lesson Cards 10-1, 10-2, and 10-3—activities that are appropriate for kindergarteners, first graders, or children who need a review. Lesson Card 10-1 involves comparisons made perceptually. In the beginning of this activity all irrelevant perceptual attributes have been masked; that is, the objects are the same except for length. This allows you to build the concept of length as an attribute of long, thin things. As the activity progresses and vocabulary is reviewed and extended, the objects compared differ on several attributes, but the focus is on length.

Lesson Card 10-2 uses the procedure of making direct comparisons. In the case of length, this involves

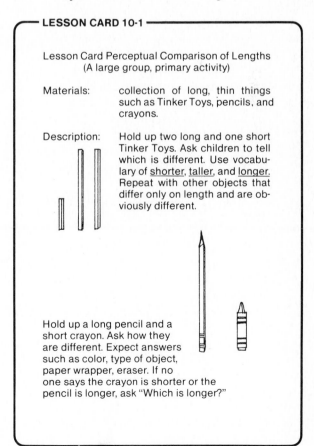

LESSON CARD 10-1

Lesson Card Perceptual Comparison of Lengths
(A large group, primary activity)

Materials: collection of long, thin things such as Tinker Toys, pencils, and crayons.

Description: Hold up two long and one short Tinker Toys. Ask children to tell which is different. Use vocabulary of <u>shorter</u>, <u>taller</u>, and <u>longer</u>. Repeat with other objects that differ only on length and are obviously different.

Hold up a long pencil and a short crayon. Ask how they are different. Expect answers such as color, type of object, paper wrapper, eraser. If no one says the crayon is shorter or the pencil is longer, ask "Which is longer?"

taking two objects and placing them side by side on a common baseline. This activity may be extended to seriating objects on length—that is, arranging them from shortest to tallest. For the young child this is a more difficult task because of the multiple comparisons.

Lesson Card 10-3 presents the problem of comparing two objects when they cannot be placed side by side. The children must use a third object to help them make the comparison. Thus, they are making an indirect comparison. This is what we do when we use a ruler to assign measurements: it is the third object that assists us in making a comparison.

Through activities such as these children should develop an understanding of length as an attribute of long, thin objects. However, there are other ways that we use length. Length is the distance around your waist. Young children can use yarn to compare their waists or to compare their own wrist with their ankle. An activity for older children is guessing whether the height or the distance around a variety of cylindrical cans is longer and then checking their guess by using string.

The distance between two points is also measured by length. In this case, we may use vocabulary such as *nearer* and *farther* when comparing two distances. Distance is more difficult to perceive than the length of a long, thin object, so it should be introduced later.

Capacity. If one considers capacity to be an attribute of containers, then this attribute can be introduced to young children by asking, "Which holds more?"

While perceptual comparisons can be made between the two containers, young children often make the comparisons on length (height) rather than on capacity. When asked which holds more, a tall container or a short container, most children will choose the taller container even if the shorter one actually holds more. Thus, it is probably best to begin the study of capacity by using direct comparisons.

To make direct comparisons we need some type of filler; water and sand are easy for young children. Given a variety of containers, children can fill one and pour it into the other to see which holds more. After children have done some experimenting on their own, you may want to have more structured activities. By labeling a pair of containers with letters, you can have children circle the letter of the container that holds more. You can also have a great guessing contest in which children guess which holds more and then check the results together.

We use indirect comparisons when two containers cannot be compared perceptually or directly. Suppose you have two containers with small openings that make it difficult to pour from one into another. By pouring each into a pair of large-mouth containers, the capacities

---

LESSON CARD 10-2

Direct Comparison of Length
(An individual, primary activity)

Materials: a box of long, thin objects many of which are about the same length, and three sheets of construction paper labeled as shown:

SHORTER	SAME	LONGER

Description: Have a child choose one object and put it on SAME. The child then compares each object with the object on SAME and puts it on the appropriate piece of paper.

SHORTER	SAME	LONGER

LESSON CARD 10-3

Indirect Comparison of Length
(A large group activity followed by individual practice for primary children)

Materials: a piece of string for each child, index cards, tape, and pen.

Description: Choose two objects that cannot be moved and are about the same length, or two dimensions of the same object—for example, the height and width of your desk. Ask which is longer and how you could show which is longer. Show the children how to use the string to represent each length and how to compare those representations.

After children are familiar with this, give each a string and let them choose an object you've marked with an index card. They should make a representation and then compare it with several others. At the end you can make a "graph" of all the lengths.

can be compared. Note that this is similar to what we do when we use graduated cylinders.

Weight. To compare weights perceptually, we need to be able to lift the two objects. Children should be given a variety of pairs of objects (one of which is much heavier than the other) and asked to hold one in each hand. Children often think that a larger object weighs more. Thus, some of the objects should be small and heavy while others are larger and light. For children to understand that to find which is heavier they must do more than look, they need experience in comparing two objects that look the same but weigh different amounts. An easy way to accomplish this is to put different weights into identical containers with lids (such as cottage-cheese containers).

When you cannot feel the difference between the weight of two objects, you need a balance to assist in the comparison. To introduce the balance, choose an object that the children know is heavier than another, so they can see that the heavier object "goes down" on the balance just as their hands probably did.

Many activities may be set up in which children compare two objects on weight. Can you think of one similar to the length activity on Lesson Card 10-2? A challenging activity is to compare five identical containers, with lids secured and each filled with different amounts of weight, and put them in order from lightest to heaviest.

Indirect comparisons are not necessary until units of weight are introduced, because whenever you could compare each of two objects to a third on the balance it would be much simpler to compare the two directly.

Area. Area is an attribute of plane regions that can be compared by sight if the differences are large enough and the shapes similar enough. That is, it is easy to tell this page is larger than a driver's license, but it may be difficult to compare the areas of the three regions A, B, and C in the sketch.

If the regions can be cut out, then it is fairly easy to compare regions B and C by placing one on top of the other. It is more difficult to compare either B or C with A. Not until children have some idea of conservation of area, especially that one can cut a region and rearrange it without changing the area, can this be a meaningful experience. Thus, the first direct comparisons should be made with two regions, one of which "fits" within the other.

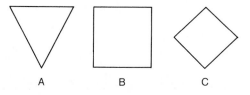

If you cannot move the objects to place one on top of the other, you may want to trace one object and use this representation to make an indirect comparison. For example, to compare the area of a desk to the area of a bulletin board, you could cut a piece of paper the size of the desk and put it on the bulletin board.

To help children understand that regions can be rearranged and not affect the area, many geometry activities would be helpful, such as the shape search on Activity Card 10-2.

Volume. If volume is considered as "how much space a three-dimensional object takes up," then it is difficult to make anything but perceptual comparisons before units are introduced. Thus, volume is an attribute to which not too much attention should be paid until grade 4 or 5. However, since there is a close connection between volume and capacity, some background will be obtained if containers are filled with nonliquids, such as blocks, balls, or other objects.

Temperature. We can certainly sense great differences in temperatures. Before introducing thermometers, we can have children compare to see which of two objects is colder (or hotter). We can also talk about things (or times) that are hot or cold; however, there are few other comparisons we can make without an instrument to help.

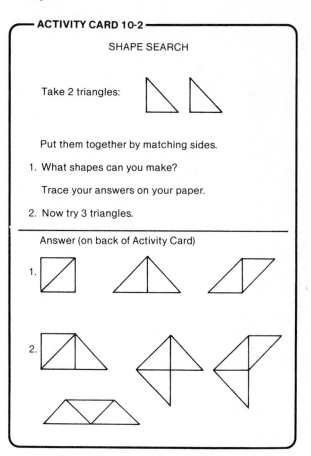

Time. There are two attributes of events that can be measured, *time of occurrence* and *length of duration*. We can begin describing the time of occurrence by giving a time span: it happened today, in the morning, in October. Thus, we need to develop the vocabulary of days, months, and periods of the days with young children.

We can tell which of two events takes longer (duration) if their lengths are greatly different. Does it take longer to brush your teeth or read this chapter?

If the events are closer in duration, we can tell which lasts longer if they both begin at the same time (note the similarity to deciding which object is longer when both are placed on a baseline). You can think of many contests that use this idea: whose paper plane flew longer, whose eyes were shut longer, who hopped longer.

Units of Measure

If we want to answer the question, "How long is the pencil?" we can say, "It's longer than my thumb" or "It's shorter than my arm." These are relative statements that place a range of possibilities on the length but do not do a very accurate job of describing it. To be accurate, we need to compare the pencil to a unit. We can use an arbitrary unit such as a paper clip and say that the pencil is seven paper clips long, or we can use a standard unit and say it is 16 centimeters long. Once we have described the length, we can compare it to other lengths. That is, we will use the symbolic description to assist us in indirectly comparing. The unit of measurement gives us much power; we can communicate with others and we can make many comparisons that were previously difficult to make.

The unit of measurement is one of the most important aspects of measurement. Research results from the national assessment show that children do have some knowledge of units and can apply "this knowledge in simple tasks, but appear to abandon this knowledge in more complex settings" (3, p. 42). For example, over three-fourths of nine-year-olds could find the volume of the rectangular solid as shown here. When the solid was more complicated, they counted the faces of the cubes that were visible.

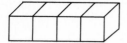

There are many concepts related to the unit of measurement that we need to help children develop. These, with examples of activities to help develop them, are discussed next.

Concepts Related to Units. The concepts described here are developed over time. A single activity will not suffice; you need to be aware of the concepts, include similar activities with other attributes, and look for opportunities within any measurement activity to further the development.

1. *A measurement must include both a number and the unit.* How many times do you remember a teacher telling you to be certain to write inches? And how many times did you not see the necessity—probably because on the whole page you were measuring in inches?

If we begin by having children measure the same object with many different arbitrary units, research indicates that they are more likely to see the need to include the unit. Having children measure the length of a book with paper strips, erasers, and cubes or weigh an object with washers, pennies, or paper clips is the type of task that will encourage younger children to write (or draw) the unit.

2. *Two measurements may be easily compared if the same unit is used.* Young children often rely only on the number or possibly only on the unit to make a comparison. Thus, if one pencil is 6 paper clips long and another pencil is 2 strips long, the child will say that the one that is 6 is longer. They have not yet reached the

---

┌─ LESSON CARD 10-4 ─

Length-Units

Measure. Use given unit.
1. length of desk - erasers
2. height of door - your shoe
3. distance around globe - chains
4. cabinet drawer - paper clips
5. wastebasket height - hands
6. distance across room - book

How long were they?
1. 15 erasers   5. 18 hands
2. 10 shoes   6. 36 books
3. 8 chains   7. . . .
4. 32 paper clips

Which is longest? shortest?

Discuss which is longer—for example, the cabinet drawer or the distance around the globe. Settle by measuring each with the same unit.

stage where they can coordinate the number with unit. If they are at the stage where they just fail to see the necessity, then activities such as the one on Lesson Card 10-4 should help.

3. *One unit may be more appropriate than another to measure an object.* The size of the unit chosen depends upon the size of the object and upon the degree of accuracy desired. If children are allowed to choose the unit, the idea of the unit's size depending upon the size of the object will be clearer. See Activity Card 10-3 for an example of this type of activity.

4. *There is an inverse relationship between the number of units and the size of the unit.* When measuring the same object with different units, children soon realize that the larger the unit, the fewer are required. For example, you could have each child weigh a different object with pennies, washers, and cubes. If each child made a graph of the results, a pattern would soon be apparent when comparing all the graphs.

5. *Standard units are needed to communicate effectively.* Many concepts about units can be well developed with arbitrary units. At the same time you will be teaching procedures of measuring with units (how to line up units, use a balance, cover a region, keep track of how many, and so on).

At some point, depending upon the attribute, you want to begin using standard units. Standard units are either customary (inch, pint, pound, etc.) or metric (meter, gram, liter, etc.). Children have already heard of standard units but may not realize why we use them.

Stories about difficulty in communicating sizes when there is no standard of measurement are one way to present the necessity of a standard unit. Another way is to have children make a recipe of Kool-Aid, using a very "large cup" for the water and a very "small spoon" for the sugar. (Be sure to have enough Kool-Aid and sugar to "doctor" it up so they can then drink it afterward.)

6. *A smaller unit will give a more exact measurement.* First, children need to realize that all measurements are approximate. If you have had them do a lot of measuring of real objects, they will have been reporting approximate measurements but perhaps without being fully aware of it. A practice of saying "about 6 inches," "more than 6 inches," or "between 6 and 7 inches" will help.

To set up the need for a more precise measurement, give each of two children, sitting far apart, a paper strip between 2 and 3 decimeters (say, 26 and 27 centimeters) and decimeter strips. Have each measure the

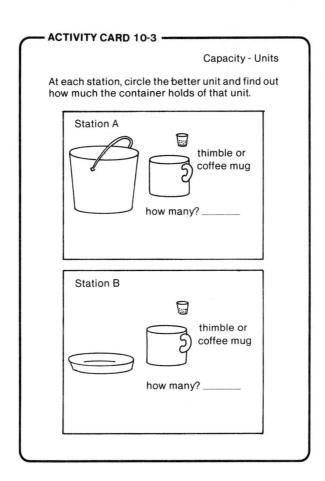

ACTIVITY CARD 10-3

Capacity - Units

At each station, circle the better unit and find out how much the container holds of that unit.

Station A

thimble or coffee mug

how many? _____

Station B

thimble or coffee mug

how many? _____

strip and tell its length in decimeters. Then ask the class which strip is longer (no fair comparing the strips directly). Next, have them measure with centimeters. Discuss with the class why a smaller unit was needed.

How to Introduce Units. As we noted earlier, many concepts can be developed while using arbitrary units. How then do you introduce arbitrary units?

Length is the first attribute that children measure. In order to do this, they take a unit and copies of that unit and put them end to end until the units are as long as the object they are measuring. From previous direct comparing of two objects, they should know when the lengths are the same. However, they have not lined up the units in a straight line with no gaps in between or no overlaps, nor have they counted the units. Units that connect, such as Unifix cubes or Lots-a-Links, are good to begin with because they are easy to handle and "line up" easily without gaps or overlaps.

After an example or two, you need only set up objects to be measured and supply the units and then let children proceed under your guidance. Later, children can take one unit and move it (iteration). This is a more advanced skill, one that is needed for proper use of a ruler when measuring objects longer than the ruler. It is a skill that should not be pushed too early. If you find children who cannot move, mark, and count, postpone this until later.

If children have been measuring with arbitrary units, then the move to using standard units should be easy. They will have much understanding about the process of measuring, so the purpose now should be to give them a feel for the standard unit. Let us take the decimeter as an example and consider some ways to build the feel for it as a standard unit.

Give each child a paper strip (say, of index card) that is 10 cm by 2 cm. Do a variety of activities that have the children compare things to the decimeter strip. Some are suggested here.

Decimeter List-Up. Put a list on the board of objects children find in the room that are the same length as a decimeter. Be sure to include things on them such as fingers, pockets, soles of shoes.

Decimeter Hold-Up. Pair the children and have one child try to hold two forefingers a decimeter apart, vertically, horizontally, and obliquely. The partner should check each time; then roles should be reversed.

Decimeter Stack-Up. Set up stations with pennies, chips, clips, beans, cubes, and the like. At one chip station the children should try to stack the chips a decimeter high. At another chip station they should try to make a line of chips a decimeter long. Then they should use their decimeter strip to see how close they were.

After the children are somewhat familiar with the decimeter, have them measure with decimeters. This is a good time to have them estimate the length of objects and then check. As children are measuring with the strips, they (and you) should notice that putting down strip after strip is not the easiest way to measure. Have them tape their strips together, end to end, alternating colors if two colors are available. Now they have a "decimeter ruler," except they still have to count the units. After they have done some counting, see if anyone will suggest numbering the strips. This will help children understand how rulers are made and that we are counting units.

When children are familiar with the decimeter, have them measure something very long. Have each child make a 10-decimeter ruler. Tell the children that this unit is called a meter and is used to measure longer distances. Then, have them become familiar with meters through activities similar to those suggested with decimeters. The new unit should be related to ones they have used; this will help the children understand the new unit as well as assist in conversions from one unit to another.

Children become familiar with standard units through comparing, measuring, estimating, and constructing. The experiences you provide should include all these processes.

It is important that not too many standard units are introduced at one time, that the unit is not too small or too large for a child of that age to handle, and that the numbers generated are not too large. Table 10-1 is a

TABLE 10-1

Attribute	Metric Units	Customary Units
Length	Decimeter (1–2)*	Inch (1–2)
	Centimeter (2–3)	Foot (2–3)
	Meter (2–3)	Yard (2–3)
	Millimeter (3–4)	Mile (4–5)
Weight	Kilogram (2–3)	Ounce (2–3)
	Gram (4–5)	Pound (2–3)
Capacity	Liter (1–2)	Quart (2–3)
	Milliliter (4–5)	Cup (1–2)
		Gallon (2–3)
Area	Square centimeter (4–5)	Square inch (4–5)
	Square meter (5–6)	Square foot (4–5)
		Square yard (4–5)
Volume	Cubic centimeter (5–6)	Cubic inch (5–6)
	Cubic meter (5–6)	Cubic foot (5–6)
		Cubic yard (5–6)
Temperature	Celsius degree (2–3)	Degree Fahrenheit (2–3)
Time		Hour (1–2)
		Minute (1–2)
		Second (3–4)
		Day (K–1)
		Week (1–2)
		Month (K–1)

*Approximate grade level.

guide to the most common standard units used in elementary school and the approximate grade levels at which it would be appropriate to introduce them.

Instruments

There are some attributes that instruments are used to measure. In elementary school the more common instruments are rulers, scales, graduated containers, thermometers, protractors, and clocks. Other attributes (such as area and volume) are assigned a measurement by the use of a formula after an instrument has been used to measure some dimensions. Still other attributes are derived from measurements of more than one attribute (e.g., speed is derived from distance and time).

Much of the emphasis in the elementary curriculum is on instruments and formulas, and children encounter difficulty with both. One probable source of difficulty is that the children do not understand what they are measuring and what it means to measure. The activities and suggestions we have presented thus far have dealt with building this understanding. Here we will look at some common problems children have with particular instruments and ways to assist in developing the correct skills.

Ruler. A ruler will automatically count the number of units if we realize what unit we are using and if we line up the ruler properly. To help children realize the unit being used, it is beneficial for them to be familiar with it and for the scale on the ruler to have only that unit. That is, if the unit is centimeters, then choose a ruler marked in centimeters, not in centimeters and millimeters. Or if the unit is inches, then choose a ruler without the markings of fourths or eighths. At the bottom of this page is an exercise similar to the one from national assessment (2, p. 90). What do you think was the most common answer of nine-year-olds? Yes, 77 percent said the segment was 5 inches. Forty percent of the 13-year-olds also gave this response. Children must be helped to see that the 1 on a ruler means that one unit has already been used. How would you help a child who was making this error? Remember the direct comparing? You could also use separate units, or just mark the inches on the segment and count.

It is important that children measure real objects with the ruler. Make certain that you assess the children's ability before you give them objects longer than one ruler. Can they move the ruler (iterate), and do they have the addition skills to add the units? For example, suppose the children have a 25-cm ruler and they are to measure something that is 43 cm long. Can they add 25 and 18? Of course, they could use counting or techniques that rely on their place value and counting background: 25, 35, 36, 37, . . . , 43.

You should also be aware that children may have difficulty in measuring to the nearest fourth, eighth, or sixteenth of a unit. Forty-seven percent of the 13-year-olds had difficulty measuring to the nearest one-fourth inch (2, p. 89). What causes this difficulty? It may be the smallness of the unit (there is more room for error), but the difficulty probably stems from their lack of confidence and understanding of fractions, their lack of understanding of the unit (they are now measuring in fourths), and their lack of consciousness of how to measure to the nearest unit. Up to now in measuring to a unit they have been able to tell just by looking what unit is nearer. The example in Figure 10-1 gives you some idea of how to make this process more explicit. It will also be helpful to emphasize the units by asking: "What two units is it between, two-fourths and three-fourths or three-fourths and four-fourths?" Children must be able to answer this before deciding which it is nearer. This is why a firm foundation of fractions, and especially fractions as they relate to length, will help with measuring to the nearest unit.

Although we have concentrated on the problems, do not be discouraged. Children love to use rulers, and overall they do quite well with them. Make certain you have children not only measuring objects but also constructing line segments or objects of given length.

Scaled Instruments. Instruments such as bathroom scales, graduated cylinders, and thermometers cause children some trouble because each unit is not marked. On the second national assessment, only 12 percent of nine-year-olds and 46 percent of 13-year-olds could read a thermometer (2, p. 93). The difficulty was caused by each mark's representing 2 degrees.

One way to help children become more aware of the markings on a scale is to give and read with them many scales with different markings, but a more powerful way is to have them make their own instruments. They can make graphs, for example, using different scales (see Chapter 14), or they can mark their own graduated cylinders. Activity Card 10-4 gives children

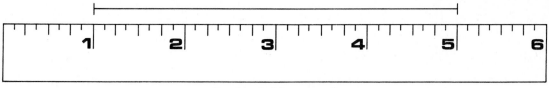

How long is this segment?

instructions on how to make the "cylinder." After they have made it, have them measure the amounts other containers hold. Note that this activity also is good practice in finding multiples of a number.

Clocks. The ordinary dial clock or watch is one of the most complicated instruments to read and yet often one of the first to be taught. Not only are there two or more ways to read the scale on it (hour, minute, and second), but it moves in a circular fashion. Children appear ready to learn how to tell time at no set age; you will often notice a wide variety of ability within a class. The following is a suggested list of skills needed in telling time:

1. Identify the hour hand and the minute hand and the direction they move.
2. Orally tell time by the hour (noting that the minute hand is on the 12) and moving the hands of a clock to show those times.
3. Identify the hour that a time is "after" (e.g., it's after 4).
4. Count by fives.
5. Tell time to the nearest 5 minutes and report it orally (e.g., as 4 o'clock and 20 minutes after).
6. Write the time in digital notation (4:20).
7. Count on from multiples of five (e.g., 25, 26, 27).
8. Tell time to the nearest minute and write time in digital notation.
9. Match the time on a digital clock to a regular clock.
10. Identify the hour that a time is "before" (e.g., it's before 10) and count by fives to tell about how many minutes before the hour.

These skills need to be developed over a long period of time, and children need to have clocks with movable hands. To give you some idea of what nine-year-olds, in general, are able to do, let's examine the results of the national assessment (2, p. 92): "Ninety-three percent could tell time on the hour, 86 percent could tell time at 15 minute intervals (e.g., 8:15, 6:45), 69 percent could tell time at 5 minute intervals (e.g., 6:25, 11:55), and 59 percent could tell time at one minute intervals (e.g., 2:53)." While nine-year-olds were at this level in telling time, "only about one-third could solve problems involving time such as telling the time 8 hours after a given time."

You can begin problem solving very early if children have clocks or watches to help them. For example, as soon as children can tell time on the hour, you can ask questions such as, "What time will it be in 2 hours?" As the children become more familiar with the clock, you can give more challenging questions, such as those on the worksheet in Activity Card 10-5.

Reading digital clocks is easier than reading regular clocks; however, solving the types of problems just given is more difficult with a digital clock. Do you see why? In learning to read a regular clock, a child learns the relationship of the minutes and hours and has a model to use in solving such problems. Thus, if all clocks were to become digital, we would need to spend less time on reading time but more on how our time system works.

Formulas

Formulas for area, perimeter, volume, and surface area are usually introduced in the upper grades. While formulas are necessary and useful tools for measuring, they should not take the place of careful development of the attributes and the measuring process. One skill that needs to be developed is that of using formulas—but not at the expense of helping students see how formulas are derived. The main emphasis in this section will be on ways to build meaning of the area formulas. The formulas for the other attributes may be developed similarly.

Before developing formulas, students should be given the opportunity to compare regions on area with and without units. We have already discussed comparing areas without the aid of units by placing one region on top of the other and by cutting one region in order to make the comparison.

In being introduced to units of area, the students should experience covering the region with a variety of types of units—squares, triangles, rectangles. At this stage they would count the number of units as well as learn that square units are the standard shape used in area. Many different shapes can be covered to help students see the need to approximate and to use smaller units. In the accompanying sketch a region was first covered by one size of squares and then by smaller squares.

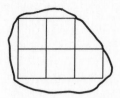 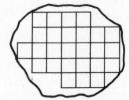

When students are thoroughly familiar with covering with and counting units of many shapes and especially of rectangles, it is time to introduce the formula for area of a rectangle. We will examine steps to develop this formula and then show how to use it to develop the formulas for parallelograms, triangles, trapezoids, and other figures. After learning how to use these formulas, children should be given exercises such as those on Activity Card 10-6 in which they have to combine formulas.

ACTIVITY CARD 10-5

HOW TIME FLIES!

Name_____

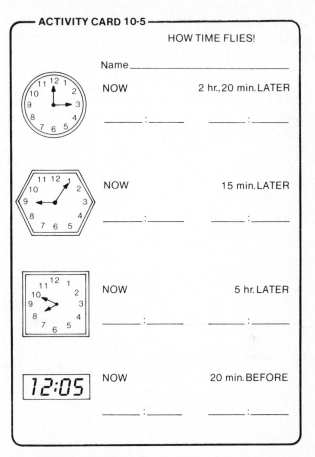

NOW	2 hr., 20 min. LATER
____:____	____:____

NOW	15 min. LATER
____:____	____:____

NOW	5 hr. LATER
____:____	____:____

12:05 NOW 20 min. BEFORE

____:____   ____:____

ACTIVITY CARD 10-4

Make Your Own Measure

Materials: Large glass, spoon, small container, masking tape, water, felt-tip pen

Directions:
1. Put a piece of tape on the side of the glass as shown below.
2. Fill the small container with spoonfuls. Count how many it takes. Empty it into the glass. Mark the level of the water and the number of spoonfuls.

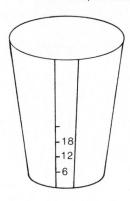

3. Fill the small container again. Empty into glass and mark.

4. Continue to the top.

Now you have your own measure. Use it to see how much other containers hold.

ACTIVITY CARD 10-6

AREAS, AREAS, AREAS

Find the area of each of these. Do not forget that you can find a part at a time.

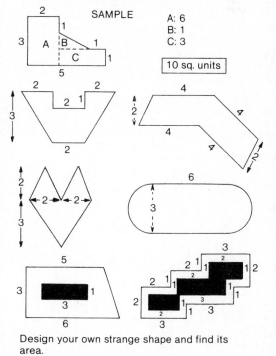

SAMPLE

A: 6
B: 1
C: 3

10 sq. units

Design your own strange shape and find its area.

Rectangle. The formula for the area of a rectangle is often the first formula children meet. This is appropriate because it can be developed easily, building upon models that children may have used for multiplication.

You will note in the series of suggested steps (see Figure 10-2) that the formula $A = b \times a$ is being developed (A is area, b is base, and a is altitude). This form of the formula generalizes better than $A = l \times w$; do you see in the opening lesson how the length-and-width interpretation led to initial confusion with the trapezoidal table? Children need to look at a rectangle in both ways, so that the intuitive development is begun with length and width, but before the formula is introduced the shift is made to base and altitude.

While some of these steps could be combined into a single lesson, it is suggested that Step 3 not be done until the objectives in Step 1 are secure. A problem may arise when children are doing Step 7 if they have not had prior experience in covering real objects. When they measure, the base and altitude will not be an exact number of units. You may have them estimate how many more squares it would take to cover this. Later you can develop the idea of using smaller units or fractional parts of the unit.

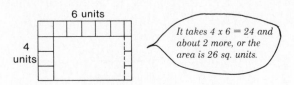

Figure 10-2. Suggested sequence for area formula of a rectangle.

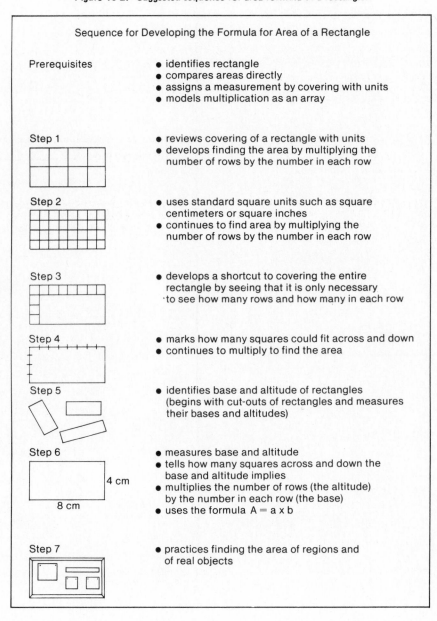

One difficulty that children often have with area of a rectangle is learning rotely that the area is the length times the width (or base times altitude) and not developing the underlying concepts. Thus, when they are faced with finding the area of a square, they run into difficulty (it has no longer side!). The results of the national assessment showed that 13-year-olds' performance dropped from 51 percent correct for rectangles to 12 percent correct for squares (2, p. 95).

Parallelogram. Once the area formula for a rectangle has been mastered, the area formula for a parallelogram can be developed. Children need background in geometric experiences in which they have compared parallelograms with rectangles and have tried to cut the parallelograms to rearrange them into rectangles. Then, they should identify the base and altitude of parallelograms. Note that any side can be designated as a base, and the altitude depends on what side was chosen.

Next, develop the relationship of the area of a parallelogram with base b and altitude a and the corresponding rectangle. From exercises such as Activity Card 10-7, children should see the area of a parallelogram is the same as the corresponding rectangle, $A = b \times a$.

Triangle. From this point the area of a triangle can be developed from the realization that a triangle is always half of a parallelogram. This development depends upon a strong background of geometry, experiences like those described in Chapter 15, and activities such as Activity Card 10-8. Even when students see that the area of a triangle is half that of a corresponding parallelogram or $A = \frac{1}{2}(b \times a)$, they have difficulty identifying the altitude, especially in triangles like E.

Trapezoid. There are many ways to develop the formula for the area of a trapezoid. One of the easiest is to rely again on the area of a parallelogram.

Find the area of this trapezoid.

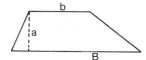

Take a copy of the trapezoid and place it like this.

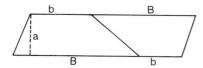

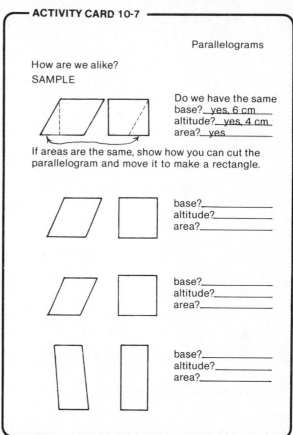

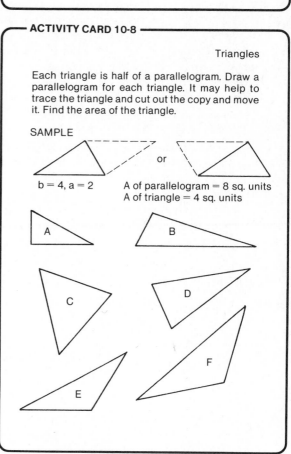

What figure have you formed? [A parallelogram.]
What is its base? [$B + b$]
What is its altitude? [a]
What is its area? [$A = a(B + b)$]
How does the area of the trapezoid compare to the area of the parallelogram? [Half as much]
Therefore, area of trapezoid $= \frac{1}{2}a(B + b)$.

Circle. The circle is the one common geometric figure whose area is not related to the previous procedures. Students can be convinced the formula is logical by cutting it into segments and rearranging them to form a parallelogram, as shown below. This depends upon their knowledge of the circumference being $2\pi r$.

cut and arrange

the length of the "parallelogram" is half of the circumference or πr

the altitude is the radius, r, of the circle.

$A = (\pi r) r$ or
$A = \pi r^2$

Equivalences and Conversions

After making a measurement, we often use it to solve a problem involving a comparison or an arithmetic operation. In so doing, we may need to change from one unit to another (conversion), which relies upon the equivalence relation of the two units. In this section we will examine equivalences and conversions within either the customary or the metric system. It is not recommended that you teach conversions between systems, such as from inches to centimeters.

Equivalences. As you introduce new standard units you should relate them to the others. For example, suppose you are introducing a millimeter; you should relate it to a centimeter by showing it is smaller and it is one-tenth of a centimeter.

After using different units and being given the equivalences, there comes a point at which you expect children to know certain equivalences. Some of these, such as 7 days = 1 week, 60 minutes = 1 hour, and 12 inches = 1 foot, will become known through repeated use. Children need to know that they are expected to know other equivalences. There was a time when we required children to memorize long tables of equivalences. This is no longer the case; those which you expect to be memorized should be ones that are commonly used. When we change to the metric system, this task will become easier because of the standard prefixes and tens relationship between units. Table 10-2 summarizes this relationship and gives the most commonly used metric units.

Since not all equivalences will be memorized, children must become familiar with using a table of equivalences. You will need to help them develop the different skills related to a table. The table and questions that follow illustrate these skills.

$$1 \text{ day} = 24 \text{ hours}$$
$$1 \text{ hour} = 60 \text{ minutes}$$
$$\text{minute} = 60 \text{ seconds}$$

How many hours in a day? (This is a straightforward reading.) What part of a day is 1 hour? (This involves knowledge of fractional relations.) How many seconds in an hour? (This involves a conversion.)

Area and volume equivalences can be difficult for children because they often are derived from the linear equivalences. From knowing that 1 m = 10 dm, we can derive that $1 \text{ m}^2 = 100 \text{ dm}^2$ and $1 \text{ m}^3 = 1000 \text{ dm}^3$. Children need experiences in seeing these basic relationships through models, drawings, and questions such as on Lesson Card 10-5.

Conversions. To change from one unit to another, you must know the relation between the two units. However, this is not sufficient. Let us look at an example of a class discussion.

Mr. Bane: "It seems that several of you are stumped on the assignment. Devon, please read the first exercise and let's look at it together."

Devon: "Blank dm equals 5 m."

The teacher writes on the board: _____ dm = 5 m.

Mr. Bane: "Can you tell me what we are looking for?"

TABLE 10-2

	10 kilo (k)	10 hecto (h)	10 decka (da)	Base unit	10 deci (d)	10 centi (c)	10 milli (m)
Length	kilometer (km)			meter (m)		centimeter (cm)	millimeter (mm)
Capacity				liter (l)			milliliter (ml)
Mass	kilogram (kg)			gram (g)			

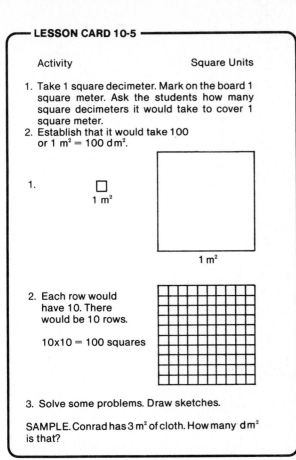

LESSON CARD 10-5

Activity   Square Units

1. Take 1 square decimeter. Mark on the board 1 square meter. Ask the students how many square decimeters it would take to cover 1 square meter.
2. Establish that it would take 100 or 1 m² = 100 dm².

1.   □
      1 m²

                          1 m²

2. Each row would have 10. There would be 10 rows.

   10 x 10 = 100 squares

3. Solve some problems. Draw sketches.

SAMPLE. Conrad has 3 m² of cloth. How many dm² is that?

George: "How many decimeters there are in 5 meters."

Mr. Bane: "What do you know about decimeters and meters?"

Alana: "A decimeter is about this big and a meter is about this big."

Mr. Bane: "That's right. Could everyone see Alana's hands? Which unit is larger, the meter or the decimeter? . . . Right, so will it take more than 5 decimeters or less than 5 to make 5 meters?"

Melinda: "It'll take more. It takes 10 decimeters to make 1 meter."

Mr. Bane draws this on the board:

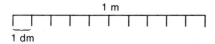

                    1 m

   1 dm

Mr. Bane: "If 1 meter is 10 decimeters, then what would 5 meters be?"

Devon: "I see, it's 5 groups of the 10 decimeters or 50 decimeters."

Mr. Bane: "Good. Let's try one more. 20 cm = _____ dm."

Carl: "Centimeters are smaller, they take more; so it won't be as many as 20 dm."

Mr. Bane: "Good. We know our answer must be less than 20."

Randy: "Let's draw a picture like this. Oh, there's no use drawing in all 20 marks. We know 10 cm makes 1 dm. So we want to know how many tens in 20."

Mr. Bane: "Right, in this case we can just look at the picture and see that it is 2 decimeters. But what if it was 184 centimeters?"

Dave: "We still need to know how many tens in 184—we divide."

Jim: "There are 18 decimeters."

Mr. Bane: "What about the 4 left over?"

Paula: "Those are centimeters. We have 18 full decimeters and 4 left-over centimeters."

Mr. Bane: "Let's write that down. 184 cm = 18 dm 4 cm. OK. Try some on your own and I'll help you if you have questions."

This discussion, although not an initial presentation to the class, points out many good techniques to use in developing conversions. First, Mr. Bane had the children decide whether their answer would be larger or smaller than the other number. This relied on the children's knowing the relative sizes of the units and their understanding that the smaller the unit, the more it takes. Second, Mr. Bane tried to have the children visualize the relationship between the units. Third, he related the operation to be used to their understanding of what multiplication and division mean.

If one is doing a lot of metric conversions, there are shortcuts. These depend upon the facility to multiply and divide by powers of ten. (See Chapter 13 on estimation.) These shortcuts are helpful but should not replace a careful building of the process.

Estimation

Estimating is the mental process of arriving at a measurement without the aid of measurement instruments. There are many reasons to include estimating in the curriculum. It helps to reinforce the size of units and the relationships among units. It is a practical application; think of all the times you want to know approximately how long, how heavy, or how much something holds.

There are two main types of estimation. In the most common type, the attribute and object are named and the measurement is unknown. For example, how long is your arm? In the other type, the measurement is known and the object is to be chosen. For example, what piece of furniture in your room is about 1 meter long? By keeping the two classes of estimation in mind, you will be able to expand your repertoire of estimation activities. The strategies that are described next can be used in either kind of estimation.

Several strategies are commonly used in making estimations. You can help children develop these strategies by talking through the different ways that different children use to make an estimation and by presenting these strategies.

One strategy is to compare to a *referent*. If you know that you are 1 m 70 cm tall, then you can estimate the height of a child who comes up to your waist. Or, if you have to choose a board that is 2 m long, you will have some idea of the size. Can you think of other times when you use a referent?

Another strategy is that of *chunking* (12, p. 62). In this process you break the object into subparts and estimate each part. For example, you want to know about how far you walked from your room to the library and store and then back to your room. If you know that from your room to the library is about $\frac{1}{2}$ mile, that it's about that same distance from the library to the store, and twice as far from the store back to your room, you walked about 2 miles.

A refinement of chunking is that of *unitizing*. In this case you estimate one part and see how many parts are in the whole. For example, someone asks you to cut a string that is about 3 meters long. You estimate 1 meter and take 3 of these. This is a good strategy to emphasize when you are teaching multiplication, since it provides an application of multiplication.

How can you include estimating in your program? First, it should be a natural part of many measurement activities. Children should be encouraged to see if they can tell about how long, heavy, etc. the object they are going to measure is. Second, look for ways to include

Figure 10-3. Ideas for estimation.

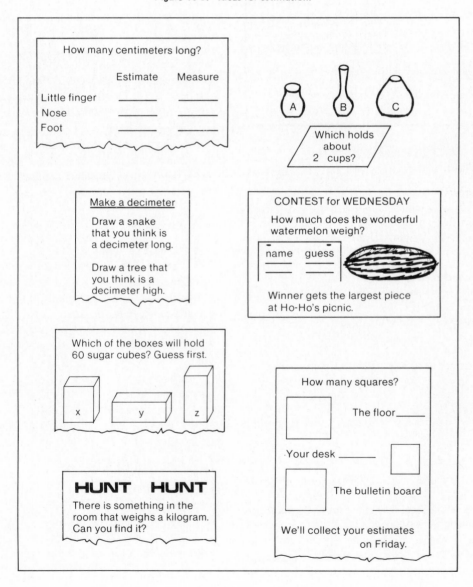

estimation in other subject areas. About how far did you jump? What size of paper do you need? About how long did it take you? Third, plan estimating activities for their own sake or use brief ones as daily openers for several weeks throughout the year.

The activities in Figure 10-3 give some ideas to get you started. Once you begin thinking about the things in your room, you will be able to come up with a lot of variations. One thing to remember: do not mark an estimation as right or wrong. Help children develop ways to make better estimates (the strategies and practice will help), but do not discourage them. Let them check their estimates by measuring. They will know whether they were close or not. You may be surprised to find out who are the good estimators in your class.

Relationships Between Attributes

Activities involving two attributes can help children see how the attributes are related or how one attribute is not dependent upon the other. For example, by doubling the dimensions of a rectangle, children may see how the area is changed. By examining figures with the same area but different shape, children may see that area is independent of shape. We have included sample activities with suggestions of other variations or extensions. If you do not know the answer, you will be able to find it by doing the activity.

Area and Shape. Use Activity Card 10-9 to have children (grades 2-4) investigate what different shapes they can make using two to four squares. For older children, you can extend this activity to more squares and place the restrictions that the squares must have touching sides (not corners) and that two shapes are the same if one is a reflection or rotation (see Chapter 15) of the other. A variation is to use triangular paper rather than the square. You can also have children look at figures with the same shapes but different areas.

Volume and Shape. An activity such as the one on Activity Card 10-9 could be done with cubes. Activity Card 10-10 not only has older children (grades 6–8) examine different shapes with constant volume, but also ties the investigation to number theory (primes and composites).

Perimeter and Area. There is often much confusion between perimeter and area. This is due partly to a lack of understanding of area and to premature introduction of the formulas. There are many activities that can help children see that a figure with a given perimeter may have many different areas. One is found on Activity Card 10-11. Activity Card 10-13 touches on this activity. Children should also realize that figures with the same area can have different perimeters. You could modify Activity Card 10-11 for older children by asking them to find the perimeter of each of the shapes or by challeng-

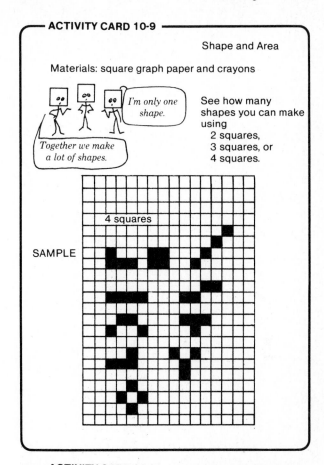

ACTIVITY CARD 10-9

Shape and Area

Materials: square graph paper and crayons

I'm only one shape.

Together we make a lot of shapes.

See how many shapes you can make using
2 squares,
3 squares, or
4 squares.

4 squares

SAMPLE

ACTIVITY CARD 10-10

Shape and Volume

Materials: cm cubes (or sugar cubes)

Take 12 cubes. See how many different rectangular solids you can make. Record the dimensions of each.

Now try some of these:
7, 9, 16, 11, 13, 18, 15 cubes

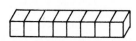

I'm 8 cubes
8 by 1 by 1

I'm 8 cubes
2 by 2 by 2

How many different solids can you make if the number of cubes is prime? _____

a product of two primes? _____

a perfect square? _____

How many solids can you make with 24 cubes? _____ Try it!

ACTIVITY CARD 10-11

Perimeter and Area

Materials: string, ruler, cm graph paper, stick pins.

Cut a string 14 cm long:

How many different rectangles can you make with a perimeter of 14 cm? Keep the sides a whole number of cm. Find the area of each.

Here is one. There are others.

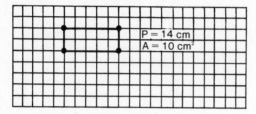

P = 14 cm
A = 10 cm²

Now try 20 cm.

What about 13 cm?

---

ing them to take five squares and see what shape they can make that has the largest perimeter or the smallest perimeter.

Volume and Surface Area. Just as the area of a figure does not depend entirely on the perimeter, the volume does not depend solely on the surface area. The experiment on Activity Card 10-12 looks at the relation of the lateral surface area to the volume. You can vary this by having children fold the papers into thirds (sixths) both ways or make cylinders (a long, thin one and a short, fat one).

In junior high, after the formula for rectangular solid has been developed, you could have the children calculate the volume of each of the tubes on Activity Card 10-12.

Perimeter and Dimensions. On Activity Card 10-13 the pattern that emerges relating the length of each side to the number of sides is expected, but the pattern of the number of sides and the height might be unexpected.

Metric Relations. Activity Card 10-14 helps the children find some of the important relationships among different metric units. These relationships make the metric system convenient to use, since it gives an easy translation from solid measures to liquid measures.

ACTIVITY CARD 10-12

Volume and Surface Area

Materials: 4 sheets of heavy construction paper, masking tape, and solid filler.

Make tubes and tape them as shown:

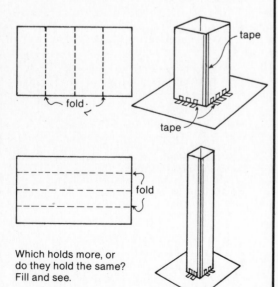

Which holds more, or do they hold the same? Fill and see.

ACTIVITY CARD 10-13

Perimeter and Dimensions

Materials: 6 strips (2 cm by 21 cm) of stiff paper, ruler, scissors, and tape.

Fold one strip into thirds. Make a fence triangle. Tape.

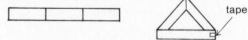

Fold the other strips into fourths, fifths, sixths, sevenths, and eighths. Make fences.

Make a chart and fill it in.

number of sides	length of each side in mm	height (stand it on one side and see how tall)
3	——— mm	——— mm
4		
5		
6		
7		
8		

Which has the largest area?
Which has the smallest area?

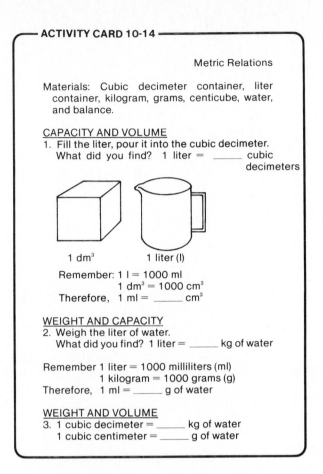

ACTIVITY CARD 10-14

Metric Relations

Materials: Cubic decimeter container, liter container, kilogram, grams, centicube, water, and balance.

CAPACITY AND VOLUME
1. Fill the liter, pour it into the cubic decimeter. What did you find?   1 liter = _____ cubic decimeters

1 dm³   1 liter (l)

Remember: 1 l = 1000 ml
                1 dm³ = 1000 cm³
Therefore, 1 ml = _____ cm³

WEIGHT AND CAPACITY
2. Weigh the liter of water. What did you find?   1 liter = _____ kg of water

Remember 1 liter = 1000 milliliters (ml)
                1 kilogram = 1000 grams (g)
Therefore, 1 ml = _____ g of water

WEIGHT AND VOLUME
3. 1 cubic decimeter = _____ kg of water
    1 cubic centimeter = _____ g of water

examples of how measurement fulfills that reason.

4. You have a child in your class who physically cannot handle a ruler. How would you solve this situation?

5. Describe activities that you could use to introduce a centimeter, a kilogram, a liter, or a square decimeter.

6. Design an activity card that relates a fixed area to varying perimeters.

7. Describe how you would help to convince a child that the triangles shown here have the same area.

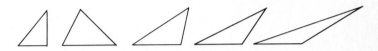

8. Design three task cards for the opening lesson, one of which is an extension for gifted students.

9. There are several problem-solving activities involving measurement throughout the chapter. Find, in books, journals, or elsewhere, at least five more. Categorize them as to grade and attribute.

10. Check the scope-and-sequence chart of a textbook series to see how their introduction of units corresponds to Table 10-1.

11. Try the activity on page 142 with students. What difficulties did they encounter? How did you help them? How would you change the activity?

12. Write a lesson for Step 4 on page 152. How do you think your lesson compares to the one that Wes alluded to in the opening lesson?

13. Examine upper-level textbooks to see how they introduce the formula for the area of a rectangle. Contrast their introduction with the one suggested in this chapter.

14. Design five estimation activities that include both classes of estimation for a grade level of your choice.

15. Try one of the activities in the section on relating attributes with children. Write up your experiences, including whether or not the children could do the activity and whether they gather the point of the activity.

16. Outline a series of steps for developing the volume formula for rectangular solids similar to those for developing the area of a rectangle.

17. Find a model that will help you develop the volume of a pyramid and develop a lesson.

A GLANCE AT WHERE WE'VE BEEN

Measuring is a process that may be used for many attributes. Basically each attribute is measured in the same way, but the unique characteristics of each make the actual steps differ. Most important in these steps is knowing the attribute that is being measured. This chapter has given many suggestions about ways to develop premeasurement ideas by comparing perceptually, directly, and indirectly. These ideas are built upon as children begin to use units. At this point they may assign a number by counting and later by using instruments or by formulas. Other suggested ways to help children learn about measuring are estimating and relating two attributes.

By including measuring in your program, you have the opportunity to show how mathematics is practical, to develop problem-solving skills, to develop other mathematical ideas, to relate mathematics to other topics, and to make mathematics fun for many children.

THINGS TO DO: ADDING TO YOUR PICTURE

1. What are the five steps in the measuring process?
2. What attributes, units, and instruments are found in most elementary programs?
3. Why should you include measurement in your mathematics program? Choose one reason and give

SELECTED REFERENCES

1. Bright, George W. "Estimation as Part of Learning to Measure." In *Measurement in School Mathematics* (ed. Doyal Nelson). Thirty-eighth Yearbook of the National Council of Teachers of Mathematics. Reston, Va.: NCTM, 1976.

2. Carpenter, Thomas P.; Corbitt, Mary Kay; Kepner, Henry S., Jr.; Lindquist, Mary Montgomery; and Reys, Robert E. *Results from the Second Mathematics Assessment of the National Assessment of Educational Progress.* Reston, Va.: National Council of Teachers of Mathematics, 1981.

3. Hiebert, James. "Units of Measure: Results and Implications from National Assessment." *Arithmetic Teacher,* 28 (February 1981), pp. 38–43.

4. Hirstein, James J.; Lamb, Charles E.; and Osborne, Alan. "Student Misconceptions about Area Measure." *Arithmetic Teacher,* 25 (March 1978), pp. 10–16.

5. Hirstein, James J. "The Second National Assessment in Mathematics: Area and Volume." *Mathematics Teacher,* 74 (December 1981), pp. 704–708.

6. Inskeep, James E., Jr. "Teaching Measurement to Elementary School Children." In *Measurement in School Mathematics* (ed. Doyal Nelson). Thirty-eighth Yearbook of the National Council of Teachers of Mathematics. Reston, Va.: NCTM, 1976.

7. Leutzinger, Larry P., and Nelson, Glenn. "Meaningful Measurements." *Arithmetic Teacher,* 27 (March 1980), pp. 6–11.

8. Lindquist, Mary Montgomery, and Dana, Marcia E. "The Neglected Decimeter." *Arithmetic Teacher,* 25 (October 1977), pp. 10–17.

9. Lindquist, Mary Montgomery, and Dana, Marcia E. "Measurement for the Times." *Arithmetic Teacher,* 26 (April 1978), pp. 4–9.

10. Montgomery, Mary E. "The Interaction of Three Levels of Aptitude Determined by a Teach-Test Procedure with Two Treatments Related to Area." *Journal for Research in Mathematics Education,* 4 (November 1973), pp. 271–278.

11. O'Daffer, Phares G., and Clemens, Stanley R. *Geometry: An Investigative Approach.* Boston: Addison-Wesley, 1976.

12. Osborne, Alan. "Measurement: How Much?" In *Selected Issues in Mathematics Education* (ed. Mary Montgomery Lindquist). Berkeley, Calif.: McCutchan Publishing Corp., 1980.

13. Romberg, Thomas A.; Harvey, John G.; Moser, James M.; and Montgomery, Mary E. *Developing Mathematical Processes* (DMP). Chicago: Rand McNally, 1971–1976.

14. Thomas, Diane. "Geometry in the Middle Schools: Problem Solving with Trapezoids." *Arithmetic Teacher,* 26 (February 1979), pp. 20–21.

11

Developing Fractions and Decimals

———— SNAPSHOT OF A LESSON ————

A fifth-grade class has reviewed ways to model fractions given the whole. When we join the class, the teacher is making the transition from the review to the lesson for today, in which a fractional part of a whole is given and the whole must be constructed.

Mrs. Benson: "Good, you know a lot about fractions. Today, we are really going to test our brains. You found that it is pretty easy to show a fractional part of a whole. What if I give you a fractional part and you have to show me the whole?"

Justin: "I'm not certain what you mean."

Mrs. Benson: "Well, if I told you that this picture represents three-fifths of a cake, could you draw the whole cake?"

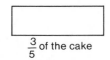

$\frac{3}{5}$ of the cake

Rosa Lee: "It sure would be a skinny cake."

Camille: "That depends upon how the two-fifths was cut off."

Mrs. Benson: "You are both right; you won't be able to tell exactly what the shape of the cake was before it was cut unless I tell you where it was cut. Let's pretend you can see that it was cut right here. [Pointing to the right side.] What do you know?"

Gilbert: "You have three of the five equal pieces. If we divide this into three equal parts, we know how large one-fifth is."

Mrs. Benson: "Let's do that. Who can tell me how to finish the problem?"

$\frac{3}{5}$ of the cake

Olav: "All you have to do now is add the missing two-fifths. Rosa Lee, you are right, it is a skinny cake. It would look like this." [Coming to the board he draws two more parts.]

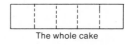

The whole cake

Mrs. Benson: "How about another one? I have two-sevenths of a piece of licorice. How long was the licorice to begin with? Each of you draw a small line segment and label it two-sevenths."

Justin: "Does it matter how long that is?"

Mrs. Benson: "No, Justin, but we'll each be doing a slightly different problem. How long did you draw yours?"

Justin: "About five centimeters."

Mrs. Benson: "Do each one of you have a picture something like this?"

$\frac{2}{7}$ of the licorice

"What do you do then?"

Winifred: "That must be two of the seven parts, so one part would be about this long (holding up her fingers). Now, we need seven of those."

Mrs. Benson: "Has everyone drawn the licorice stick?... Now, what if I know that three-fifths of the candy in a box was 12 pieces, how many pieces were in the box originally?"

Denise: "I drew 12 pieces, but then I don't know what to do."

Mrs. Benson: "Let's think, what does this picture tell you?"

```
x x x x
x x x x
x x x x
```
$\frac{3}{5}$ of the candy

Denise: "That means this must have been three of the five parts; this is three equal parts. Oh, there are 12 so there must be four in each part."

Mrs. Benson: "Good, let's circle the three sets of four."

$\frac{3}{5}$ of the whole

Denise: "You need two more sets of four. So there must have been 20 pieces to begin with."

Mrs. Benson: "Does that make sense? Is 12 three-fifths of 20?"

After a few more examples using improper fractions and mixed numbers, the students do the sheets Mrs. Benson had ready for them.

INTRODUCTION

Fractions and decimals have long been a stumbling block for many students. This may be because we rush to symbolization and operations without developing strong conceptual underpinnings of the numbers and the operations. Thus, much of this chapter is devoted to the concept development and the processes underlying the operations.

As we will see in examining the concepts associated with fractions and decimals, they are complex. However, two rather simple but powerful ideas, *partitioning* and *equivalence,* can help tie many of the ideas together (8, p. 75). Partitioning is the process of sharing equally, and equivalence focuses on different ways to represent the same amount.

One idea related to equivalence you should keep in mind is that decimal fractions are another notation for common fractions. For example, .5 and $\frac{5}{10}$ are just two different ways to represent the same fractional part. In turn, each is equivalent to one-half.

Both common fractions and decimal fractions can represent fractional parts, but decimal fractions represent only partitionings of tenths, hundredths, and so on, while common fractions can represent any partitionings. We have chosen to begin with common fractions because they are more general than decimal fractions. While the discussion first concentrates on common fractions (called simply *fractions* from here on), this should not imply that the entire study of fractions be done before decimals. Once a beginning foundation has been built with fractions, the decimal notation can be introduced. In fact, many of the operations with decimals are easier than the corresponding operations with fractions and can be taught meaningfully before the entire study of operations with fractions is completed.

CONCEPTUAL DEVELOPMENT OF FRACTIONS

In reporting the results of the second national mathematics assessment, the interpretative team stated, "Concepts and models underlying fractions are not well developed by age 9. Although older students do not have much difficulty in relating fractions to pictorial models, they do not seem to realize that these models may be helpful in other situations" (4, p. 31). In a careful examination of the items on the assessment, it is evident that there are many holes in the 13-year-old's understanding of fractions, and these leave the child unable to use fractions in many situations. Fractions often seem to be some weird numbers that you do something with, but it's not clear what.

Meanings

Three distinct meanings of fractions—part-whole, quotient, and ratio—are found in most elementary programs. Most fraction work is based upon the part-whole; often there is little development of the other two meanings.

Part-Whole. The part-whole interpretation of a fraction such as $\frac{3}{5}$ indicates that a whole has been partitioned into 5 equal parts and 3 of those parts are being considered. The sketch shows one model of three-fifths; soon we will see other ways that three-fifths may be modeled as part of a whole.

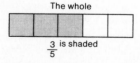

The whole

$\frac{3}{5}$ is shaded

Quotient. The fraction $\frac{3}{5}$ may also be considered as a quotient, $3 \div 5$. This also arises from a partitioning situation. Suppose you had some big cookies to give to 5 people. How would you do this if you actually had the cookies? You would probably give each person one cookie, then another, and so forth until you had distributed the same amount to each. If you had 20 cookies, then you could represent this process mathematically by $20 \div 5$; each person would get 4 cookies. Now, suppose you had only 3 big cookies for 5 people, or $3 \div 5$. How much would each person get? Would anyone get a whole? (No.) Let's look at one way to solve the problem using pictures of the cookies (see Figure 11-1). This is the interpretation of fractions that we use when we express a remainder in a division problem as a fraction. It is also the interpretation that is needed to change a fraction to decimal notation.

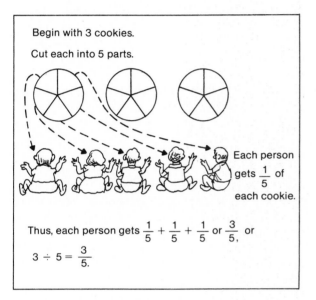

Begin with 3 cookies.

Cut each into 5 parts.

Each person gets $\frac{1}{5}$ of each cookie.

Thus, each person gets $\frac{1}{5} + \frac{1}{5} + \frac{1}{5}$ or $\frac{3}{5}$, or $3 \div 5 = \frac{3}{5}$.

Figure 11-1

Ratio. The fraction, $\frac{3}{5}$, may also represent a ratio situation such as: there are 3 boys for every 5 girls. A model for this would be:

You can see that this is conceptually quite a different interpretation of fractions. This interpretation is discussed in Chapter 12; in the present chapter we will consider the other two meanings.

Models of Part-Whole

We will concentrate on four models—region, length, set, and area—for the part-whole meaning. Any of these models may also be used for the quotient interpretation; however, the region model is most often

used because it is the simplest. Other attributes such as capacity, volume, or time can also be used as models.

Region. The region model is the most concrete form and is easily handled by children. The whole (the unit) is a region and the parts are congruent (same size and shape). This region may be any shape, such as circle, rectangle, square, triangle. In presenting this model a variety of shapes should be used, so that the children do not think that a fraction is always a "part of a pie." The rectangle, however, is probably the easiest for children to draw and to partition. Try to partition a rectangle, a circle, and a triangle into three equal parts. Which was the easiest? (See Figure 11-2.) The circle does have one advantage; it is easy to see as a whole. Since the region is the most common model, we will give many uses of it throughout the chapter.

Length. Any unit of length can be partitioned into fractional parts with each part being equal in length. Children can fold a long, thin strip of paper (partition it) into halves, fourths, and so forth. Later this activity should lead to indicating fractions as points on a number line. In so doing, the children must realize that each unit has been partitioned. That is, the point $4\frac{1}{3}$ is found by partitioning the unit from 4 to 5 into thirds, finding one-third of that unit, and realizing that this is $\frac{1}{3}$ more than 4 or $4\frac{1}{3}$.

Set. The set model uses a set of objects as the whole (the unit). This model sometimes causes difficulty, partly because students have not often considered a set of, say, 12 objects as a unit. The more likely reason for difficulty is that the students have not physically partitioned objects; furthermore, the symbolization is rushed for this model.

Without mentioning fractions, children should be given experiences partitioning sets. This will provide a background for division as well as for this model of fractions. For example, a child may be asked to give 12 objects to four children. Later, attention should be focused on whether or not a given number of objects can be

Figure 11-2

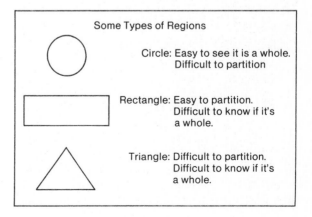

Some Types of Regions

Circle: Easy to see it is a whole. Difficult to partition

Rectangle: Easy to partition. Difficult to know if it's a whole.

Triangle: Difficult to partition. Difficult to know if it's a whole.

partitioned equally among a given number of people. For example, can 15 objects be partitioned equally among 5 people? [Yes.] 4 people? [No.] 3 people? [Yes.] 2 people? [No.]

Now, this can be related to fractions. What do we do to find fifths? We partition the region, length, and now the set into five equal parts. Look at Figure 11-3; the 15 marbles have been partitioned into 5 equal parts. Each part is a fifth of the whole set. From this one can answer the questions: What is one-fifth of 15? [3.] Two-fifths of 15? [6.] Three-fifths of 15? [9.] Experience of this type allows children to solve many practical problems and gives background for multiplication of fractions.

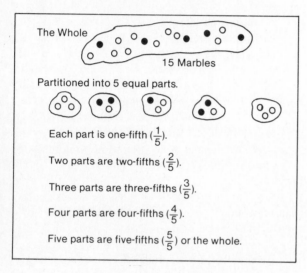

Figure 11-3

Area. The area model is a sophisticated one that encompasses the region model. We remove the restriction that the parts must be the same shape; they must only be equal in area. Before using this model, children must have some idea of when two different shapes have equal areas. Look at the squares partitioned into fourths. This model is more appropriate for older children (at least fourth grade) than for younger children.

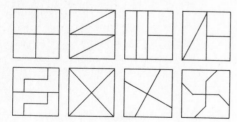

How to Introduce Fractions

All the meanings and models presented in the previous parts were explained to you at one time. This does not mean that this is the way you teach fractions. You want to begin with the simplest meaning and model, something that will be meaningful for the children. That would be the part-whole meaning and the region model. After introducing this model and the language and symbols associated with fractions, you can introduce other part-whole models. The other meanings of fractions can be introduced after children become more familiar with fractions through ordering and finding equivalent fractions and with improper fractions and mixed numbers.

Partitioning. Underlying the idea of part-whole is the meaning of part and of whole. The *whole* is whatever is specified as the unit. At first this should be an obvious whole. The *part* must be an "equal" part, and children must learn to partition the whole into equal parts.

To begin, give examples of regions that are and are not partitioned. Then, let the children do the partitioning. For example, each child could be given a "candy bar" (a piece of paper the size of a large candy bar) to share with a friend. Have them fold the "candy bar" to show how they would share. Talk about whether a fold like the one sketched here would be "fair." Through other examples, develop sharing equally among 4, 3, 6, and 5 people.

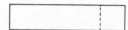

Words. As soon as you have developed the idea of equal parts, introduce the words halves, thirds, fourths, and so on. Be sure to ask such questions as, "How many equal parts would I have if each part was a fifth? an eighth?" (and even a twenty-fourth).

Counting. Once children are familiar with the fractional part words, it is time to begin counting those parts. This should not be any more difficult than counting apples, but you need to know what you are counting. An example of an activity card to practice counting is given on Lesson Card 11-1.

Symbols. Research has shown that children's understanding of fractions is stronger if the symbols are delayed until the right-hand side of this triangle is firmly in place (7):

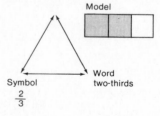

When the children can match the words with the model, tell them that we write $\frac{2}{3}$ for two-thirds.

You now have to connect the other parts of the triangle:

1. Given a model, the child writes the symbol.
2. Given a symbol, the child chooses the model.

Let's Count

Materials: One piece of light colored construction paper cut into fourths and a crayon for each child.

Preparation of the models: Have each child fold one piece of the paper into halves and draw a dark crayon mark on the crease. Label the back of this piece halves. Do the same for thirds, fourths, and sixths.

Now practice counting--one-third, two-thirds, a whole--while pointing to the appropriate model and parts. Continue with other examples.

Hold up the sixths model and fold it to show five-sixths. Ask the children how many sixths. Continue with other examples.

Then, have the children show with their models a variety of fractions.

Now, play a quick game. Tell the children you are thinking of a number: "It's a number of fourths." Have them model their guesses with the paper models. Give a point to those who guess and model correctly.

Extension: Make models of fractions by shading parts. Have the children count the shaded parts. Don't forget they first need to know what they are counting! (That is, they must first know whether it is halves, thirds, fourths...or twenty-fourths.)

3. Given a symbol, the child says the word.
4. Given a word, the child writes the symbol.

Textbooks usually concentrate on objectives 1 and 2, so you will find plenty of examples of these. Objectives 3 and 4 require a lot of oral work; reading problems and answers will assist in this.

Drawing a Model. In this developmental sequence, children have modeled fractions by folding paper or by choosing a picture. You want them also to be able to draw a picture. The rectangle is probably the easiest shape to use to show a "good approximation" to a fractional part. Encourage the children to be as accurate as possible, but do not worry if these drawings are not perfect. Which of the two accompanying drawings would you accept as a picture of $\frac{2}{3}$? While Bob's is neater than Marilyn's, he seems to have missed the point that the three parts have to be equal. You might help Marilyn be a little neater, but she does seem to have the idea of two-thirds.

Bob

Marilyn

Extending the Model. Look at the results in Table 11-1. There is no doubt that this model is more complicated than the ones we have been using, but it is a very useful one for introducing equivalent fractions and for ordering fractions.

TABLE 11-1

What fractional part of the figure is shaded?

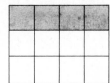

Responses	Percent Responding	
	Age 9	Age 13
Acceptable responses		
$\frac{1}{3}$, $\frac{4}{12}$, .33	20	82
Unacceptable responses		
$\frac{1}{4}$, .25	5	4
Top 4, top part, $\frac{4}{8}$	36	6
Other	15	6
I don't know	17	1
No response	7	1

Reprinted with permission of the National Council of Teachers of Mathematics (4).

You can use paper-folding again to introduce this model and to introduce equivalent fractions. For example, give each child a fourth of a sheet of plain paper. Have each child fold the paper into thirds and color two-thirds. Now fold the paper in half the other way. Ask how many parts and what kind of parts (6, sixths). Then, ask what part is shaded. Encourage both $\frac{2}{3}$ and $\frac{4}{6}$. Tell the children that we call $\frac{2}{3}$ and $\frac{4}{6}$ *equivalent* fractions because they represent the same amount.

After many more examples with paper-folding, draw the picture of what was happening with the paper-folding. Draw a picture of the paper folded in thirds and shade $\frac{2}{3}$; then draw the fold made when partitioning it into halves.

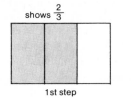
shows $\frac{2}{3}$
1st step

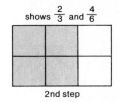
shows $\frac{2}{3}$ and $\frac{4}{6}$
2nd step

Next, move to pictures showing only the second step. Make certain the students can identify the way it was "folded" in both directions. Have them show $\frac{1}{3}$, $\frac{2}{3}$, $\frac{1}{4}$, $\frac{3}{4}$, and so on and give an equivalent fraction.

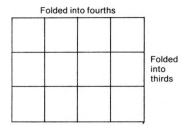
Folded into fourths

Folded into thirds

This sequence, along with activities like those in the opening lesson, provides a strong background for further development of fractions and the operations.

Ordering Fractions

Part of understanding fractions is realizing that they are numbers and can be ordered, added, subtracted, multiplied, and divided. Our goal is to have children order fractions symbolically, but we can build the bridge from the concrete to the symbolic. Not only will this bridge help children realize what they are doing when they are ordering fractions, it will also give another context in which to practice relating fractions and the models. Many problems involving ordering capture children's interest because they want to know which is more, which is shorter, which is larger.

Concrete Models. If children have made concrete models, then it is not difficult to order fractions. Suppose that you have the children fold a given sized strip into halves, thirds, and so on. Then, to find out which is larger, $\frac{2}{3}$ or $\frac{3}{4}$, fold the thirds strip so it is $\frac{2}{3}$ long and the fourths strip so it is $\frac{3}{4}$ long, and compare the lengths of the two folded strips. To give children enough practice ordering fractions using concrete models, you need

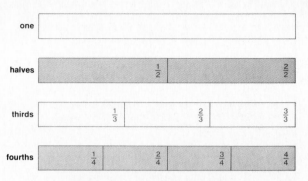

Figure 11-4.   From Romberg (13).

to provide variety, including games such as the one in Activity Card 11-1.*

Pictorial Models. Children are able to order fractions if given pictures of the models. For example, the strips in Figure 11-4 could be used as shown. A picture of two identical pie pans with $\frac{3}{4}$ of one pie and $\frac{2}{3}$ of the other pie still in the pan could show that $\frac{3}{4}$ is more than $\frac{2}{3}$. If the models of the two fractions are not pictured, then the children need to be able to draw pictures accurately enough to tell. It is not easy to draw a picture to

*Activity Cards 11-1, 11-3, 11-4, 11-5, 11-6, and 11-8 are from Romberg (13).

ACTIVITY CARD 11-1

Whole Hog

This is a quick and easy game for two.

Each of you must trace the H (for Hog). This will be your gameboard.

Cut ten squares of paper. Write one of these fractions on each square:

$\frac{1}{2}$ $\frac{1}{3}$ $\frac{1}{6}$ $\frac{2}{6}$ $\frac{1}{9}$ $\frac{2}{9}$ $\frac{3}{9}$ $\frac{1}{18}$ $\frac{2}{18}$ $\frac{3}{18}$

Each of you needs a crayon. Now you are ready to go Whole Hog.

Game rules

1. Put the fraction cards in a pile face down.

2. Both of you pick a card from the top of the pile.

3. Turn your cards over and decide who has the larger fraction.

4. The player with the larger fraction must color that fractional part of her or his H.

5. Put both cards at the bottom of the pile

6. Choose two more cards and play as before.

7. If a player with the larger fraction cannot color the fractional part shown on the card, put both cards back and pick two more.

8. Continue playing until one person has colored the whole H. That person is the first to go Whole Hog and loses the game.

9. Trace two more H's and play again.

see which of two fractions such as $\frac{1}{3}$ and $\frac{2}{7}$ is larger. There is a logical procedure, however, that always works and does not depend upon the accuracy of the parts.

To order thirds and sevenths, you need a picture that shows both thirds and sevenths. This may be accomplished by drawing a rectangle partitioned into thirds in one way and into sevenths in the other. Children need to be able to identify one-third, two-thirds, one-seventh, two-sevenths, three-sevenths, and so forth on this sketch. Then it can be used to order any fractions less than 1 whose denominators are threes and sevens. (See Activity Card 11-2.) After the children are familiar with this type of picture, they should be encouraged to draw their own.

Symbolic. It is easier to compare two measurements given in the same unit (78 meters with 20 meters) than two measurements given in different units (83 meters with 4318 centimeters). Likewise, it is easier to compare two fractions with the same subunit ($\frac{3}{5}$ with $\frac{2}{5}$) than two fractions with different subunits ($\frac{2}{3}$ with $\frac{5}{7}$). The secret in a more difficult situation is to turn them into a simpler case—that is, express them in the same unit. With the fractions this means expressing each fraction as an equivalent fraction in the same subunit (or common denominator). The pictorial model shown in Activity Card 11-2 can help with this. Once the rectangle is partitioned into both thirds and sevenths, it is par-

titioned into twenty-firsts. Thus $\frac{2}{3}$ is 14 of the 21 parts or $\frac{14}{21}$, and $\frac{5}{7}$ is 15 of the 21 parts or $\frac{15}{21}$. The notation we could use is:

$$\frac{2}{3} = \frac{14}{21} \quad \text{and} \quad \frac{5}{7} = \frac{15}{21}, \quad \text{therefore } \frac{5}{7} > \frac{2}{3}$$

Before becoming proficient with this method, the children must be familiar with how to find equivalent fractions. They must also be able to choose a common denominator. The pictorial model will help with this, as will suggestions made in the next part on equivalent fractions.

Equivalence of Fractions

We have looked at models that could be represented in more than one way, such as by $\frac{2}{3}$ and $\frac{4}{6}$. Thus, students with this background are familiar with the concept of equivalent fractions, but they may not have developed many of the skills associated with equivalent fractions.

Finding an Equivalent Fraction Without a Model. To find an equivalent fraction, we want the generalization that both the numerator and denominator may be multiplied (or divided) by the same number. We will begin with the paper-folding model and symbolically describe what is happening.

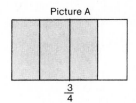
Picture A

$\frac{3}{4}$

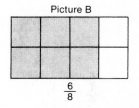
Picture B

$\frac{6}{8}$

Make a model of $\frac{3}{4}$ by folding a piece of paper (picture A); then fold it in half the other way (picture B). Establish that $\frac{3}{4} = \frac{6}{8}$. Now, look at what happened when the paper was folded in half. You created twice as many equal parts (or 2×4) and twice as many shaded parts (or 2×3). We can write this:

$$\frac{2 \times 3}{2 \times 4} \quad \text{or} \quad \frac{3 \times 2}{4 \times 2} = \frac{6}{8}$$

After more examples such as these, the students should make the generalization that both the numerator and denominator may be multiplied by the same number and the resulting fraction is equivalent.

Conversely, one could begin with picture B and describe how to get to picture A. In picture B, we began with 8 equal parts and grouped them by 2, or $8 \div 2$. This also groups the number of parts under consideration by 2, or $6 \div 2$. Thus,

$$\frac{6}{8} = \frac{6 \div 2}{8 \div 2} = \frac{3}{4}$$

ACTIVITY CARD 11-2

sevenths

thirds

A.
$\frac{1}{3}$ is _____ pieces of the whole

$\frac{2}{7}$ is _____ pieces of the whole

Which is larger? $\frac{1}{3}$ or $\frac{2}{7}$ _____

B.
$\frac{2}{3}$ is _____ pieces of the whole

$\frac{5}{7}$ is _____ pieces of the whole

Which is larger? $\frac{2}{3}$ or $\frac{5}{7}$ _____

C.
$\frac{1}{3}$ is _____ pieces of the whole

$\frac{3}{7}$ is _____ pieces of the whole

Which is larger? $\frac{1}{3}$ or $\frac{3}{7}$ _____

Again, this type of example should lead to the generalization that the numerator and denominator may be divided by the same number.

Finding an Equivalent Fraction Given Its Denominator. Once the students have made the generalization that both the numerator and denominator may be multiplied or divided by the same number, then they are ready to move to problems such as:

$$\frac{2}{3} = \frac{\square}{12}, \quad \frac{4}{6} = \frac{\square}{3}$$

In the first example, the students need to think, "What is 3 multiplied by to get 12?" Once they have established it is 4, they should write:

$$\frac{2 \times 4}{3 \times 4} = \frac{8}{12}$$

In the second example, they should realize that 6 was divided by 2 to obtain 3 so that 4 would also have to be divided by 2, or

$$\frac{4 \div 2}{6 \div 2} = \frac{2}{3}$$

The first example is the type of thinking one needs in finding a common denominator; the second, the type needed in simplifying many problems.

Children should also be helped to see that you can-not always change a common fraction to an equivalent one with certain specified denominators if the numerator must be a whole number. For example, $\frac{5}{12}$ cannot be changed to thirds even though you can divide 12 by 4 to get 3. When you divide 5 by 4, you do not get a whole number. Likewise, you cannot change $\frac{2}{3}$ to fifths:

$$\frac{2}{3} = \frac{?}{5}$$

There is no whole number that you can multiply 3 by to get 5. Exercises such as those in Activity Card 11-3 focus on these skills.

Finding a Common Denominator. In the past there has been much emphasis on finding the least common denominator. With a decreased emphasis on fractions, this skill is not as essential as it once was. However, to add or subtract fractions one must find a common denominator. For example, given the fractions $\frac{2}{5}$ and $\frac{3}{4}$, finding a common denominator requires finding a fraction equivalent to $\frac{2}{5}$ and a fraction equivalent to $\frac{3}{4}$ with the same denominator. This amounts to finding a number that both 5 and 4 will divide. Of course, the product of these two denominators will always give a common denominator. The modeling that we showed in ordering fractions indicates why this works (see Figure 11-5).

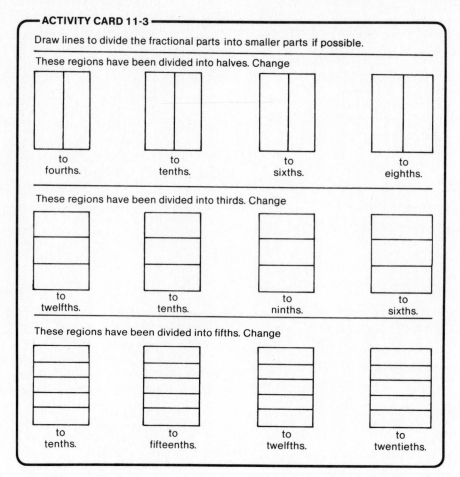

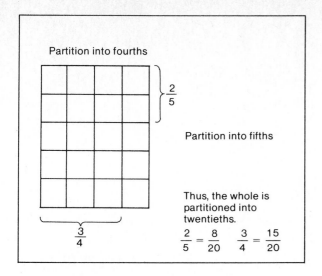

Figure 11-5

At times this method will not give the least common denominator. For example, a common denominator of $\frac{5}{6}$ and $\frac{3}{4}$ is 6×4 or 24, but the least common denominator is 12. The least common denominator is the smallest number that both 6 and 4 will divide. With small denominators, this can often be found by inspection, probably a more beneficial approach than learning a routine.

Mixed Numbers and Improper Fractions

Through models you can lead naturally into mixed

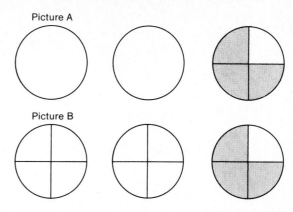

numbers and improper fractions. As much as possible have the children write both the mixed number and the improper fraction to represent a model. Look at the picture A; the most natural description is $2\frac{1}{4}$. How can we see the improper fraction representation? Drawing in the fourths as in picture B helps with the initial counting of nine-fourths.

After becoming familiar with both improper fractions and mixed numbers, students need to be able to change from one form to the other without the use of models. However, familiarity with the models should help in the process. Do not rush to a routine, but have the students think through the problem, as in the examples on Activity Card 11-4. Then they can learn the

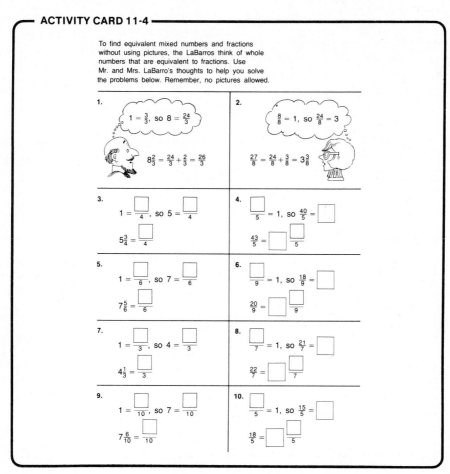

shortcut you probably use. They can think: "$8\frac{2}{3}$, 8 is 8 times 3 thirds or 24 thirds, plus the 2 thirds is 26 thirds, or $8 \times 3 + 2$ is 26. Thus, $8\frac{2}{3} = \frac{26}{3}$."

OPERATIONS WITH FRACTIONS

The key to presenting meaningfully the operations of fractions is to establish a firm background with fractions, especially with equivalent fractions. Then, some introduction is needed that explains the operations and relates them to operations with whole numbers. Finally, the algorithms need to be introduced and mastered.

Addition and Subtraction

Instead of beginning with a symbolic sentence such as $\frac{2}{3} + \frac{1}{4}$, we will begin with joining and separating situations. The problem will be solved by using the pictorial model; then a sentence will be written to describe the situation. The purposes of this procedure are (1) to help children see that adding and subtracting of fractions solve problems similar to those with whole numbers, (2) to give them an idea of what a reasonable answer will be, and (3) to help them see why a "common denominator" is necessary when adding or subtracting.

Let us look at how you could introduce these ideas. You will need blank transparencies and one with a copy of the strips in Figure 11-4, a transparency marker, and an overhead projector. Here is a list of questions to ask and things to do.

1. Show the transparency with strips and ask questions to make certain the children are able to tell what kind of strips are shown (halves, thirds, fourths, etc.).

2. Ask: "If I had 8 whole strips and you gave me 3 more, how many would I have altogether?" They will think this is easy, but make the point that they are going to look at fractions like they used to look at whole numbers. Now ask, "I have $\frac{1}{4}$ of a strip and you give me $\frac{1}{3}$ more of a strip. How much do I have altogether?"

3. Discuss their ideas. If no one suggests putting $\frac{1}{3}$ together with $\frac{1}{4}$, take the blank transparency and draw a copy of $\frac{1}{4}$, then "add" to it a strip $\frac{1}{3}$ long. This is how long a strip you would have altogether. Now try to find a name for this length. You will find that it matches the $\frac{7}{12}$ strip.

4. Then, write $\frac{1}{3} + \frac{1}{4} = \frac{7}{12}$.

5. Continue with other joining situations that lead to the sentences, such as the following:

$$\frac{3}{12} + \frac{4}{12} \quad \text{(like denominators)}$$
$$\frac{1}{6} + \frac{5}{12} \quad \text{(unlike denominators)}$$

6. Now, move to separating or take-away situations, again reminding the students of how they solve such situations with whole numbers.

7. Ask: "If I had $\frac{3}{4}$ of a strip and I gave you $\frac{1}{3}$ of a strip, how much would I have left?"

8. Accept their ideas and solutions; they are more likely to suggest drawing on the blank transparency, now that they have seen it used for addition. If not, draw a strip that is $\frac{3}{4}$ long, then from one end cross out a strip that is $\frac{1}{3}$ long and check to see what is left. You should find that $\frac{5}{12}$ is left.

9. Write: $\frac{3}{4} - \frac{1}{3} = \frac{5}{12}$.

10. Continue with other separating situations, including at least one in which the subtraction is impossible; for example: "I have $\frac{1}{3}$ of a strip and I give you $\frac{7}{12}$. How much do I have left?"

After such an introduction the students need to solve such problems on their own. A more challenging sheet is given on Activity Card 11-5, where the children have to first find each of the fractions in the picture.

Like Denominators. If you have been following the teaching sequence for developing fraction concepts, the children orally have been given much experience in adding and subtracting fractions with like denominators, but they have not been given the problems symbolically. Use like denominators to introduce the vertical format. If children have any difficulty in adding or subtracting like fractions, use the fraction words to help:

$$
\begin{array}{ll}
\frac{1}{5} & \text{1-fifth} \\
+\frac{3}{5} & \text{3-fifths} \\
\hline
\frac{4}{5} & \text{4-fifths}
\end{array}
$$

It will also help to have the children read the problem orally. Adding and subtracting like denominators should not take long if the foundation of fractions has been built, and you should move on to unlike denominators.

Unlike Denominators. The main idea to be developed when adding or subtracting fractions with unlike denominators is that we cannot add or subtract them symbolically without first changing them to like denominators. In order to help children see that fractions with unlike denominators cannot be added or subtracted, emphasize each of the following:

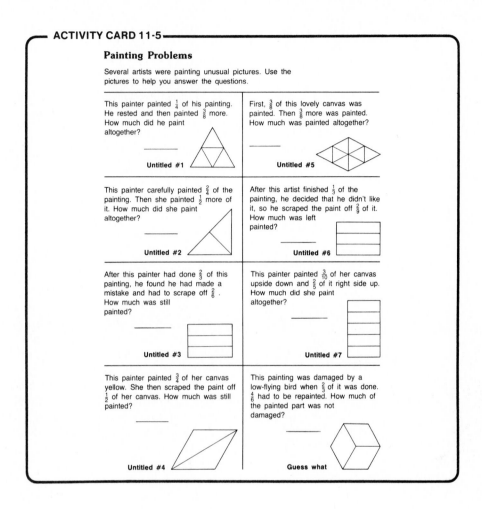

1. Return to the words: 1-*fourth* plus 1-*third* would be what? Thirds, fourths, or some other fraction?

2. Return to measurement: If you measured one thing in inches and another in feet, how long would the two be together? Before adding, you must change both to the same unit. Likewise, if you measure something in thirds and something in fourths, you must change both of them to the same unit.

3. Return to the transparency with the strips (Figure 11-4) to help children see that when you add (subtract) fractions with unlike denominators, the result is a fraction with a denominator different from at least one of the two. For example:

$$\frac{1}{3} + \frac{1}{4} = \frac{7}{12}, \qquad \frac{1}{3} + \frac{1}{6} = \frac{1}{2}, \qquad \frac{1}{3} + \frac{5}{6} = \frac{7}{6}$$

Now look at the strips (Figure 11-4) and consider adding $\frac{1}{3}$ and $\frac{1}{4}$ by adding $\frac{4}{12}$ and $\frac{3}{12}$, or

$$\begin{array}{r} \frac{1}{3} = \frac{4}{12} \\ + \frac{1}{4} = \frac{3}{12} \\ \hline \end{array}$$

So we need first to change the fractions to "like" fractions or to find a common denominator. You will need to continue to work with the students on how to do this (see the discussion of equivalent fractions).

Fractions Greater Than One. Adding fractions whose sum is greater than one or adding mixed numbers is not particularly difficult provided that (1) adding fractions less than one has been mastered; (2) changing from an improper fraction to a mixed number has been mastered, and (3) these numbers have meaning. There are two new skills that have not been emphasized. Look at the example in Figure 11-6. Can you find the new skills?

First, the child must be able to see why it is best to add the fractions first and then the whole numbers. The other new skill is changing $7\frac{17}{12}$ to $8\frac{5}{12}$. While children may have encountered this when changing from improper to mixed numbers, usually they have concentrated on changing an improper fraction such as $\frac{25}{8}$ to a mixed number. They have not changed a mixed number whose fraction part is an improper fraction to another mixed number.

On the other hand, subtracting is often more difficult, partly because they have not changed a mixed number to another mixed number and also because they lack understanding of regrouping. Look at the example in Figure 11-7. Children must understand in regrouping

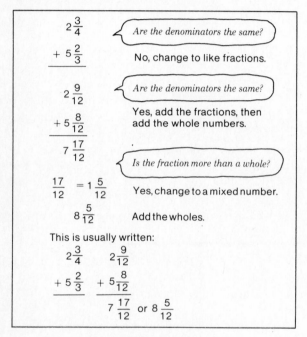

$$2\frac{3}{4}$$

Are the denominators the same?

No, change to like fractions.

$$+\,5\frac{2}{3}$$

$$2\frac{9}{12}$$

Are the denominators the same?

Yes, add the fractions, then add the whole numbers.

$$+\,5\frac{8}{12}$$

$$7\frac{17}{12}$$

Is the fraction more than a whole?

$$\frac{17}{12} = 1\frac{5}{12}$$

Yes, change to a mixed number.

$$8\frac{5}{12}$$

Add the wholes.

This is usually written:

$$2\frac{3}{4} \qquad 2\frac{9}{12}$$
$$+\,5\frac{2}{3} \qquad +\,5\frac{8}{12}$$
$$\overline{} \qquad \overline{7\frac{17}{12} \text{ or } 8\frac{5}{12}}$$

Figure 11-6

Figure 11-7

$$6\frac{3}{7}$$

Are the denominators the same?

Yes. (If not, change them to like fractions.)

$$-\,2\frac{4}{7}$$

Can I take 4/7 from 3/7?

$$5\frac{10}{7}$$

No, I must regroup $6\frac{3}{7}$.

$$-\,2\frac{4}{7}$$

(One whole is seven-sevenths, so altogether, I have $\frac{10}{7}$.)

$$3\frac{3}{7}$$

Now subtract the fraction parts, then the whole parts.

$6\frac{3}{7}$ to $5\frac{10}{7}$ that 1 is $\frac{7}{7}$, and 6 is $5 + 1$ or $5 + \frac{7}{7}$. Hence, $6\frac{3}{7}$ is $5 + \frac{7}{7} + \frac{3}{7}$ or $5\frac{10}{7}$. Does the accompanying sketch help you see that $6\frac{3}{7} = 5\frac{10}{7}$?

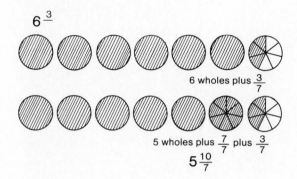

$6\frac{3}{7}$

6 wholes plus $\frac{3}{7}$

5 wholes plus $\frac{7}{7}$ plus $\frac{3}{7}$

$5\frac{10}{7}$

Multiplication

The algorithm for multiplication of fractions is one of the simplest: multiply numerators to find the numerator, multiply denominators to find the denominator. It can be taught in minutes (to be forgotten in seconds, unless a great amount of practice is provided). More important, this method of teaching the algorithm does not provide background into why it works or when to use it. We are suggesting a development that gives the underlying meanings of multiplication, an idea of the size of an answer, and the reason why the algorithm works before the algorithm itself is presented.

We will look at four different cases: a whole number times a fraction or mixed number; a fraction times a whole number; a fraction times a fraction; and a mixed number times a mixed number. In each case we will tie the multiplication to a meaning of multiplication of whole numbers. We will use the knowledge that 3×4 means 3 groups of 4 and 3×4 is the area of a 3-by-4 rectangle.

Whole Number Times a Fraction. Let's begin with a problem: "You have 3 pans each with $\frac{4}{5}$ of a pizza. How much pizza?" How is this problem like having 3 bags each with 4 marbles? See if the accompanying sketch helps you to see the similarity between multiplying whole numbers and multiplying a whole number times a fraction.

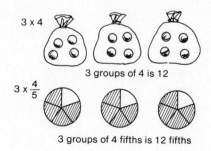

3×4

3 groups of 4 is 12

$3 \times \frac{4}{5}$

3 groups of 4 fifths is 12 fifths

If we consider 3 groups of 4 to be 3 × 4, then it makes sense to consider 3 groups of $\frac{4}{5}$ to mean 3 × $\frac{4}{5}$. How did we first find 3 groups of 4? We could have put out 3 groups of 4 marbles and counted them; likewise, if we want to find 3 groups of $\frac{4}{5}$, we can put out 3 pans each having $\frac{4}{5}$ in it and count the number of fifths. Or, to find 3 × 4, we could consider repeated addition: 4 + 4 + 4 = 12. Likewise, 3 × $\frac{4}{5}$ is $\frac{4}{5}$ + $\frac{4}{5}$ + $\frac{4}{5}$ = $\frac{12}{5}$.

After the students have solved problems like this with pictures, see if they can solve them without the pictures or repeated addition. Place strong emphasis on the words. Listen carefully as you read this:

5 × $\frac{2}{3}$ is 5 groups of 2-thirds
which is <u>5 groups of 2</u> or <u>10</u> (thirds) or $\frac{10}{3}$

Fraction Times a Whole Number. Again, let's begin with a problem: "You have $\frac{3}{4}$ of a case of 24 bottles. How many bottles have you?"

If children have worked with the set model, they have the background to solve this with physical objects. Here, we want to move to solving it symbolically and to tie it to multiplication.

First, let us look at why it makes sense to consider this as multiplication. If we had 5 cases with 24 bottles in each, what would we do to find out how many? We would multiply 5 × 24. Likewise, 20 cases would be 20 × 24, 53 cases would be 53 × 24, and thus, $\frac{3}{4}$ case would be $\frac{3}{4}$ × 24.

Now let's review how we find $\frac{3}{4}$ of 24. We first partition the set into 4 equal parts (each part would have 6), or, in other words, we find $\frac{1}{4}$ of 24. Thus, $\frac{3}{4}$ would be 3 times as many, or 3 × 6 = 18.

$$\frac{3}{4} \times 24 = ?$$

Think: $\frac{1}{4}$ × 24 = 6

Think: $\frac{3}{4}$ is 3 times as many, or 3 × 6 = 18

At first glance, this looks slightly different from the algorithm of multiplying numerators and multiplying denominators. Actually, the results are the same:

$$\frac{3}{4} \times 24 = \frac{3}{4} \times \frac{24}{1} = \frac{3 \times 24}{4} = \frac{72}{4} = 18$$

One way to approach these problems is to use commutativity. Since 3 × 4 = 4 × 3, then we want $\frac{3}{4}$ × 24 = 24 × $\frac{3}{4}$. We can then find $\frac{3}{4}$ × 24 by the procedures discussed in multiplying a whole number times a fraction. While this approach may be easier, you lose the opportunity to present the "of" meaning.

Fraction Times a Fraction. "If you own $\frac{3}{4}$ of an acre of land and $\frac{5}{6}$ of this is planted in trees, what part of the acre is planted in trees?" Let's begin solving this by drawing pictures. Why is this multiplication? Remember that 3 × 4 may be interpreted as the area of a 3 × 4 rectangle. What we have in the tree picture is a $\frac{3}{4}$ by $\frac{5}{6}$ rectangle and its area is $\frac{3}{4}$ × $\frac{5}{6}$. And we see that $\frac{3}{4}$ × $\frac{5}{6}$ = $\frac{15}{24}$. Looking at the third picture, we see that $\frac{15}{24}$ of the acre is planted.

This model will need to be developed slowly, and only after children have had experience with finding areas of rectangles. After doing this, find out whether any children can see a shorter way to find the product. Make a list of multiplication exercises and products (do not reduce the answers). See if the children notice the pattern (multiply the numerators, multiply the denominators). You can refer to the picture to see why this works. You have partitioned the acre into fourths one way and sixths the other way, thus creating 4 × 6 or 24 equal parts (this is the denominator). Trees were planted in 3 rows of 5 or 15 of these parts, or 3 × 5 is the numerator. Writing this in terms of fractions, we have:

$$\frac{3}{4} \times \frac{5}{6} = \frac{3 \times 5}{4 \times 6} = \frac{15}{24}$$

At this point, return to the previous two cases and let the children know that this process holds for these cases also.

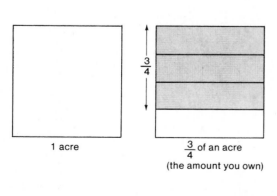

1 acre $\qquad$ $\frac{3}{4}$ of an acre
(the amount you own)

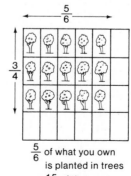

$\frac{5}{6}$ of what you own
is planted in trees
or $\frac{15}{24}$ of the acre

A word of caution: do not rush to "cancelling." Be certain that children can do multiplication this way, reducing answers if necessary, and applying multiplication to problems before introducing cancelling.

Mixed Number Times a Mixed Number. Figure 11-8 shows a couple of models that could be used to solve the problem: "You have some material that is $2\frac{1}{4}$ yards by $1\frac{1}{2}$ yards. How many square yards do you have?" Picture A changes both mixed numbers to improper fractions, while picture B shows how to multiply mixed numbers without first changing them to improper fractions.

Division

As with multiplication, one can model many division situations. The models get rather complicated, how-ever, so we present only one model and then show how the division algorithm can be developed symbolically. If you are presenting the division algorithm to children who are not ready for a symbolic treatment, then you should find other models for other situations.

Consider the problem: "Suppose you have $\frac{3}{4}$ of a square pizza and you want to share it equally among 5 people. How much of the pizza would each person receive?"

This problem can be solved by division: $\frac{3}{4} \div 5 = ?$ You know how you would solve this with a pizza. Let's draw a picture of that. Each person would get 3 out of 20 pieces. Or $\frac{3}{4} \div 5 = \frac{3}{20}$. You immediately notice that this is the same picture as $\frac{1}{5} \times \frac{3}{4}$ or $\frac{3}{4} \times \frac{1}{5}$. This begins to develop the rule that $\frac{3}{4} \div 5 = \frac{3}{4} \times \frac{1}{5}$.

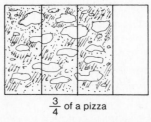

$\frac{3}{4}$ of a pizza

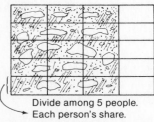

Divide among 5 people.
Each person's share.

Figure 11-8

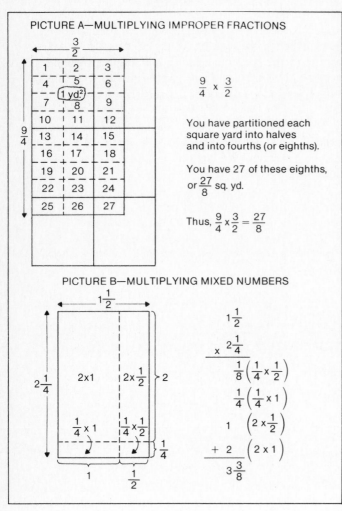

PICTURE A—MULTIPLYING IMPROPER FRACTIONS

$\frac{9}{4} \times \frac{3}{2}$

You have partitioned each square yard into halves and into fourths (or eighths).

You have 27 of these eighths, or $\frac{27}{8}$ sq. yd.

Thus, $\frac{9}{4} \times \frac{3}{2} = \frac{27}{8}$

PICTURE B—MULTIPLYING MIXED NUMBERS

$$
\begin{array}{r}
1\frac{1}{2} \\
\times\ 2\frac{1}{4} \\
\hline
\frac{1}{8}\left(\frac{1}{4} \times \frac{1}{2}\right) \\
\frac{1}{4}\left(\frac{1}{4} \times 1\right) \\
1\ \left(2 \times \frac{1}{2}\right) \\
+\ 2\ \left(2 \times 1\right) \\
\hline
3\frac{3}{8}
\end{array}
$$

There are several ways to show why the algorithm for dividing fractions works. We will consider only one way, which depends upon: (1) knowing that $a \div b = \frac{a}{b}$ and (2) knowing that if the numerator and denominator of a fraction are multiplied by the same number, the resulting fraction is equivalent.

Suppose we want to solve: $\frac{3}{4} \div \frac{5}{8} = \square$. We will talk through this problem in this way:

$$\frac{3}{4} \div \frac{5}{8} = \frac{\frac{3}{4}}{\frac{5}{8}}$$
  "We rewrite $\frac{3}{4} \div \frac{5}{8}$ as this, just like $5 \div 6$ is written $\frac{5}{6}$."

$$= \frac{\frac{3}{4} \times \frac{8}{5}}{\frac{5}{8} \times \frac{8}{5}}$$
  "We can multiply the numerator and denominator by the same number."

$$= \frac{\frac{3}{4} \times \frac{8}{5}}{1}$$
  "We chose $\frac{8}{5}$ because we want the denominator to be one."

$$= \frac{3}{4} \times \frac{8}{5}$$
  "A number divided by one is the number."

Thus $\frac{3}{4} \div \frac{5}{8} = \frac{3}{4} \times \frac{8}{5}$

Once this is understood, you should make certain that the students can verbalize the rule: "To divide two fractions, invert the divisor and multiply." Do not forget that students can check a division problem by multiplying:

$$15 \div 5 = 3 \quad \text{because} \quad 3 \times 5 = 15$$

$$\frac{3}{4} \div \frac{5}{8} = \frac{6}{5} \quad \text{because} \quad \frac{6}{5} \times \frac{5}{8} = \frac{30}{40} = \frac{3}{4}.$$

Take some time to talk about the answers. Note that in this example, the quotient ($\frac{6}{5}$) is larger than either of the other two numbers. This is quite different from whole numbers, and students should realize this is possible. You can give a logical explanation by considering a problem such as $6 \div \frac{3}{4}$.

DEVELOPMENT OF DECIMALS

In introducing decimals you should link them to other knowledge—in particular, to common fractions and to place value. While you will need to interweave both of these in your teaching, we have separated them for ease of discussion.

Relationship to Common Fractions

Decimal fractions are just another notation for tenths, hundredths, and other "powers-of-ten" parts of a unit. Thus, basic to decimals is understanding of these fractional parts. Hopefully, that understanding has been built in introducing common fractions. We will assume so as we first look at tenths.

Tenths. Before introducing the decimal notation for tenths, let's review what students know about tenths from their background with fractions. They should know that to partition a unit into tenths, there must be 10 equal parts. They should also be able to make the connection between the model, the oral name, and the fraction. And they should know that 10 tenths makes a whole, that $\frac{7}{10}$ is less than a whole, and that $\frac{27}{10}$ is more than a whole.

With this background the children should be ready to learn that .3 is a new symbol for $\frac{3}{10}$. At this point you should link the place value ideas to the new notation (see the discussion on place value). You also need to stress that .3 is read just like $\frac{3}{10}$. Also look at $\frac{27}{10}$ or $2\frac{7}{10}$. This is written 2.7 and read "2 and seven-tenths." Note that the word *and* is said for the decimal point. Reading decimals in this way helps to connect decimal and fraction ideas. A quick game to play that practices writing decimal and fraction notation is described on Lesson Card 11-2. Before introducing hundredths, you should make certain that the students have made all the connections in this triangle:

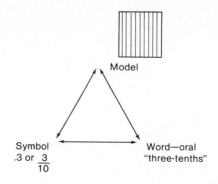

Model

Symbol
.3 or $\frac{3}{10}$

Word—oral
"three-tenths"

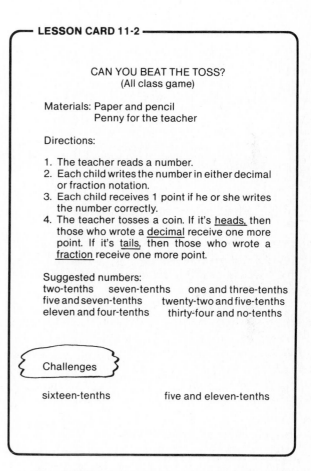

LESSON CARD 11-2

CAN YOU BEAT THE TOSS?
(All class game)

Materials: Paper and pencil
Penny for the teacher

Directions:

1. The teacher reads a number.
2. Each child writes the number in either decimal or fraction notation.
3. Each child receives 1 point if he or she writes the number correctly.
4. The teacher tosses a coin. If it's <u>heads,</u> then those who wrote a <u>decimal</u> receive one more point. If it's <u>tails,</u> then those who wrote a <u>fraction</u> receive one more point.

Suggested numbers:
two-tenths   seven-tenths   one and three-tenths
five and seven-tenths   twenty-two and five-tenths
eleven and four-tenths   thirty-four and no-tenths

Challenges

sixteen-tenths   five and eleven-tenths

Hundredths. To begin extending decimals to hundredths, provide each child with a copy of the model of hundredths and 10 strips 2 cm $\times$ 20 cm (see next page). Make certain that the children know that each part is a hundredth. Have them show $\frac{3}{100}, \frac{7}{100}, \frac{10}{100}, \frac{21}{100}$, and so on.

Then develop the idea that one strip is $\frac{1}{10}$. Have them use two strips to cover the tenths column in the model and lightly mark 3 more squares. Ask what part of the whole is covered. Elicit both responses, $\frac{2}{10} + \frac{3}{100}$ and $\frac{23}{100}$. Write: $\frac{23}{100} = \frac{2}{10} + \frac{3}{100}$.

Now turn to the place-value interpretation and the decimal notation .23. Use the model to show that

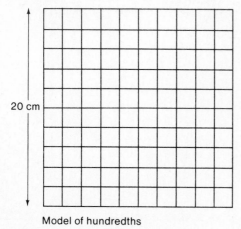

20 cm

Model of hundredths

.2 = .20, and so on. Continue having children make the connections shown in the triangle—that is, connecting the model, symbol, and oral (and written) word.

Thousandths and Other Decimals. "Although 13- and 17-year-olds appeared to have facility with tenths and hundredths, their competency was less developed for thousandths and smaller decimal numbers" (4, p. 39). This is partly because there is less emphasis on these decimals but also because we often expect children to generalize after hundredths to all the other places. Most of the work with smaller decimals should be done primarily through the place-value interpretation, since the fractions become unwieldy. However, thousandths should be developed as one-tenth of a hundredth, and the understanding that 10 thousandths is $\frac{1}{100}$ should be developed through a model.

Decimals and Other Common Fractions. One skill that needs to be developed is the ability to relate fractions to decimals. Hopefully, if decimals have been introduced carefully, students will be able to write fraction notation for a decimal and the decimal notation for any fraction expressed in tenths, hundredths, and so on. However, this will not assure that they can express other fractions as decimals.

Look at the results in Table 11-2 (4). Analyze the errors made in both examples. What do they indicate about students' grasp of fractions and decimals? Would you not hope that students would realize that $\frac{5}{8}$ is just a little more than one-half and thus could not equal .85, which is almost a whole?

Before moving to an algorithm for changing any fraction to a decimal, let us look at some common fractions that can be changed to tenths, hundredths, and thousandths and, thus, be expressed as decimals. Activity Card 11-6 will give you some idea of how to proceed.

Once you have established that many fractions can be written as decimals, you can turn to the meaning of a fraction as division. Begin with an example that can be easily changed to a decimal—for example, $\frac{4}{5}$. Students should know that $\frac{4}{5} = \frac{8}{10} = .8$ and that $\frac{4}{5}$ means $4 \div 5$. In

TABLE 11-2

Exercise	Percent Responding Age 13
A. Which decimal is equal to $\frac{1}{5}$?*	
.15	12
● .2	38
.5	38
.51	3
I don't know	6
B. Which decimal is equal to $\frac{5}{8}$?*	
.6	7
● .625	27
$.\overline{714285}$	3
$.8\overline{5}$	30
I don't know	30

*This exercise is similar to an unreleased exercise.
Reprinted with permission of the National Council of Teachers of Mathematics (4).

order to divide 4 by 5, one needs to be able to divide decimals and to realize that 4 is also 4.0. Then one can reason:

$$\frac{4}{5} = 4 \div 5 \quad \text{which is} \quad 5\overline{)4} \quad \text{or} \quad 5\overline{)4.0}^{.8}$$

Therefore,

$$\frac{4}{5} = .8$$

Make certain you encourage the children to tell first whether the answer is more or less than one.

Once you have introduced the procedure, you can explore many interesting patterns, some of which can be investigated with a calculator. For example, look at the fraction equivalents for ninths:

$$\frac{1}{9} = .11111\ldots$$
$$\frac{2}{9} = .22222\ldots$$
$$\frac{3}{9} = .33333\ldots$$
$$\vdots$$

If you use only the calculator, the students may think that $\frac{1}{9} = .11111111$. You should do a few of these by hand to show that the pattern continues forever. Students can also be helped to see that $\frac{1}{3}$ does not equal .33, .333, or .3333 by looking at the meaning of $\frac{1}{3}$. If $\frac{1}{3} = .33$, then each of 3 equal parts of a whole would be .33. Thus, the whole would be .33 + .33 + .33 or .99, but this is not 1. Likewise, $\frac{1}{3} \neq .3333$, even though this is a better approximation.

Relationship to Place Value

The place-value interpretation of decimals is most useful in understanding computation with decimals. We

┌───┐
ACTIVITY CARD 11-6

More Tenths, Hundredths, and Thousandths

Can you write an equivalent fraction in tenths,
hundredths, or thousandths for each kind of
fractional part named below? If not, write **no**.
If you can, write **yes** and then fill in the box
to complete the sentence.

Kind of fractional part	tenths	hundredths	thousandths
thirds	Example: $\frac{1}{3} = \frac{\square}{10}$ NO	$\frac{1}{3} = \frac{\square}{100}$ NO	$\frac{1}{3} = \frac{\square}{1000}$ NO
fourths	Example: $\frac{1}{4} = \frac{\square}{10}$ NO	$\frac{1}{4} = \frac{25}{100}$ YES	$\frac{1}{4} = \frac{250}{1000}$ YES
fifths	$\frac{1}{5} = \frac{\square}{10}$ ___	$\frac{1}{5} = \frac{\square}{100}$ ___	$\frac{1}{5} = \frac{\square}{1000}$ ___
sixths	$\frac{1}{6} = \frac{\square}{10}$ ___	$\frac{1}{6} = \frac{\square}{100}$ ___	$\frac{1}{6} = \frac{\square}{1000}$ ___
eighths	$\frac{1}{8} = \frac{\square}{10}$ ___	$\frac{1}{8} = \frac{\square}{100}$ ___	$\frac{1}{8} = \frac{\square}{1000}$ ___
twentieths	$\frac{1}{20} = \frac{\square}{10}$ ___	$\frac{1}{20} = \frac{\square}{100}$ ___	$\frac{1}{20} = \frac{\square}{1000}$ ___
twenty-fifths	$\frac{1}{25} = \frac{\square}{10}$ ___	$\frac{1}{25} = \frac{\square}{100}$ ___	$\frac{1}{25} = \frac{\square}{1000}$ ___
fortieths	$\frac{1}{40} = \frac{\square}{10}$ ___	$\frac{1}{40} = \frac{\square}{100}$ ___	$\frac{1}{40} = \frac{\square}{1000}$ ___

└───┘

will look now at how to develop this interpretation and how to use it in ordering decimals and in rounding decimals.

Interpretation. Return to whole numbers and think about what we know about place value. Take, for example, the number 2463. We can identify the places (ones, tens, hundreds, and thousands) as well as what number is in each (3, 6, 4, and 2). We know, for example, that the 4 means 4 hundreds. We have also learned how the places were formed: we began with ones as a unit, grouped ten of these to form a new unit (tens), grouped ten of these to form a new unit (hundreds), and so forth.

In introducing place-value ideas with decimals, we begin with the ones as the unit. Instead of grouping by tens, we take one-tenth of the one to form the new unit of tenths. To indicate this new unit in our place-value system we use a decimal point after the ones. Children should also be helped to realize that 10 of the tenths make a one (just like 10 of any unit make the next larger unit). They should also be able to identify the tenths place in a number. This interpretation should be integrated with the interpretation of decimals as fractions.

Again, when introducing hundredths the place-value interpretation should be made. Given a number such as 51.63, the child should be able to tell what number is in the tenths place and the hundredths place as well as to tell the relationships among the places (hundredths is $\frac{1}{10}$ of the tenths, or 10 hundredths is 1 tenth). After introducing thousandths in a similar way, the children should be able to generalize to any decimal place.

Let us see how the grid can assist with decimals. When learning about decimals it is most important that a decimal such as 24.09 be read as twenty-four *and* 9 hundredths and not two, four, point, zero, nine. The words "tenths" and "hundredths" help students keep the tie between fractions and decimals.

Consider the following example:

T	O	tth	hth	
				32 *and* 43 hundredths
				or
3	2	4	3	32 *and* 4 tenths, 3 hundredths

Tie this to the modeling we did with hundredths and tenths in the fraction interpretation. Do you see that the 43 hundredths that we found as 4 tenths and 3 hundredths on the model shows up in the grid?

Now let's use the grid for writing other decimals. We use it first in conjunction with models.

Write 8 hundredths.

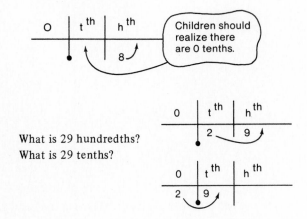

What is 29 hundredths?
What is 29 tenths?

Do you see how this last example can help children write $\frac{29}{10}$ as a decimal? Look at 4.3 on the grid. (Remember to use models when first explaining this.) How many tens are there? (0) We could write a 0 in the tens place, but this is not customary. How many hundredths are there? (0) We could write a 0 in the hundredths place and sometimes it is helpful. What does that tell us?

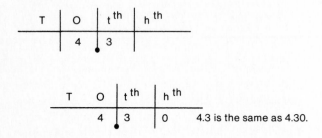

4.3 is the same as 4.30.

Once children are well acquainted with the models and the grid, they should be able to handle decimals with ease.

Ordering and Rounding Decimals. The ordering and rounding of decimals should follow directly from an understanding of decimals and the ability to order and to round whole numbers. This understanding must include being able to interpret the decimals in terms of place value and being able to think of .2 as .20 or .200.

Here is an example of a discussion that you might use in ordering two decimals:

Which is larger—23.61 or 23.9?

Questions	*Expected Responses*
What do we do first?	Compare the numbers in the largest place.
What is the largest place?	Tens.
Since those numbers are the same, what do we do next?	Compare the numbers in the ones place.
Since those are the same, what do we do?	Compare the numbers in the tenths.
Which is larger?	The 9.
Therefore, which is larger—23.61 or 23.9?	23.9
Can anyone tell us another way to look at this?	23.9 is 23.90 and 90 hundredths is more than 61 hundredths.

In rounding a decimal such as 24.78 to the nearest tenth, you need to ask the same types of questions as you do with whole numbers, but you must also understand that 24.7 = 24.70.

Questions	*Expected Responses*
What "tenths" is 24.78 between?	It's between 24.7 and 24.8 (or 24.70 and 24.80).
Is it nearer 24.7 or 24.8?	Looking at 24.70 and 24.80, it's nearer 24.80.
How will you round it?	To 24.8.

DECIMAL OPERATIONS

Certainly one advantage of decimals over fractions is that computation is much easier and basically follows the same rules as whole numbers. In teaching the algorithms you should build upon the place-value interpretations and the corresponding whole-number algorithms. With the availability of calculators, it is important that you spend as much time on seeing whether answers are reasonable as on the algorithms. Thus, the estimation skills described in Chapter 13 become crucial.

Addition and Subtraction

If your students have done a lot of estimation with whole numbers, you might begin the study of adding and subtracting with finding approximate answers to problems. This, of course, depends upon the children's understanding of decimals. As you look at the data on Activity Card 11-7, see if you can formulate questions. Then examine the ones listed to get you started. The answers you get should be about what is given, but accept any reasonable answer.

Once you have introduced problem situations with decimals, you need to develop algorithms for adding and subtracting. These are exactly the same algorithms as for whole numbers, so that you need to stress (1) add-

THE SIZE OF GREAT BRITAIN

COUNTRY	AREA (Thousands of km²)	POPULATION (Millions)
England	50.363	46.351
N. Ireland	5.452	1.537
Scotland	30.415	5.196
Wales	8.019	2.768

QUESTIONS
1. About how much larger is England than Scotland?
2. About how large is Great Britain?
3. Do more than a million people live in N. Ireland?
4. What is the population of Great Britain?
5. Do twice as many people live in Wales as live in N. Ireland?

ANSWERS
1. About 20 thousand km².
2. About 95 thousand km².
3. Yes.
4. About 55 million.
5. No; this may cause some discussion and lead to the need of considering more than the whole numbers.

ing or subtracting like units and (2) regrouping in the decimal places. A few examples with models will usually allow children to generalize from the whole-number algorithms.

Difficulty with adding or subtracting (1, p. 43) arises mainly when the exercise is given in horizontal format or in terms of a story problem and the decimals are expressed in different units—for example, 51.23 + .4 + 347. To deal with this, it is wise to have children first focus on an approximate answer. Will it be more than 300? 500? 1000? It is a help for some children to use a grid:

H	T	O	tth	hth
	5	1	2	3
			4	0
+3	4	7	0	0

Once the algorithms are introduced, continue to use them in problem-solving situations to approximate

answers and to practice adding and subtracting (it's a good way to keep these skills sharp).

Multiplication and Division

Before we examine how to teach multiplying or dividing two decimals, let's consider multiplying and dividing a decimal by a whole number. These operations are conceptually easier to explain and allow for some development that will assist when multiplying or dividing two decimals.

Consider the following problem:

> Six tables are lined up end-to-end. Each table is 2.3 meters long. How long is the line of tables?

Students should be able to solve this problem by adding decimals, and from their previous work with multiplication they should realize this is a multiplication problem. Thus, they should see that $6 \times 2.3 = 2.3 + 2.3 + 2.3 + 2.3 + 2.3 + 2.3 = 13.8$. However, just as we moved away from repeated addition to find the product of two whole numbers, we need to do so with this type of problem. Here is another way to think about it: this method depends upon a firm foundation of the place-value interpretation of decimals.

$$\begin{array}{r} 2.3 \\ \times\ 6 \\ \hline \end{array} \quad \text{is} \quad \begin{array}{r} 23 \text{ tenths} \\ \times\ 6 \\ \hline 138 \text{ tenths, which is } 13.8 \end{array}$$

or

$$\begin{array}{r} 2.37 \\ \times\ 6 \\ \hline \end{array} \quad \text{is} \quad \begin{array}{r} 237 \text{ hundredths} \\ \times\ 6 \\ \hline 1422 \text{ hundredths, which is } 14.22 \end{array}$$

The work with the grid will help students remember that 138 tenths is 13.8. In using this method, you should first have the students decide on a reasonable answer. Is 6×2.37 more than 12? As much as 18? They can also check by repeated addition.

In dividing a decimal by a whole number, the distributive algorithm that was used for dividing whole numbers may be used. Consider the following problem:

> A vinegar company distributed 123.2 million liters of vinegar equally to 8 customers. How much vinegar did each customer receive?

First, ask for reasonable answers. Did each customer get more than 10 million liters? (Yes, that would only be 80 million liters.) Did each get more than 20 million liters? (No, that would be 160 million liters.) So, we know the answer is between 10 and 20 million liters. Talk through the division as follows:

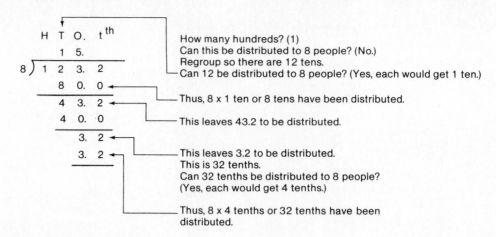

After this method is introduced, do some problems with remainders and then develop division to a specified number of places (see Examples A and B).

$$
\begin{array}{r}
15.4 \\
8\overline{\smash{)}123.8} \\
80.0 \\
\hline
43.8 \\
40.0 \\
\hline
3.8 \\
3.2 \\
\hline
.6
\end{array}
$$

Example A: Remainder is .6
Note that keeping the decimal in the algorithm helps one see the remainder is .6, not 6.

$$
\begin{array}{r}
15.47 \\
8\overline{\smash{)}123.80} \\
80.0 \\
\hline
43.8 \\
40.0 \\
\hline
3.8 \\
3.2 \\
\hline
.60 \\
.56 \\
\hline
.04
\end{array}
$$

Example B: You need to carry out the division to two places (hundredths) and round to the nearest tenth.

Again, students need to know 123.8 = 123.80.

There are several ways to teach multiplication of a decimal by a decimal. One way is to just give the rule for placing the decimal point. Another is to have children discover a rule by using the calculator. A third way is to change the decimals to fractions and develop the rule. A fourth is to use the place-value interpretation as shown here to develop the rule:

$$
\begin{array}{r}
3.2 \\
\times 1.6 \\
\hline
\end{array}
$$
is
$$
\begin{array}{r}
32 \text{ tenths} \\
\times 16 \text{ tenths} \\
\hline
512 \text{ hundredths} \\
\text{or } 5.12
\end{array}
$$

Note: One must develop that tenths times tenths is hundredths.

No matter which of these you choose, the important thing for this age group is to be able to check to see that their answer is reasonable.

To divide a decimal by a decimal, you essentially turn the problem into one that you already know how to do. That is, you make the divisor a whole number. To do this you multiply the divisor by a power of 10, such as 10, 100, 1000. In order not to change the problem, you must also multiply the dividend by that same number. For example:

$$.5\overline{\smash{)}1.25} \quad \text{change to} \quad 5\overline{\smash{)}12.5}$$

multiply
by 10

This procedure can be shortened to "Move the decimal point the number of places in the divisor needed to make it a whole number, then do the same in the dividend."

While this rule can be quickly learned, there is still the question of why it works. Students can easily be told why we do this (to turn the problem into one we can already do) and can easily be convinced that it works (using the calculator or multiplying to check). However, what would you say to the inquisitive child who asks why it works? One way is to appeal to fractions. We know that

$$1.25 \div .5 = \frac{1.25}{.5}$$

And we know that we can multiply the numerator and denominator by the same number. Thus,

$$\frac{1.25}{.5} = \frac{1.25 \times 10}{.5 \times 10} = \frac{12.5}{5} \quad \text{or} \quad 1.25 \div .5 = 12.5 \div 5$$

Students need more practice with multiplication and division of decimals than they did with addition and subtraction. This is partly because multiplication and division of whole numbers is not as firmly fixed as addition and subtraction. It is also because new rules are needed. You will find a great variation of skill level among children in your class. You might want to begin collecting some challenging activities such as the one on Activity Card 11-8 as well as games and other practice materials.

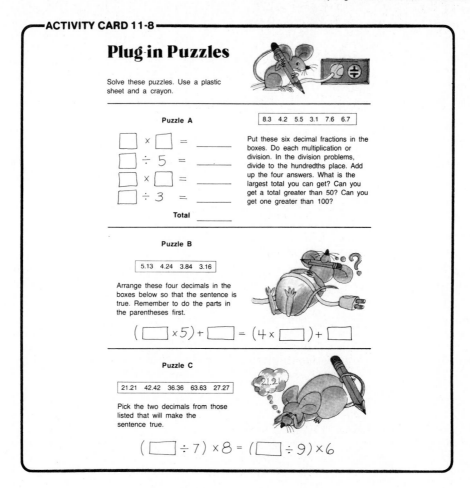

ACTIVITY CARD 11-8

Plug-in Puzzles

Solve these puzzles. Use a plastic sheet and a crayon.

Puzzle A

8.3 4.2 5.5 3.1 7.6 6.7

☐ x ☐ = _____

☐ ÷ 5 = _____

☐ x ☐ = _____

☐ ÷ 3 = _____

Total _____

Put these six decimal fractions in the boxes. Do each multiplication or division. In the division problems, divide to the hundredths place. Add up the four answers. What is the largest total you can get? Can you get a total greater than 50? Can you get one greater than 100?

Puzzle B

5.13 4.24 3.84 3.16

Arrange these four decimals in the boxes below so that the sentence is true. Remember to do the parts in the parentheses first.

(☐ x 5) + ☐ = (4 x ☐) + ☐

Puzzle C

21.21 42.42 36.36 63.63 27.27

Pick the two decimals from those listed that will make the sentence true.

(☐ ÷ 7) x 8 = (☐ ÷ 9) x 6

A GLANCE AT WHERE WE'VE BEEN

We have examined how to approach fractions and decimals in a meaningful way. This can be done through thoughtful teaching that first develops an understanding of the numbers through models and appropriate language. It involves careful sequencing and a pace that does not rush to the symbolic alone. The operations with these numbers can also be presented in a meaningful way instead of through rules learned by rote. A firm foundation of the numbers and the operations will assist students in using these numbers to solve problems. Thus, throughout the development in this chapter applications have been included to let students see how these numbers are used and to give meaning to the numbers and operations.

Ages or grade levels have not been given because we have found that often older children will profit from some of the beginning concepts. It will be your job to realize what pieces of this topic your students are missing. This will not be as difficult as it sounds if you are familiar with the background and how the concepts and skills interweave.

THINGS TO DO: ADDING TO YOUR PICTURE

1. Show four different part-whole models for $\frac{3}{4}$.

2. Create five ·story problems that ask children to order fractions.

3. Design a worksheet that would be a good follow-up to the opening lesson. Include all three models —region, length, and area—and a couple of challenging problems.

4. Make up a worksheet that follows the introduction to adding and subtracting fractions. Use halves, fourths, fifths, tenths, and twentieths, providing the appropriate picture of strips as in Figure 11-4.

5. Make up five problems that can be solved by multiplying fractions, and draw the area model to find the solution.

6. Examine two texts to see how they introduce division of fractions, and contrast each to the method in the book.

7. Illustrate (using the hundredths square) the steps in the algorithms for each of these problems:

$$
\begin{array}{r}
5.69 \\
+\,9.35 \\
\hline
\end{array}
\qquad
\begin{array}{r}
15.2 \\
-\;7.9 \\
\hline
\end{array}
$$

8. Read the description of the film "Weird Numbers" and its review in *Films in the Mathematics Classroom* [reference (1) in Chapter 12]. Preview the film if it is available. Plan a lesson using this film; include a list of questions or activities to be used as a follow-up to the film.

SELECTED REFERENCES

1. Ashlock, Robert B. "Introducing Decimal Fractions with the Meterstick." *Arithmetic Teacher,* 23 (March 1976), pp. 201–206.

2. Bright, George W., and Harvey, John G. "Using Games to Teach Fraction Concepts and Skills." In *Mathematics for the Middle Grades (5–9)* (ed. Linda Silvey). 1982 Yearbook. Reston, Va.: National Council of Teachers of Mathematics, 1982. Pp. 205–216.

3. Brown, Christopher N. "Fractions on Grid Paper." *Arithmetic Teacher,* 27 (January 1979), pp. 8–10.

4. Carpenter, Thomas P.; Corbitt, Mary Kay; Kepner, Henry S., Jr.; Lindquist, Mary Montgomery; and Reys, Robert E. *Results from the Second Mathematics Assessment of the National Assessment of Educational Progress.* Reston, Va.: National Council of Teachers of Mathematics, 1981.

5. Carpenter, Thomas P.; Corbitt, Mary Kay; Kepner, Henry S., Jr.; Lindquist, Mary Montgomery; and Reys, Robert E. "Decimals: Results and Implications from National Assessment." *Arithmetic Teacher,* 28 (April 1981), pp. 34–37.

6. Dana, Marcia, and Lindquist, Mary Montgomery. "From Halves to Hundredths." *Arithmetic Teacher,* 27 (November 1979), pp. 4–8.

7. Ellerbruch, Larry W., and Payne, Joseph N. "A Teaching Sequence from Initial Fraction Concepts through the Addition of Unlike Fractions." In *Developing Computational Skills* (ed. Marilyn N. Suydam). Reston, Va.: National Council of Teachers of Mathematics, 1978.

8. Kieren, Thomas E. "Knowing Rational Numbers: Ideas and Symbols." In *Selected Issues in Mathematics Education* (ed. Mary Montgomery Lindquist). Berkeley, Calif.: McCutchan Publishing Corporation, 1980.

9. Lankford, Francis G., Jr. *Some Computational Strategies of Seventh Grade Pupils.* Charlottesville, Va.: University of Virginia, 1972. ERIC: ED 069 496.

10. Lichtenberg, Betty K., and Lichtenberg, Donovan R. "Decimals Deserve Distinction." In *Mathematics for the Middle Grades (5–9)* (ed. Linda Silvey). 1982 Yearbook. Reston, Va.: National Council of Teachers of Mathematics, 1982. Pp. 142–152.

11. Payne, Joseph N. "Sense and Nonsense about Fractions and Decimals." *Arithmetic Teacher,* 27 (January 1980), pp. 4–7.

12. Post, Thomas. "Fractions: Results and Implications from National Assessment." *Arithmetic Teacher,* 29 (May 1981), pp. 26–31.

13. Romberg, Thomas A.; Harvey, John G.; Moser, James M.; and Montgomery, Mary E. *Developing Mathematical Processes (DMP).* Chicago: Rand McNally, 1974–1976.

14. Scott, Wayne R. "Fractions Taught by Folding Strips." *Arithmetic Teacher,* 28 (January 1981), pp. 18–22.

15. Suydam, Marilyn N., and Dessart, Donald J. *Classroom Ideas from Research on Computational Skills.* Reston, Va.: National Council of Teachers of Mathematics, 1976.

12

Examining Ratio, Proportion, and Percent

INTRODUCTION

"Family income this year increased by 10 percent."
"Jon did only half the work Mary did."
"Her salary is three times my salary."
"The cost of living tripled during the last eight years."

Such statements are heard frequently; much of our own quantitative thinking is relational. In such thinking, what is important is the relationship between numbers, rather than the actual numbers themselves. For example, consider the prices of three carpets. The difference in price between these carpets (A and B or B and C) is $1 per square yard. Yet B is twice as expensive as A and C is 50 percent more expensive than B. In comparing relative cost, it is the ratio relationship of the prices rather than the prices themselves that becomes important.

CARPET SALE

A
$1.00
sq. yd.

B
$2.00
sq. yd.

C
$3.00
sq. yd.

RATIO

Ratios involve matching things in different ways. It is essential that early experiences with ratio stimulate children to think of two related numbers simultaneously. Consider, for example, Activity Cards 12-1 and 12-2.* Each question encourages children to think about ordered pairs of numbers, such as: (4 bagels, 2 bananas). Each question helps link the operation of multiplication directly to ordered pairs and ratio. It is essential that ratios be closely linked to multiplication.

Money (the number of pennies in a dime, nickels in a quarter, and so on) provides natural and meaningful illustrations of ratio. Organizing such information (see Figure 12-1) not only visually displays many ratios but helps students realize that a ratio is a multiplicative comparison of two or more numbers in a given order.

Children should recognize that the one-to-five ratio for quarters and nickels can be written several different ways, such as 1:5, an ordered pair (1, 5) or 1/5 (read "one is to five"). Any of these forms is acceptable. This model also provides a natural extension of ratio to more than two numbers. For example, the ordered triple

*Activity Card 12-1 is from Romberg (13).

183

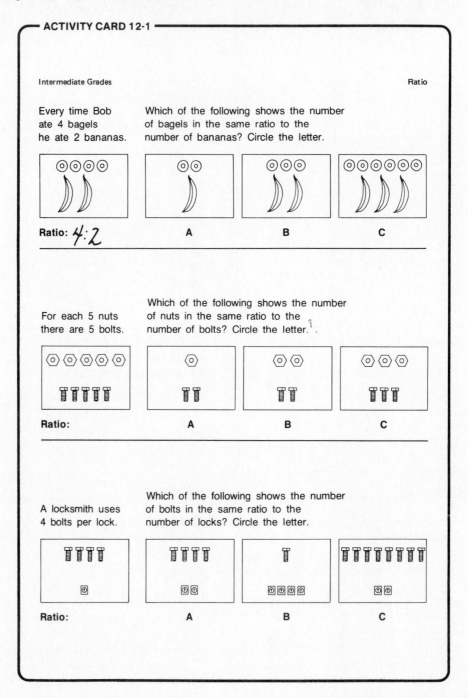

Intermediate Grades   Ratio

Every time Bob ate 4 bagels he ate 2 bananas.

Which of the following shows the number of bagels in the same ratio to the number of bananas? Circle the letter.

Ratio: 4:2   A   B   C

For each 5 nuts there are 5 bolts.

Which of the following shows the number of nuts in the same ratio to the number of bolts? Circle the letter.

Ratio: A   B   C

A locksmith uses 4 bolts per lock.

Which of the following shows the number of bolts in the same ratio to the number of locks? Circle the letter.

Ratio: A   B   C

(2, 10, 50) relates 2 quarters, 10 nickels, and 50 pennies.

Children encounter ratio in many different forms: "three video games for a dollar," "twice as long," "half as much," and so on. Real-world examples of ratio help develop a greater awareness and understanding. Consumer purchases, such as 2 cans for 99¢, 3 pounds for $1.99, and 88¢ a dozen, are frequently encountered and each illustrates ratios in action. The statement of values (8, 12, 20) on a sack of lawn fertilizer uses ratio to report the percent of phosphorous, nitrogen, and potash contained. This reminds us of the importance of the order of the entries and the need to understand what each entry represents. An ordered pair from Figure 12-1, such as (5, 25) could represent 5 quarters and 25 nickels or 5 nickels and 25 pennies. Whether a ratio has two, three, or more entries, it has little meaning until the entries are known.

Although multiplication problems provide opportunities to discuss ratio informally, the concept of ratio is typically not studied until fifth grade. Suppose you are ready to extend some ideas on multiplication to study ratio. After completing and discussing Activity

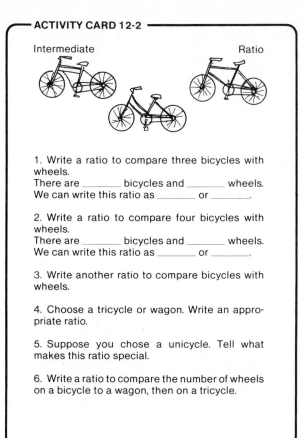

ACTIVITY CARD 12-2

Intermediate   Ratio

1. Write a ratio to compare three bicycles with wheels.
There are _____ bicycles and _____ wheels.
We can write this ratio as _____ or _____.

2. Write a ratio to compare four bicycles with wheels.
There are _____ bicycles and _____ wheels.
We can write this ratio as _____ or _____.

3. Write another ratio to compare bicycles with wheels.

4. Choose a tricycle or wagon. Write an appropriate ratio.

5. Suppose you chose a unicycle. Tell what makes this ratio special.

6. Write a ratio to compare the number of wheels on a bicycle to a wagon, then on a tricycle.

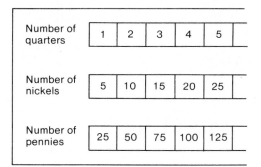

Number of quarters	1	2	3	4	5
Number of nickels	5	10	15	20	25
Number of pennies	25	50	75	100	125

Figure 12-1

Card 12-1, you might consider how some of those tasks lead directly toward writing ratios, as on Activity Card 12-2.

Pupils are sometimes confused with the different symbolization used to record ratio. This confusion can be minimized by linking the symbols to appropriate models and promoting class discussion. Chips or cut-out wheels could be used to model these tasks before the ratios are written. A table might be made to help organize the information. Once recorded, guided discussion centering on the information and the situation helps children talk about the mathematics. For example, questions such as the following will provide early practice in verbalizing and describing some of the mathematics surrounding the concept of ratio:

> If I have three bicycles and six wheels, the ratio is three to six or (3, 6).
> If the ratio is four to eight, how many bicycles do I have?
> If the ratio is five to ten, how many wheels do I have?
> If I have six bicycles, can you tell how many wheels are needed? What is the ratio?

It is important that ratios be correctly applied to all types of numbers. In elementary school, however, the emphasis is typically on smaller numbers such as 1-to-2, 2-to-3, and 3-to-4 relationships. These ratios are the most frequently used and much easier to model and conceptualize than 7-to-9 or 11-to-14. It is also common to express a relationship as 1-to-2 rather than 2-to-1.

Far more important than how the ratio is expressed is the understanding of the relationship. Young children with a good understanding of numbers use "twice as much" just as often and as comfortably as "half as much." Instruction should take advantage of these different expressions to develop further reversible thinking.

PROPORTION

Proportions relate two or more ratios and are frequently used in problem situations. Consider, for example, this problem:

SALE
Hot Cross Buns

3 for 49¢

How much will a dozen cost?

In approaching such a problem, using words along with the numerical values helps children not only organize the information but understand it more clearly. It is helpful, too, to get students to talk about reasonable answers before getting into specific computation. For example, in light of our earlier work with estimation we might think:

$\frac{1}{4}$ dozen is almost 50¢, so

$\frac{1}{2}$ dozen is almost \$1, so

1 dozen will be almost \$2

ACTIVITY CARD 12-3
Intermediate

Two Views
Proportions

Proportions: Two Views

METHOD 1

3 : 12 = 5 : □
BAGS THINGS BAGS THINGS

THERE ARE 3 BAGS AND 12 THINGS.
THE SECOND NUMBER IS 4 TIMES THE FIRST.

3 × 4 = 12
SO
5 × 4 = 20

×4   ×4
3 : 12 = 5 : 20
BAGS THINGS BAGS THINGS

METHOD 2

6 : 26 = 3 : □
BAGS THINGS BAGS THINGS

HOW MANY THINGS IN A BAG ? THE
SECOND NUMBER IS HOW MANY TIMES
THE FIRST ? THAT'S NOT EASY TO
FIGURE OUT.

HMM, 26 THINGS IN 6 BAGS. 3 BAGS
IS 1/2 OF 6 BAGS. SO THERE HAVE TO BE
1/2 OF 26 THINGS.

6 ÷ 2 = 3   26 ÷ 2 = 13

6 ÷ 2   26 ÷ 2
6 : 26 = 3 : 13
BAGS THINGS BAGS THINGS

Solve the following proportions.
Use whatever method is easiest for you.

A. 20 : 30 = 40 : □
doors walls doors walls

B. 9 : 81 = 15 : □
teams players teams players

C. 15 : 30 = 220 : □
books pupils books pupils

D. 43 : 13 = □ : 39
horses owners horses owners

E. 24 : 8 = 27 : □
fish gulls fish gulls

F. 5 : 16 = □ : 32
dogs tricks dogs tricks

G. 8 : 56 = □ : 21
workers $ workers $

H. 11 : □ = 8 : 64
kg objects kg objects

I. 48 : 14 = 24 : □
ml tubes ml tubes

J. 500 : 25 = 100 : □
liters cans liters cans

K. □ : 8 = 12 : 32
bars ¢ bars ¢

L. 100 : □ = 12 : 3
tacks ¢ tacks ¢

Such thinking is very productive. It should be both encouraged and rewarded. It uses estimation along with ratios to produce ballpark answers. Frequent experiences similar to this will improve students' judgment, making them less likely to fall victim to unreasonable answers resulting from indiscriminate number crunching.

Students should also realize that a single problem can be represented by several proportions. For example, here are some ways of writing proportions for the hot cross buns:

$$\frac{3}{49} = \frac{12}{\square} \qquad 3:49 = 12:\square \qquad \frac{49}{3} = \frac{\square}{12} \qquad 49:3 = \square:12$$

$$\frac{3}{12} = \frac{49}{\square} \qquad 3:12 = 49:\square \qquad \frac{12}{3} = \frac{\square}{49} \qquad 12:3 = \square:49$$

Although students should recognize the equivalence of these statements, they should feel free to use the form of their choice.

Many problems involving proportions are solved mentally without any paper-and-pencil computation:

ACTIVITY CARD 12-4

Intermediate   Equivalent Ratios

Swap Shop Swaps

Complete each chart with equivalent ratios.

A.   3 : 5
mops   dustpans

mops	dustpans
3	5
9	15
6	10
12	
	50
	25
	30

B.   8 : 2
lamps   rugs

lamps	rugs
4	1
12	3
24	6
40	
20	
	7
	9

C.   1 : 6
hammer   sponges

hammers	sponges
1	6
5	30
3	18
7	
	60
	54
8	

D.   12 : 8
yo-yos   banks

yo-yos	banks
12	8
15	10
18	12
	16
9	
	40
72	

E.   10 : 50
paperbacks   spoons

paperbacks	spoons
10	50
40	200
30	150
5	
	250
	500
60	

F.   8 : 3
ties   shirts

ties	shirts
8	3
16	6
	9
	24
88	
	27
32	

---

this approach should be encouraged whenever possible. However, when the computation becomes too messy, the proportion can be solved algorithmically. Activity Card 12-3 highlights two different strategies.* Providing two ways of solving proportions encourages students to analyze the problem situation before choosing an approach to use.

*Activity Cards 12-3, 12-4, and 12-5 are from Romberg (13).

The pennies-nickels comparisons in Figure 12-1 contain many equivalent ratios (1:5 = 2:10, 2:10 = 3:15, and so on). The concept of equivalent ratios is very important and can be anchored in different ways. For example, Activity Card 12-4 provides practice exercises that a child could model if necessary and that also promote and reward the discovery of patterns.

Once equivalent ratios are established, they can be used in a variety of ways. For example, comparative shopping relies heavily on determining if two ratios are in fact proportional. Suppose the same product is packaged in two different sizes:

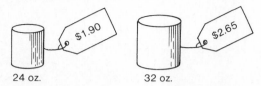

24 oz.   32 oz.

Which size has the lowest unit price? Although this question can be solved in different ways, it involves ratios. More specifically, are these ratios equal?

$$\frac{\$1.90}{24} \overset{?}{=} \frac{\$2.65}{32}$$

This can be solved several ways, but one of the most natural is by finding equivalent ratios:

$$\frac{\$1.90 \times 4}{24 \times 4} = \frac{\$7.60}{96} \qquad \frac{\$2.65 \times 3}{32 \times 3} = \frac{\$7.95}{96}$$

Not Equal

Since the ratios are not equal, the prices are not equivalent, and the smaller size selling at $1.90 is the better buy.

As proportions are studied, students should realize that maps and scale drawings use ratio. Activity Card 12-5 provides opportunities for students to use measurement skills along with ratio in some practical problem solving.

Extending these skills along with ratio to proportions leads to solutions of many practical geometry problems. Using similar triangles to find proportions is a very practical way of finding distances and lengths not easily measured, such as heights of skyscrapers and distances between mountain peaks or across canyons or lakes (see Figure 12-2).

Before closing this discussion on ratio and proportion, let's look at some additional geometric applications involving similarity. Two figures are similar if their respective sides are in the same ratio—i.e., proportional. Thus, all squares are similar but all rectangles are not. Look for some patterns in the similar triangles in the accompanying sketch.

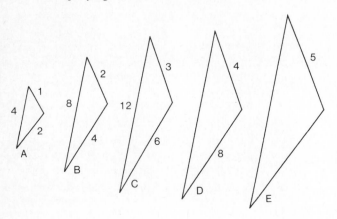

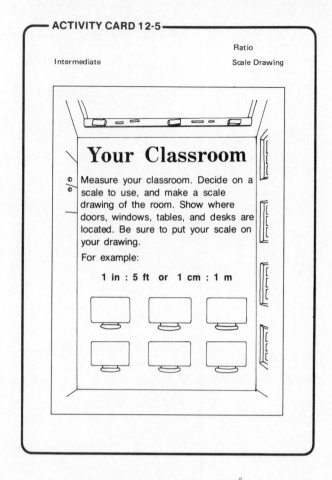

Your Classroom

Measure your classroom. Decide on a scale to use, and make a scale drawing of the room. Show where doors, windows, tables, and desks are located. Be sure to put your scale on your drawing.

For example:

1 in : 5 ft or 1 cm : 1 m

The girl is 150 centimeters tall, and her shadow is 30 centimeters long. The shadow of the flagpole is 120 centimeters long. The triangles formed by the flagpole and the girl are similar. What is the height of the flagpole?

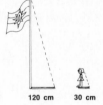

120 cm   30 cm

Figure 12-2.   From Romberg (13).

Triangle A is similar to triangle B because the extended ratios 1:2:4 and 2:4:8 are equal. Likewise, triangles B and C are similar. Now let's use triangles D and E for some additional problem solving. If triangle D is similar to A, describe how to find the length of the longest side of triangle D. If triangle E is also similar to A, describe how the lengths of the other two sides can be found. Since the resulting ratios in E involve multiples of five, we could also relate these values to the coins on page 185. This illustrates multiembodiment and reminds students that the same numerical patterns can occur in very different settings.

An interesting application of ratio and proportion appears in architectural designs. The ratio of the sides of a rectangle varies, but one ratio, known as the *golden ratio*, has occurred in many architectural structures and works of art (14).

PERCENTS

Save 23 to 55%

MONEY MARKET CERTIFICATES

14.70%

YIELDS

16.07%

City asks for 40% budget increase

Serious crimes drop 5 percent

Wholesale Price Index Up 0.6 Pct.

38 Percent Plunge In Profits

One need only read a newspaper or watch television to be reminded that percent is one of the most widely used and abused mathematical concepts. Its understanding is taken for granted, even though there is plenty of evidence to the contrary. Incorrect usage of percent is frequent among both secondary students and adults. Flagrant errors abound, suggesting that often the most basic ideas are unclear. For example, a question similar to the one below was asked during the first national mathematics assessment (5):

> If 5 percent of the students are absent today, then 5 out of how many are absent?

About one-third of the 17-year-olds and adults missed this question; apparently they did not know 100 was the comparison base for percent.

Misconceptions, distortions, and confusion surrounding percent are surprisingly easy to find. Here are examples:

1. *"Prices reduced 100%."* If this advertisement were correct, the items would be free. Probably the prices were reduced 50%. If an item that cost $400 originally was on sale for $200, then the ad based the 100% on the sale price, when it should have been based on the original price.

2. *"Of all doctors interviewed, 75% recommended our product."* Such a claim, if true, could be a bonanza for a company. If, however, the ad said "3 out of the 4 doctors we interviewed recommended our product," the consumer reaction might be different. Percents can often be used to disguise the number involved. This is a double-edged sword. Percents allow for easy comparisons because of the common base of one hundred, but they may appear to represent a larger sample than actually exists.

Ironically, the understanding of percent requires no new skill or concepts beyond those used in mastering fractions, decimals, and ratios. In fact, percent is not a mathematical topic per se, but rather the application of a particular type of notational system. The justification for teaching percent in school mathematics programs rests solely on its social utility. Consequently, percent should be taught and learned in application situations.

Like decimals and fractions, percents express a relationship between two numbers. Percents are ratios and without a doubt are the most widely used of all ratios. Percent is derived from the Latin words *per centum* which mean "out of a hundred" or "for every hundred." Thus the origin of percent and its major uses are more closely associated with ratio than with either decimals or fractions.

When is percent understood? Students understand percent when they can use it many different ways. For example, if someone understands 25 percent, he or she can:

1. Find 25 percent in various contexts. For example: Cover 25 percent of a floor with tiles. Determine 25 percent off the price of a given item. Survey 25 percent of the students in class. In many of these situations, estimates of 25 percent are not only appropriate but essential.

2. Identify characteristics of 25 percent. For example, 25 percent of the milk in a glass is less than half. Or, if 25 percent of the milk in a glass is spilled, then 75 percent remains.

3. Compare and contrast 25 percent with a range of other percents such as 5 percent, 50 percent, and 100 percent. For example, 25 percent is half as much as 50 percent, one-fourth as much as 100 percent, and five times as much as 5 percent.

Getting Started

Percents should be introduced only after students thoroughly understand fractions and decimals and have had experiences with ratio. Percent is not studied extensively in elementary school, although it is typically introduced around fifth or sixth grade. Only the fundamental ideas for using percent are established; most computation applying percent in problem-solving situations is reserved for later.

Instruction should begin by explaining that 25% means 25 per hundred. It should expand to a wide range of percents, such as 50%, 90%, 5%, 100%, 99%, 1%, and 200%. These percents should be illustrated in a variety of different situations. For example, a meter stick provides an easily accessible and effective model. Cover part of the meter stick and ask children to estimate the percent of the meter stick that is covered. Students could be shown the meter stick face down (if the scale is on both sides, cover one side with masking tape) and then asked:

	Red	Blue
Side A		
Side B	70%	30%

Estimate what percent of the meter stick is covered. About what percent of the meter stick is not covered?

How can we check our estimate? (Turn the stick over.)

This model provides many different situations (25%, 50%, 1%, etc.) that can be presented and discussed quickly. Patterns may also emerge as students realize that the sum of the covered and uncovered portions will total 100 percent.

A related activity involving area could have students using a stack of 20 cards with the B side down. On the A side, specific percents of the card are colored blue (0%, 10%, 20%, . . . , 100%) and the remainder (100%, . . . , 0%) red. Make two cards of each type. Ask students to take turns trying to win cards by looking only at side A and trying to predict the percents shown on side B. Lesson Card 12-1 provides some additional tasks that use models to develop important concepts of percent. Each of these tasks provides ideas that can be used to relate percents and fractions.

These early experiences with percent should be

LESSON CARD 12-1

USING PERCENT MODELS

Materials: Several different models, each of which displays clearly the 100 parts in a whole.

Activity: Pose additional questions to accompany the following teacher-led discussions.

1. Construct a model that has 100 parts but at the same time has the potential of displaying equivalent subsets of these 100 elements. Here are two models.

Rope with 100 discs arranged 10 black, 10 red, 10 black, 10 red, . . .

Rectangle 5 x 20 all small squares shown.

2. Find representations of various percents on each model. For example, when representing 50 percent, help students realize that any 50 of the parts could be chosen—for example, in either of the two ways shown here.

3. Have students consider the model as a whole and ask for all the fractions that show the same amount as 50 percent. Write the results informally—something like:

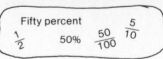

Fifty percent
$\frac{1}{2}$ 50% $\frac{50}{100}$ $\frac{5}{10}$

4. Repeat step 3 using 20 percent. A display similar to this would emerge.

Twenty percent
$\frac{2}{10}$ 20% $\frac{1}{5}$ $\frac{20}{100}$

5. Compare the representations for 50 percent and 20 percent on each model. Ask questions such as:
   Which is greater, 50 or 20 percent?
   What fractional part is covered by 20 percent?
   What fractional part remains uncovered?

6. Any multiple of ten can be illustrated easily with these models. Continue to model different percents and their corresponding fractions until generalizations of these relationships are established.

followed by activities that center around direct translation experiences involving 100. Figure 12-3 illustrates how the same diagram can be represented symbolically by a fraction, a decimal, and a percent. It should be emphasized that each small square represents 1% and the entire square represents 100%. Practice activities using this model to convert percents to fractions and decimals, and vice versa, should be plentiful. For example, Figure 12-1 also provides a visual reminder that 17% (read "seventeen percent") can also be thought of as $17 \times \frac{1}{100}$, so the symbol % can be thought of as equivalent to the fraction $\frac{1}{100}$. Also, 17% can be thought of as 17/100, so that the concept of ratio is reinforced. It is important that students feel comfortable with different interpretations of a percent.

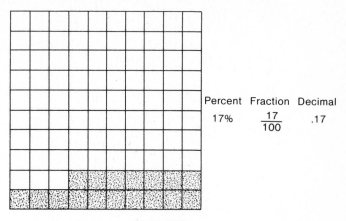

Percent	Fraction	Decimal
17%	$\frac{17}{100}$	.17

Figure 12-3

The importance of establishing 100 as the base for percent cannot be overemphasized, and 50% should be recognized as the fraction $\frac{50}{100}$ or $50 \times \frac{1}{100}$. However, it is also important that students know that an infinite number of equivalent fractions ($\frac{1}{2}, \frac{2}{4}, \frac{3}{6}, \ldots, \frac{50}{100}, \ldots$) also represent 50 percent.

Activity Card 12-6 provides a natural means of developing some important ideas in an informal and yet meaningfully structured way. Examine the four activities (a) through (d). Each should further develop children's concept of percent. Activities (b), (c), and (d)

require some collection and recording of data prior to reporting the percents. The use of three different base numbers (10 logs, 100 pennies, and 20 chips) will strengthen the link between a ratio and percent. Even though answers on each activity depend on the data recorded, some patterns will emerge. A few questions from the teacher should trigger some stimulating discussion. For example, do the percents on each card total 100%? Why does this happen? Can you think of a time when it would not? Tell something special about activity (c).

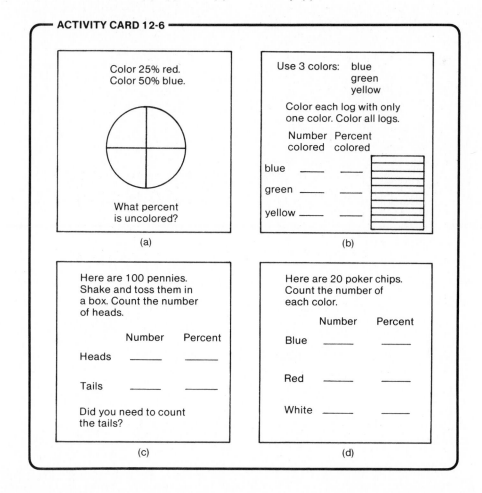

ACTIVITY CARD 12-6

(a)
Color 25% red.
Color 50% blue.

What percent is uncolored?

(b)
Use 3 colors: blue
                 green
                 yellow

Color each log with only one color. Color all logs.

	Number colored	Percent colored
blue	____	____
green	____	____
yellow	____	____

(c)
Here are 100 pennies. Shake and toss them in a box. Count the number of heads.

	Number	Percent
Heads	____	____
Tails	____	____

Did you need to count the tails?

(d)
Here are 20 poker chips. Count the number of each color.

	Number	Percent
Blue	____	____
Red	____	____
White	____	____

One particularly troublesome aspect of percent involves very small percents (between 0% and 1%). For example, $\frac{1}{2}\%$ as in "$\frac{1}{2}\%$ milk fat," is not well understood. A visual representation can help show that $\frac{1}{2}\%$ is indeed less than 1% (see Figure 12-4). This understanding rests on the earlier agreement that each small square represents 1%, and this cannot be mentioned too often. This percent can also be shown symbolically as both a fraction and a decimal. However, it is far more important in elementary school to establish the intuitive notion of relative size of small percents than to devote extensive time to the algebraic gymnastics of showing the fraction and decimal equivalent.

Development of percents more than 100 is challenging and should be done with models. Once the idea is established that a given region represents 100%, more than one region can be used to represent percents greater than 100%. For example, 235% could be represented by two completely shaded regions and one partially shaded region (see Figure 12-5). Using every opportunity to show equivalence between percents, fractions, and decimals will help establish and maintain these relationships.

Keeping It Going

Although percents are regularly encountered in many different real-life problem-solving situations, there are only three basic types of problems involving percents. Several different methods can be used to solve percent problems, and two of them (ratio and equation) are illustrated. The effective use of these methods re-

quires a firm understanding of the concept of percent and ratio as well as the ability to solve simple equations. Such skills are developed over a period of several years and need not be rushed. In fact, the necessary steps toward solving percent problems are taken in the elementary grades and built upon in secondary school. In the elementary school it is absolutely essential to help students solve percent problems meaningfully and to avoid rushing them toward symbolic methods. More formal methods will be developed and anchored in secondary school.

Now let's take a brief look at each type of problem:

1. Finding the percent of a given number.

    Lucas receives $60 a month for a paper route, and next month he will get a 10% raise. How much is his raise?

    The context of this problem suggests that the raise will be something considerably less than $60. It might be modeled like this:

$60

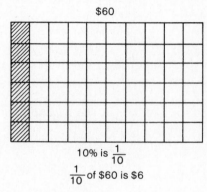

10% is $\frac{1}{10}$

$\frac{1}{10}$ of $60 is $6

Percent	Fraction	Decimal
$\frac{1}{2}\%$	$\frac{\frac{1}{2}}{100} = \frac{1}{200}$	.005

Figure 12-4

Figure 12-5

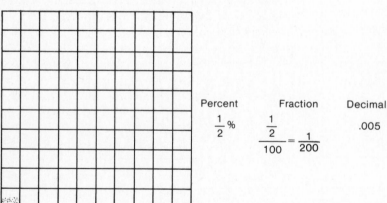

Percent	Fraction	Decimal
234%	$\frac{234}{100} = 2\frac{34}{100}$	2.34

It could also be solved other ways.

Ratio method: $\dfrac{10\%}{100\%} = \dfrac{R}{60}$, $\quad R = \$6$

Equation method: $R = 10\%$ of $\$60$
$$= .1 \times \$60$$
$$= \$6$$

The computation is simple and may disguise the level of difficulty this type of problem presents. For example, only 10% of the 13-year-olds in the second national mathematics assessment answered a similar question correctly (6).

2. Find what percent one number is of another number.

The Cardinals won 15 of their 20 games. What percent did they win?

Intuitively, it is clear that the Cardinals did not win all their games, so the answer must be less than 100%. Similarly, they won more than half their games, so it must be more than 50%. It could be modeled like this:

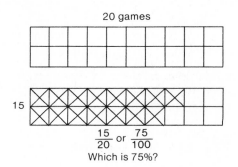

20 games

$\dfrac{15}{20}$ or $\dfrac{75}{100}$
Which is 75%?

Here are two more ways to find the solution:

Ratio method: $\dfrac{P\%}{100\%} = \dfrac{15}{20}$, $\quad P = 75\%$

Equation method: $P \times 20 = 15$
$$P = \dfrac{15}{20} = .75$$
$$P = 75\%$$

Once again the computation is easy, but only 21% of the 13-year-olds in the assessment answered correctly on a similar question (6).

3. Find the total (100%) when only a percent is known.

The sale price was $40, and it was marked down 50%. What was its original price?

Common sense suggests that the sale price should be more than $40. Guess-and-test is often a very effective strategy in solving this type of problem. For example, if we guess an original price of $60, then the sale price of $30 is too low. Still, we are

on the right track, and if this approach is continued, it will eventually lead to the correct price of $80. It could be modeled like this:

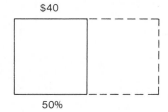

$40

50%

This model provides a base for either of these solutions.

Ratio method: $\dfrac{50\%}{100\%} = \dfrac{\$40}{OP}$ (*OP*—original price)
$$OP = \$80$$

Equation method: 50% of $OP = \$40$
$$OP = \$80$$

This type of problem is typically more difficult to solve. This was confirmed by results from the second mathematics assessment, where less than 5% of the 13-year-olds responded correctly (6).

The consistently poor performance on percent problems means that instruction must become more systematic. If stress is placed on a particular method before the problem is thought through and well understood, the result will probably be confusion and poor performance. Instructional emphasis in the elementary school must be on thinking aloud and talking about what should be done and what would be a reasonable answer. These teacher-led discussions should occur before any serious paper-and-pencil efforts are made to solve the problem. Early emphasis on writing a solution to a percent problem forces many students to operate mechanically (without any conscious thinking) on the numbers to produce an answer.

Students should be encouraged to think quantitatively in solving problems involving percent. Research does not support the teaching of a single method such as ratio or equation to solve such problems (4); instruction should therefore be flexible and not locked into a single method. It is recommended that problems involving percent be presented and then student leads followed flexibly toward solutions. More specifically, some verbalization of the solution should accompany the actual problem-solving process. This helps clarify what was done (either right or wrong) and provides some closure to the process. It also allows for some consideration of the reasonableness or sensibleness of an answer.

This less formal, intuitive approach lacks the structure and security of emphasis on a particular method.

Yet it has several important advantages. In particular, it encourages students to understand the problem in their own minds along with possible solutions, and it decreases the likelihood of their applying a method blindly.

A GLANCE AT WHERE WE'VE BEEN

Ratios compare two or more numbers. They take different forms and have many applications—money (pennies for nickels), measurement (12 inches in a foot), consumer purchases (3 for 29¢), scale drawings and blueprints, to name but a few. Together with proportion, ratios provide an opportunity to practice many computational skills as well as strengthen problem-solving skills. Ratios also provide a natural means of studying percent, which has a comparison base of 100. Since few mathematical topics have more practical use than percents, it is essential that meaningful and systematic development of percent be provided. That has been the direction of our discussion.

THINGS TO DO: ADDING TO YOUR PICTURE

1. Give an example of a ratio and a proportion. How could you help children distinguish between them?
2. Ratios may be used to determine the best buy. Use local newspaper advertisements to find information and set up ratios to compare different sizes of the same product. Can you refute the claim, "The larger the quantity, the lower the unit price"?
3. Many excellent articles on ratio and percent appear in *Arithmetic Teacher*. For some examples, check *Activities for Junior High School and Middle School Mathematics* (8). Select an article and then prepare an activity card based on it to help children learn a particular concept.
4. Describe how ratios are used in photography and identify some "popular sizes."
5. Examine some of the references on the "golden ratio" suggested by Schaaf. Prepare a summary of a few interesting applications in architecture and nature for your class.
6. Read the description of the film "Ratio" and its review in *Films in the Mathematics Classroom* (1). Preview the film if it is available. Tell whether or not you would use this film in a sixth-grade class that is studying ratio.
7. Make up a story for each of these sentences:
   (a) $\frac{5}{12} = \frac{x}{\$1.80}$
   (b) 40% of 95 = □
8. Describe how you could use a meter stick, graduated in millimeters, to illustrate each of the following percents:
   (a) `35%
   (b) 3.5%
   (c) .35%

9. Here is a partially completed chart:

Decimal	Fraction	Percent
.1	$\frac{1}{10}$	10%
____	____	5%
____	$\frac{1}{4}$	____
.333 . . .	____	____
.5	____	____
____	$\frac{2}{3}$	____
____	____	75%

Explain why it would be helpful to have sixth-grade children memorize these popular percents and their related fraction and decimal form.

10. Rose was making $22,000 a year. She received a 10% raise. Later in the year the company started losing money and reduced all salaries 10%. Rose said, "I'm making what I was before." Is her thinking correct? Describe how you would explain the procedure to Rose.
11. In our discussion of percent problems we emphasized the importance of "talking" or "thinking" through a solution before setting up equations to solve. Do you agree with this emphasis? Defend your position.
12. Describe how you would "think through" a solution to this problem: The population of a city increased from 200,000 to 220,000. What is the percent of inccrease?

SELECTED REFERENCES

1. Bestgen, Barbara J., and Reys, Robert E. *Films in the Mathematics Classroom.* Reston, Va.: National Council of Teachers of Mathematics, 1982.
2. Brown, Gerald W., and Kinney, Lucien B. "Let's Teach Them About Ratio." *Mathematics Teacher,* 66 (April 1973), pp. 352–355.
3. Bruni, James V., and Silverman, Helene J. "Let's Do It! From Blocks and Model Making to Ratio and Proportion." *Arithmetic Teacher,* 24 (March 1977), pp. 172–180.
4. Callahan, Leroy G., and Glennon, Vincent J. *Elementary School Mathematics: A Guide to Current Research,* 4th ed. Washington, D.C.: Association for Supervision and Curriculum Development, 1975.
5. Carpenter, Thomas P.; Coburn, Terrence G.; Reys, Robert E.; and Wilson, James W. *Results from the First Mathematics Assessment of the National Assessment of Educational Progress.* Reston, Va.: National Council of Teachers of Mathematics, 1978.
6. Carpenter, Thomas P.; Corbitt, Mary Kay; Kepner, Henry S., Jr.; Lindquist, Mary Montgomery; and Reys, Robert E. *Results from the Second Mathematics Assessment of the National Assessment of*

Educational Progress. Reston, Va.: National Council of Teachers of Mathematics, 1981.

7. Cole, Blaine L., and Weissenfluh, Henry S. "An Analysis of Teaching Percentage." *Arithmetic Teacher,* 21 (March 1974), pp. 226–228.

8. Easterday, Kenneth E.; Henry, Loren I.; and Simpson, F. Morgan. *Activities for Junior High School and Middle School Mathematics.* Reston, Va.: National Council of Teachers of Mathematics, 1981.

9. *Experience in Mathematical Ideas,* Vol. 2. Washington, D.C.: National Council of Teachers of Mathematics, 1970.

10. Hauch, Eldon. "Concrete Materials for Teaching Percentage." *Arithmetic Teacher,* 1 (December 1954), pp. 9–12.

11. Mathematics Resource Project: *Ratio, Proportion and Scaling.* Palo Alto, Calif.: Creative Publications, 1977.

12. Reys, Robert E.; Rybolt, James F.; Bestgen, Barbara J.; and Wyatt, J. Wendell. "Processes Used by Good Computational Estimators." *Journal for Research in Mathematics Education,* 13 (May 1982), pp. 183–201.

13. Romberg, Thomas A.; Harvey, John G.; Moser, James M.; and Montgomery, Mary E. *Developing Mathematical Processes.* Chicago: Rand McNally, 1974–1976.

14. Schaaf, William L. *A Bibliography of Recreational Mathematics,* Vol. 4. Reston, Va.: National Council of Teachers of Mathematics, 1978.

13

Estimating with Numbers

SNAPSHOT OF A LESSON

Key Ideas for Lesson (Grade 7):

1. Use computational skills in applied settings.
2. Encourage use of estimation to get a ballpark answer.
3. Be alert for unreasonable answers.

Orientation:

Some situations designed to check on reasonableness of answers are being presented in some consumer settings.

Teacher: "I went shopping and bought a package of ground beef that weighed 1.1 pounds and was priced at $2.33 per pound. The total price was marked $2563 but no decimal point could be read. How much did it cost? [After giving the class some time to think . . .] Marcus?"

Marcus: "It should be about two and one-half dollars, so the price would be $2.56 and just forget about the 3."

Teacher: "Good job, Marcus."

Mrs. Best visually surveys the rest of the class and everyone except Susan seems to agree.

Teacher: "Susan, you look puzzled."

Susan: "I am! I worked it all out and got $25.63."

Teacher: "Let me see if I can help. While I am looking at Susan's work, I want everyone else to make up an application problem using the numbers 3.4 and 9.89."

Susan: "Here's my work."

Teacher: "How did you decide where to place the decimal point?"

Susan: "I just looked at the first two decimals and then kept going straight down underneath for the answer."

$$
\begin{array}{r}
1.1 \\
\times\ 2.33 \\
\hline
.33 \\
3.30 \\
22.00 \\
\hline
25.63
\end{array}
$$

Mrs. Best recognizes this as a mechanical error. Susan is applying a rule that works for adding and subtracting decimals. In this situation Susan has focused so completely on this rule that she is blinded to the unreasonableness of her answer.

Teacher: "Susan, let's try it again. Your multiplication is correct, so we are only going to look at placing the decimal. This time I am erasing these decimal points.

```
      1.1
 ✕   2.33
      33
     3 30
    22 00
    25 63
```

Now, if you bought one pound of ground beef, it would cost how much?"

Susan: "$2.33."
Teacher: "OK, now what about two pounds?"
Susan: "$4.66."
Teacher: "So what can you tell me about this answer?" (She points to the computation that is missing the decimals.)
Susan: "It should be more than $2.33 but less than $4.66, so the decimal point goes between the two and five."

WHAT CHARACTERIZES COMPUTATIONAL ESTIMATION?

Look at the examples of computational estimation in Figure 13-1. All of them have three common characteristics. In each case these applications require computation that:

1. Is done mentally, without paper-and-pencil computation;

2. Is done quickly; and

3. Produces answers that are adequate for the decisions to be made, even though they are not exact.

Another example will further illustrate some of the processes involved in computational estimation. Suppose you were asked the question in Figure 13-2. In examining this problem, if you thought the answer should be less than $3.00 because 97 cents (or 24¼ ✕ 4)

Figure 13-1

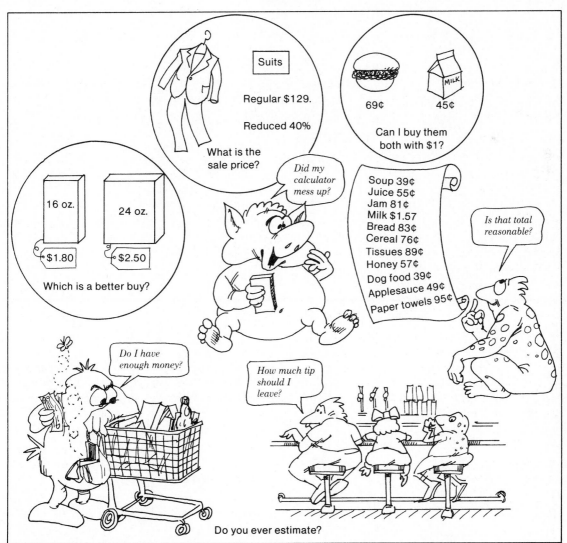

Do you ever estimate?

```
                "About how much do a dozen oranges cost?"


                      GIANT NAVEL ORANGES

                           4 for 97¢


        RESPONSE                        COMMENT

    Record the problem on paper and     Although this response is correct,
    compute a result of $2.91.          it is clearly not the result
                                        of computational estimation,
                                        which is a process done internally
                                        without the aid of an external
                                        calculating or recording tool.


    Mentally compute 3 x 97 and         The reporting of an exact
    report $2.91 or about $3.00.        answer is a reflection of rapid
                                        and accurate mental computation
                                        which is intertwined with the
                                        process of computational estima-
                                        tion.  In many cases it is
                                        easier to do mental computation and
                                        report an exact answer rather
                                        than an approximation.  Only
                                        careful probing of the respondent
                                        can determine if estimation was
                                        involved.


    Think of the oranges as 4 for       These two processes are different.
    $1.00 and answer "about $3.00."     The first uses a ratio approach
                                        and the second uses a unit price
                                        approach, but both involve compu-
    Think of the oranges as about       tational estimation.  In each
    25¢ each and 25¢ x 12               case information has been changed
    (or 1/4 x 12) is $3.00.             to more mentally manageable numbers
                                        such as thinking 4 for $1.00 instead
                                        of 4 for 97¢.  Thus rounding and
                                        determination of the correct place
                                        value are also integral parts of
                                        computational estimation.
```

Figure 13-2

had been rounded up, then you would be making a refinement of the original answer. This refinement or adjustment reflects an important process known as *compensation,* about which more will be said soon. The extent of compensation typically depends on the amount of time available to make an estimate or on the importance of a close estimate.

The context of the problem often influences the computational estimation process used. For example, in the orange problem the amount of tax is unknown. In most real-world situations, such information influences the answer and may result in an estimate of more than $3.00 instead of less than $3.00. The significance of such contextual clues depends on the maturity and experiences of the respondent, but it cannot be ignored when considering acceptable answers to questions requiring computational estimation.

Computational estimation requires an interaction of mental computation, number concepts, and technical arithmetic skills such as rounding. It is a mental process that is performed quickly (without any recording tools) and that results in answers that are reasonably close to a correctly computed result.

LAYING THE FOUNDATION

Getting Started

Research has confirmed that students can develop and learn computational estimation skills, but they must have the opportunity to do so. Although some significant improvement can occur quickly, the development of good computational estimation skills is a lengthy process that will be accomplished only over a period of years. Such instruction should begin early, but no later than third grade.

It must begin with an awareness of what estimation is about, so that students develop a tolerance for error. This is an important but difficult task. Many students are accustomed only to exact answers in mathematics and must be encouraged to accept answers from estimation. Thus, estimation involves a mental set different from that used to compute an exact answer. An "exact-answer mentality" must be changed before specific estimation strategies are taught. This change will begin when estimation is recognized as an essential and practical skill. That's why we must consistently emphasize computational estimation within different problem situations and along with traditional computation procedures. Directed discussion helps eliminate the attitude among students that an estimate is a "second-rate" answer, not quite as good as an exact answer.

Bulletin and poster boards can provide visual reminders of everyday uses of computational estimation. Problem settings such as those in Figure 13-1 can kick off discussion of different uses of estimation and help highlight its importance. In addition, students can be asked for which of the following situations an estimate is expected, or for which an exact answer is needed:

What is your telephone number?
How long have you worked at your job?
How old are you?

How many brothers and sisters do you have?
What is your address?
How much will the lunch cost?
What time is it?

For some questions, an exact answer is essential and an estimate would make little sense (What is your telephone number?). In other instances, such as one's age, an exact answer (years, months, days, and so on) would be cumbersome and probably provide no better information than an estimate.

Here are some actual applications where not only are estimations accepted but exact answers would not seem "realistic":

At what altitude did the pilot say we were flying?
What is the population of the United States?
What kind of gas mileage are you getting with your new car?
The world's largest hamburger chain has sold over how many billion hamburgers?

A survey of newspaper headlines can generate interesting and exciting searches for estimates. Look at Activity Card 13-1.* Identifying exact numbers and esti-

*Activity Card 13-1 is adapted from Reys and Reys (9).

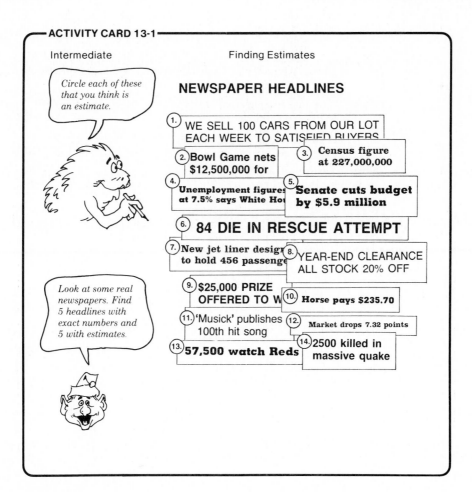

ACTIVITY CARD 13-1

Intermediate   Finding Estimates

Circle each of these that you think is an estimate.

NEWSPAPER HEADLINES

1. WE SELL 100 CARS FROM OUR LOT EACH WEEK TO SATISFIED BUYERS
2. Bowl Game nets $12,500,000 for
3. Census figure at 227,000,000
4. Unemployment figures at 7.5% says White House
5. Senate cuts budget by $5.9 million
6. 84 DIE IN RESCUE ATTEMPT
7. New jet liner designed to hold 456 passengers
8. YEAR-END CLEARANCE ALL STOCK 20% OFF
9. $25,000 PRIZE OFFERED TO W
10. Horse pays $235.70
11. 'Musick' publishes 100th hit song
12. Market drops 7.32 points
13. 57,500 watch Reds
14. 2500 killed in massive quake

Look at some real newspapers. Find 5 headlines with exact numbers and 5 with estimates.

mates in these different contexts not only is interesting but will sharpen students' discrimination skills. It will also remind them about how often numbers appear in the world around them.

Once students become aware of some common uses of estimation, they become sensitive to other situations involving estimates. Such activities promote a deeper understanding of the purpose of estimating and greater appreciation of its power. Once this attitude is developed, instruction on some very basic and powerful notions of estimation can begin.

Focusing on Front-End Digits

The front-end strategies are a very basic, yet powerful approach that can be used in a variety of situations and taught to children as early as third and fourth grades. Two important things must be checked: (1) the leading or front-end digits in a number, and (2) the place value of those digits. Unlike computing with paper-and-pencil algorithms, where work often begins on the back-

end digits, an estimate requires a quick and accurate answer most efficiently arrived at by focusing on the front-end digits.

To help understand this idea, hide a three-digit number behind a sheet of paper on the board. Ask students to guess a three-digit number and see how close they get to the hidden number. Before guessing, give them the opportunity to see one digit of their choosing.

As students try this activity, some choose the hundreds digit:

This gives the most useful information. Others might ask to see the ones digit:

Can this information be of as much help? Why? A few experiences such as this help students see that the leading digit is powerful because it together with its place value represents a good approximation to the original number.

This background, accompanied by a command of basic facts, related mental computational skills, and place value, is all that is necessary for learning the general front-end approach to estimation. To introduce the front-end strategy for addition, you might suggest that a portion of the problem has been torn away and some information is missing. If the missing piece cannot be found, can an exact answer be determined?

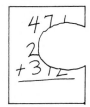

Since the leading digits are visible, we can use them to formulate an estimate. For example, $4 + 2 + 3 = 9$. Is 9 a good estimate? It looks as if each number in the problem contains three digits, so 900 rather than 9 is a reasonable estimate. Other discussion might touch upon questions such as:

Is 900 an over- or underestimate?
How might we get a closer estimate?

Practice is important. Initially, provide the cover for the back-end digits as illustrated here. Students can be given similar problems where they hide the back-end digits by covering them with a hand or card.

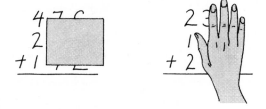

Immediate feedback on how well students have done in providing estimates is important. Be lenient in accepting responses initially, but do ask students to explain how they obtained their estimates. The discussion offered by students will help clarify procedures and may even suggest new approaches to estimating in a given problem.

Compensation

Compensation is the process used to add or subtract something to or from an initial estimate, as shown in Figure 13-3. This process of adjusting or refining an

Figure 13-3. Adapted from Reys and Reys (9).

estimate is done naturally by most students. It is a powerful process that cuts across all estimation strategies; that is why it is described first here. It should not be taught separately, but rather be developed naturally along with each strategy. Every opportunity should be taken to encourage compensation and to reward students that use it. Two examples demonstrating the subtle way in which compensation evolves are shown in Figure 13-4.

Compensation can be used with all operations. Consider this example for estimating products:

Figure 13-4. Adapted from Reys and Reys (9).

Here the student used the idea of compensation to refine an initial estimate. What about these examples?

	Think	*Reported Result*
42 × 61	40 × 60 = 2400	"A little more than 2400."
39 × 78	40 × 80 = 3200	"A little less than 3200."
27 × 32	30 × 30 = 900	"About 900."

For the first two examples, the rounding procedure makes it clear whether we have produced an underestimate or an overestimate. How about the last example? It is not obvious without further exploration.

Like many tools, the more we use estimation the better we get at using it. The need for compensation is easily understood, even though the exact processes used to determine the amount of compensation may be difficult to explain. Often the amount of compensation rests on a "gut feeling." As more sophisticated skills are developed, most students will become better at explaining what they did.

ESTIMATION STRATEGIES

In order to promote systematic development of computational estimation skills, we will now highlight four specific strategies:

- Front-end (truncate)
- Front-end (round)
- Compatible numbers
- Averaging

Each strategy is very powerful, but only one of them, rounding, is typically taught. We believe they should all

be taught. In addition to these strategies one key process, namely compensation, should be established.

The successful development of estimation skills will result from a sequential program involving instruction, practice, and testing. Some guidelines for these phases follow the ensuing discussion of strategies.

Front-End (Truncate)

Key ideas for introducing this strategy to children are illustrated in Figure 13-5. This approach enables the student virtually to see the numbers used. It involves error, as does the more traditional rounding strategy, but later this error may be compensated for by "adding on some" for the back-end digits. This approach can be extended to subtraction and multiplication as well as other numbers. Thus, this front-end truncation strategy can be introduced to young children but extended to a variety of applications for older students (see Activity Card 13-2).

The unique advantage of the front-end truncation strategy over the traditional rounding approach is that all the numbers to be operated on are visible in the original problem. It provides young students with a means of arriving at an estimate quickly and easily. This feeling of success or "I can do it!" is important.

Front-End (Rounding)

Rounding is more sophisticated than truncation. It requires rounding skills be developed in addition to the prerequisites cited for the front-end truncation strategy. Rounding is the dominant method used by current textbooks that teach estimation skills. It is particularly appropriate for addition, subtraction, and multiplication

Figure 13-5.   Adapted from Reys and Reys (9).

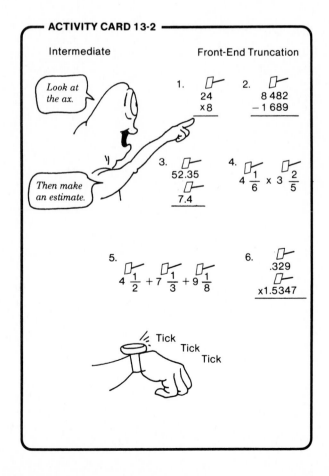

of all types of numbers (Figure 13-6). Activity Cards 13-3 and 13-4 show ways to sharpen front-end estimation skills.

Rounding, like truncation, also involves error, but this error may be compensated for later as greater command and confidence with the strategy are attained. While rounding is a useful and powerful strategy, it presents certain problems for students. For example, estimate the answer to:

$$4219 + 7912 + 2446$$

If students are asked to round and add, they are involved in a series of internal mental steps: round 4219 to 4000; round 7912 to 8000; round 2446 to 2000. Now, what is 4000 + 8000 + 2000? Thus, the rounding strategy for estimation involves a two-step process. The number(s) must first be rounded, then used in mentally computing the estimate. This process involves more mental visualization of the numbers than the truncation strategy, which is why we recommend that rounding follow truncation.

Compatible Numbers

In this strategy compatible numbers—i.e., manageable numbers that are easy to compute mentally—are used to make an estimate. Figure 13-7 demonstrates how compatible numbers might be used in division.

The numbers in the problem are literally changed to compatible numbers that are close to the original numbers but easier to work with. The process involves changing one or more numbers. Compatible numbers is the most difficult strategy to develop, but its usefulness makes it worth the effort. It requires careful development and rewards good number sense. It is a particularly powerful strategy for division, and it can be applied to

all types of numbers. For example, Activity Card 13-5 shows how compatible numbers might be applied to fractions and percents.

In many ways, the development of the compatible-numbers strategy epitomizes the process of problem solving. For example, in problem solving there are usually several different solution paths. Likewise, the choice of sets of compatible numbers is usually not unique. In fact, it is far more important to choose some numbers that are compatible than to spend much time searching for the best pair. Furthermore, in problem solving it is important to possess various strategies and recognize when a particular strategy is appropriate. Likewise, it is essential that compatible numbers be recognized as a legitimate estimation strategy, and that its use be encouraged whenever appropriate. Also, if this compatible-number strategy is not taught, it will not be available for use by students.

Averaging

The averaging strategy uses a mean for an estimate. It is a two-step process and is useful whenever a group of numbers cluster around a common value. Figure 13-8 gives a glimpse of the strategy in action.

In the first step, a reasonable group average is selected; the second step involves multiplying it by the total number of values in the group. The estimated average is determined by selecting a convenient multiple around which all the data cluster. This estimated average should be produced quickly and yield a comfortable number to multiply. This estimate can then be refined or adjusted through compensation. Thus the averaging strategy builds onto the compatible-numbers strategy. It also involves the process of compensation.

Figure 13-6. Adapted from Reys and Reys (9).

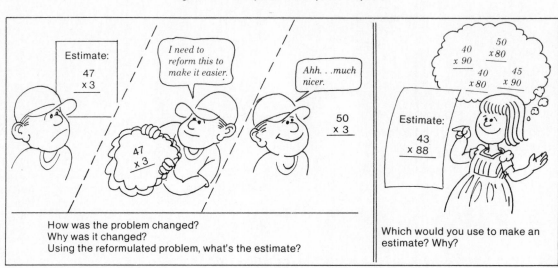

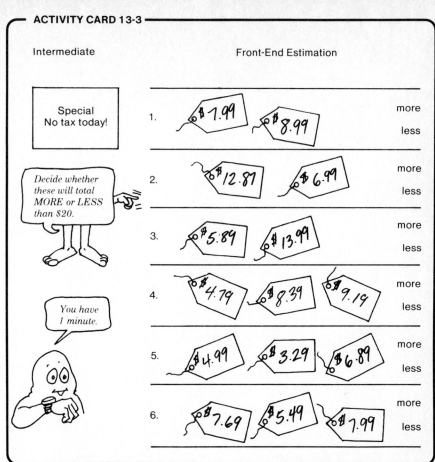

ACTIVITY CARD 13-3

Intermediate | Front-End Estimation

Special
No tax today!

Decide whether these will total MORE or LESS than $20.

You have 1 minute.

1. $7.99 $8.99 — more / less
2. $12.87 $6.99 — more / less
3. $5.89 $13.99 — more / less
4. $4.79 $8.39 $9.19 — more / less
5. $4.99 $3.29 $6.89 — more / less
6. $7.69 $5.49 $7.99 — more / less

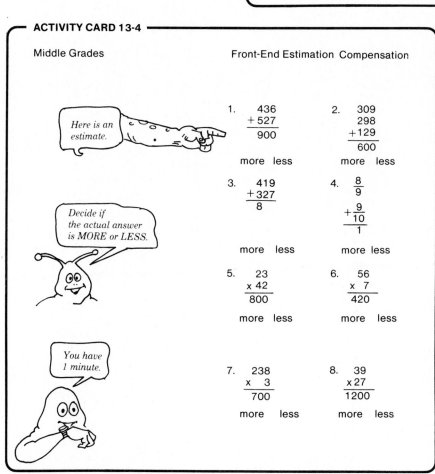

ACTIVITY CARD 13-4

Middle Grades | Front-End Estimation Compensation

Here is an estimate.

Decide if the actual answer is MORE or LESS.

You have 1 minute.

1. 436
   + 527
   ─────
    900

   more   less

2. 309
    298
   + 129
   ─────
    600

   more   less

3. 419
   + 327
   ─────
      8

   more   less

4. 8/9
   + 9/10
   ─────
      1

   more   less

5.   23
   x 42
   ────
    800

   more   less

6.   56
   x 7
   ────
    420

   more   less

7. 238
   x   3
   ────
    700

   more   less

8.   39
   x 27
   ────
   1200

   more   less

205

Figure 13-7. Adapted from Reys and Reys (9).

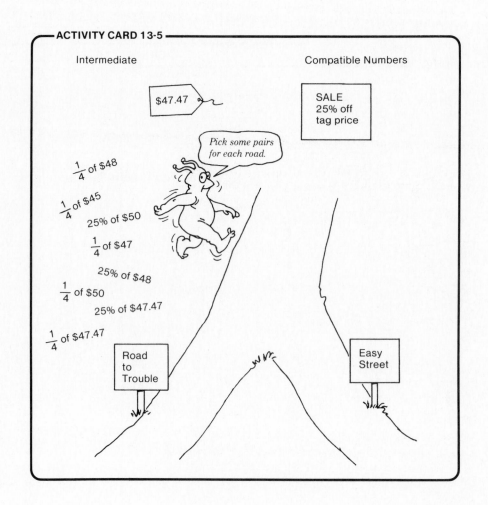

Figure 13-8. Adapted from Reys and Reys (9).

This is a limited strategy but a powerful one. Many different problem situations, such as those shown on Activity Cards 13-6 and 13-7, should be presented so that students recognize various applications. The averaging strategy is appropriate for estimating sums of groups of numbers quickly. A strength of this strategy is that it eliminates the mental tabulation of a long list of front-end or rounded digits.

PUTTING IT TOGETHER

Like problem-solving techniques, estimation strategies are developed through careful instruction, discussion, and use. For best development of estimation skills, it is recommended that the following three phases be included:

- *Instruction.* Unless computational estimation strategies are taught, most students will neither learn nor use them. Prerequisite skills (such as mastery of basic facts and place value) must be reflected in the instruction and development of a strategy. Greater understanding and appreciation of a strategy will result when it is related to different applied situations. Practice is important, but instruction on each of these estimation strategies will complement, direct, and motivate meaningful practice.

- *Practice.* It is important to have a wide variety of practice, preceded by specific instruction. Short practice sessions of five to ten minutes each week are recommended. Such regular practice will help maintain basic facts, improve mental computation skills, and provide opportunities for further developing computational estimation skills.

- *Testing.* Periodic testing provides motivation for developing computational estimation skills. The

Figure 13-9. A short test on estimating addition and subtraction of fractions.

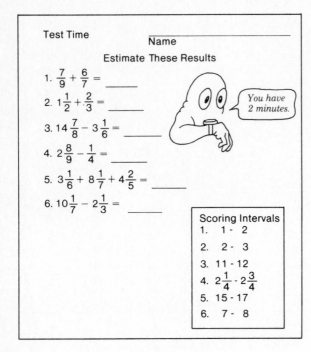

testing time should be carefully controlled. Figure 13-9 is an example of a timed test on fractions. Some suggested scoring intervals are shown in the box in the lower righthand corner. These intervals are large enough to reward different estimation strategies but small enough to penalize unreasonable answers. The size of intervals should be relaxed or tightened to reflect students' ability as well as specific instructional goals. As with practice sessions, such tests should be short. Problems may be chosen to focus on a specific strategy, concentrate on certain kinds of numbers, or provide a mixture of different estimation situations.

MORE TEACHING TIPS

Guiding students through a meaningful and lasting development of estimation strategies and subskills cannot be accomplished in a single unit. Instruction should systematically build onto the necessary prerequisites (such as basic facts, mental computation, rounding, and place value) as estimation strategies are established. Here are some specific teaching suggestions:

1. Students should realize that computational estimation skills are important and they are expected to develop them.

2. Destroy the one-right-answer syndrome early. Help students develop a tolerance for error and to realize that several different yet acceptable estimates might be made for the same problem.

3. Give immediate feedback in all phases of estimation (instruction, practice, and testing). This helps students make self-corrections and adjustments that are essential during this formative stage of development.

4. Control time carefully on estimation activities, or at least make sure students are aware that they are expected to obtain their estimates mentally and that there will not be enough time to compute an exact answer. If too much time is allowed, only a measure of paper-and-pencil computation may result. If too little time is allowed, only wild guessing may occur. Somewhere between these two extremes will be appropriate timing, which you can determine only by experimenting with your students.

5. Provide numbers that encourage and reward computational estimation. For example, 78 + 83 could be mentally computed, but 78,342 + 83,289 would more likely promote estimation.

6. Take advantage of real-world consumer settings to develop and practice estimation strategies.

7. Identify acceptable intervals for good estimates. Discussing intervals with students provides additional learnings, as students gain insight into other solution strategies and become more comfortable with the notion that several correct but different estimates exist.

8. Ask students to tell how their estimates were made. Research suggests that students often develop individual and unique approaches to computational estimation problems. By sharing them, they develop an appreciation of different estimation processes.

A final word of caution: Avoid an error that is inadvertently introduced within many elementary basal textbooks. Do not ask pupils to estimate answers to computational problems and then do the paper-and-pencil computation to check their "estimate." Such an activity encourages pupils to reverse the order and do the computation before making the estimate. Thus, "estimation" becomes a perfunctory rounding task done at the end of the computation and yielding a second-rate answer. This should never happen! All early experiences with computational estimation should be devoted exclusively toward estimation. As pupils develop more sophistication, they should of course be able to determine "by inspection" whether paper-and-pencil computation results are reasonable. However, this application of computational estimation will result only from careful and systematic instruction over a long period.

A GLANCE AT WHERE WE'VE BEEN

Computational estimation is a basic skill and should be an important component of every mathematics program. If progress is going to be made in teaching computational estimation, we must depart from the exclusive reliance on rounding found in current mathematics programs. This chapter has highlighted a workable approach. We feel that it gives all students the opportunity to develop computational estimation skills that heretofore only a few people have acquired on their own.

THINGS TO DO: ADDING TO YOUR PICTURE

1. Identify some characteristics of computational estimation.

2. List some prerequisites that should be established before teaching front-end estimation approaches.

3. Explain why it is important that students have a clear understanding of the goal of computational estimation.

4. Distinguish between the front-end truncation and front-end rounding strategies. Explain which you should use first, and tell why.

5. Consider this interesting and true story.

A team of surveyors was sent to Mt. Everest to take an official measurement of its height. They decided to make six independent height measures, then average them to determine the "official" height. The six measurements were:

$$
\begin{array}{r}
28{,}990 \\
28{,}991 \\
28{,}994 \\
29{,}998 \\
29{,}001 \\
\underline{29{,}026} \\
174{,}000 \div 6 = 29{,}000 \text{ ft.}
\end{array}
$$

The team studied the obtained average and was concerned that readers might view 29,000 ft. as a rough estimate rather than a fairly precise measure. So they recorded their official calculation as 29,002 ft.

Discuss why the surveyors might have been concerned with an official measure of 29,000 ft. Describe how this type of activity might increase student's awareness of whether numbers are exact.

7. Examine a fifth- or sixth-grade book of an elementary mathematics series for computational estimation activities.
   (a) About how many lessons involved estimation?
   (b) Was a proper mental set for estimation established? If so, describe how.
   (c) List all the strategies taught.

8. Discuss how the process of compensation applies to all estimation strategies.

9. Describe a real-world situation that would use an averaging strategy.

10. Describe a computational estimation problem where a compatible-numbers strategy would be used.

11. Why is this not a good assignment? "I want you to estimate the answers to these problems, then compute the correct answers, and then see how far your estimate was off."

12. Observe people doing computational estimation. Many situations—such as shoppers in stores, clerks in checkout stands, and people determining the total for a restaurant bill—provide opportunities to watch and listen to procedures being used. Identify the specific strategies.

13. Choose one activity, such as Activity Card 13-9, and identify acceptable intervals for each question.

14. Review a standardized achievement test. Are any questions included to assess computational estimation? Discuss their strengths and weaknesses.

15. Briefly describe some instructional guidelines that should be used when teaching computational estimation.

SELECTED REFERENCES

1. Buchannan, Aaron. "Estimation as an Essential Mathematical Skill" (Professional Paper 39). Los Angeles: Southwest Regional Laboratory for Educational Research and Development, August 1978.

2. Carpenter, Thomas P.; Corbitt, Mary Kay; Kepner, Henry S., Jr.; Lindquist, Mary Montgomery; and Reys, Robert E. *Results from the Second Mathematics Assessment of the National Assessment of Educational Progress.* Reston, Va.: National Council of Teachers of Mathematics, 1981.

3. Driscoll, Mark J. *Research Within Reach: Elementary School Mathematics.* St Louis: CEMREL, Inc., 1980.

4. Johnson, David C. "Teaching Estimation and Reasonableness of Results." *Arithmetic Teacher,* 27 (September 1979), pp. 34-35.

5. Mathematics Resource Project: *Number Sense and Arithmetic Skills.* Palo Alto, Calif.: Creative Publications, 1977.

6. O'Daffer, Phares. "A Case and Techniques for Estimation: Estimation Experiences in Elementary School Mathematics—Essential Not Extra." *Arithmetic Teacher,* 27 (February 1979), pp. 46-51.

7. Reys, Robert E.; Rybolt, James F.; Bestgen, Barbara J.; and Wyatt, J. Wendell. "Processes Used by Good Computational Estimators." *Journal for Research in Mathematics Education,* 13 (May 1982), pp. 183-201.

8. Reys, Robert E., and Bestgen, Barbara J. "Teaching and Assessing Computational Estimation Skills." *Elementary School Journal,* 82 (November 1981), pp. 117-127.

9. Reys, Barbara J., and Reys, Robert E. *Guide to Using Estimation Skills and Strategies (GUESS).* Palo Alto, Calif.: Dale Seymour Publications, 1983.

10. Reys, Robert E.; Bestgen, Barbara J.; Coburn, Terrence G.; Schoen, Harold L.; Shumway, Richard J.; Wheatley, Charlotte L.; Wheatley, Grayson H.; and White, Arthur L. *Keystrokes: Calculator Activities for Young Students.* Palo Alto, Calif.: Creative Publications, 1980.

11. Schoen, Harold L.; Friesen, Charles D.; Jarrett, Joscelyn A.; and Urbatsch, Tonya D. "Instruction in Estimating Solutions of Whole Number Computations." *Journal for Research in Mathematics Education,* 12 (May 1981), pp. 165-178.

12. Seymour, Dale. *Developing Skills in Estimation.* Palo Alto, Calif.: Dale Seymour Publications, 1981.

13. Trafton, Paul. *SRA TUTORdisc Programs—Estimation Skills.* Chicago: Science Research Associates, 1981.

14. Trafton, Paul. "Estimation and Mental Arithmetic: Important Components of Computation." In *Developing Computational Skills* (ed. Marilyn N. Suydam and Robert E. Reys). 1978 Yearbook. Reston, Va.: National Council of Teachers of Mathematics, 1978.

14

Using Statistics and Probability

Key Ideas:

1. Construct some graphs.
2. Promote graph reading skills.
3. Increase awareness and importance of different scales on graph.

Necessary Materials:

Several different colors of blocks, sheets of grid paper, and markers or crayons.

Orientation:

Most children need experience in building and constructing graphs. This second-grade lesson provides some valuable experiences and, while doing so, moves naturally from concrete toward symbolic representation of data.

Teacher: "These blocks show the number of people absent from our room each day last week. Let's graph this information on grid paper. (Graphs trigger many questions that help develop graph reading skills and lead to better understanding of data. The teacher knows that involving students in formulating questions is an important part of problem solving, so as soon as the graph is completed, she continues.) Look at our graph carefully. I want you to ask a question

that could be answered from this graph. Bob, your hand was up first."

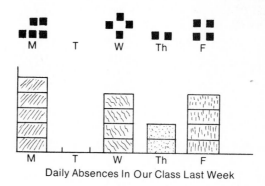

Daily Absences In Our Class Last Week

Bob: "How many students were sick in our school?"

Gloria (after a long wait): "Our graph doesn't answer that question. It only shows information about our room."

Teacher: "That's right, Gloria. This graph only shows what happened in our room. Also, it doesn't tell us how many were sick, only how many were absent. That reminds us to read the title of the graph so everyone will know what it represents. Now, let's hear another question. Aaron?"

Aaron: "How many people were absent Wednesday?"

Sharon: "Four."

Teacher: "Doug, let's hear your question."

Doug: "On which day was everyone in class?"

Sharon: "Tuesday."

Doug: "That's right, because no one was absent."

Teacher: "Do you have a question, Kelly?"

Kelly: "Which day had the most absences?"

Sharon: "Monday had the most. There were five students absent."

Other questions are posed and discussed. A bit later in the lesson, the teacher continues.

Teacher: "Let's look at the absences for the last two weeks. Here are tallies of the absences for each day.

Let's make a graph of them on this paper."

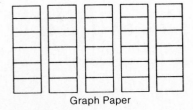

Graph Paper

Sandy: "Our graph paper isn't tall enough!"

Teacher: "What do you mean?"

Sandy: "We can only show six absences on the paper, but there were eight absences on Monday."

Teacher: "Could we do any trading here?"

Sandy: "What do you mean?"

Teacher: "In place value, when we get ten ones we trade for one ten."

Sandy: "But we don't have ten."

Teacher: "Maybe we can make other trades. For example, we trade five pennies for a nickel or . . ."

Sandy: "Two nickels for a dime."

Sharon: "I got it—we can trade two absences for one square on the grid."

Teacher: "That's a nice idea, let's try it. We would color four squares for Monday. How many for Tuesday?"

Sharon: "One. And two for Wednesday."

Sandy: "Three for Thursday and five for Friday."

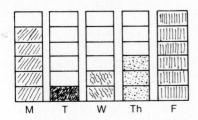

Daily absences in our class for the last two weeks.

Teacher: "This graph is *almost* finished."

Sandy: "It looks done to me . . . what else could we do?"

Teacher: "We need to show on the graph what each box represents."

This code is recorded in a highly visible place beside the graph.

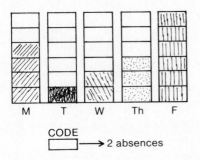

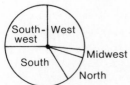

CODE

→ 2 absences

INTRODUCTION

Until recently, statistics and probability would have been considered out of place in most elementary school mathematics programs. This is no longer the case. All current elementary school mathematics textbook series give attention to probability and statistics. Graphs are often included within the probability and statistics strand because they provide a powerful means of representing information. Some graphing techniques are presented in this chapter, but you have already found graphs used throughout this book to illustrate many different mathematical ideas.

It is recognized that every educated person must be able to process information effectively and efficiently. Often such information is encountered in graphical, statistical, or probabilistic form. For example:

(Graphical) Where are the jobs?

(Statistical) The mean salary of professional baseball players is $195,000 a year.

(Probabilistic) The probability of rain today is .35.

Each of these statements needs to be understood if meaningful interpretations are to be made.

The context and format of the way such information is presented varies greatly, but correctly interpreting the information often requires the application of a variety of mathematics. Consider, for example, the mathematical concepts involved in weather reports (decimals, percents, and probability); public opinion polls (sampling techniques and errors of measurement); advertising claims (hypothesis testing); monthly government reports involving unemployment, inflation, and energy supplies (percentages, prediction, and extrapolation).

All the media rely on techniques of summarizing information. Radio, television, and newspaper bombard us with statistical information. The current demand for information-processing skills is much greater than 25 years ago, and technological advances will place a far greater premium on such skills in the years ahead.

Graphs, statistics, and probability are closely intertwined. Consider, for example, the life-expectancy information shown in Figure 14-1. It visually summarizes much information. Questions such as:

Which country has the greatest life expectancy?
Which country has the shortest life expectancy?
In which countries do females live longer than males?

can be answered quickly from the graph. Extending this discussion to questions such as:

What is the life expectancy in Sweden for females?
How much longer can women in the United States expect to live than men?
How is life expectancy determined?

involves statistics. Further extensions might include:

If I am born in the United States, what are my chances of living to be 75?
If my spouse and I are both 23 years old, what is the probability that we will both be alive at age 40?

These questions not only require additional data, but provide direct applications of probability. For example,

such questions related to life expectancy are answered regularly by insurance companies.

Graphing, statistics, and probability should not be viewed or treated in isolation. Their study provides numerous opportunities to review and apply different mathematics in a variety of real-world situations. For example, understanding of whole numbers, fractions, decimals, percents, ratios, and proportion is essential and is often called upon. Many computational skills are reviewed and polished as they are applied in graphing or doing statistics and probability.

GRAPHING

Graphing skills include constructing and reading graphs as well as interpreting graphical information. They should be introduced early in the primary grades.

Here is a way of getting started. First, ask children each to choose one piece of their favorite fruit from a basket and position this piece of fruit on a flat table top [see Figure 14-2(a)]. The resulting rows of fruit represent the children's preference in a real-world, concrete fashion. Next ask them each to draw the fruit they chose on an index card and then use the cards to build a picture-bar graph [Figure 14-2(b)]. Although this is a less concrete means of showing information, for most children it is still a very meaningful way to represent their preferences. Finally, this same information can be expressed more symbolically in the bar graph in Figure 14-2(c). Regardless of how the data are presented, pertinent questions can be asked to encourage thoughtful interpretation of the graphs. Such questions might include:

How many children prefer apples?
What is the favorite fruit?
How many different fruits are shown?
How many children contributed to the graph?

All good graphing activities are based on two premises:

Figure 14-1

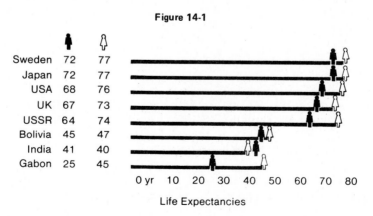

Sweden 72 77
Japan 72 77
USA 68 76
UK 67 73
USSR 64 74
Bolivia 45 47
India 41 40
Gabon 25 45

0 yr 10 20 30 40 50 60 70 80

Life Expectancies

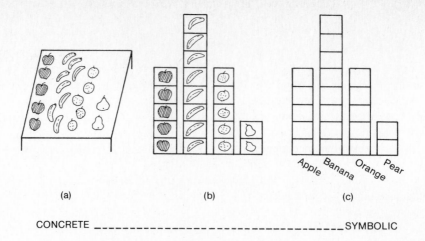

(a)   (b)   (c)

CONCRETE _____SYMBOLIC

Figure 14-2

1. Students must be involved with the data.
2. The data should be understood by and be of genuine interest to the students.

Data that come from nowhere frequently go nowhere when graphing is attempted. The actual data used will depend on student interest and maturity; here are a few kinds of survey data that could be collected in the classroom:

- *Physical characteristics*—heights, weights, color of eyes, shoe sizes
- *Sociological characteristics*—birthdays, number in family, amount of allowances
- *Personal preferences*—favorite television shows, favorite books, favorite sports, favorite color, favorite drinks

Each of these examples gives students the opportunity to collect data themselves. A lesson built around Activity Card 14-1 will sharpen data-gathering techniques, and a host of idea starters are available (19). In completing Activity Card 14-1, students are required to refine and polish their questions to get whatever information they are seeking; this in itself is an important and valuable experience.

Once information has been collected, graphs are often used to summarize and help others digest the results. Many different graphs exist. Skills related to constructing and interpreting them constitute an important part of mathematics instruction. We will examine the four most popular graphs introduced in elementary school. In each figure, (a) illustrates a graph typical of those found in elementary programs while (b) demonstrates how the same graphical notations are extended and used in real life.

Line Graphs

Points on a grid are used to represent data. Each axis is clearly labeled, so that the data shown can be interpreted properly. A wide variety of line graphs exist

ACTIVITY CARD 14-1

Fifth Grade   Sharpening Data-Gathering Skills

Let's find how many cars, buses, and trucks pass by our school.

Before beginning this survey, we need to agree on some things.

Why do these questions need to be answered before starting?

1. What streets will we survey?
2. What day will the survey be conducted?
3. What time will the survey start?
4. How long will the survey last?

Name two more important questions.

and are used. As Figure 14-3(a) shows, line graphs are particularly good for showing variations, such as hours of daylight, temperatures, rainfall, and so on. They are also an effective visual means of comparing several sets of data, as illustrated in Figure 14-3(b).

Picture Graphs

Data are represented by pictures. A picture can represent one object or several (see Figure 14-4). In order to properly interpret picture graphs, children must know how much each object represents. Research shows that 60 percent of nine-year-old students ignored such coding information when interpreting graphs (1).

214

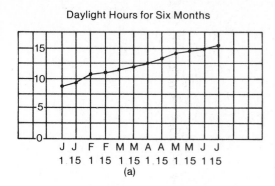

Daylight Hours for Six Months

(a)

Percent

Fewer than 5 years of elementary school

4 years of high school or more

4 or more years of college

Note: Data are based upon sample surveys of the population.
Source: U.S. Department of Commerce, Bureau of the Census.

(b)

Figure 14-3

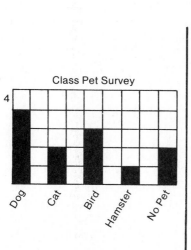

Favorite Ice Cream Flavors

Chocolate

Vanilla

Strawberry

Estimated Retention Rates, Fifth Grade
Through College Graduation: United States
1972 to 1984

Each figure represents 10 persons

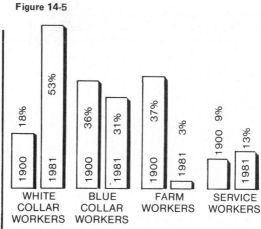

For every 100 pupils in
the 5th grade in fall 1972

75 graduated
from high school in 1980

23 are likely to earn
bachelor's degrees in 1984

Source: Surveys, estimates, and projections of the
National Center for Education Statistics.

Figure 14-4

Bar Graphs or Histograms

Bars represent data and/or percentages. As Figure 14-5 shows, the values sometimes are read from the axis and at other times are reported directly on the graph.

Bar graphs are similar to line graphs except that bars are drawn from the data points to the axis, rather than connecting data points with a line. They show how things relate to each other for quick visual comparisons.

Figure 14-5

Class Pet Survey

4

Dog Cat Bird Hamster No Pet

18% — 1900
53% — 1981
36% — 1900
31% — 1981
37% — 1900
3% — 1981
9% — 1900
13% — 1981

WHITE COLLAR WORKERS   BLUE COLLAR WORKERS   FARM WORKERS   SERVICE WORKERS

Division of American Workforce

215

Circle or Pie Graphs

A pie graph is a circle representing the whole, and its wedges report percentages of the whole (see Figure 14-6). The pie graph is popular because it is easy to interpret. It has major limitations in that it represents only a fixed moment in time and it cannot exceed 100 percent.

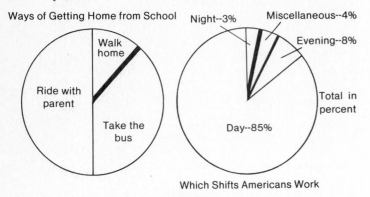

Figure 14-6

Interpreting graphs and answering specific questions from them helps students better understand and appreciate their value. It also leads toward recognition of strengths and limitations of different graphs.

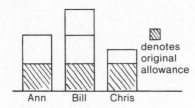

Sometimes graphs may be deceptive. For example, the graph shown here reports changes in allowances for three children. It shows that Ann's allowance was doubled, Bill's tripled, and Chris's increased by one-half. Based on this information, we may imagine Bill feeling philanthropic and Chris complaining of hard times. What is wrong with the graph? Technically it is correct, but it doesn't tell the entire story because the original allowances were not the same. Let's look at the data:

	Original Allowance	Size of Increase	Amount of Increase	New Allowance
Ann	$3.00	doubled	$3.00	$6.00
Bill	1.50	tripled	3.00	4.50
Chris	4.00	half	2.00	6.00

A graph with a labeled vertical axis would reflect the situation more accurately. These "different" graphs of the same data demonstrate how graphs can distort and sometimes misrepresent information. Developing a healthy skepticism of graphical displays is an important part of developing graphing skills.

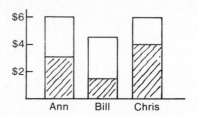

It takes many years to develop the graphing skills necessary to cope with the wide variety of real-life needs, and school provides many opportunities. Here are a few specific suggestions to guide graphing experiences:

1. Use information that interests students.
2. Provide opportunities for students to collect their own data and decide how to best represent these data graphically.
3. Consider alternate ways of graphically representing the same data. This includes changing the scales as well as the kinds of graphs.
4. Have some data that are hard to digest or at least difficult to grasp without a graph.
5. Pose questions that go beyond direct reading of graphs, and encourage students to both describe and interpret the information.

STATISTICS

Statistics is the collection and handling of data. So much information exists today that it must be simplified or reduced in ways other than by graphs. The collection, organization, presentation, and interpretation of data is called *descriptive statistics*. Here are some familiar examples:

Most children in the fifth grade are 12 years old.
The median family income is $20,250.
The average temperature today was 29°.

Each of these statements uses statistics to describe a situation or current condition. Descriptive statistics are in common use. They are introduced in the primary grades through data collection and graphs, then extended with further practice activities in the intermediate grades.

Average

As statistical knowledge grows more specific, descriptive statistical measures should be discussed. For example, "average" is a popular statistical term that many children have heard even before entering school. It is used to report such things as "average temperature for today," "average family income," "test average," "batting average," and "average life expectancy."

Any number that is used to represent a series of values is called an average of those values. Many different "averages" exist, but only three—mean, median, and mode—are commonly experienced in elementary school. Each of these can be developed meaningfully through concrete activities before computation is introduced. Such experiences will provide greater understanding of the concept of average. Furthermore, it will help the later acquisition and development of symbolic formulas in secondary school.

Care must be taken to insure that statistics is viewed as more than a series of skills or techniques. How to find an average is an important skill that should be developed. However, statistics must not stop with the "how to"; rather, it must raise questions such as: Why should the average be reported? What average is most appropriate? Why? These questions are essential and must be asked regularly. The teaching of statistics in elementary school must aim higher than skill development. Students should know how to "get" a statistic, but must also know what they have "gotten."

Mean. The *mean* is the arithmetic average. It is determined by adding all the values involved and dividing by the number of addends. Here is one way to model the mean (see Figure 14-7). Return test scores to children on pieces of adding machine tape, where the length of each strip is determined by the score. Thus, a score of 88 would be 88 cm long and a score of 64 would be 64 cm long. Scores can be physically compared with the tapes,

so it is clear that the score on Test 2 was much improved. To show the average score, simply tape these two strips of paper together and then fold the resulting strip in half. This technique is very appealing and enlightening. Although it becomes unwieldy if many scores are involved, this unwieldiness actually helps develop greater appreciation for and understanding of the symbolic formula.

A somewhat different but similar concrete approach can be taken to find the mean. The blocks in Figure 14-8(a) show the number of absences in a class reported for one week. If children are asked to "even out" the blocks as much as possible, this evening-out process produces a mean of three blocks per day [Figure 14-8(b)]. The mean could have also been determined by computing:

$$\text{mean} = \frac{5 + 0 + 4 + 2 + 4}{5} = \frac{15}{5} = 3$$

For some children manipulating the physical model not only will help them understand the formula, but will promote greater retention.

The words *average* and *mean* are often used interchangeably. Care should be taken to help children recognize and become familiar with both words. The second national mathematics assessment revealed that few elementary students know what the words mean (5). For example, a majority of 13-year-olds reported the average for a set of data, but only 6 percent computed the mean.

Figure 14-7

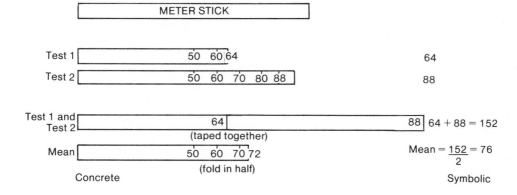

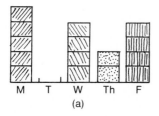

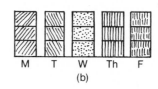

Figure 14-8

Grasp of average is a powerful tool in estimation and problem solving, as represented in the previous chapter. Problems such as the one in Figure 14-9 provide opportunities to apply averages and estimation in everyday situations.

Figure 14-9

Median. The *median* is the middle value in a set of data. Thus the same number of values are above as below the median. It is easy to illustrate. Consider the ages of five children: 2, 3, 7, 9, 9. The middle age or median is 7 years.

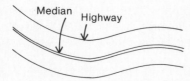

Reference to a highway median will remind students that a median in statistics is a middle position. It is another measure of central tendency, although generally unfamiliar to most elementary students. It, too, can be modeled. For example, consider the five test scores shown on the index cards in Figure 14-10(a). Take the cards and begin ordering them from lowest to highest [Figure 14-10(b)]. This provides practice in using *greater than, less than,* and ordering. To find the middle score or median, simply remove the highest and

Figure 14-10

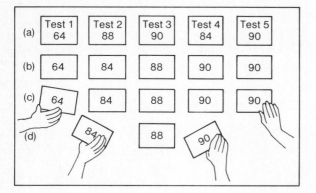

lowest cards simultaneously [Figures 14-10(c) and (d)]. Continue this process until the middle card remains; this score, 88, is the median.

There were five scores in Figure 14-10. Suppose a sixth test was made and a score of 17 was made. A new arrangement could be made by ordering the test scores [Figure 14-11(a)]. Again remove the highest and lowest cards simultaneously until two cards remain. In this case, the median will be the middle point between these two scores, namely 86 [Figure 14-11(b)].

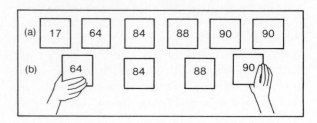

Figure 14-11

Summary of Test Scores Reported in Figures 14-10(a) and 14-11(a)		
	Mean	*Median*
Five Tests	83	88
Six Tests	72	86

Check the accompanying summary of the means and medians for these two sets of tests. It illustrates that the median was affected very little by the extreme low score on the last test, whereas the mean dropped greatly. One characteristic of the mean is that its value is affected by extreme scores.

Suppose you are preparing a report of average incomes and you want to present the fairest picture. Should the mean—which would be affected by the extremely high salaries of movie stars, professional athletes, and corporate heads—be used? Many governmental agencies handle this problem by reporting median family incomes.

Mode. The *mode* is the value that occurs most frequently in a collection of data. In physical terms, this is the high point on a graph, or the tallest column. In Figure 14-10(a) the most frequently occurring test score was 90 (it occurred twice), so the mode is 90. The mode is easy to find and is affected very little by extreme scores.

Students' ages within a class provide an excellent application of mode, since within a given class a large number of children will be the "same" age. Businesses also frequently rely on the mode to select merchandise. Suppose, for example, that you own a shoe store. The mean and/or median size of shoe you sell has no practical value for restocking, but the modal shoe size holds clear implications, since you want to stock the size most people wear.

Finding the mean, median, and mode for the same data can generate discussion about when certain averages should be used. For example, look at Activity Card 14-2. Calculating the mean, median, and mode provides practice on computational skills. More important, however, would be deciding which of these averages to report. The median salary of $50,000 or the modal salary of $48,000 seems more representative than the mean salary of $103,000. If salary negotiations were taking place, the players might cite one "average" while the owners cited a very different "average." Discussing which averages are appropriate for what purpose helps students better understand why different ones exist and are used.

"Averages" are experienced in many different ways during elementary school. Each can be modeled and developed in ways that are appealing, interesting, and meaningful. No new mathematics is required, yet the learning of average—mean, median, and mode—provides a vehicle for applying many mathematical concepts and skills that students are developing.

ACTIVITY CARD 14-2

Intermediate   Averages

$38,000	60,000
42,000	74,000
48,000	270,000
48,000	350,000
48,000	
52,000	

Here are yearly salaries of one professional basketball team!

Decide the best average to report for the team. Tell why your choice is better than the other averages.

What is the mean? median? mode?

PROBABILITY

Probability is encountered daily. Here are some probabilistic statements such as we frequently encounter and are expected to interpret:

> The chance of rain today is 40 percent.
> The Cards are a 3-to-1 favorite to win.
> The probability of an accident today is less than 1 in 100.
> The patient has a 50-50 chance of living.
> If I study, I will probably pass the test.
> I am sure we will have a test Friday.
> We will have milk at the cafeteria today.

The first three statements are commonly heard and relate directly to probability. The last four illustrate a subtle but frequent use of probability in many everyday situations. In situations of both kinds it is the utilitarian role of probability that makes it an important basic skill. One way to increase awareness that probability surrounds our lives is to have students make a daily or weekly list of probability statements they have seen (newspaper, magazines, or television) or heard (radio and television).

Probability will not and should not be learned from formal definitions; rather, the presentation of varied examples will help illustrate and clarify its important concepts. At all stages of instruction, we as teachers must use correct language to describe what is happening. This language serves as a model for children as they begin developing probability concepts and simultaneously add new probabilistic terms to their vocabulary.

We next discuss some key concepts and terms in ways appropriate for elementary students to experience.

Probability of an Event

Look at these statements that involve probability:

> The probability of tossing a head is $\frac{1}{2}$.
> The probability of rolling a four on a die is $\frac{1}{6}$.
> The probability of having a birthday on February 30 is 0.

In these examples "tossing a head," "rolling a four," and "having a birthday on February 30" are events or outcomes. Probability assigns a number (from zero to one) to an event. The more likely an event is to occur, the larger the number assigned to it, and so the probability is 1.0 when something is certain to happen. For example, the probability of students in this room having been born in the twentieth century is 1. On the other hand, the probability of something impossible happening is zero. For example, the probability of students in this room having been born in the nineteenth century is zero.

Long before probabilities of specific events are calculated, it is important that terms such as *certain, uncertain, impossible, likely,* and *unlikely* be introduced and discussed. Most students, even in primary grades, are familiar with the terms *impossible* and *certain* and can give examples of them. Although *likely* and *unlikely* will be less familiar and will require more careful development, Activity Card 14-3 provides a good start. As each card is sorted, an explanation or argument for placing it in that specific box should be given. This rationale is essential in refining and developing clear understanding of these important terms. An excellent follow-up is to have students write statements to be sorted into these categories. Each would write several original statements and then exchange papers so that someone else classifies them. Once these general probabilistic terms become familiar, more specific probabilities can be determined.

Sample space is a fundamental concept that must be established or at least understood before the probabilities of specific events can be determined. The sample space for a probability problem represents all possible outcomes. Activity Card 14-4 is designed to help children think about what outcomes are possible for a particular event. Consider, for example, the situation where cups are tossed. Some children may realize that the cup will not land on its edge, nor will it float. Thus only three outcomes can happen, and these possible outcomes comprise the sample space. Likewise, when a coin is being flipped, it will neither float nor land on its edge, so only two outcomes are possible.

Once the sample space is known, the calculation of specific probabilities usually follows naturally. When a coin is flipped, as described on Activity Card 14-5, the probability of a head is the number of ways a head can

Figure 14-12.   Summary of sample spaces of some events and their probabilities.

QUESTION	SAMPLE SPACE	NUMBER OF SUCCESSES	PROBABILITY
What is the probability of getting a head on a single toss of a coin?	H, T	1	$\frac{1}{2}$
What is the probability of getting two heads when two coins are tossed?	HH, HT, TH, TT	1	$\frac{1}{4}$
What is the probability of getting a five on a single roll of a die?	1, 2, 3, 4, 5, 6	1	$\frac{1}{6}$
What is the probability of drawing a spade from a deck of 52 playing cards?	52 cards - ace through deuce of each of four suits	13	$\frac{13}{52}$ or $\frac{1}{4}$
If each letter of the alphabet is written on a piece of paper, what is the probability of drawing a vowel?	26 letters of the alphabet	a, e, i, o, u	$\frac{5}{26}$

Intermediate Grades

Probability
Identifying Sample Spaces

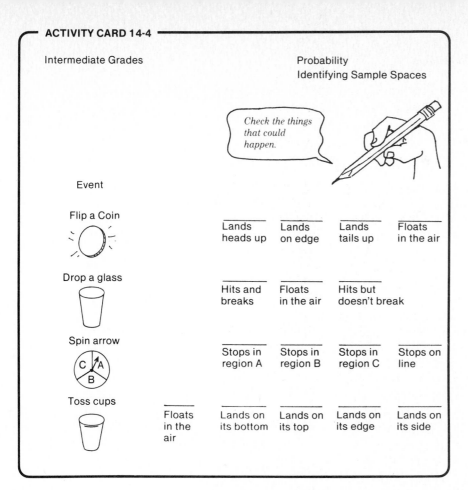

Check the things that could happen.

Event

Flip a Coin

____ Lands heads up ____ Lands on edge ____ Lands tails up ____ Floats in the air

Drop a glass

____ Hits and breaks ____ Floats in the air ____ Hits but doesn't break

Spin arrow

____ Stops in region A ____ Stops in region B ____ Stops in region C ____ Stops on line

Toss cups

____ Floats in the air ____ Lands on its bottom ____ Lands on its top ____ Lands on its edge ____ Lands on its side

Intermediate Grades

Data Collection
More Likely-Less Likely

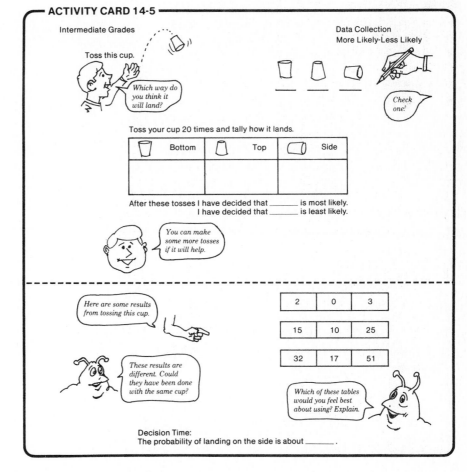

Toss this cup.

Which way do you think it will land?

____ ____ ____

Check one!

Toss your cup 20 times and tally how it lands.

Bottom	Top	Side

After these tosses I have decided that _____ is most likely.
I have decided that _____ is least likely.

You can make some more tosses if it will help.

Here are some results from tossing this cup.

2	0	3
15	10	25
32	17	51

These results are different. Could they have been done with the same cup?

Which of these tables would you feel best about using? Explain.

Decision Time:
The probability of landing on the side is about _____ .

occur divided by the total number of outcomes (head or tail), or $\frac{1}{2}$. Specific probabilities rest heavily on fractions, which provide a direct and convenient means of reporting and interpreting probabilities.

Discussion of possible outcomes helps identify the sample space and clarify notions of probability. Questions along these lines might get the discussion started. Can the spinner shown on Activity Card 14-4 stop in region C, if there is no area marked C? Can the spinner stop on a line? Even though this outcome is unlikely, it can happen, and a plan of action should be decided if it does. (Maybe you spin again.)

Consider the sample space for tossing the cups, as shown on Activity Card 14-4. Is the cup equally likely to land on its top, its side, or its bottom? Without additional information, it would be foolhardy to decide. Activity Card 14-5 provides a possible start. In addition to deciding which outcomes are more or less likely, this exploration may lead to more precise statements. For example, one reasonable conclusion from Activity Card 14-5 is that the probability of the cup landing on its side is about one-half.

Randomness

Randomness is an important concept underlying all learning in probability. It is encountered in many different forms. The term "fair" is often used in describing a situation. For example, to say that we toss a "fair coin" or "fair dice" makes it clear that no inherent biases exist that would affect randomness. In another context, a person is asked to toss (not scoot) a die to insure that one face is not favored. If ping-pong balls are drawn from a bowl, it is important that the balls be thoroughly mixed and the person doing the drawing be blindfolded to insure randomness. All these experiences remind us of the importance of randomness. It is a cornerstone of probability and should be embedded in a variety of activities. Discussions on the consequences of unfairness and absence of randomness should be a part of planned instruction activities.

Independence of Events

Independence of events is an important concept in probability, but one that does not develop naturally from intuition. If two events are *independent,* one event in no way affects the outcome of the other. Thus if a coin is tossed, lands heads, and then is tossed again, it is still equally likely to land heads or tails. This sounds simple enough, but consider this question:

Suppose four consecutive sixes have occurred on four rolls of a fair die. What is the probability of getting a six on the next roll?

The majority of 13-year-olds tested on the second national mathematics assessment missed this question; in fact, only 21 percent answered correctly (5). Many suggested that the die had a "memory" and things would "even out." Most did not conclude that the probability would be $\frac{1}{6}$, regardless of what had already happened. If an event has occurred a number of times in a row, we fallaciously presume that the "law of averages" makes it unlikely that the event will occur on the next trial. This basic misunderstanding contradicts the notion of independence of certain events.

Having children collect data and discuss the results can help dispel some of this erroneous thinking. Activity Card 14-6 will produce different results for different students, yet the answers to the questions will be very similar. Why? Because these events, namely the rolls of a die, are independent of one another.

Tossing a coin and recording the outcomes in sequence will likely generate some long "runs" of an occurrence even though each outcome is independent of others. Although the probability of a head is $\frac{1}{2}$, we might flip a coin ten times and get 8, 9, or even 10 heads in a row. Consider this record of 20 tosses of a coin:

T T T T H T H H H H T T H H T H H H H

It produced a sequence of four consecutive heads and one of five consecutive tails. Overall, 11 heads appeared. Such analysis and discussion helps children understand that things don't even out on each flip. However, as the number of flips gets very large, the ratio of heads to the total number of flips will get closer and closer to $\frac{1}{2}$. This latter point is very important, but its significance is beyond the grasp of most elementary students.

There are, of course, times where one event may depend on another. For example, suppose you wanted to roll two dice and obtain a sum of eight. If 1 is shown on the first die, it is impossible to get a sum of eight. This leads toward notions of *conditional probability* that will be explored later in secondary school.

Several key probability concepts that should be established in the elementary school have been identified. Activity Card 14-7 provides a single setting that will address each of them. The questions direct attention to these concepts and should produce valuable discussion. The interrelatedness of these concepts is also illustrated.

Instruction is needed to develop the necessary techniques to solve simple probability problems. There are, of course, other situations that are very complicated and where probabilities are difficult to calculate. What is the probability of New York winning the World Series? of World War III occurring during this decade? of a woman being elected president? Such questions do not

Intermediate   Independence

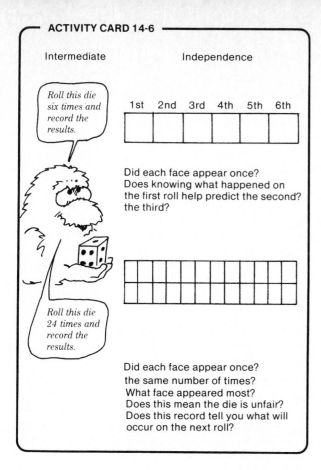

Roll this die six times and record the results.

1st	2nd	3rd	4th	5th	6th

Did each face appear once?
Does knowing what happened on the first roll help predict the second? the third?

Roll this die 24 times and record the results.

Did each face appear once?
the same number of times?
What face appeared most?
Does this mean the die is unfair?
Does this record tell you what will occur on the next roll?

Intermediate   Probability Review

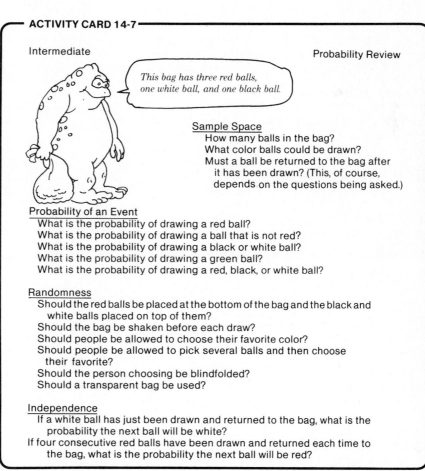

This bag has three red balls, one white ball, and one black ball.

<u>Sample Space</u>
How many balls in the bag?
What color balls could be drawn?
Must a ball be returned to the bag after it has been drawn? (This, of course, depends on the questions being asked.)

<u>Probability of an Event</u>
What is the probability of drawing a red ball?
What is the probability of drawing a ball that is not red?
What is the probability of drawing a black or white ball?
What is the probability of drawing a green ball?
What is the probability of drawing a red, black, or white ball?

<u>Randomness</u>
Should the red balls be placed at the bottom of the bag and the black and white balls placed on top of them?
Should the bag be shaken before each draw?
Should people be allowed to choose their favorite color?
Should people be allowed to pick several balls and then choose their favorite?
Should the person choosing be blindfolded?
Should a transparent bag be used?

<u>Independence</u>
If a white ball has just been drawn and returned to the bag, what is the probability the next ball will be white?
If four consecutive red balls have been drawn and returned each time to the bag, what is the probability the next ball will be red?

lend themselves to simple solutions, but their probabilities can be approximated by experts. Regardless of who determines the numerical probabilities, the knowledge and interpretative skills developed in simpler probability situations can be successfully applied.

A GLANCE AT WHERE WE'VE BEEN

Probability and statistics represent important basic skills. In addition to their practical use in reading and interpreting information, such as graphs, they provide many opportunities to apply much mathematics such as fractions, decimals, and ratios as well as computational skills and problem solving. In fact, the elements of uncertainty in probability and statistics present situations that require critical thinking skills.

Meaningful learning is always important. It is difficult to imagine any mathematical topic that allows for more involvement and stimulates more enthusiasm for learning than probability and statistics. Even though the importance of probability and statistics is unchallenged, performance on these topics leaves much to be desired. Hopefully, this discussion will encourage you to give greater instructional priority to statistics and probability in your classroom.

THINGS TO DO: ADDING TO YOUR PICTURE

1. Read "Making and Interpreting Graphs and Tables: Results and Implications from National Assessment" by Bestgen (1). Identify some of the common errors and misconceptions reported. Describe some of the suggestions and recommendations she offers.

2. Examine a newspaper or magazine. Make a list of the different kinds of graphs used. Tell why you think a particular graph (picture graph, circle graph, bar graph) was used in each situation.

3. Statistics can be obtained from different sources. For example, what is the average number of:
   (a) Peas in a pod?
   (b) Seeds in an apple?
   (c) Sections in an orange?
   In each case discuss why you chose the average stated. Name several other averages from nature.

4. Suppose you have opened some Nutty Bars to check a company's claim of an "average" of 8 peanuts per bar.

Bar	Number of Peanuts
1st	5
2nd	8
3rd	8
4th	8
5th	11
6th	7
7th	8
8th	6
9th	6
10th	6

   (a) What is the mean number of nuts?
   (b) What is the median number?
   (c) What is the modal number?
   (d) Which "average" did the company probably use?

5. Here are the results on three tests: 68, 78, 88. What is the mean? the median? Explain why the mode is of little value. What score would be needed on the next test to get an "average" of 81? Describe two different ways this could be done.

6. Arrange interlocking cubes together in lengths of 3, 6, 6, and 9.
   (a) Describe how you could use the blocks to find the mean, median, and mode.
   (b) Suppose you introduce another length of 10 cubes. Has the mean changed? the median? the mode?

7. Examine the scope-and-sequence chart for an elementary textbook series. At what level was graphing first introduced? What kinds of graphing skills are highlighted? What important statistical topics were included? At what levels were they taught?

8. Use a newspaper or weekly news magazine to look for statistical information about family incomes. What kind of average was reported? Did the article explain that average? Did it give a rationale for reporting that particular average?

9. Examine the 1981 Yearbook of the National Council of Teachers of Mathematics entitled *Teaching Statistics and Probability* (23). Select an article to read and use as a basis for preparing a lesson plan.

10. Check the topical index in the book *Films in the Mathematics Classroom* (2). Identify two films that you would like to use in developing concepts of statistics. Examine their description and, if they are available, preview them.

11. Select a probability article from *Activities for Junior High School and Middle School Mathematics* (7) related to probability and statistics.
    (a) Prepare a lesson plan based on one of the activities described.
    (b) Present this lesson to an appropriate group of children or to your peers.

12. Games are fun and can help develop better understanding of probability. Play several games from "Fair Games, Unfair Games" (3). Identify some of the mathematics being learned. Tell how you might use these games with students.

13. Describe how the activities in Activity Card 14-4 could be used to discuss probabilities of zero and one.

14. Pick five questions from Activity Card 14-7 that you would include in an introductory fifth-grade lesson on probability. Tell why you picked those questions.

15. Ten cards are marked 0, 1, 2, 3, . . . , 9 and placed face down. If the cards are shuffled and then one card drawn, tell why the following statements are true:
    (a) The sample space has 10 events.
    (b) The probability of drawing the 6 is $\frac{1}{10}$.
    (c) The probability of drawing the 3 is the same as the probability of drawing the 7.

(d) The probability of drawing a card with an even number is $\frac{1}{2}$.

(e) The probability of drawing a card with a number greater than 8 is $\frac{2}{10}$.

(f) This activity involves independent events.

SELECTED REFERENCES

1. Bestgen, Barbara J. "Making and Interpreting Graphs and Tables: Results and Implications from National Assessment." *Arithmetic Teacher,* 28 (December 1980), pp. 26–29.

2. Bestgen, Barbara J., and Reys, Robert E. *Films in the Mathematics Classroom.* Reston, Va.: National Council of Teachers of Mathematics, 1982.

3. Bright, George W.; Harvey, John G.; and Wheeler, Margarette Montague. "Fair Games, Unfair Games." In *Teaching Statistics and Probability* (ed. Albert Shulte and James Smart). 1981 Yearbook. Reston, Va.: National Council of Teachers of Mathematics, 1981.

4. Bruni, James V., and Silverman, Helen J. "Let's Do It—Graphing Is a Communication Skill." *Arithmetic Teacher,* 22 (May 1975), pp. 354–366.

5. Carpenter, Thomas P.; Corbitt, Mary Kay; Kepner, Henry S., Jr.; Lindquist, Mary Montgomery; and Reys, Robert E. "What Are the Chances of Your Students Knowing Probability?" *Mathematics Teacher,* 74 (May 1981), pp. 342–344.

6. Craver, John S. *Graph Paper from Your Copier.* Tucson: Fisher Publishing Co., 1980.

7. Easterday, Kenneth E.; Henry, Loren I.; and Simpson, F. Morgan. *Activities for Junior High School and Middle School Mathematics.* Reston, Va.: National Council of Teachers of Mathematics, 1981.

8. *Experiences in Mathematics Ideas,* Vol. 2. Washington, D.C.: National Council of Teachers of Mathematics, 1970.

9. Gawronski, Jane Donnelly, and McLeod, Douglas B. "Probability and Statistics: Today's Ciphering." In *Selected Issues in Mathematics Education* (ed. Mary Montgomery Lindquist). Chicago: National Society for the Study of Education and National Council of Teachers of Mathematics, 1980.

10. Girard, Roth A. "Development of Critical Interpretation of Statistics and Graphs." *Arithmetic Teacher,* 14 (April 1967), pp. 272–277.

11. Johnson, Donovan A.; Hansen, Viggo P.; Peterson, Wayne H.; Rudnick, Jesse A.; Cleveland, Ray; and Bolster L. Carey. *Applications in Mathematics, Course A: Prediction and Probability.* Glenview, Ill.: Scott, Foresman, 1972.

12. Johnson, Donovan A.; Hansen, Viggo P.; Peterson, Wayne H.; Rudnick, Jesse A.; Cleveland, Ray; and Bolster, L. Carey. *Applications in Mathematics, Course A: Sampling and Statistics.* Glenview, Ill.: Scott, Foresman, 1972.

13. Jones, Graham. "A Case for Probability." *Arithmetic Teacher,* 27 (February 1979), pp. 37, 57.

14. Lorton, Mary Baratta. *Mathematics Their Way.* Menlo Park, Calif.: Addison-Wesley, 1976.

15. Mathematics Resource Project: *Statistics and Information Organization.* Palo Alto, Calif.: Creative Publications, 1978.

16. Nuffield Mathematics Project, *Pictorial Representation.* New York: John Wiley, 1967.

17. Nuffield Mathematics Project, *Probability and Statistics.* New York: John Wiley, 1969.

18. *Organizing Data and Dealing with Uncertainty.* Reston, Va.: National Council of Teachers of Mathematics, 1979.

19. Pagni, David L. "Applications in School Mathematics: Human Variability." In *Applications in School Mathematics* (ed. Sidney Sharron and Robert E. Reys). 1979 Yearbook. Reston, Va.: National Council of Teachers of Mathematics, 1979.

20. Pincus, Morris, and Morgenstern, Frances, "Graphs in the Primary Grades." *Arithmetic Teacher,* 17 (October 1970), pp. 499–501.

21. Shulte, Albert P. "A Case for Statistics." *Arithmetic Teacher,* 26 (February 1979), p. 24.

22. Shulte, Albert, and Choate, Stuart. *What Are My Chances? Books A and B.* Palo Alto, Calif.: Creative Publications, 1977.

23. Shulte, Albert, and Smart, James, eds. *Teaching Statistics and Probability.* 1981 Yearbook. Reston, Va.: National Council of Teachers of Mathematics, 1981.

24. Smith, Rolland R. "Probability in the Elementary School." In *Enrichment Mathematics for the Grades.* 27th Yearbook. Washington, D.C.: National Council of Teachers of Mathematics, 1963.

15

Exploring Geometry

Students are in interest centers in a kindergarten. Mrs. Pedro moves over to a small group of children who are building with blocks and decorating their structures with wooden geometric solids. There is some disagreement about who can use some of the solids.

Mrs. Pedro: "Jonathan, what seems to be the problem?"

Jonathan: "We want these [pointing to some of the solids]; those won't stack."

Mrs. Pedro: "Let's all solve a puzzle. Whoever can solve it, gets that solid. We'll need two of each solid."

Earl: "I can't find one that matches this."

Joanne: "I've got it. How about this one?"

Mrs. Pedro: "We've got all the pairs now and the mystery box."

Maria: "Oh, I remember this game. We have to find out what's in the box."

Mrs. Pedro: "Right. I'll put one solid in the mystery box and the rest away so we can't see them. [She turns around so they cannot see her.] The pair of one of these three solids is in the box."

Jonathan: "Can we shut our eyes and feel?"

Mrs. Pedro: "No, this time we must only listen. Anthony, you may try listening to the box first. But all of you listen because you may be able to tell."

Anthony: "It's not rolling like a ball."

Jonathan: "Let me hear. You're right, so it can't be the ball."

Mrs. Pedro: "Does everyone agree? Joanne, could you hear?"

Joanne: "No, let me try. Yeah, it sort of rolls but not like that one."

Mrs. Pedro: "Let's put this one away, since everyone agrees it isn't the one. Now, it must be one of these two."

Maria: "This one [pointing to the third one] would just slide—slunk, slunk—and wouldn't roll at all."

Earl: "This one [pointing to the first one] would roll if it was like this."

Anthony: "Not if you shook the box. It might not roll."

Jonathan: "Right, so it can't be this one."

Mrs. Pedro: "So, which is it?"

All: "This one! Let us see."

Mrs. Pedro opens the box to let them see it was the cone.

Joanne: "Let's try again."

Kathy: "Can I play?"

Mrs. Pedro: "Yes, here's one that will really make all of you think."

They play several more rounds.

Earl: "Let us try to stump you."

Mrs. Pedro: "All right. I'll be back in a minute."

Mrs. Pedro hears talking and laughing. They hand her the box.

Mrs. Pedro: "Oh, you rascals. You filled the box. You really stumped me."

TEACH GEOMETRY—WHY?

You may find yourself working with some teachers who respond to geometry in the following ways:

"Oh, I never could do proofs."

"The children don't understand it, so why do it?"

"We do it if we finish everything else."

There are many reasons for such responses. Some are based on personal past experiences—an unsatisfactory geometry course in high school or no geometry in their own elementary school. Some are based on inappropriate geometry curriculum materials—an abstract, definitional approach. Some are based on a historical emphasis on computation—even though geometry has been recommended by various professional groups for over one hundred years.

You may find that you are working with some teachers who respond:

"It amazes me who is good in geometry; it's not always my best arithmetic students."

"What a joy it is to see a child's eyes light up as she discovers . . . ."

"Some of my students could work on a geometry problem for hours."

"Geometry gives me an opportunity to work on communication skills and to help children to follow instructions."

"The change in the spatial ability of children after they work with geometric shapes always surprises me."

"I love to learn with my students; I never liked geometry before."

What has this second group of teachers discovered about teaching geometry? While they may be just as frustrated as the first group about the lack of time to fit everything into the curriculum, it is evident that geometry will be a part of their program. They have found some or all of the following reasons to include geometry:

1. To provide for the child's everyday needs.
2. To provide for the child's developmental needs.
3. To achieve subject-matter and content goals.
4. To achieve process goals (9, p. 84).

Can you relate these reasons to the responses of the second group of teachers?

You may find many other reasons to teach geometry if only you will adopt the philosophy of the teacher who said, "I love to learn with my students . . . ." As you read through the rest of this chapter, begin this process. You may meet many new ideas, but by trying the activities and brushing up on some things you once learned, you will begin to extend your geometric knowledge as well as your knowledge of how to teach geometry in elementary and junior high schools.

SOLID GEOMETRY

Studying the geometric properties of three-dimensional objects provides a grand opportunity to emphasize the process goals of geometry. This section is built around some of these processes—describing and classifying, constructing, exploring, and discovering, as well as relating three-dimensional shapes to two-dimensional shapes. In this section we will often refer to a three-dimensional shape as a solid, although the object may not be "solid."

If wooden or plastic solids are not available, you could make models as suggested in the constructing part of this section. You and your students should also collect real objects—balls, cans, boxes, cones—that are of a particular geometric shape as well as some more unusual ones.

Describing and Classifying

Children need to be able to describe properties of three-dimensional objects to see how two or more objects are alike and different according to geometric properties. Describing and classifying are processes that extend over time as we add new and more complex properties. In the activities that follow, we are suggesting vocabulary and properties appropriate for beginning, intermediate, and more advanced students. Older children who have not been exposed to three-dimensional activities will benefit from activities like the ones described in the beginning activities.

Beginning Activities. Often we teach children the names of the geometric shapes but do not build the discriminating power that children need in order to use the names with meaning. In these beginning activities you should build on the children's own vocabulary, adding new words as appropriate. Although the names of the solids can be used, they need not be formally introduced until children have done activities like these.

Activity 1. Who Am I? Put out three objects (such as a ball, a cone, and a box). Describe one of them (it is round all over, it is flat on the bottom, it is flat all over) and have the children guess which solid you are describing.

Activity 2. Who Stacks? Have the children sort the objects according to which stack (which roll, which slide). A more sophisticated sort is which solids will always stack, which will stack in some way, and which will not stack in any way.

Activity 3. How Are We Alike? Different? Hold up two solids and have children tell how they are alike or different. For example, children may contrast the two solids shown below as follows:

"They both are flat all over."
"One is tall."
"One has bigger sides."
"They have some square faces."
"They have six faces."

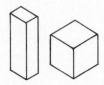

Activity 4. Who Doesn't Belong? Put out three solids such as those shown in the next sketch. Have children tell which does not belong with the other two. Since there are many ways to solve this problem, be ready to encourage lively discussion. For example, some children may say A doesn't belong because it has a point. Others may say B doesn't belong because it's short, or C doesn't belong because it's skinny or has a smaller bottom.

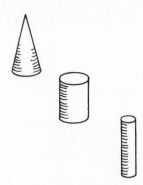

Activity 5. How Many Faces Have I? A face is a flat side. Have children count the number of faces. You can do this in many contexts, but one way is to have them collect objects with six faces (boxes, books), with two faces (cans), with zero faces (balls).

Activity 6. Can You Find an Object Like Me? Put out a solid and see if children can find real objects that have the same shape. You may get disagreement about which are alike.

Intermediate Activities. In these activities we will introduce the names of some of the solids, consider the size (or measure properties), and consider the edges, faces, and vertices of solids.

Activity 1. Edges, Vertices, and Faces. After introducing *edge* (straight segment formed by two faces) and *vertex* (point where three or more faces come together), have children solve these riddles:

I am a solid with
   8 edges; who am I?
   6 edges and 4 faces; who am I?
   5 corners; who am I?
   the same number of corners as faces; who am I?
   no faces (no corners); who am I?
   one face and no corners; who am I?

Activity 2. Cube, Cone, Pyramid, Cylinder, and Sphere. Introduce each word by putting out examples of the solid and nonexamples. (See Activity Card 15-1.) Then ask children to tell what makes a solid belong to that group.

Activity 3. Solid Search. Make up a set of activity cards that have children search the solids according to the size and shape of the faces and the length of the edges. Here are samples to get you started; the questions you make will depend upon the solids.

Find a solid with:
1. Exactly 2 faces that are the same size and shape (congruent).
2. Exactly 3 faces that are the same size and shape.

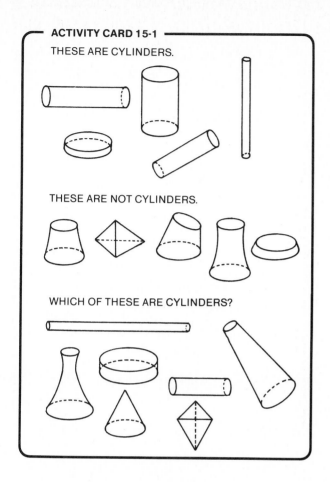

ACTIVITY CARD 15-1

THESE ARE CYLINDERS.

THESE ARE NOT CYLINDERS.

WHICH OF THESE ARE CYLINDERS?

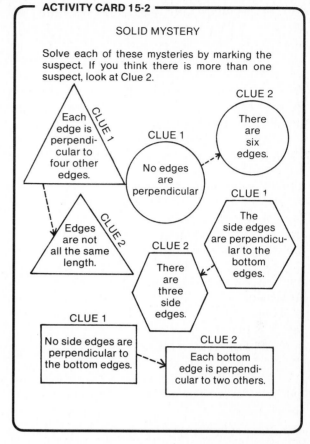

ACTIVITY CARD 15-2

SOLID MYSTERY

Solve each of these mysteries by marking the suspect. If you think there is more than one suspect, look at Clue 2.

CLUE 1 Each edge is perpendicular to four other edges.

CLUE 1 No edges are perpendicular

CLUE 2 There are six edges.

CLUE 2 Edges are not all the same length.

CLUE 1 The side edges are perpendicular to the bottom edges.

CLUE 2 There are three side edges.

CLUE 1 No side edges are perpendicular to the bottom edges.

CLUE 2 Each bottom edge is perpendicular to two others.

3. All edges the same length.
4. Three different lengths of edges.

Advanced Activities. These activities include the properties of parallel and perpendicular faces and edges as well as a more careful definition and classification of the solids.

Activity 1. Parallel Faces. This is an activity to be done after parallel faces have been introduced. It consists of questions about real objects and why faces are parallel. A few sample questions are given here to start you thinking:

1. Why are the top and bottom of soup cans parallel?
2. Why are shelves parallel to the floor?
3. Why are roofs of houses in cold climates usually not parallel to the ground?
4. Why is the front side of a milk carton parallel to the back side?

Activity 2. Perpendicular Edges. This activity (see Activity Card 15-2) asks children to construct solids from sticks and connectors. Some suggestions for materials are given in the construction section that follows.

Activity 3. What Is a Right Prism? This activity introduces the definition of right prisms and how to name them. After giving examples and nonexamples of right prisms as in Activity 2 of the intermediate activities, have children come up with the definition of a prism: a solid that has congruent and parallel bases (top and bottom) joined by rectangular faces. Then discuss how prisms are named: if the base is a triangle, it is a triangular prism, and so on.

These activities are only suggestions of ideas to develop. By the end of eighth grade, children should have developed the ability to identify solids (cones, prisms, cylinders, spheres, pyramids) and name special ones. More important, they should be able to contrast the different solids by the properties mentioned in this discussion. The activities in the rest of this section reinforce and extend these ideas.

Constructing and Then Exploring and Discovering

One of the difficulties that children have with three-dimensional geometry is visualizing the solid. It is essential to have models. If models are not available, there are many ways that you can have children make them.

As children are making the models, they often discover many things about the solids. There are, however, other properties or relationships that they may not discover or other ways to explore the solids. The activities we now discuss provide examples of ways to structure their investigations.

Paper Tubes. Some of the easiest and most versatile models can be made from heavy construction paper. Cylinders and prisms may be made as shown in Activity Card 15-3. Top and bottom faces may be added by tracing the top of the tube, cutting, and taping it to the tube. Many variations of prisms can be made, and these can be cut to create many strange shapes.

Discovery with Paper Tubes. The exploration in Activity Card 15-4 is a variation of a famous formula—Euler's (pronounced "oil-ers") formula—which relates the numbers of edges (E), faces (F), and vertices (V) to each other ($V + F = E + 2$). Because the tubes have no top or bottom face, the formula found here is $V + F = E$, which is more readily evident. Several other relations are also noted that hold for these prisms.

"Stick" Models. Models can be made from straws and pipe cleaners, toothpicks and clay (or small marsh-

---

ACTIVITY CARD 15-4

DISCOVERY WITH PAPER TUBES.

Make 3 different tubes as shown on Activity Card 15-3.

	TUBE 1	TUBE 2	TUBE 3
FACES			
EDGES			
CORNERS			

1. Count the number of faces of Tube 1. (Remember there is no top or bottom, so don't count them.) Write the number in the chart.
2. Count the number of edges of Tube 1. (Don't forget the top and bottom edges.)
3. Repeat 1 and 2 for Tube 2.
4. QUESTION. Do you see an easy way to tell how many edges if you know the number of faces? HYPOTHESIS: _____
5. Count the corners of Tube 1 and Tube 2.
6. QUESTION. Do you see an easy way to tell how many corners if you know the number of faces and edges? HYPOTHESIS:_____

---

7. Check your hypotheses with Tube 3.

ACTIVITY CARD 15-3

PAPER TUBES
Materials: construction paper, masking tape

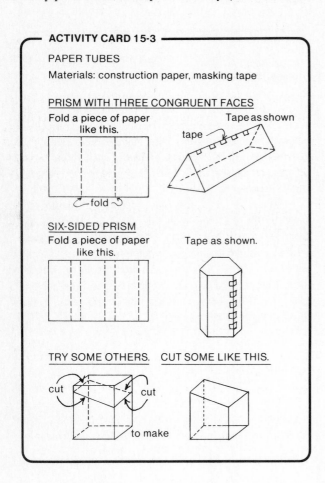

PRISM WITH THREE CONGRUENT FACES
Fold a piece of paper like this.   Tape as shown
tape
fold

SIX-SIDED PRISM
Fold a piece of paper like this.   Tape as shown.

TRY SOME OTHERS.   CUT SOME LIKE THIS.
cut   cut
to make

ACTIVITY CARD 15-5

NEWSPAPER AND TAPE MODELS

Materials: newspaper, scissors, and tape.

STEP 1. Take three sheets from a newspaper and roll tightly from corner to corner.
STEP 2. Tape to hold rod.

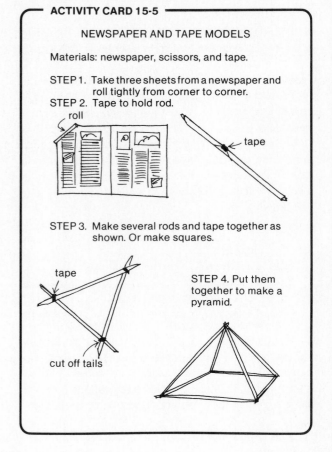

roll   tape

STEP 3. Make several rods and tape together as shown. Or make squares.

tape

STEP 4. Put them together to make a pyramid.

cut off tails

230

mallows), or from other "sticks" and holders. There are also reasonably priced, commercial materials that are designed for this purpose. Activity Card 15-5 illustrates a three-dimensional figure made from newspaper sticks and tape.

In building three-dimensional objects with the newspaper sticks the children can investigate rigidity of triangles, squares, or other polygons. Have them build a pyramid and a cube. What happens? They should find that the triangular pyramid is a rigid structure while the cube needs bracing.

Networks. The pattern of a solid may be given so that when edges are attached by the tabs, the solid will be created. Activity Card 15-6 illustrates networks for several solids. Can you name the solid that each will make?

ACTIVITY CARD 15-6

NETWORKS

Materials: scissors, glue, ruler, and construction paper

Directions: Enlarge these patterns on construction paper. Cut out. Fold on lines. Glue tabs under adjoining side.

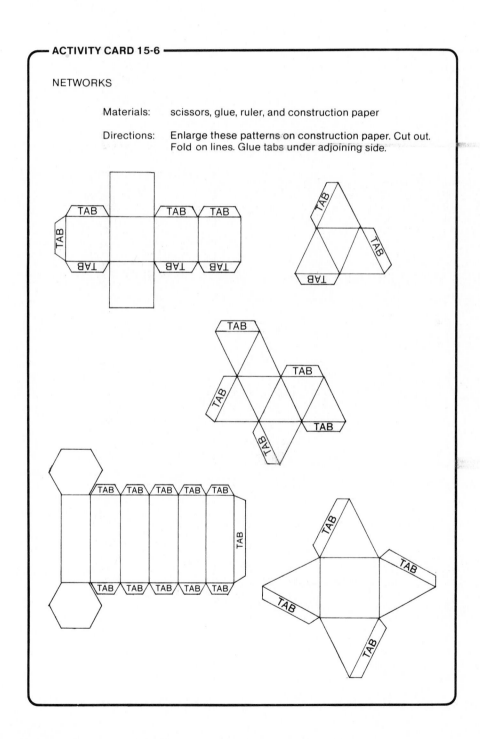

Some networks can be "folded" to create a solid; others cannot be. Activity Card 15-7 gives the students a chance to see if they can tell from a network whether or not a solid can be constructed. Children can verify their answers by cutting out the network and folding.

Relating Three Dimensions to Two

Since three-dimensional objects often must be pictured in two dimensions, children must be able to relate the objects to pictures. They also need to be able to look at a three-dimensional object and ascertain its two-dimensional parts. Constructing solids assists in this skill, but there are activities that focus on it directly.

Making Imprints of Faces of Solids. Make imprints in playdough (home-made works great) of the faces of solids. Have children match the solid with a matching face. (You can also trace the faces instead of making imprints, but younger children can see the fit in the imprint.) See Activity Card 15-8 for a challenging activity for youngsters.

Different Views of a Solid. Have children choose which views of solids are possible and which are not. It is important to have the solids available and to discuss the children's answers with them. Activity Card 15-9 gives two variations.

Cross Sections. Cross sections of solids are often difficult for people to visualize. The cutting of the tubes

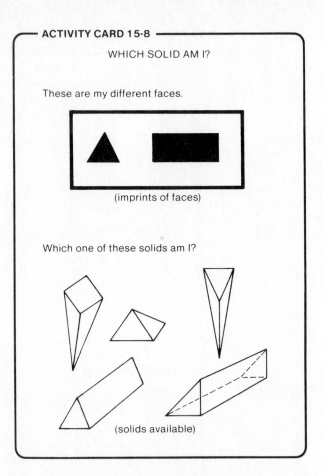

ACTIVITY CARD 15-8

WHICH SOLID AM I?

These are my different faces.

(imprints of faces)

Which one of these solids am I?

(solids available)

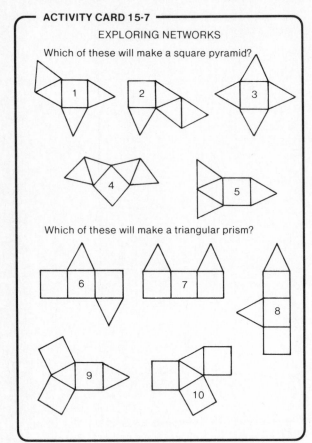

ACTIVITY CARD 15-7

EXPLORING NETWORKS

Which of these will make a square pyramid?

1   2   3

4   5

Which of these will make a triangular prism?

6   7

8

9   10

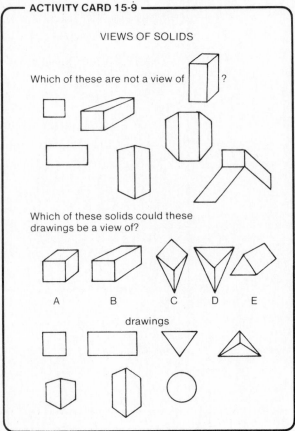

ACTIVITY CARD 15-9

VIEWS OF SOLIDS

Which of these are not a view of ⬜ ?

Which of these solids could these drawings be a view of?

A   B   C   D   E

drawings

in the process of construction helps children to see the cross section. If you have other objects that can be cut (oranges, carrots shaped in cones, or zucchini shaped in different solids), you can help the children see the cross sections.

PLANE GEOMETRY

In this section we will consider two-dimensional shapes, their properties, relationships among shapes, and classification schemes. The ideas mainly are presented through sample activities involving many types of physical materials—geoboards, geometric pieces (see Figure 15-1),

paper strips, compasses, as well as paper and pencil. You will need to try the activities as you read in order to see the complete picture.

Just as in examining three-dimensional shapes we often focus on the faces (two-dimensional), in examining the two-dimensional shapes we often focus on the sides or vertices (one-dimensional). We will build these one-dimensional concepts as they occur naturally within a two-dimensional context.

Properties of a Shape

While we have an intuitive feel about the difference between shapes, we need ways to describe that

Figure 15-1. From Romberg (10).

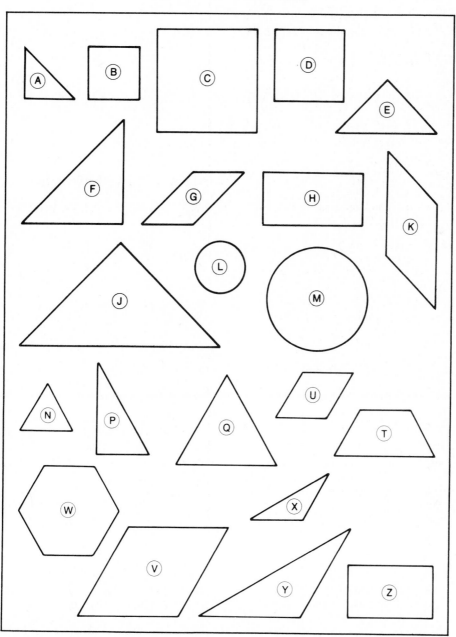

difference. By considering the properties of shapes we can develop that ability. There are many ways of describing a geometric shape: the number of sides, the number of corners, its name, whether or not it is symmetric, length of sides, size of angles, parallel and perpendicular sides, whether or not it is convex. For ease of discussion we have separated the different properties, but we bring them back together later when we discuss classification. Some of the easier properties for children to learn are presented first, but within these there are often more sophisticated activities.

Number of Sides. Children readily count the number of sides (straight parts) of a shape. If the shape has many sides, you may need to mark the place where you begin counting.

How Many Sides? This is a simple activity using geometric pieces that can involve all your children. Give each child a geometric piece. If you do not have plastic pieces as in Figure 15-1, cut pieces from heavy paper or construction paper. Call a number and have the children who have a piece with that number of sides stand. Be certain to call numbers such as two and seven for which no one will stand. Then have a search for all the different shapes that have three sides, four sides, five sides, six sides, and zero sides (the circle). Put a sample of each different shape somewhere within view of all the children. Be sure to have the children tell how the three-sided shapes differ (some are bigger than others, some seem skinny, and so on). It is important for them to realize that the number of sides does not entirely specify the shape.

Can You Make a _____? An activity that can be challenging has children make a figure of a given number of sides on a geoboard. (See Activity Card 15-12 for a picture of a geoboard.) Give each child a geoboard and one rubber band. Begin by asking questions such as, "Can you make a four-sided figure?" Gradually add other conditions. "Can you make a four-sided figure that touches only four pegs? That touches six pegs? That has two pegs inside (not touching) it?"

Can You Beat That? A more advanced activity has children put the geometric pieces together to make new shapes with a specified number of sides. Two children each "blindly" choose three geometric pieces from A–K (or from N–Z). Each tries to put the pieces together to make a shape with as few sides as possible. (See Activity Card 15-10.) Play several rounds to determine a winner.

Number of Corners. Closely related to counting the number of sides is counting the number of corners. Children will soon realize that any polygonal figure has the same number of sides as corners if they count both on each shape. The activities suggested for counting the number of sides can be modified for counting corners.

Symmetry. Two types of symmetry—line and rota-

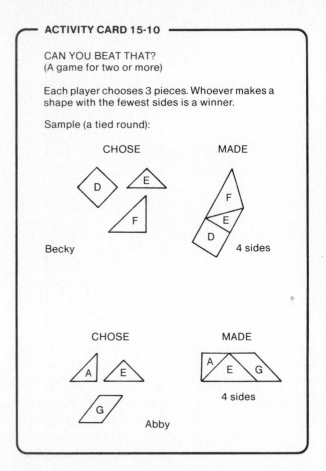

ACTIVITY CARD 15-10

CAN YOU BEAT THAT?
(A game for two or more)

Each player chooses 3 pieces. Whoever makes a shape with the fewest sides is a winner.

Sample (a tied round):

CHOSE   MADE

Becky   4 sides

CHOSE   MADE

Abby   4 sides

tional—may be used to describe geometric shapes as well as other figures.

To introduce line symmetry have children compare two snowmen. When they say one looks lopsided,

show them how they can fold the other one so the sides match. Then, have them find the line(s) of symmetry of other shapes. (See Activity Card 15-11.) Be sure to let them try a square (four lines of symmetry), an equilateral triangle (three lines of symmetry), and a circle (an infinite number). Older children can often see the lines of symmetry without folding, but some shapes are misleading. One of these is a parallelogram. Many children will say, at first glance, that a parallelogram has two lines of symmetry. Try it yourself.

It is important that children also see symmetry in things around them. You might want them to make a bulletin board of pictures that are symmetric. It is also fun to make symmetric shapes. One way is to fold a piece of paper and cut the folded piece, leaving the fold

ACTIVITY CARD 15-11

SYMMETRY - LINE

Fold these to see how many lines of symmetry.

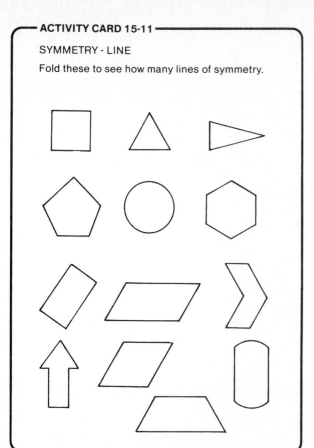

intact. Can you figure out how to make a shape with two lines of symmetry?

Length of Sides. Many of our definitions of geometric shapes as well as classification schemes depend upon the length of sides. Activity Card 15-12 presents a more advanced activity in which children make shapes on a geoboard according to certain specifications about the lengths of the sides. Try some of the cards and classify them as to whether they are easy, medium, or challenging!

Size of Angles. There are many ways to examine the angles of geometric figures. Here are some of the properties related to angles that children may discover:

1. The sum of the angles of a triangle is 180°.
2. The sum of the angles of a quadrilateral is 360°.
3. The base angles of an isosceles triangle are equal.
4. Opposite angles of a parallelogram are equal.
5. A polygon with more than three sides can have equal sides without having equal angles.
6. The angle opposite the longest side of a triangle is the largest.

ACTIVITY CARD 15-12

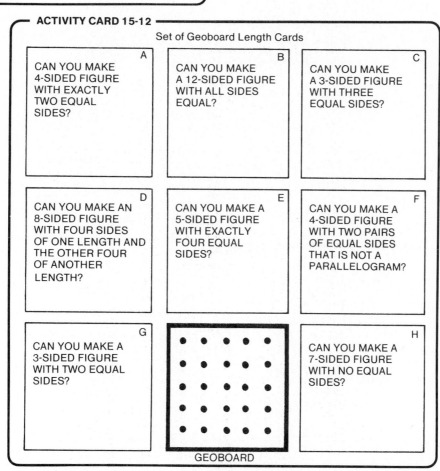

A guided discovery lesson to help students see that the angles of a quadrilateral sum to 360° is given on Activity Card 15-13.

Parallel and Perpendicular Sides. Besides examining parallel and perpendicular lines in geometric shapes, children need to be able to identify parallel lines and perpendicular lines in a plane and, later, in space. Two lines in a plane are parallel if they never intersect. (Remember, a line can be extended indefinitely in either direction.) Another useful definition states that two lines are parallel if they are always the same distance (perpendicular distance) apart. Two lines are perpendicular if they intersect at right angles. The worksheet (Activity Card 15-14) is a straightforward one on which the children identify parallel lines.

It is important that children recognize perpendicular and parallel lines in the world around them. Have them search for them in the room. You might together start a list on the board, letting children add to it as they find other examples. Here is a start:

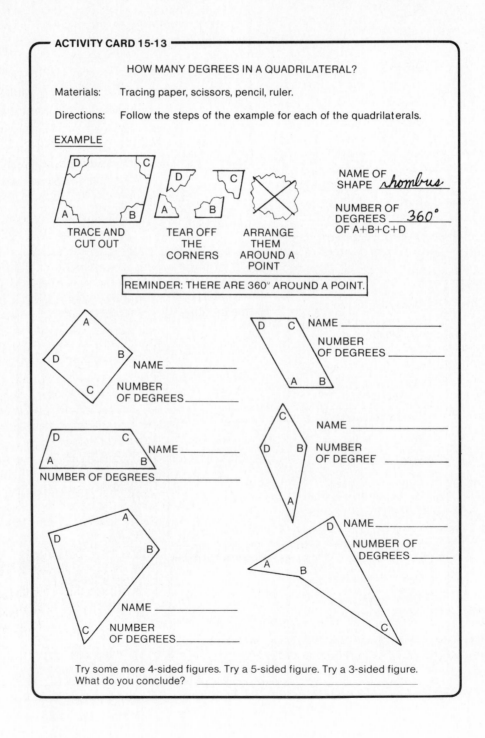

ACTIVITY CARD 15-13

HOW MANY DEGREES IN A QUADRILATERAL?

Materials: Tracing paper, scissors, pencil, ruler.

Directions: Follow the steps of the example for each of the quadrilaterals.

EXAMPLE

TRACE AND CUT OUT   TEAR OFF THE CORNERS   ARRANGE THEM AROUND A POINT

NAME OF SHAPE *rhombus*

NUMBER OF DEGREES *360°* OF A+B+C+D

REMINDER: THERE ARE 360° AROUND A POINT.

NAME _____
NUMBER OF DEGREES _____

NAME _____
NUMBER OF DEGREES _____

NAME _____
NUMBER OF DEGREES _____

NAME _____
NUMBER OF DEGREE _____

NAME _____
NUMBER OF DEGREES _____

NAME _____
NUMBER OF DEGREES _____

Try some more 4-sided figures. Try a 5-sided figure. Try a 3-sided figure. What do you conclude? _____

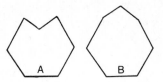

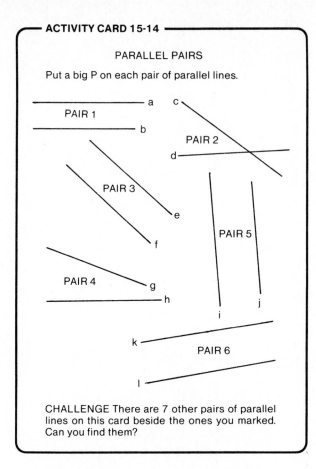

ACTIVITY CARD 15-14

PARALLEL PAIRS

Put a big P on each pair of parallel lines.

PAIR 1 · PAIR 2 · PAIR 3 · PAIR 4 · PAIR 5 · PAIR 6

CHALLENGE There are 7 other pairs of parallel lines on this card beside the ones you marked. Can you find them?

Parallel lines

Opposite sides of a book

The horizontal lines in E

The top and bottom of the board

Perpendicular lines

Adjacent sides of a book

The vertical and horizontal lines in E

You may also have the children identify parallel and perpendicular sides on the geometric pieces (see Figure 15-1). Find all the pieces that have one pair of perpendicular sides. Find all the pieces with more than one pair of perpendicular sides. Find a piece with one pair of parallel sides. The activity on Activity Card 15-15* is a challenging one in which children have to arrange two pieces to make shapes with a specified number of parallel sides.

Convex and Concave. Often we expose children only to convex shapes (a polygon with all angles less than 180°) because those are the ones with names. Many of the activities suggested thus far have included concave shapes. If you have children making shapes, the concave ones will often give interesting variety.

*Activity Card 15-15 is from Romberg (10).

Show children two shapes such as those sketched above and have them describe how they are alike and different. They will probably express the idea that shape A "comes back" on itself or "caves" in (concave). Introduce the terms *concave* and *convex*. After having children classify shapes as convex or concave, you might have them investigate questions such as the following:

1. Can you draw a four-sided (five-sided, six-sided, seven-sided) figure that is concave?
2. Can you draw a five-sided (six-sided, seven-sided) figure that is "concave in two places" (or that has two angles greater than 180°)?
3. Can you draw a six-sided (seven-sided, eight-sided) figure that is "concave in three places"?

Altitude. The altitude (or height) of a geometric shape depends upon what is specified as a base. Since identifying the altitude (or height) is essential in finding most areas, children should develop the ability to identify the altitudes of a given figure. The first part of Activity Card 15-16 is designed to help children realize that a geometric object has different heights. The second part is designed to transfer the idea of height to altitude (or from a geometric object to a drawing or piece of paper).

Names of Geometric Shapes. Often we teach children the geometric names without providing much opportunity to explore the properties or to solve problems. On the second national mathematics assessment 84 percent of the nine-year-olds and 96 percent of the 13-year-olds could recognize a rectangle, but only 14 percent of the 13-year-olds realized that just having opposite sides congruent in a quadrilateral was not sufficient for a quadrilateral to be a rectangle (5, pp. 73–75).

Children should begin to recognize types of shapes through examples and nonexamples and not through definitions. By experiencing examples and discussing the properties, they can begin to realize what properties define a figure. Look at Activity Card 15-17, which gives examples and nonexamples of triangles. Do you see why the different figures were included?

If a child says that C, B, F, or G is a triangle, what property of triangles do you think is being ignored in each case? If a child fails to realize that D is a triangle, what do you think may be the reason?

Children also need to be able to recognize real objects for which the geometric shapes are models. For example, you might have young children write a "book"

ACTIVITY CARD 15-15

PIEZLES

Solve any five of these piece puzzles (piezles).

1. Use one Ⓖ and one Ⓚ. Make a shape with two pairs of parallel sides. Can you make another shape with three pairs of parallel sides? with four pairs?

2. Use one Ⓟ and one Ⓣ. Make a shape with zero pairs of parallel sides; then with one pair of parallel sides; then with two pairs of parallel sides.

3. Is there a shape with three Ⓚ's that has four pairs of parallel sides?
　Is there a shape with four Ⓚ's that has three pairs of parallel sides?

4. Which piece can you use with one Ⓒ to make a shape having three pairs of parallel sides?

5. Use one Ⓐ and one Ⓣ. Can you make a shape with more than one pair of parallel sides?

6. Which two pieces make a shape with an even number of pairs of parallel sides?

1Ⓖ and 1Ⓣ　　1Ⓦ and 1Ⓩ
1Ⓒ and 1Ⓗ　　1Ⓗ and 1Ⓩ
1Ⓖ and 1Ⓤ　　1Ⓥ and 1Ⓨ

7. Which two pieces make a shape with an odd number of pairs of parallel sides?

1Ⓑ and 1Ⓗ　　1Ⓣ and 1Ⓤ
1Ⓝ and 1Ⓦ　　1Ⓗ and 1Ⓚ
1Ⓔ and 1Ⓖ　　1Ⓒ and 1Ⓥ

8. Which two pieces make shapes that have the same number of pairs of parallel sides?

1Ⓑ and 1Ⓤ　　1Ⓗ and 1Ⓥ
1Ⓤ and 1Ⓩ　　1Ⓖ and 1Ⓩ
1Ⓟ and 1Ⓠ　　1Ⓒ and 1Ⓚ

9. Which two pieces make a shape with every side parallel to at least one other side?

1Ⓝ and 1Ⓟ　　1Ⓑ and 1Ⓦ
1Ⓤ and 1Ⓩ　　1Ⓖ and 1Ⓚ
1Ⓒ and 1Ⓣ　　1Ⓔ and 1Ⓕ

10. Which two pieces make a shape with at least one nonparallel side?

1Ⓔ and 1Ⓚ　　1Ⓠ and 1Ⓣ
1Ⓖ and 1Ⓗ　　1Ⓕ and 1Ⓣ
1Ⓝ and 1Ⓦ　　1Ⓗ and 1Ⓦ

ACTIVITY CARD 15-16

WHAT'S MY ALTITUDE?

Make a triangle from a stiff piece of paper. Cut a strip 2 cm by 20 cm. Mark off segments of 9 cm, 4 cm, and 7 cm and label them A, B, and C, respectively. Fold and tape as shown:

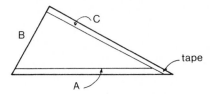

1. Set the triangle on side A. This is the base.
   How long is the base? ___9 cm___
   What is the altitude? ___cm___

2. Set the triangle on side B. This is the base now.
   How long is the base? _____
   What is the altitude? _____

3. Set the triangle on side C. This is the base now.
   How long is the base? _____
   What is the altitude? _____

On a large sheet of paper: Trace the triangle and show the altitude for each of the bases.

ACTIVITY CARD 15-17

THESE ARE TRIANGLES.

THESE ARE NOT TRIANGLES.

WHICH OF THESE ARE TRIANGLES?

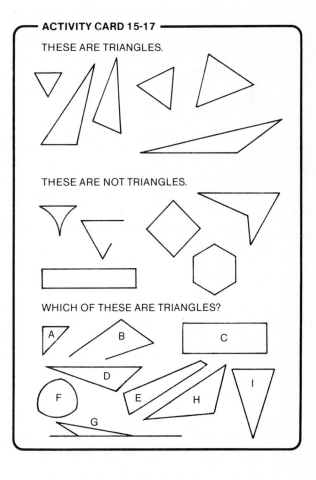

about circles. What is shaped like a circle? Let them find examples and draw pictures. Older children can be challenged to tell why certain objects are shaped in a certain way. Why are most buttons shaped like a circle? Why is paper rectangular? Why are walls rectangular? Why are braces triangular?

The most common shapes are triangle, square, rectangle, circle, and parallelogram. (Other names will be suggested shortly, when we discuss classification.) Other words besides the properties we have discussed also are used with figures. For example, we expect children to be able to identify the center, radius, diameter, and circumference of a circle. The most important thing with all vocabulary is that, after it is introduced, it be used.

Relationships Between Shapes

In the preceding section we looked at properties of individual shapes. To emphasize those properties, it is often helpful to compare two or more shapes. In so doing, we may use the relationships of congruence and similarity. After examining these two relationships, we will see how children at different levels might respond to comparing two shapes on all the properties mentioned thus far.

Congruence. Two shapes are said to be *congruent* if they have the same size and the same shape. For young children, this means that one shape could be made to fit exactly on the other. If the two shapes are line segments, then they are congruent if they have the same length. If the two shapes are two-dimensional, then, if they are congruent, they have the same area. The converse is not true: two shapes with the same area may not be congruent. Children have difficulty with this, as evidenced in the second national mathematics assessment (5, p. 78). Fifty percent of the 13-year-olds thought that the parallelogram shown below was congruent to the rectangle. This is probably more a function of the technical word *congruence* than of the concept. Young children have little difficulty identifying the figures with the same shape and size. Thus, the task becomes one of asking young children to match figures to see if they are the same size and shape, and gradually introducing and using the word *congruence.*

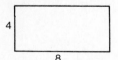 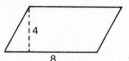

You may have children begin to investigate the relationship between same area but different shape through activities such as that on Activity Card 10-2.

Congruence can be examined through matching activities such as the one on Activity Card 15-18.

Congruence is often investigated through motion geometry. If two shapes are congruent, they can be made to fit by one or more of the three motions illustrated in Figure 15-2. It sometimes takes more than one motion, as shown by the glide.

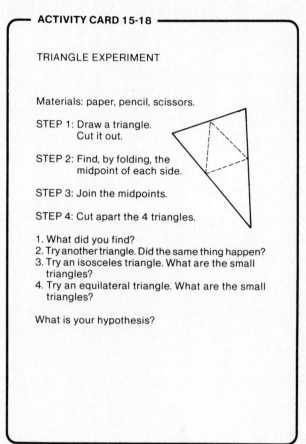

ACTIVITY CARD 15-18

TRIANGLE EXPERIMENT

Materials: paper, pencil, scissors.

STEP 1: Draw a triangle.
Cut it out.

STEP 2: Find, by folding, the midpoint of each side.

STEP 3: Join the midpoints.

STEP 4: Cut apart the 4 triangles.

1. What did you find?
2. Try another triangle. Did the same thing happen?
3. Try an isosceles triangle. What are the small triangles?
4. Try an equilateral triangle. What are the small triangles?

What is your hypothesis?

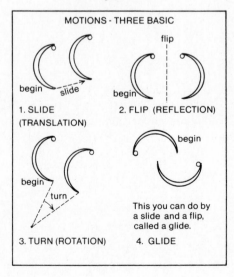

Figure 15-2

MOTIONS - THREE BASIC

1. SLIDE (TRANSLATION)

2. FLIP (REFLECTION)

3. TURN (ROTATION)

4. GLIDE

This you can do by a slide and a flip, called a glide.

Similarity. Children have some idea of similarity, but some shapes are misleading (see Figure 15-3). This intuitive notion has to be refined to a mathematical definition: two figures are *similar* if corresponding angles are equal and corresponding sides are in the same ratio.

This definition is too formal for a beginning. Instead you can begin by using a geoboard and "geopaper." Children can make a design on the geoboard and transfer it to smaller geopaper, or they can copy designs from one size of graph paper to another.

After students have been introduced to ratio, they can investigate similarity in a more rigorous way. The knowledge of similarity is used in many practical situations such as photography. (The use of similar triangles is discussed in Chapter 12.)

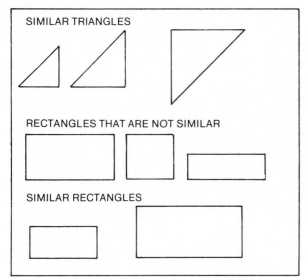

Figure 15-3

Comparing Two Figures. As children are learning about the properties of geometric figures, they should be given many opportunities to compare figures. Look at the responses the children give as they compare the two figures in Figure 15-4.

Classification Schemes

We have examined many properties of, and relationships among, geometric figures. Now we will look in more detail at the defining properties of two-dimensional shapes—what makes a parallelogram be a parallelogram, when is a rhombus a square, what is a regular polygon?

Triangles. We classify triangles either by sides or by angles:

By sides

equilateral—three congruent sides

isosceles—at least two congruent sides

scalene—no sides congruent

Figure 15-4

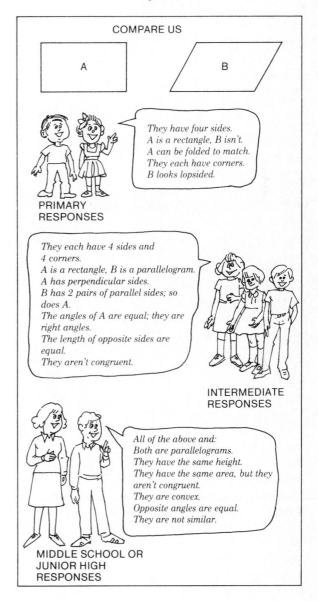

By angles

acute—all angles less than 90°

right—one angle equal to 90°

obtuse—one angle greater than 90°

Once children have learned to identify triangles by sides and by angles, the two properties may be put together as on Activity Card 15-19.

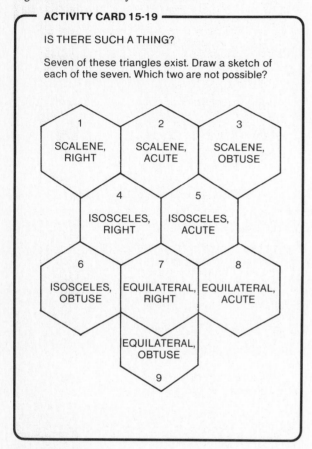

ACTIVITY CARD 15-19

IS THERE SUCH A THING?

Seven of these triangles exist. Draw a sketch of each of the seven. Which two are not possible?

1. SCALENE, RIGHT
2. SCALENE, ACUTE
3. SCALENE, OBTUSE
4. ISOSCELES, RIGHT
5. ISOSCELES, ACUTE
6. ISOSCELES, OBTUSE
7. EQUILATERAL, RIGHT
8. EQUILATERAL, ACUTE
9. EQUILATERAL, OBTUSE

Quadrilaterals. There are many special names for quadrilaterals; the most common are parallelograms, rectangles, squares, rhombuses, trapezoids, and kites. These classes are not disjoint as were those of triangles classified by sides (or by angles). That is, a rectangle is also a parallelogram. This type of classification scheme is more difficult for children than one that partitions the whole set into disjoint classes. It requires more than just recognizing examples of figures; it requires knowing the definition. For example, a parallelogram is a quadrilateral with two pairs of parallel sides. Assuming you know that a quadrilateral is a four-sided, closed simple figure, can you identify which of the following are parallelograms?

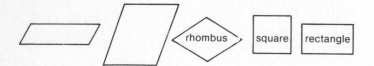

rhombus   square   rectangle

You are correct; they all are. This means that a square, a rhombus, and a rectangle are all special types of parallelograms.

What is a rhombus? A rhombus is a parallelogram with all sides congruent. Does that mean that a square is a rhombus? What is a rectangle? A rectangle is a parallelogram with right angles. Does that mean a square is a rectangle? Here is a picture of these relationships.

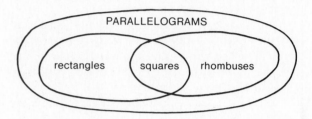

PARALLELOGRAMS

rectangles   squares   rhombuses

How do we begin to teach such relationships? Do you see that children must first begin to verbalize many properties of the figure? For example, they must be able to describe a square as:

1. A four-sided figure
2. Opposite sides parallel
3. All right angles
4. All sides congruent

Properties 1 and 2 make it a parallelogram; properties 1, 2, and 3 make it a rectangle; properties 1, 2, and 4 make it a rhombus; properties 1, 2, 3, and 4 make it a square. Activity Card 15-20 helps children with this idea.

Polygons. We name polygons by the number of sides:

3 sides:	triangles
4 sides:	quadrilaterals
5 sides:	pentagons
6 sides:	hexagons
7 sides:	heptagons
8 sides:	octagons
9 sides:	nonagons
10 sides:	decagons

This is not a difficult type of classification, but often we show children only regular polygons. Thus, among the shapes shown here, a child sees only the first as a hexagon, instead of realizing they all are hexagons. Can you think of real objects that are shaped like these?

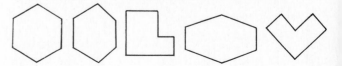

ACTIVITY CARD 15-20

CLASSIFYING QUADRILATERALS

Mark each of the figures below with a
1--if it is a quadrilateral,
2--if it has two pairs of parallel sides,
3--if it has all right angles,
4--if it has all congruent sides.

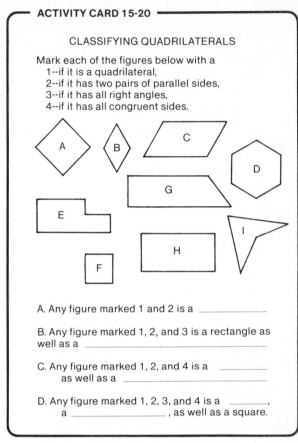

A. Any figure marked 1 and 2 is a _____

B. Any figure marked 1, 2, and 3 is a rectangle as well as a _____

C. Any figure marked 1, 2, and 4 is a _____
as well as a _____

D. Any figure marked 1, 2, 3, and 4 is a _____,
a _____ , as well as a square.

ACTIVITY CARD 15-21

CAN YOU FIND A _____?

See if you can find each of these in the design below.

(A) triangle - isosceles
(B) triangle - scalene
(C) quadrilateral - not symmetric
(D) quadrilateral - 4 lines of symmetry
(E) pentagon - concave
(F) pentagon - convex
(G) hexagon - exactly 2 pairs of parallel sides
(H) hexagon - symmetric
(I) heptagon (7 sides) - symmetric
(J) heptagon - not symmetric
(K) octagon

The names of pentagons, heptagons, nonagons, and decagons are not widely used, so that in doing activities you may have to remind children of these names. Activity Card 15-21 uses the names as well as other properties.

A GLANCE AT WHERE WE'VE BEEN

Geometry is a topic that is often neglected in elementary school, yet it has many benefits for children if presented in an intuitive, informal manner. We have given you a variety of examples of activities that provide this type of informal experience. These activities can be modified in many ways to suit the topic and the level of your students. In the solid geometry we looked at processes. You can use these same processes (as we did in many of the activities) with plane figures. Likewise, like the plane figures, the solid figures may be considered in terms of their properties, relationships among them, and classification schemes.

We have touched on only a few things you can do to help children build concepts and skills in geometry, as well as only a few ways to present problems and apply geometry. There are many other fascinating topics and activities that you can use. Begin to collect these and use them in your teaching.

THINGS TO DO: ADDING TO YOUR PICTURE

1. Give four reasons why geometry should be included in an elementary mathematics program. Explain, in your own words, what one of these reasons means to you.
2. Construct three solids using at least two of the different methods suggested in this chapter.
3. Name three properties of solids that should be learned at each of the levels: beginning, intermediate, and advanced.
4. Defend spending time on constructing models of solids.
5. List eight geometric properties of plane shapes that children can describe.
6. Give the reason for including each example and nonexample of a triangle on Activity Card 15-17.
7. Design a classifying activity for intermediate students based on one of the ideas in the beginning activities.
8. Make a list of ten questions and find a solution for each for the activity: "Can You Make a _____?" (page 234).
9. Find an activity involving students in an art project that deals with symmetry.
10. Design a discovery lesson for one of the properties of angles on page 235.
11. Try one of the geometry activities in this chapter with children. Write up the plan and the children's reaction.
12. Look at the geometry in a textbook at a given grade level. Make a list of the activities from this chapter that would complement the text.

13. The Geometry section in *Films in the Mathematics Classroom* (1) lists over 60 films. Read some of the descriptions and reviews, then suggest a film that you would like to use and tell why.

SELECTED REFERENCES

1. Bestgen, Barbara J., and Reys, Robert E. *Films in the Mathematics Classroom.* Reston, Va.: National Council of Teachers of Mathematics, 1982.

2. Bezuszka, S. J.; Kenney, Margaret; and Silvey, Linda. *Tessellations: The Geometry of Patterns.* Palo Alto, Calif.: Creative Publications, 1979.

3. Bruni, James V. *Experiencing Geometry.* Belmont, Calif.: Wadsworth, 1977.

4. Brydegaard, Marguerite, and Inskeep, James E. *Readings in Geometry from the Arithmetic Teacher.* Reston, Va.: National Council of Teachers of Mathematics, 1972.

5. Carpenter, Thomas P.; Corbitt, Mary Kay; Kepner, Henry S., Jr.; Lindquist, Mary Montgomery; and Reys, Robert E. *Results from the Second Mathematics Assessment of the National Assessment of Educational Progress.* Reston, Va.: National Council of Teachers of Mathematics, 1981.

6. Dana, Marcia E., and Lindquist, Mary Montgomery. "The Surprising Circle." *Arithmetic Teacher,* 25 (January 1978), pp. 4–11.

7. Dana, Marcia E., and Lindquist, Mary Montgomery. "Let's Try Triangles." *Arithmetic Teacher,* 26 (September 1978), pp. 2–9.

8. Lindquist, Mary Montgomery, and Dana, Marcia E. "Strip Tease." *Arithmetic Teacher,* 25 (March 1980), pp. 4–9.

9. O'Daffer, Phares, and Clemens, Stanley R. *Geometry: An Investigative Approach.* Boston: Addison-Wesley, 1976.

10. Romberg, Thomas A.; Harvey, John G.; Moser, James M.; and Montgomery, Mary E. *Developing Mathematical Processes (DMP).* Chicago: Rand McNally, 1974–1976.

11. Van de Walle, John, and Thompson, Charles S. "A Triangle Treasury." *Arithmetic Teacher,* 28 (February 1981), pp. 6–11.

16

Searching for Number Patterns

An eighth-grade class is studying a chapter on "Number Theory," in which they have learned to identify primes and to express composite numbers as products of primes. The class has just opened, and they are reviewing previous work.

Miss Bell: "Yesterday we looked at prime factors. Who can tell how to find the prime factors of 429?"

Hans: "That one is easy, because you can look at 429 and see that 3 is a factor. 429 = 3 · 143."

Miss Bell: "That's quick, but why did you stop with the 143?"

Hans: "143 is prime, I think."

Miss Bell: "How would we check?"

Lee: "Use the calculator and start dividing."

Miss Bell: "That's fine; what would you try first?"

Nicole: "Begin with 2 and try every prime afterward. What happens if we accidentally use a composite?"

Laurie: "That wouldn't matter. If it did divide 143, then you could just factor it. Just like we did with the factor tree."

Jesse: "OK, but it seems like you could be trying a lot of numbers before you get to 143."

Miss Bell: "That's what we all thought, but yesterday when you were absent we found a shortcut. Who can tell Jesse what we found?"

Andra: "You can stop when you get halfway there."

Miss Bell: "Andra, what do you mean by halfway?"

Andra: "Guess it's not half, but it sort of is a funny half. You know (going to the board), when we found all the factors of 28 we listed them:

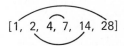

$$[1, 2, 4, 7, 14, 28]$$

When you get to 4 you have them all. That's what I mean by half."

Miss Bell: "You have the right idea, but how do we know where to stop trying if we don't list all the factors?"

Hans: "You can stop when you get to the square root of the number. That's what we found out yesterday."

Andra: "That's what I meant by halfway."

Miss Bell: "OK. Now what numbers do we have to try for 143?"

Lee: "The calculator says that the square root of 143 is 11.95."

Hans: "So we need to try 2, 3, 5, 7 and, let's see . . . 11."

Laurie: "But we don't have to try 2 and 5 because we know they don't divide 143."

.
.
.

WHY TEACH NUMBER THEORY?

Number theory is the branch of mathematics most concerned with the properties of the natural numbers. Odd and even numbers, primes, prime factorization, number patterns, least common multiple, and greatest common divisor are number-theory topics often found in elementary and junior high schools. Besides its being a rich area for problem solving, there are many reasons to teach number theory at this level. We will consider five of these reasons and illustrate them with activities.

Fascination with Numbers and Number Patterns

From the time of ancient civilizations, people have been fascinated with numbers and number patterns. Ancients often thought numbers had mystical qualities, and the branch of mathematics called *numerology* was studied in great depth by some. Others were fascinated by patterns of numbers such as those that occur in the 100-triangle-chart on Activity Card 16-1. Many of your students, given an opportunity, will also be fascinated by numbers and some of their unusual properties. Thus, one reason to study number theory is to awaken and encourage the fascination of numbers in settings that require looking for relationships and solving problems.

A Chance to Discover Mathematics

Many conjectures in number theory are easy to state, even though some may be difficult to prove. For example, the famous conjecture by Goldbach is easy enough for fourth and fifth graders to understand. In 1742, Goldbach conjectured that any even number greater than 2 could be written as the sum of two primes. For example, $8 = 3 + 5$, $18 = 11 + 7$, and $162 = 79 + 83$. After children have shown that this conjecture is reasonable for the first 100 even numbers, they can explore some conjectures of their own. See Activity Card 16-2 for some starting places. It is important that each child keep a record, or you keep a class record, of conjectures that fail. It is just as important to know what will not work as what will work. Be sure to emphasize that they have not proved a conjecture by trying examples; they can only find out that it works for their examples. In fact, no one has proved or disproved Goldbach's conjecture.

A chance to discover their own pattern in the 100-triangle-chart, a conjecture, or a divisibility test is probably as close as a lot of students will ever come to discovering original mathematics. While some of the things your students may discover may not be original, there is still a joy in one's own idea or realization.

ACTIVITY CARD 16-1

WHAT DO YOU SEE IN ME ? ? ? ?

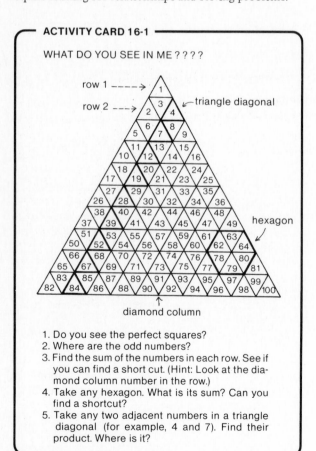

row 1 ----→
row 2 ----→
triangle diagonal
hexagon
diamond column

1. Do you see the perfect squares?
2. Where are the odd numbers?
3. Find the sum of the numbers in each row. See if you can find a short cut. (Hint: Look at the diamond column number in the row.)
4. Take any hexagon. What is its sum? Can you find a shortcut?
5. Take any two adjacent numbers in a triangle diagonal (for example, 4 and 7). Find their product. Where is it?

ACTIVITY CARD 16-2

DO YOU BELIEVE THAT?

Try one of these conjectures about positive whole numbers. None of them are true, but you can change them slightly so they will be.

TINBACH'S CONJECTURE Every number can be expressed as the difference of two primes.
Examples: $14 = 17 - 3$ $5 = 7 - 2$ $28 = 31 - 3$

ZINCBACH'S CONJECTURE Every number can be expressed as the sum of 3 squares (0 is permitted).
Examples: $3 = 1^2 + 1^2 + 1^2$ $14 = 1^2 + 2^2 + 3^2$
$9 = 3^2 + 0^2 + 0^2$

ALUMINUMBACH'S CONJECTURE Every odd number can be expressed as the sum of 3 primes.
Examples: $15 = 5 + 5 + 5$ $11 = 3 + 3 + 5$

BRASSBACH'S CONJECTURE Every square number has exactly 3 divisors.
Examples: $2^2 = 4$, 4 has 3 divisors 1, 2, and 4

COPPERBACH'S CONJECTURE The product of any number of primes is odd.
Examples: $5 \times 3 \times 7 = 105$ (3 primes)
$7 \times 3 \times 3 \times 5 = 315$ (4 primes)

Extension of and Practice in Mainline Topics

We often need ways to help individualize within a topic. For example, suppose we are beginning the year in a fifth-grade class and we need to review multiplication and division with some children. While all children would probably benefit from some review, they will not all need the same amount. What do you do with those students who do not need as much review? Number theory often provides an extension. In this case, you might have them investigate abundant, deficient, and perfect numbers (see Activity Card 16-3). This will give a lot of practice with multiplication and division.

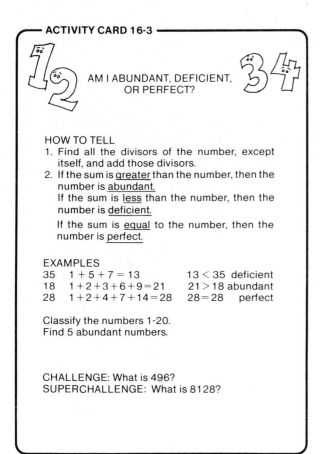

ACTIVITY CARD 16-3

AM I ABUNDANT, DEFICIENT, OR PERFECT?

HOW TO TELL
1. Find all the divisors of the number, except itself, and add those divisors.
2. If the sum is <u>greater</u> than the number, then the number is <u>abundant.</u>
   If the sum is <u>less</u> than the number, then the number is <u>deficient.</u>
   If the sum is <u>equal</u> to the number, then the number is <u>perfect.</u>

EXAMPLES
35	$1 + 5 + 7 = 13$	$13 < 35$	deficient
18	$1 + 2 + 3 + 6 + 9 = 21$	$21 > 18$	abundant
28	$1 + 2 + 4 + 7 + 14 = 28$	$28 = 28$	perfect

Classify the numbers 1-20.
Find 5 abundant numbers.

CHALLENGE: What is 496?
SUPERCHALLENGE: What is 8128?

Recreation

Did you ever think of mathematics as a recreation? Number theory provides many puzzle-type activities that many children will find recreational. Just as not all children enjoy the same sports or games, not all will find puzzles enjoyable. However, if you begin with simple puzzles and treat them as such, many children will become interested.

In solving such puzzles they are practicing skills, learning about how numbers act, and using problem-solving strategies. For example, in the magic square shown below, children soon learn that the two largest numbers cannot go in the same row, column, or diagonal. While this activity can be done solely with paper and pencil, it is suggested that you use cards. First, it makes the activity more like a puzzle to many children. Second, it saves erasing wrong tries until holes appear in the paper! The disadvantage of the cards is that children have no records of their tries and may repeat the same attempt over and over. This may lead to the need for a record of the attempts.

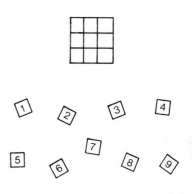

Arrange the numbers in the grid so that every row, column, and diagonal has a sum of 15.

Use in Other Mathematics Topics

We have seen how number theory can be used for practice in the four operations and in problem solving, but it can also be used in other mathematics topics. For example, we may use the least common multiple in finding common denominators, or we may use greatest common divisors in reducing fractions. At one time, many of the number-theory topics were of assistance in doing or checking computation. For example, the divisibility tests were a quick way to see if a number was a factor of another, and "casting out nines" was a quick check on long computations. While none of these may retain its former importance, they can be justified if they also fulfill some of the other reasons to study number theory.

SPECIFIC NUMBER-THEORY TOPICS

Certain skills related to number theory are expected of most students. In this section we will examine some ways to develop these skills. Like any skills, once they are developed they need to be maintained. To teach children what a prime number is in fourth grade and then never use it again assures that it will be forgotten.

Only about 58 percent of 13-year-olds could choose the definition of a prime number (5, p. 18).

Beyond the skills to be developed, it is important to keep in mind the reasons for studying number theory. If all we do is have children learn definitions and rules, then we have missed the real power of number theory.

Odds and Evens

Classifying numbers as odd or even is one of the first number-theory topics that children encounter. As children count by twos—2, 4, 6, 8, 10—they learn there is something different about these numbers; these are the even numbers, and the others are the odds. More precisely, an even number is a number that is divisible by 2.

You can begin the study of odds and evens by having young children model the numbers with square tiles. Give each child a number (1–20) of square tiles. The children may pretend they are making candy bars that are two squares wide. If a "number" can be arranged in a rectangle that is two squares wide, then it is even. If not, it is odd. See the candy bars made here.

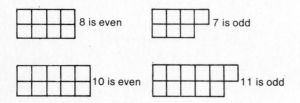

8 is even   7 is odd

10 is even   11 is odd

Have the children list all the odd and even numbers. They should see the pattern that every other number is even and that the even numbers end in 0, 2, 4, 6, or 8.

Later, children can use this candy-bar model to investigate the sum of two evens or two odds or the products of evens and odds. For example, two odds can always be put together to make an even, or the sum of two odds is even. Likewise, the product of an even and an odd will always be even, as shown below.

Evens and odds arise on many occasions, but you should look for experiences in which the ideas of odds and evens are used. For example, students might find the sum of the first 50 odd numbers (see patterns), find the probability of throwing an even number with two dice, or find the first odd number that is divisible by 11.

Factors, Primes, and Prime Factorization

While learning about multiplication and division, children have begun learning about multiples and factors. In this section we will examine how to extend and use these ideas.

Factors. Each of two numbers multiplied together to give a product is called a *factor* of that product. For example, 3 and 4 are factors of 12, since 3 times 4 is 12.

Children can begin exploring factors by using materials. For example, begin with 12 objects. See if they can group the 12 objects by ones, twos, threes, . . . , twelves. There are 12 groups of ones, 6 groups of twos, 4 groups of threes, 3 groups of fours, 2 groups of sixes, and 1 group of twelves, but 12 cannot be grouped by fives, sevens, and so on. Later have them express this in terms of products:

The 12 Story

12 = 12 × 1	12 = 3 × 4
12 = 6 × 2	12 = 2 × 6
12 = 4 × 3	12 = 1 × 12

Later, we want children to find all the factors of a given number. For example, what are all the factors of 84? One place to begin is to see what numbers will divide 84. Have the children begin with the simplest divisor. You might lead them through a discussion such as this:

"We know that 1 will divide 84, so 1 and 84 are factors." Write:

[1,   , 84]

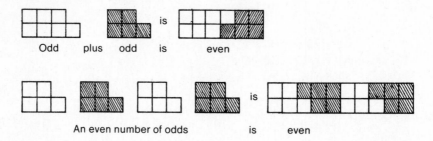

Odd   plus   odd   is   even

An even number of odds   is   even

Now try 2 (use your calculator). [2 × 42 = 84, so 2 and 42 are factors.] Write:

[1, 2 ⌒ 42, 84]

"How about 3?" [3 × 28 = 84, so 3 and 28 are factors.] Write:

[1, 2, 3 ⌒ 28, 42, 84]

"How about 4?" [4 × 21 = 84, so 4 and 21 are factors.] Write:

[1, 2, 3, 4 ⌒ 21, 28, 42, 84]

"How about 5? No, so try 6." [6 × 14 = 84, so 6 and 14 are factors.] Write:

[1, 2, 3, 4, 6 ⌒ 14, 21, 28, 42, 84]

"How long do you continue? Do you see that we are closing in on it? At this point you can conclude that you don't need to try anything beyond 14 because anything larger than 14 would have to be multiplied by something smaller than 6 and we've tried that. So, let's try 7." [7 × 12 = 84, so 7 and 12 are factors.] Write:

[1, 2, 3, 4, 6, 7 ⌒ 12, 14, 21, 28, 42, 84]

"How about 8? 9? Do you need to try 10?" Children will need to try 10, 11, and perhaps some more before they realize that if they divide 84 by 10, 11, and so on they always get a quotient smaller than 9, and they have checked each one of these. This is the process on which the students in the opening lesson had been working. Activity Card 16-4 is a game that requires the children to find the factors of numbers 2–36 and to use some strategy. Try it with a friend. It's not as easy to win as you may think!

Multiples. A *multiple* of a number is the *product* of that number times any whole number. For example, 36 is a multiple of 4, since 36 is 4 times 9. In looking at multiples we usually begin with the number and generate multiples of it. The positive multiples of 4 are:

4, 8, 12, 16, 20, 24, 28, . . .

How did we generate this list? (We multiplied 4 by 1, 2, 3, 4, and so forth.)

Several materials can be used to illustrate multiples —the number line, Cuisenaire rods, and the hundred chart. The children should be familiar with the smaller multiples of the numbers 1–10 through the multiplication facts.

The concept of a multiple is not difficult—remember, it is a product. It is a new word that we are using, and children often confuse it with the other new word, factor or divisor. Confusion arises also when we ask, "What is 36 a multiple of?" We are actually asking children to find the factors of 36. Then when we ask, "What is 4 a factor of?" we are actually asking the children to find the multiples of 4. We need to be able to think in both directions—for example, to list all the multiples of 7 and to find what 42 is a multiple of. But when you are first beginning the study of multiples and factors, keep the language clean!

ACTIVITY CARD 16-4

FACTOR ME OUT
A game for two

Materials: paper and pencil
Make a chart like this:

●	2	3	4	5	6
7	8	9	10	11	12
13	14	15	16	17	18
19	20	21	22	23	24
25	26	27	28	29	30
21	32	33	34	35	36

Rules:
1. Player 1 choses a number. He or she gets that many points. The opponent gets all the factors of the number (except the number).

SAMPLE	SCORE
Player 1 chooses 10	Player① | Player②
Player 2 gets 2 and 5	10 | 7

2. Mark out the number and the factors; these cannot be used again.
3. Repeat with Player 2 choosing the number.
4. Alternate turns until no numbers are left.

WINNER: Player with most points.

Primes and Composites. A number is prime if it has exactly two factors: one and itself. Otherwise, it is composite. There are several concrete models that you may use to introduce the idea of primes. The activity on Lesson Card 16-1 illustrates one model.

After children have been introduced to primes, give them the definition. Then, they need to be able to

---

LESSON CARD 16-1

ACTIVITY--THE HOPPERS

Materials: A copy of the worksheet.

Directions: Have the children do the sheet and discuss the following
questions with them.

1. What numbers had two hopper stoppers? (2,3,5,7, etc.)
2. What numbers had more than two hopper stoppers? (4,6,8,9, etc.)
3. What number had only one hopper stopper? (1)

Introduce the terms prime and composite.

THE HIP HOPPERS HOP

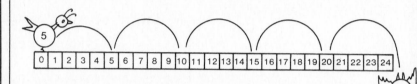

The hoppers are strange characters that can only hop a certain length. For
example, the 5-hopper hops 5 spaces each time. They all begin at 0.

See where each hopper will land. The 1-hopper and the 2-hopper have
been done for you.

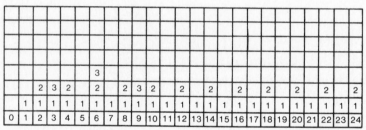

Be a 3-hopper. You will land at 3 (write a 3 above the 3), you will land at 6
(write a 3 above the 6)...Keep going. (You should have 3's above 9, 12, 15,
18, 21, 24).

Do the same for the 4-hopper, the 5-hopper, all the way to a 24-hopper.
Then, answer the questions your teacher has.

---

identify what numbers are primes and which are composites. The opening lesson illustrates a procedure they may use to classify numbers as prime or composite.

There are other explorations that focus on primes, such as the sieve described in the next section. One can also investigate twin primes (pairs of primes that are two apart, such as 11 and 13), reversal primes (pairs of primes such as 79 and 97), or the infinitude of primes.

Prime Factorization. The fundamental theorem of arithmetic says that every composite number may be expressed as a product of primes in only one way. Many patterns and formulas in number theory as well as some algorithms for finding the greatest common factor and the least common multiple depend upon expressing a number as a product of primes (prime factorization). How would you begin to find the prime factors of 3190?

FACTOR TREE METHOD   DIVISION METHOD

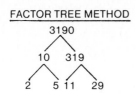

Two methods are commonly used to find the prime factorization of a number. One is making a factor tree and the other is dividing the number by primes. We illustrate above the use of these methods in finding the prime factors of 3190.

What is the difference between the two methods? In the factor-tree method the first step is to factor the number into any two factors. In the division method you must divide by a prime. If in the factor-tree method you made the rule that one factor must always be a prime, then the two methods would be the same except for notation. Do you see the similarity?

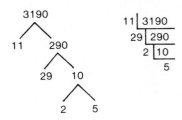

No matter which method you choose, make certain that the students finally write the prime factorization. That is, they should express 3190 as 2 × 5 × 11 × 29.

Greatest Common Factor and Least Common Multiple

We have looked at factors and multiples of individual numbers; now we will examine pairs of numbers and ask, "What is the largest number that is a factor of both of the numbers (greatest common factor)?" or "What is the smallest number that is a multiple of both the numbers (least common multiple)?"

Understanding these concepts depends mainly on knowing how to find factors and multiples and keeping straight which is which. Algorithms for finding the greatest common factor (GCF) and the least common multiple (LCM) are very similar. This is good, but it can confuse students who do not really understand what they are doing. In the second national mathematics assessment nearly half of the 17-year-olds showed this confusion, while few of the 13-year-olds had developed either concept (5, p. 17).

Often we teach GCF and LCM one right after the other and then do not use them. Or, if we teach them at separate times, we never bring the two ideas back together to compare and contrast them. If we teach them, we should present them in a meaningful manner. Several algorithms may be used for finding the GCF and LCM; the listing algorithm and the factorization algorithm are commonly used. Since the listing algorithm is the more concrete of the two, we will present it here. As you read, ask yourself what questions you could ask students when presenting it to them.

The Listing Algorithm. To find the GCF with the listing algorithm, we first list all the factors of the two (or more) numbers. For example, to find the GCF of 18 and 24 we list:

The factors of 18:   1, 2, 3, 6, 9, 18
The factors of 24:   1, 2, 3, 4, 6, 8, 12, 24

Then we look for the common factors (1, 2, 3, 6) and choose the largest. Therefore, 6 is the greatest common factor.

Similarly, to find the LCM, we list the multiples of each number until we find common multiples. For example, to find the LCM of 18 and 24 we list:

The multiples of 18:   18, 36, 54, 72, 90, 108, 126, 144, . . .
The multiples of 24:   24, 48, 72, 96, 120, 144, . . .

By inspection 72 is the smallest number common to both sets, thus the LCM is 72.

Children may use the LCM as they find the least common denominator of two fractions and they may use the GCF when they reduce fractions, yet often we fail to teach them what they are using. For example, to reduce $\frac{18}{24}$, they may first reduce it to $\frac{9}{12}$ and then to $\frac{3}{4}$. If they see that the greatest common divisor of 18 and 24 is 6, then they can do it in one step. However, the time saved by finding the greatest common divisor first is probably not worth the effort.

Likewise, at times it is important to find the least common denominator, but often it is sufficient to find a common denominator. Today, with calculators and less emphasis on complicated fractions, the finding of GCF and LCM is not as crucial as it was. If you do teach these, however, develop them carefully and at a stage in the students' maturity when they can grasp what they are doing.

Patterns

We begin looking at patterns with very young children. At first we may look at color patterns (red, yellow, red, yellow), size patterns (big, small, big, small), or type-of-object patterns (cat, dog, cat, dog). In each case we want children to focus on the relationships among the elements of the pattern. That means that they must know something about the individual elements. The same things are true about more sophisticated patterns.

One way that patterns are used in number theory is in sequences. When we first begin examining sequences, we usually ask students to give a few more terms of the sequence and to tell the rule they are using. Later, in algebra, we have the children express this rule in general, so that any term of the sequence may be specified. The background you provide will make this latter task easier.

You have seen patterns throughout this book—in the calculator chapter (Chapter 2), in the basic facts and algorithm chapters (Chapters 8 and 9), and at other places within this chapter. We focus now on how to teach patterns. Here are several hints that may help you.

First, you need to realize that some children enjoy looking for patterns and relationships, while others do not. For the latter, part of the difficulty may be that the question is rather open-ended; that is, there is no one route to follow. It also may be that the student has not had success in finding patterns. This does not mean that you should not expose these children to sequences; it is a valuable skill and one in which each of us can be trained to be more successful.

Students need to be aware that many number sequences follow some rule. The rule may be simple, such as "Add 2 to the previous term," or complicated, such as, "Subtract one from the square of the previous number." Begin with simpler sequences and progress to the more difficult ones, making certain that knowledge about individual terms has been acquired. No one would be very successful finding that 215 may be the next number in the following pattern [0, 7, 26, 63, 124, _____ , _____], unless he or she were familiar with the perfect cubes 1, 8, 27, 64, 125, 216, ...

Students need to make up their own sequences by starting with a rule and generating the sequence. You can then use those and have other students continue the pattern.

As in most problem solving, if you get off on the wrong track, it is hard to get back on. Sometimes it is best to leave the sequence and return to it later with a fresh outlook.

Another use of patterns in number theory is in finding sums of sequences. If the sequence is formed by adding a constant to each preceding term (an arithmetic sequence), there is a very easy way to find the sum. Let us look at this technique by solving a problem. What is the sum of the first 100 positive integers? We could actually plug away (either with or without a calculator) and find a sum, but a much more elegant and simpler way is shown in Activity Card 16-5. Gauss, a famous mathematician, found this method when a teacher gave the young lad the task of adding the first 100 numbers as a way to keep him occupied. Doing it his way certainly did not keep him busy very long, did it?

You will help children see the beauty of mathematics when you begin to look for patterns and for things that do not follow a pattern. Do not let them think that everything has a pattern or that everyone sees the same pattern. What do you think is the next number in this pattern?

$$1, -2, 4, \underline{\hspace{1cm}}$$

Did you think -8? That could be the next if your rule were to multiply each preceding number by -2. But we were thinking it would be -5. Can you tell why? (We were adding $-3, 6, -9, \ldots$.)

Divisibility Tests

At one time the divisibility rules were important. Today, they are an interesting sidelight in mathematics. It is the discovery of some of the rules or the investigation to see why they work that makes them a topic worth the study.

Many children discover on their own the rules for 2 and 5 through observing patterns in the multiplication and division facts for 2 and 5. The rules for other numbers are not quite as evident. Activity Card 16-6 provides a guided discovery lesson for the divisibility rules for 3 and 9. It is important to discuss the results of the table with the class and to give more examples if the students don't answer the questions clearly. Good questions to raise would be: Does this divisibility test work for larger numbers? Is this a test only for 3 and 9? Why does this work?

You can help students reason through this last question by examining a model of a different way to divide, say, 456 by 3. Figure 16-1 shows how to rethink the division of 456 by 3 so the divisibility test makes sense. Do you see why this also works for 9?

You can look at other divisibility tests in a similar manner. For example, do you see why the divisibility

A SHORT WAY TO FIND SPECIAL SUMS

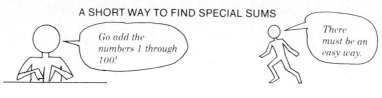

Go add the numbers 1 through 100!

There must be an easy way.

I'll write down the sum like this

$1 + 2 + 3 + ... + 98 + 99 + 100$

And I'll write it like this

$100 + 99 + 98 + ... + 3 + 2 + 1$

Aha, I see 101's!

$\underbrace{101 + 101 + 101 + ... + 101 + 101 + 101}_{100}$

"Since there are 100 of the 101's, the sum must be 100 x 101. But I've added each number twice, so it's just half of that. 50 x 101 = 5050."

Use this method to find:
1. 2 + 4 + 6 + 8 + ... + 18 + 20 (How many
2. 3 + 6 + 9 + 12 + ...+ 30 + 33   terms?)
3. 5 + 10 + 15 + ...+ 95 + 100
4. 1 + 3 + 5 + ...+ 97 + 99

Will this method work for these sums?
1. 1 + 4 + 9 + 16 + 25 + ...+ 100
2. 2 + 3 + 6 + 7 + 11 + 12 + 17 + 18
3. 2 + 5 + 8 + 11 + 14 + 17 + 20 + ...

DIVISIBILITY DISCOVERY

Use your calculator. Fill in the chart and look for patterns.

Number	Divisible By 3?	9?	Sum of Digits	Sum Divisible By 3?	By 9?
456	yes	no	4+5+6=15	yes	no
891					
892					
514					
37					
78					
79					
1357					
1358					
1359					
1360					
1361					
1362					

WHAT DO YOU THINK?
DISCUSS THESE IN CLASS.

1. A number is divisible by 3. Is it always divisible by 9?
2. A number is divisible by 9. Is it always divisible by 3?
3. What does the sum of the digits tell you?
4. What did you notice about the sequence of numbers 1357, 1358, 1359,...1362?

Figure 16-1

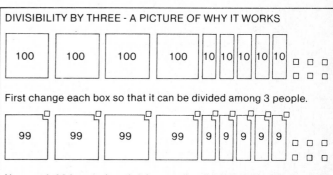

DIVISIBILITY BY THREE - A PICTURE OF WHY IT WORKS

First change each box so that it can be divided among 3 people.

Now each 99 box and each 9 box can be divided among the 3 people. We are left with 4 ones from the 4 hundred boxes, 5 ones from the 5 ten boxes, and the 6 ones. So if we can distribute 4 + 5 + 6 to 3 people, 456 is divisible by 3.

test for 4 depends upon only the 10 boxes and the ones? What can you do with 100 boxes, 1000 boxes, and so on? You can always distribute them to 4 people. A 10 box cannot be broken into 4 equal parts, so a number's divisibility by 4 depends upon how many tens and ones it has. Thus, 526 is not divisible by 4 since 26 is not, but 536 is divisible by 4 because 36 is.

Other Ideas to Investigate

There are many other topics in number theory that you can have students investigate. Some ideas are given here, but only as a starter. You can find much more about these topics as well as others mentioned in this chapter in the references listed at the end of the chapter. Most of these topics are suitable for middle school students.

Pascal's Triangle. Pascal's triangle is most closely associated with probability. However, there are many number patterns in it. Some are suggested on Activity Card 16-7.

Pythagorean Triples. A Pythagorean triple is a triple of numbers (a, b, c) such that $a^2 + b^2 = c^2$. For example, $(3, 4, 5)$ is a Pythagorean triple. There are many ways to generate Pythagorean triples and many

---

ACTIVITY CARD 16-7

PASCAL'S TRIANGLE

```
          1         row 0
         1 1        row 1
        1 2 1       row 2
       1 3 3 1
      1 4 6 4 1
     1 5 10 10 5 1
    1 6 15 20 15 6 1
   1 7 - - - - - -
```

1. Finish row 7.
2. Write rows 8 and 9.
3. What patterns do you see?
4. Find the sum of each row. Fill in the table.

row	sum
0	1
1	1+1=2
2	1+2+1=4
3	
4	
5	

What do you think the sum of the eighth row is? Try it. How about the twentieth row?

5. Look at the numbers in any odd row (ignore the ones). What do you notice? Do you think this will be true in row 9?

ACTIVITY CARD 16-8

PYTHAGOREAN PATTERNS

Here is a table of Pythagorean Triples.

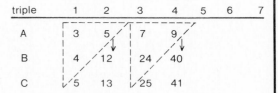

triple	1	2	3	4	5	6	7
A	3	5	7	9			
B	4	12	24	40			
C	5	13	25	41			

I. Use a calculator and check to see if (3,4,5), (5,12,13), (7,24,25), and (9,40,41) are Pythagorean triples. (See if $A^2 + B^2 = C^2$)

II. Create the fifth triple.
  A. What would A be?
  B. To find B, look at the three numbers in the dotted triangle. What do you do with the three numbers to get the B marked with an arrow?
  C. If you know B, how do you get C?
  D. Did you get (11,60,61)?

III. Create the sixth, seventh, and eighth Pythagorean triples.

---

patterns in the triples. The chart on Activity Card 16-8 gives a way to generate Pythagorean triples and looks at some patterns.

Fibonacci Sequence. Fibonacci's sequence of numbers is:

$$1 \quad 1 \quad 2 \quad 3 \quad 5 \quad 8 \quad 13 \quad 21 \quad 34 \quad \ldots$$

Do you know the next number in the sequence? Can you tell how the sequence is formed? Many patterns in nature follow this sequence; one is shown on Activity Card 16-9.

Number Patterns in Geometry. Many patterns in geometry lead to interesting number patterns. A sample is given on Activity Card 16-10.*

Sieves. The most famous of the sieves is the *sieve of Eratosthenes*. In this sieve the numbers are arranged in ten columns. The sieve gives an easy method for generating the primes. At first the process will seem long, but soon you will realize how quickly the primes can be generated. The beauty of the arrangement of the sieve on Activity Card 16-11 is that after 2 and 3, all the primes occur in the first or the fifth column. Do you see why?

---

*Activity Card 16-9 is from Romberg (12).

ACTIVITY CARD 16-9

Natural Growth

Do at least two of the three problems about natural growth on this page and page 19.

1. Small animals made up of one cell reproduce by dividing; the old cell remains and a new one is born. Suppose you had a type of cell that kept on dividing and producing a new cell each day. After a new cell was one-day old, it became an old cell and could produce new cells of its own—one each day. The drawing shows how a family of cells would grow from one new cell.

Copy and continue this table that describes the cell growth.

Day 6 Ⓞ—Ⓝ—Ⓝ—Ⓞ—Ⓞ—Ⓝ—Ⓞ—Ⓞ

Day 5 Ⓞ————Ⓞ—Ⓝ————Ⓞ—Ⓝ

Day 4 Ⓝ————Ⓞ————Ⓞ

Day 3 ————Ⓞ————Ⓝ

Day 2 ————Ⓞ

Day 1 ————Ⓝ

Ⓝ new cell   Ⓞ old cell

Day	1	2	3	4	5	6	7	8	9	10	11	12
Number of new cells	1	0	1	1	2	3						
Number of old cells	0	1	1	2	3	5						
Total number of cells	1	1	2									

---

2. Some trees grow new branches each month by having every old branch put out a new twig which then becomes an old branch within one month. The drawing illustrates the growth record of part of a tree, beginning with a new twig, and shows how it looked for each of five months.

Copy and complete this table to show the growth record of these twigs and branches for eight months.

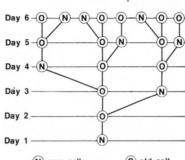

Month 5

Month 4

Month 3

Month 2

Month 1

Green, new twig
Brown, old branch

Month	1	2	3	4	5	6	7	8
Number of new twigs	1	0	1	1	2			
Number of old branches	0	1	1					
Total number of limbs	1	1	2					

ACTIVITY CARD 16-10

COUNT THOSE RECTANGLES

How many rectangles?

This may be hard to count. Let's look at some simpler examples first

1 square
0 nonsquare rectangles
1 total

2 squares
1 nonsquare rectangle
3 total

3 squares
3 nonsquare rectangles
6 total

Fill in this table. Look for the shortcut.

Number of squares	1 2 3 4 5 6 7 ... 15

Number of
nonsquare
rectangles   0 1 3 ?

Total   1 3 6

ACTIVITY CARD 16-11

SIEVE 6

1. Circle 2, then mark out every second number.
2. Circle 3, then mark out every third number (6, 9, 12,...) Some may already be marked out.
3. Circle 5 (since 4 is marked out) and mark out every fifth number. Continue to 96.

	②	3	X	5	X
7	8	9	10	11	12
13	14	15	16	17	18
19	20	21	22	23	24
25	26	27	28	29	30
31	32	33	34	35	36
37	38	39	40	41	42
43	44	45	46	47	48
49	50	51	52	53	54
55	56	57	58	59	60
61	62	63	64	65	66
67	68	69	70	71	72
73	74	75	76	77	78
79	80	81	82	83	84
85	86	87	88	89	90
91	92	93	94	95	96

What numbers are circled?
In what columns are they?

A GLANCE AT WHERE WE'VE BEEN

We have examined some reasons for studying number theory or for searching for number patterns or relationships. At this level, number theory is a topic that can be used to teach students how to learn mathematics. Some of its objectives—such as identifying odd and even numbers; primes and composites; and finding the prime factorization of a number, greatest common factors, and least common multiples—are expected of most literate mathematics students. It offers an abundance of ideas suitable for students to investigate that can be used for problem solving, for extension of mainline topics, for arithmetic practice, and—to enliven your classroom.

THINGS TO DO: ADDING TO YOUR PICTURE

1. List four reasons for teaching number theory. Give an example of an activity, other than the one in the text, to illustrate one of your four reasons.
2. Find a number-theory activity that provides practice with one of the four operations.
3. Explain with a picture why the divisibility test works for 8.
4. Challenge: Use the picture method to discover a divisibility test for 11.
5. In a junior high text, locate the factoring algorithm for finding the GCF and LCM. Compare that method with the listing algorithm presented here as to level of difficulty in developing meaning and ease of use, given a number expressed as a product of primes.
6. Show how one can develop multiples with Cuisenaire rods, number line, or any other concrete model.
7. Make a worksheet that uses materials and encourages the discovery of the following: The sum of two evens is even, the sum of two odds is even, and the sum of an even and an odd is odd.
8. Try one of the conjectures on Activity Card 16-2 with a student. Record the student's procedure, comments, and hints that you provided.
9. Write a lesson plan for one of the following:
   (a) Finding all the factors of a number.
   (b) Finding the prime factors of a number.
   (c) Finding the least common multiple.
10. Collect activities that you can use in teaching in one of these areas: Pascal's triangle, Pythagorean triples, sieves, divisibility tests, magic squares, geometric number patterns, Fibonacci sequences, or number patterns.
11. Preview the film "Number Patterns" [referenced in *Films in the Mathematics Classroom*, reference (1) in Chapter 15]. State the objectives of the film and how you would use it in the classroom.

SELECTED REFERENCES

1. Bright, George W. "Using Tables to Solve Some Geometry Problems." *Arithmetic Teacher*, 25 (May 1978), pp. 39–43.

2. Burton, David M. *Elementary Number Theory.* Boston: Allyn and Bacon, 1976.

3. Burton, Grace M., and Knifong, J. Dan. "Definitions for Prime Numbers." *Arithmetic Teacher,* 27 (February 1980), pp. 44–47.

4. Cacha, Frances B. "Exploring the Multiplication Table and Beyond." *Arithmetic Teacher,* 25 (November 1978), pp. 46–48.

5. Carpenter, Thomas P.; Corbitt, Mary Kay; Kepner, Henry S., Jr.; Lindquist, Mary Montgomery; and Reys, Robert E. *Results from the Second Mathematics Assessment of the National Assessment of Educational Progress.* Reston, Va.: National Council of Teachers of Mathematics, 1981.

6. Dalton, LeRoy C., and Snyder, Henry D. *Topics for Mathematics Clubs.* Reston, Va.: National Council of Teachers of Mathematics, 1973.

7. Hervey, Margaret A., and Litwiller, Bonnie H. "The Addition Table: Experiences in Practice-Discovery." *Arithmetic Teacher,* 19 (March 1972), pp. 179–182.

8. Jacobs, Harold R. *Mathematics: A Human Endeavor,* 2d ed. San Francisco: W. H. Freeman, 1982.

9. O'Daffer, Phares, and Clemens, Samuel R. *Geometry: An Investigative Approach.* Boston: Addison-Wesley, 1976.

10. Oliver, Charlene. "Gus's Magic Numbers: A Key to the Divisibility Tests for Primes." *Arithmetic Teacher,* 19 (March 1972), pp. 183–191.

11. Omejc, Eve. "A Different Approach to the Sieve of Eratosthenes." *Arithmetic Teacher,* 19 (March 1972), pp. 192–196.

12. Romberg, Thomas A.; Harvey, John G.; Moser, James M.; and Montgomery, Mary E. *Developing Mathematic Processes (DMP).* Chicago: Rand McNally, 1974–1976.

13. Shoemaker, Richard W. *Perfect Numbers.* Reston, Va.: National Council of Teachers of Mathematics, 1973.

14. Strangman, Kathryn B. "The Sum of *N* Polygonal Numbers." *Mathematics Teacher,* November 1974, pp. 655–658.

15. Zalewski, Donald L. "Magic Triangles—Practice in Skills and Thinking." *Arithmetic Teacher,* 21 (October 1974), pp. 486–491.

Index